# The Selected Letters
# of Charlotte Perkins Gilman

Tues. April 19th. 1887.
26 Humboldt Ave. Providence R. I.

Dr. Weir Mitchell,
'Dear Sir,
I write this for you, fearing that I shall soon be unable to remember even this much. I am coming to Philadelphia next week, to see you, but a week does a great deal now. Excuse me if I write un-nessary facts, it is through ignorance. My desire is to make you acquainted with all the facts of the case, that you may form a deeper judgement than from mere casual examinatio.

To cure disease says Dr. Holmes, we must begin with the grand-fathers. Here are mine.

Maternal grandfather. A sturdy New Englander of strong domestic disposition; intensely loving and be-nevolent. Nervous and fretful over his family as he grew old. died

Excerpt from Charlotte Perkins Stetson's letter to Dr. Weir Mitchell, April 19, 1887.
Courtesy of the Wisconsin Historical Society.

# The Selected Letters
# of Charlotte Perkins Gilman

Edited and with an Introduction
by Denise D. Knight and Jennifer S. Tuttle

THE UNIVERSITY OF ALABAMA PRESS
*Tuscaloosa*

Typeface: Caslon

∞

The paper on which this book is printed meets the minimum requirements of
American National Standard for Information Sciences-Permanence of Paper for
Printed Library Materials, ANSI Z39.48-1984.

Library of Congress Cataloging-in-Publication Data

Gilman, Charlotte Perkins, 1860–1935.
   [Correspondence. Selections]
   The selected letters of Charlotte Perkins Gilman / edited and with an introduc-
tion by Denise D. Knight and Jennifer S. Tuttle.
        p.   cm. — (Studies in American literary realism and naturalism)
   Includes bibliographical references and index.
   ISBN 978-0-8173-1648-8 (alk. paper) — ISBN 978-0-8173-8156-1 (electronic)
   1. Gilman, Charlotte Perkins, 1860–1935—Correspondence. 2. Authors,
American—19th century—Correspondence. 3. Authors, American—20th
century—Correspondence. I. Knight, Denise D., 1954– II. Tuttle, Jennifer S.,
1967– III. Title.

   PS1744.G57Z48 2009
   818'.409—dc22
   [B]

                                                                        2008037789

Cover image:
*Charlotte Perkins Stetson Gilman* by Ellen Day Hale
Oil on panel before 1880
Panel: 40.6 x 30.2 x 0.6 cm (16 x 11⅞ x ¼")
Frame: 51.4 x 40.6 x 5.4 cm (20¼ x 16 x 2⅛")
National Portrait Gallery, Smithsonian Institution, NPG.83.162

# Contents

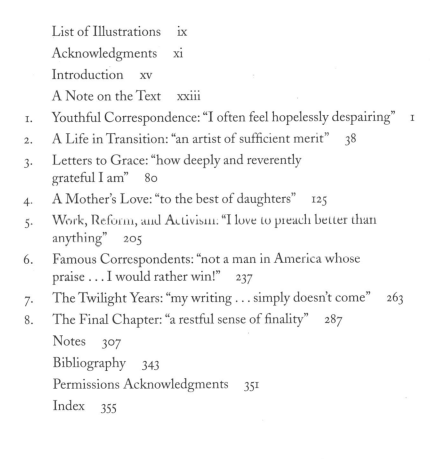

# Illustrations

# Acknowledgments

We wish to express our thanks to everyone who assisted us in the production of this volume. Although our names are the only ones to appear on the cover, many other people gave generously of their time and expertise as we worked our way through mountains of material at a host of institutions. The staff at the Arthur and Elizabeth Schlesinger Library at Radcliffe Institute, Harvard University, and particularly Ellen M. Shea, Jacalyn Blume, Sarah Hutcheon, Laurie Ellis, and Diana Carey, were unfailingly helpful in providing support through every phase of this project. Kim Walters, Director of the Braun Research Library at the Autry National Center/Southwest Museum, contributed valuable curatorial support, time, and ingenuity. Also deserving thanks are the dozens of curators, research librarians, and special collections staff at the following institutions: the Bancroft Library, University of California, Berkeley; the Barnard College Library; the Charles E. Young Research Library, UCLA; the Harriet Beecher Stowe Center; the Horrmann Library, Wagner College; the Houghton Library, Harvard University; the Huntington Library; the John Hay Library, Brown University; the Kroch Library, Cornell University; the Library of Congress; the Lilly Library, Indiana University; the New York Public Library; the Northwestern University Archives; the Otis Library, Norwich, Connecticut; the Pasadena Museum of History; the Rare Book and Manuscript Library, Columbia University; the Rhode Island Historical Society; the Sheidan Libraries, Johns Hopkins University; the Sophia Smith Collection, Smith College; the Stanford University Library; the University of Illinois Urbana-Champaign Library; the University of Rochester Library; the Vassar College Libraries; the Wisconsin Historical Society; and the Women's History Museum and Educational Center. Harry Smith of the Wisconsin Historical Society was particularly obliging of our many requests for assistance.

We are also grateful to the many people who provided us with various letters that were uncovered during their own research as well as those owned by private individuals. Walter Stetson Chamberlin, Frederick Wegener, Elizabeth and Scott De Wolfe, Sharyn Yeoman, and our friend and Gilman biographer Cynthia J. Davis provided materials that were indispensable to our work. William David Barry of the Maine Historical Society, facilitated by Roberta Gray at the University of New England, also shared materials with us. Jennifer Putzi helped point us to valuable secondary sources. Special thanks go to Gary Scharnhorst for his enthusiastic support of our project, and to the staff of The University of Alabama Press for their guidance through the various stages of this edition. Copy editor Jonathan Lawrence deserves special thanks for his meticulous reading of the manuscript. We appreciate the support offered by Gretchen M. Gogan at the SUNY Cortland Memorial Library, as well as the librarians at the University of New England, particularly Brenda Austin, for her assistance with numerous interlibrary loans; Roberta Gray, for her consistently cheerful responses to our many requests for information; and Cally Gurley, for her steady encouragement and practical assistance. Amy Henderson-Harr at the State University of New York at Cortland went far beyond the call of duty in her tireless advocacy on our behalf; Paulette St. Ours at the University of New England was a similarly generous supporter of our project; Glen C. Clarke at the SUNY Cortland also deserves thanks for his guidance, as does Pamela Schroeder for her always-helpful assistance; Staci J. Tedrow, SUNY Cortland, was an enthusiastic and dependable research assistant; and Dawn Van Hall, SUNY Cortland, provided expertise on many of the photographs used in this volume. Heartfelt thanks go to Christopher and Melinda Ratliffe for their enormous generosity in providing from their private collection the photo of an 1887 painting by Charles Walter Stetson that appears in chapter 4. We are also deeply grateful to Cindy J. Hall, a superb and meticulous researcher, who left no stone unturned in response to our queries. Karen Dandurand, who called to our attention the 1877 painting of Gilman from the National Portrait Gallery at the Smithsonian Institution (featured on the cover), also deserves our thanks, as does the Smithsonian for allowing us to use the image. Denise thanks the National Endowment for the Humanities, which funded a 2007 Summer Stipend on her behalf, and the State University of New York at Cortland for a number of research and travel grants over the years. Jennifer thanks the Historical Society of

Southern California and the John Randolph Haynes and Dora Haynes Foundation for two HSSC/Haynes Research Stipends, along with the University of New England for a University Faculty Scholarship Fund Award and for numerous College of Arts and Sciences Faculty Development Grants, all of which supported travel and research for this project. And we both are grateful to the Maine Women Writers Collection at the University of New England for providing a subvention grant. Finally, Denise thanks Michael K. Barylski, and Jennifer thanks David Kuchta, for their continued support of our work.

# Introduction

Peruse how infinite I am
To no one that You—know—
          —Emily Dickinson, Poem 636
          ("The Way I read a Letter's—this—")

Charlotte Perkins Gilman was a prolific writer of letters. Throughout her life she wrote to a wide array of correspondents, including intensely personal letters to loved ones and equally engaging communications with public figures such as Alice Stone Blackwell, William Dean Howells, Margaret Sanger, and Upton Sinclair. If, as P. D. James asserts, letters provide "a more vivid and realistic portrait of the age in which they were written than many more portentous literary forms" (vii), then Gilman's long and rich record of correspondence will do much to illuminate the times in which she lived. Her letters also shed new light upon her biography and complement her published life-writing. Similarly, they supplement her public writing by illustrating her private attempts to grapple "with almost every women's issue she publicly discussed" (M. A. Hill, *Journey* 17). On a textual level, Gilman's letters illustrate her adeptness at using—and transforming—generic conventions, along with her evolving efforts toward self-definition and self-presentation. Full of telling details, explicit professions of feeling, and even new revelations, the letters in this volume simultaneously serve as reminders of all that we do not and cannot know about Gilman—indeed, they destabilize the very idea that she was singular or unchanging. From the first extant letter in her hand, written to her grandmother, to her last note of farewell before taking her own life in 1935, however, Gilman's correspondence is alive with the engaging intellect, deep feeling, and wry humor that defined her throughout her lifetime.

Born Charlotte Anna Perkins on July 3, 1860, in Hartford, Connecticut, Gilman was a descendant of the prominent and influential Beecher family. Raised in genteel poverty by an emotionally distant mother (her father left the family during her youth), she cultivated a decidedly independent spirit that masked her private pain. She was trained in painting and drawing at the Rhode Island School of Design and then worked part-time using these skills, all the while developing the conviction that "the first duty of a human being is to ... find your real job, and do it" (Gilman, *Living* 42). Gilman was steadfast in her determination to contribute something meaningful to humanity. Her long, prolific career is testament that she did so: a writer, lecturer, and social reformer, she is best known for her short story "The Yellow Wall-Paper" (1892) and her book-length study *Women and Economics* (1898), and for her advocacy of progressive causes such as socialism, dress reform, pacifism, and women's suffrage. Less widely acknowledged but equally reflected in her correspondence are her tendencies toward xenophobia, racism, and, to a lesser extent, classism. Her career was marked by a precipitous rise and a long decline (both of which are richly documented in her letters), and her work was distinguished by an astonishing range of both genre and subject matter, bringing her into contact with a wide variety of individuals with whom to correspond. Describing herself as "only a preacher, whether on the platform or in print" (Gilman to Caroline Hill, December 4, 1921), she fashioned a pulpit out of whatever she had at hand, and she used it until her dying day.

Like her career, Gilman's personal life can be more deeply understood through attention to the letters she wrote. Her early attempts to merit the notice of an absent father, for example, provide a poignant counterpoint to the light, confident notes she dashed off to her young cousin George Houghton Gilman. Early on she vowed never to marry, preferring to devote her life to public service; yet she eventually married artist Charles Walter Stetson in 1884, and her daughter, Katharine, was born the following year. Her struggle to reconcile marriage and motherhood with her duty to world service, already well documented by scholars and biographers, is illuminated further in this volume. Her nervous breakdown, her attempt at a rest cure, her eventual divorce, her effort to raise her daughter as a single parent—all of these experiences are reflected in her correspondence. Similarly, her letters touch upon her decision to send Katharine to live with her father and his new wife, her ensuing struggle to maintain a relationship with her daughter, and her affection and esteem for her second husband, Houghton, to whom she was married from 1900 until his death in 1934. Just as Gilman's correspondence illuminates her two marriages, it sheds light upon her friendships and love affairs with women and her complex struggle with compulsory heterosexuality. And it documents her decision to die by her own hand after suffering from inoperable breast cancer, expressing her passionate advocacy of the right to die.

While the letters printed here allow readers access to a private Gilman, illuminating the personal experiences behind the public persona, by definition they expose her "in successive fragments, glimpse after glimpse" rather than offering a complete picture of her interior life (Spacks 70). As Janet Gurkin Altman argues, "The letter can be either a portrait or a mask" (185), and Gilman's serve both functions: even the most seemingly candid and private elements of her correspondence are the result of conscious authorial choices. Likewise, Rebecca Earle echoes numerous scholars of epistolary discourse in saying that letter writing allows one "to assume multiple, indeed contradictory personae" (3). Gilman's letters prove this to be true: though letter writing is conventionally understood as a form of private writing, Gilman's correspondence runs the gamut from intensely personal confessions to self-conscious attempts to construct her public image, putting her letters on a continuum with her published life-writing. Only recently having attained literary, as opposed to merely documentary, status, letters today are considered a form of autobiographical writing whose "performative, fictive, and textual dimensions" are worthy of serious analysis (Decker 4).[1] Even quick attention to Gilman's use of the letter's "stock gestures," such as "dating, salutation, and complimentary close" (Decker 22), reveals how adept she was at manipulating generic expectations.

Like many other letter writers, Gilman uses epistolary conventions to define herself vis-à-vis her addressee.[2] While letters to those of higher status typically begin with the orthodox "Dear Sir" and end "Yours Sincerely," she occasionally takes liberties that allow her more explicitly to display both deference and familiarity toward her interlocutor, such as the October 14, 1895, letter in which she salutes Charles Fletcher Lummis not as the prosaic "Dear Mr. Lummis" but instead as "O Amazing Editor!" Conversely, she claims the dominant role in the salutation she offers Martha Luther, the object of her affections who had, to Gilman's great disappointment, recently become involved with a man, continuing, rather tellingly, to address her as "Little Pet" (September 4, 1881). Even in her signature she finds ways to negotiate her relationships; she signs a November 28, 1900, letter to mentor Lester Ward as "Charlotte Perkins Gilman. (ex-Stetson!)," likely an attempt, after her marriage to Houghton, to remain visible to Ward as she continued to seek his approval. Equally interesting is her occasional decision to dispense with convention for her own ends. For the sake of humor, for instance, she opens a letter to Houghton with the salutation, "What Ho!?" (November 27, 1879). More earnestly, she addresses an early letter to Walter Stetson with a blank line to demonstrate that her love for him exceeds the language available for salutations: "_____. I have no title to address you by. They don't satisfy me, any of them" (February 13, 1882).

While Gilman's correspondence is both vast and diverse, it contains a number of telling motifs that are worth noting. As a metaphorical extension of her heart, her letters are a mechanism by which Gilman gives, receives, solicits, and withholds emotion. "Please write a real long letter to me," begs the eleven-year-old Gilman of her absent father (Gilman to Frederic Perkins, n.d.); a few years later, not wishing to offer this sign of love to one who spurns it, she confesses, "I <u>should</u> like to know whether you wish me to write to you" (April 10, 1881). Echoing this theme, running throughout her correspondence to Martha Luther is tension over Gilman's emotional investment in her letters and Martha's unwillingness to answer her in kind: "Here I show you my heart and you don't take the slightest notice, nor drop a word as to whether you enjoy the prospect or no" (July 29, 1881); a few days later, Gilman threatens to withhold her letters (and thus her affections): "Now if you don't take some notice of my letters—I'll <u>stop writing!</u>" (August 1, 1881). Clearly, Martha learned to be more appreciative, as she later earns Gilman's approval for her loving missives that validate Gilman's expressions of feeling. To Martha's request that Gilman destroy her too-revealing letters, Gilman asks, "Can't you trust me with your heart even when you feel it silly?" (September 4, 1881). More obviously, Gilman's letters to future husband Walter Stetson (like those written later to her second husband, Houghton Gilman, included in Mary A. Hill's *A Journey from Within*) are marked by emotional symbolism; this time, however, her letters suffer a lack because she is struggling to deny her feelings for Walter: "I am crushing my heart under foot," she confesses. "How can I write? Who am I writing too [*sic*]" (February 21, 1882). Most poignant of all are her letters to and about her young daughter, no longer in her custody. In typical Gilman fashion (and ironically repeating the hurtful dynamic used by her own mother), she explains to Katharine's stepmother, Grace, that in her letters to Katharine she tried "carefully to avoid such emotional touches as might make her grieve a little," confessing a few lines later that she is unsure as to whether her daughter wants "more lovingness . . . in the letters." That Gilman's emotional distance from her daughter is embodied in the epistolary form itself is clarified by the opening line of this letter, in which she asks Grace, "Will you tell me what sort of letter [Katharine] likes best?" (June 8, 1896). Seven months later she writes to Grace, "I do not know why I should sit here holding Katharine's letter to my heart and sobbing": having distanced herself from her family and finding it difficult to write letters of her own, she reveals feeling "unutterably far away and out of touch with all that is mine on earth" (January 11, 1897). While serving the obvious function of communication between herself and her loved ones, then, letters for Gilman have a much deeper symbolic meaning as well, serving as embodiments of the heart that is otherwise physically absent and wielding all of its emotional power.

Gilman's equation of the letter with the heart of its writer partakes of "the frequent conceit of familiar letters . . . that there is no essential difference between the letter-writer's *body* and her *letter*" (Hewitt 1; emphasis in source). Much like Nathaniel Hawthorne kissing Sophia Peabody's letters or Emily Dickinson mailing her tears to Sue Gilbert (Hewitt 1), Gilman frequently relies upon this conceit, speaking of letters in corporeal terms.[3] When Martha finally writes Gilman an attentive letter, for example, Gilman calls the missive "delicious"; "I taste your letter all the way down" (August 3 and 13, 1881). She confesses that another letter from Martha, left too long unanswered, is "pricking me sore" (June 17, 1890), and she tantalizes Walter by saying that she "could write letters that keep you warm in winter" (February 21, 1882). Whether it is the metonymic equation of letter and heart or the more general conceit that letters and bodies are contiguous, Gilman's corporeal language invests her correspondence with great import.

As a public figure who had reason to be wary of the yellow press, Gilman was acutely conscious that some of her letters contained information that could be damaging to her reputation and those of her loved ones, and this awareness forms another theme that recurs occasionally in her correspondence. "What horrid stuff these letters would be for the Philistines!" she writes to Martha after a particularly explicit declaration of love. "Lock 'em up, and some time we'll have a grand cremation" (July 30, 1881). The following month she continues in this vein, describing the way she lovingly carries Martha's letters in her pocket and then adding, "I was a little dubious about writing the above, but even if the Philistines ever should see it, what care I! If I am not ashamed of having sentiments I am not ashamed of admitting them" (August 8, 1881). And it would be less than a month later that Martha would ask Gilman to "tear up" her letter, to which Gilman would respond, "trust me with your heart" (September 4, 1881). Clearly, Martha did not destroy Gilman's letters, despite their containing evidence of the passionate relationship between the two. Years later, Gilman would use similar language in writing to Houghton, warning him about the scandal that would erupt if ever her letters to former lover Adeline Knapp were to surface: "I loved her, trusted her, wrote her as freely as I write to you. . . . You ought to know that there is a possibility of such letters being dragged out some day. . . . Of course she may have wisely burned them up. . . . Fancy the San Francisco papers. . . . Mrs. Stetson's Love Affair with a Woman. Is this 'Friendship'! and so on" (March 7, 1899, qtd. in Hill, *Journey* 246). Even her love letters to Houghton she considered intensely personal and revelatory. While Gilman was conscious of letters' power as evidence of privately expressed sentiments that exceeded what was acceptable in her day, she generally did not make the effort, as some in her era did, to ensure her correspondence was destroyed. Indeed, as Mary A. Hill notes, after Houghton's death Gilman decided to preserve the love letters she had long ago sent to him, which he had saved.[4] Far from destroying her epistolary record, late in life Gilman made a point of saving letters "for biographical use" (Gilman to Grace, October 13, 1925).

Gilman clearly understood that the letters she wrote throughout her life were important, that they contained valuable information about her, particularly as she became a public figure. She was also keenly aware of the fact that writing letters was hard work, and this awareness forms probably the most dominant motif in her correspondence. Writing in the age before telecommunication and living far from loved ones, Gilman used letters to transact all kinds of personal and professional business, such as keeping in touch and negotiating relationships with family and friends, arranging for speaking engagements, communicating with publishers, even saying good-bye in the months before her suicide. A few years after her first breakdown, she recollected that in the past, "in the young exuberance of hereditary pen-power . . . I sought about wildly for correspondents; pursued, discovered, created them; and could write more letters in a day, about nothing at all, than I can write now in a week on life death and money matters" (Gilman to Marian Parker Whitney, May 30, 1890);

she "look[ed] back with incredulous amazement to the time when writing was easier than talking and I sought correspondence for correspondence' sake" (Gilman to Martha Luther, August 15, 1889). Gilman's periodic depressions always affected her ability to conduct correspondence as well as to do other forms of "work"; her attitude toward writing letters first seemed to change, as noted above, with the breakdown precipitated by her first marriage and the birth of her daughter. In a telling echo of the narrator in "The Yellow Wall-Paper," Gilman writes to S. Weir Mitchell before her rest cure, "I know it isn't what I should have written but I can't do better now. . . . I am all alone in the house or I couldn't write this. <u>People</u> tire me frightfully. I'm running down like a clock—could go one [*sic*] scribbling now indefinitely—but the letters don't come right" (April 19, 1887). Here Gilman offers a striking reminder of the materiality of letter writing. Unlike those writing even a generation before, she no longer had to worry so much about the mechanics of epistolarity—she had ready access to stationery, pen and ink, postage, and mechanism for delivery—but she was restrained by her physical and mental limitations.[5] "My head is what fails you know—" she wrote to Marian Parker Whitney, "or rather the nerve force—brain power—whatever it is you write letters with" (February 19, 1894).

Gilman thus conducted her correspondence somewhat unevenly: she would write prolifically when she was feeling well, and would then go through long periods in which she was unable to do so because she was depressed or ill. A letter to William Haslam Mills offers some indication of the scale on which she operated as a correspondent: "I have brought with, for 'holiday work,['] 58 letters to answer!" ([August 9], 1915).[6] Though the apology for not having responded sooner is a well-worn epistolary convention, in Gilman's case its frequent occurrences seem most sincerely meant. She confesses to Caroline Hill that the letter she received six months earlier remains in a "conscience-crushing heap"; "I saved the letter for a fitting time to answer—and there never is any," she reveals (December 4, 1921). She writes to E. A. Ross on July 6, 1925, that she has "just now found on my desk among the 'not immediates' yours of about two years ago." And to her "Patient Friend" Alice Park she admits, "Yours of May 12th, with many interesting enclosures, duly received, read, appreciated and buried! I'm just digging 'em out now—a terrible heap" (July 18, 1930). At a particularly low point, she admitted to Martha Luther, "letters I try simply to forget, in order that they may not haunt me" (August 15,

1889). Ever conscious of her physical and mental limitations and driven to do more than she could manage in a day, Gilman was continually troubled by those yet-unwritten letters, which she numbered along with the other "work" she still hoped to accomplish. "I know, none better," she exclaimed to Katharine, "how impossible letters are!!" (September 8, 1921).

As editors, we understand that, in selecting, compiling, and editing Gilman's letters for publication, we are "chang[ing] their meaning as documents" (Spacks 74), and that published collections of letters by definition objectify the subject of the volume, turning her from an "I" to a "she" (Spacks 77).[7] And as we have already indicated, we are all too aware that the seemingly comprehensive picture of Gilman's life provided by these letters only hints at the infinite, opaque nature of her individuality. Nonetheless, we believe this collection to be valuable, for it "gives the reader an opportunity neither the author nor her individual correspondent had—that of reading a letter in context, as well as the chance to survey the correspondence with one person over a period of years." Though "assembled by the critic rather than the author," the writing herein may still "be considered a valid exposition of [Gilman's] thought" (Crecelius 259). Furthermore, while we are mindful of the ethical minefield we walk in publishing Gilman's private mail, a process that Spacks likens to gossip, our intent is to "dignify small truths rather than trivialize large ones" (Spacks 77). In providing a fuller picture of Gilman we hope precisely to complicate the stories that scholars tell about her, emphasizing her uniqueness and her subjectivity. Nearly every aspect Gilman's life and every piece of her private *oeuvre* have been published in some form; we hope that her letters will infuse this public record with a fuller, richer picture of who she was, even if this picture will always remain elusive and incomplete.

# A Note on the Text

The purpose of this edition is to make available to scholars, researchers, and students a selection of correspondence written by author and lecturer Charlotte Perkins Gilman (1860–1935). Until now, the bulk of Gilman's letters, with the exception of her correspondence to her second husband, George Houghton Gilman, have been available only through microfiche copy or by personally viewing the original documents—an accommodation that is permitted only in exceptional cases—at the Schlesinger Library at the Radcliffe Institute, Harvard University, in Cambridge, Massachusetts, which houses the largest collection of Gilman papers in the world, and in smaller holdings at a number of other libraries, museums, private collections, and historical societies. The texts used in this edition were drawn primarily from original copies of correspondence and from microfiche and photocopies; any questionable transcriptions were verified against the original letters housed at various institutions owning Gilman letters. We have also located and used letters that were purchased at flea markets and online auctions.

Included in this edition are representative selections written between approximately 1867 and August 1935. The selections illustrate Gilman's development from a restless, high-spirited, and rather opinionated young woman to a mature, internationally renowned author and lecturer whose words and wisdom touched thousands of lives as she attempted to effect social change. Passages that have been omitted because of space constraints are indicated with ellipses. Ellipses placed in the correspondence by Gilman herself are given in brackets.

Because the role of an editor is to be less interpretive than objective, we have attempted, in the chapter introductions, to let the letters stand for themselves, while still providing as background an appropriate amount of historical and biographical contextualization. Readers wishing to have a fuller biographical or psychological profile of Charlotte Perkins Gilman should consult full-length biographies listed in the bibliography. For uniformity's sake, we have chosen to refer to Gilman by the last name she assumed upon marrying her second husband, as this is the name by which she is best known.

The editorial method we used was a conservative one: our purpose has been to reproduce the original text of Gilman's letters to her correspondents rather than to "improve" it through editorial emendations. Throughout this project, textual and historical accuracy has been an overriding concern. Therefore, Gilman's spelling, capitalization, often-erratic (and sometimes missing) punctuation, underlinings, indentations, and abbreviations have been preserved. There are only two exceptions. The first has been to standardize dates; in some cases, for example, Gilman transposed month and day. As a result, dates that were clearly inverted (e.g., "17-1-'23") have been made consistent throughout, with the month preceding the day (e.g., "1-17-'23"). The second exception is our treatment of paragraph indentations, which are sometimes ambiguous; we have, therefore, made our best estimate of paragraph breaks, while conceding that in some instances our placement is subjective. In cases where parts of words are missing because of damaged or mutilated text in the extant letters, we have attempted to reconstruct the passage based on the partial word and have indicated the reconstruction with a bracketed question mark. On the rare occasion where we have included missing punctuation to enhance readability, we have enclosed the inserted punctuation in brackets. In addition, although Gilman was at times a particularly poor speller, we have transcribed the letters as they were written, occasionally adding a missing letter in brackets. In those places where there may be a question as to whether an errant spelling is Gilman's or an error in transcription, we have included a bracketed "sic" to indicate the former. Even the names of friends and/or acquaintances were occasionally misspelled, but we have let those errors stand on the theory that to correct the error may obscure information that readers might otherwise deem significant.

Gilman's circle of friends and correspondents was wide; as a result, we have identified and annotated those people with whom she shared a close relationship, those with whom she spent a substantial amount of time, and those who were well enough known to be included in biographical dictionaries. Despite our best efforts, a few people remain unidentified, primarily those to whom there is only brief mention.

In addition to having a wide range of acquaintances, Gilman—like many of her correspondents—was an avid reader; hence the Gilman letters sometimes allude to literary works. As a result, we have annotated works according to specific criteria. Annotation has not been provided for the following: historical works and biographies where the title conveys a strong sense of the content (e.g., Symonds' "Studies of the Greek Poets"); works for which Gilman has included title and author (e.g., Olive Schreiner's *Women and Labor*); and works (primarily short fiction, poems, and essays) appearing in popular press magazines for which no index is available. Otherwise, we have identified as many of the works as possible. At times, however, it was impossible to locate obscure or incomplete titles.

As a rule, we have provided annotation for Gilman's own works, particularly where publication information is noteworthy. Readers wishing complete publication histories of Gilman's works are referred to Gary Scharnhorst's virtually complete listing, *Charlotte Perkins Gilman: A Bibliography* (1985), which also provides useful information on published reports of Gilman's lectures.

In addition to inconsistencies in spelling and in punctuation noted above, Gilman used numerous abbreviations in her letters; we have expanded abbreviations where there is any question about their meaning. Allusions to places, people, events, words, or objects that might be unfamiliar to the contemporary reader or that might benefit from clarification have been elucidated to make the text more accessible.

The letters in this edition have been grouped either by correspondent or by theme and are listed chronologically within each chapter. We have provided chapter introductions and offered backgrounds and contexts for the letters in each section.

Finally, because of space restrictions, the process of selecting letters to include was a difficult one. We opted to provide the reader with letters that we deemed to be the most biographically or historically illuminating. The one exception was our decision not to duplicate letters from Gilman to her second husband, Houghton Gilman, that are readily available in Mary A. Hill's excellent edition, *A Journey from Within: The Love Letters of Charlotte Perkins Gilman, 1897–1900* (1995). We have, however, included selections of correspondence between the two that were not included in Hill's volume.

# The Selected Letters
# of Charlotte Perkins Gilman

Figure 1. Charlotte Perkins Stetson,
ca. 1884. Courtesy of Denise D.
Knight.

# I
# Youthful Correspondence
## "I often feel hopelessly despairing"

In an undated letter to her paternal grandmother, Mary Beecher Foote
Perkins, written circa 1867, when Charlotte Anna Perkins was about seven
years old, the youthful correspondent apologized for her epistolary neg-
ligence but justified her laxity by proclaiming, "I dont like to write."
Ironically, Gilman went on to become one of the most prolific writers
of the Progressive Era, publishing everything from poetry and fiction
to theoretical treatises. "To write was always as easy to me as to talk,"
she remarked in her memoir (*Living* 98), and the early habit of letter
writing that she purposely cultivated—reluctant missives to Grandma
notwithstanding—was one that she practiced throughout her life.

The correspondence in this chapter illuminates Gilman's youth—and its subsequent impact in her later life—in a variety of ways. In letters to her father, Frederic Perkins, who was estranged from the family, Gilman's emotions run the gamut. She pleads for much-needed money on behalf of her mother, who earned little as a part-time teacher; she also solicits advice, confesses to experiencing "intervals of depression," and, in her earliest correspondence, begs her often-insensitive father to respond to her letters. By the time Gilman was twenty she realized that her entreaties had fallen on deaf ears, but her disappointment over her father's lack of interest in her life is still apparent. On April 10, 1881, she wrote: "I know of old that you are too busy to write letters, even if you cared to, but I should like to know whether you wish me to write to you, for I am anything but desirous to intrude." At the same time, however, she attempts to protect herself from further rejection by assuming an air of indifference: "Do you know,—I think I should have liked you very much—as a casual acquaintance." His response was both brusque and crushing: "As for writing letters, I don't expect ever to write anything, except notes any more, & no more of those than I can help" (n.d.). Despite his rejection, Gilman still tried to forge a relationship. Shortly before her twenty-first birthday, she wrote to her father again asking for advice about a possible marriage to Charles Walter Stetson, whom she had met six months earlier: "Now it dawns on my aspiring mind that you know more than I do! And it also occurs to me that if I were in your place and had a daughter, that I should like to have her follow my suggestion in a case like this" (June 19, 1882). It was an exercise in futility. Gilman's efforts to secure a meaningful relationship with her father were again rebuffed, leaving her to conclude that although he possessed a "brilliant intellect" he had "small moral sense" (Gilman to Weir Mitchell, April 19, 1887).

This chapter also contains Gilman's early letters to her seven-years-younger cousin George Houghton Gilman, whom she would marry in 1900 at the age of thirty-nine, after divorcing Stetson in 1894. With few exceptions, the letters are playful and affectionate, as are several of the extant letters to Gilman's lifelong friend Martha Luther Lane, who also lived in Providence. The intense relationship between Gilman and Lane, well documented by biographers, garnered more commentary in Gilman's memoir than did her second marriage. "With Martha I knew perfect happiness," she wrote. "My first memory of loving any one . . . and immeasurably the dearest, was Martha. We were closely together, increasingly happy together, for four of those long years of girlhood" (*Living* 78).

The extant correspondence to Martha Lane, whom Gilman addresses as her "kitten," "pet," and "little girl," documents not only Gilman's enormous love but also the despair she suffered when she sensed that Martha's investment in the relationship was not as deep as her own. Gilman's sense of vulnerability is striking. "Fancy me strong and unassailable to all the world beside, and then coming down and truckling to you like a half-fed amiable kitten," she wrote to Martha on August 1, 1881. The letter reveals not only Gilman's insecurity but also the dichotomy between the strong and confident persona she presented to the public and the immense pain she endured privately. When Martha announced in early November that she was engaged to be married, Gilman was devastated. A little over two months later she was introduced to Stetson, a handsome Providence artist, whom she would marry in 1884.

As the letters to Stetson in this chapter reveal, Gilman was deeply divided on the issue of marriage and had long planned to devote her life to public service. She was pulled "in two directions," she acknowledged in a February 20, 1882, letter to Stetson. She did not want to make an impulsive decision; on the contrary, she saw herself as "a clearheaded woman who is weighing a lifetime in her hand." She feared that marriage might bring "a lifetime's possible pain," but she still craved the love and intimacy that had eluded her all of her life. The following day she wrote to Stetson that she had always known, "of course, that the time would come when I must choose between two lives, but never did I dream that it would come so soon, and that the struggle would be so terrible" (February 21, 1882). Although she eventually agreed to marry Stetson, just four months before their wedding she confessed to feeling suicidal: "If I were <u>sure</u> that death changed life for the better . . . I fear that even my sense of duty &c. would hardly save you from what you most dread. . . . I have a frail hope that our life together will have enough of joy to keep me sane" (January 1, 1884). Despite grave misgivings, and clinging to the "frail hope" that marriage might provide the love she both craved and feared, Gilman became Mrs. Charles Walter Stetson on May 2, 1884.

[n.d., ca. 1867]

Dear grandma[1] how are you we are all well how is grandpa dont be discuraged if I dont write oftener for I dont like to write much but I thought I woud to-day for I have not written for a long while. whenever I have a wish-bone I wish that you were well tell Catherine[2] that I can

not come and see her now but tell her to that she must not go away. . . .
from Charlotte.

[n.d., ca. 1871][3]

Dear father,

Will you please send the money for July, August, and September.
You told me to remind you of the Princess and Goblin,[4] if you forget
it. My three kits are getting large and fat. Thomas drowned the old cat
for she killed four chicks. Thomas has got a nice garden, and furnishes
us with potatos, tomatoes, melons, corn beans and squashes and pump-
kins. We have apples and pears in plenty. Please write a real long letter
to me. . . . I wish you would write to me often; . . . nobody writes to me
but you. . . . I inclose two pictures, in hopes you will do the same.

Yours affectionately,
CAP

[n.d., ca. 1875][5]

Dear father,

Now I want to have a nice long talk with you. Here I am, fifteen
years old, quite strong, . . . and instructed in the ordinary branches of
study in a reasonable degree, with a taste for literature and art, a desire (as is general I believe among girls) for well, a great many things,
and a lamentable blank in the direction of a means of livelihood. Now,
I don't want to beg, borrow or steal, I don't approve of that ordinary
mode of mending the broken fortunes of young ladies in general, viz.,
advantageous matrimony, and the question is, in the words of a rant-
ing Methodist preacher whom I once heard, "What shall I do to be
saved?" I have an inclination in the direction of authorship, but, I have
doubts as to whether I could make it pay. I also have a leaning on the
side of art; but have the same misgivings, I made a little spurt in Pho-
nographic Reporting, (a lucrative profession, I have heard,) but doubt
my own ability; I am very much much [*sic*] interested in Physiological
lectures and specimens, that we are having in school, and have vague aspirations to be an M. D.; and more than all, & worse than all, perhaps
you will say, I confess to the heinous crime of being strongly attracted
to the Stage!!!!! There! The murder is out, the cat has left the bag, the
ice is broken, and "Come one!; come all!; this rock shall fly, from its firm
base, as soon as I"!!!!![6]

"Unstable as water, thou shalt not excel"[7] said the patriarch to his son, the words often ring in my ears, and I sometimes feel, as if there was no hope, and the irrevocable Word of the Lord, had pronounced my doom. That, is in my intervals of depression, few and far between you may think, but it is not so, I often feel hopelessly despairing, at my total inability to <u>work</u>. It is, the the [*sic*] instability of character that has been the bane and poison of so many lives that might otherwise have been almost immortal. I realy [*sic*] feel it father, and it distresses me. Why one day, I'll sit down and write poetry . . . another time scribble and draw for ever so long, and again, go up to mothers room, shut the door (in pity for the rest of the household), stand in front of the glass, and give vent to the most extraordinary series of roars and shrieks that the human voice is capable of. When I feel happy, I contract my brows into a diabolical frown, when I have relapsed in the depth of despair, I assume a beatified expression, and put on a beaming smile, when I am alone I laugh promiscuously. . . . I did practice fainting on two shawls, but it hurt, so I gave it up. <u>Now</u>! I want [a] good strong dose of advice, though I cant depend sufficiently on my present happy frame of mind to promise to follow it, and in the expectation of a speedy return to this protracted epistle, I remain your perplexed daughter C. A. P.

Providence.
Nov. 23, 1879.

Dear Houghton,[8]

Although I imagine you to have written to me today, I don't wait for it, but send a beginner. . . .

I had a real good time on the boat coming home.

There was a young couple on board,
Who were each by the other adored,
The looks they were using
Were very amusing
To all the spectators on board. . . .

We have had two letters from Thomas in Nevada. He tells us divers amusing facts about the manners and customs. . . .

And he says of the Indians, Utes; "they, some of 'em, have their faces painted bright vermilion, and some of the squaws are good looking, but they are rather a disappointing lot, below medium size, grinning, chattering & dirty, male & female." So there is the noble red man!

Now take good care of your eyes, young man, and write soon to your loving cousin,

Chowperkins

Providence.<br>Nov. 27 1879.

What Ho!?

Two letters of yours received, old gentleman. And greatly pleased therewith was I, but very, very sorry to hear of your dear mama's illness. Tell her I love her, and let me know as soon as she is well enough for a letter.

By the way young friend, I will be obliged to you if you will request one of your aunts to forward to my address the grey flannel sack I left at your house; verily I will remunerate the expressman, and be extremely thankful. . . .

Ha! a thought strikes me! You can have it yourself as a testimonial of lasting affection, and a reminder of the ten commandments.

> There was a young girl much inclined,
> to leave all her treasures behind,
> and the older she grew,
> and the more ways she flew,
> the less of her things could she find. . . .

I had a joyous Thanksgiving dinner today, and devoured such an amount, as to be quite incapacitated for manual labor for the rest of the day. It is to be hoped that you have suffered no ill effects from similar indulgences.

By by dear, and don't forget to let me know how mama is. CAP.

Providence<br>Dec. 4th, 1879.

Dear Houghton,

Yours of 3rd. received. . . .

Yes, I got your aunt's letter, but not till after I had heard.[9]

Glad and beautiful your news is, and it makes me happy from the bottom of my heart to know that your dear papa is with you once more.[10] Give him my love, lots of it, all that I had for Bessie, and Aunt Katie, and what you can spare of your own share. . . .

Yours with love,

Sisperkins.

Providence
Jan 5th.
1880.

[To Houghton Gilman]
O long suffering youth!

. . . Our Christmas was most gay and festive. . . . We had a gorgeous time, and gifts numerous if not magnificent. My own private pride and glory is a gold pen with a pearl handle, ensconced in a velvet lined case. With this resplendent utensil I write such mellifluous verse, and entertaining prose as would wile the heart out of a statue. Alas & woe is me! It is now in my trunk, and my trunk has not yet returned from Boston. Yer know, Oh guileless infant, that on the day after Christmas I betook myself to that fair city, and remained there, & in Cambridge till Saturday last: What joys were mine! I went sleighing, I went to the theatre, I went to parties, and I received calls. Bye and bye, when you "are old and hideous, and the hairs of your beard are mostly grey,"[11] as the poet says, you will understand the joys of such an existence. At present, I dare say that your benighted mind regards them with unmitigated contempt. . . .

[Charlotte]

Providence.
March 11th, 1880.

Dear Ho,

. . . I have been having a very jolly week, for mother went to Boston, where she saw our mutual cousins and other friends and I reveled in solitary grandeur. I go to school as well as yourself, and it was much fun to get up early, get my breakfast, take a lunch, start out, and not come back till dark. . . .

I am glad you are becoming expert on the bicycle, for I love the beast myself, and only wish "we girls" could ride them. I have seen female velocipedeists, but they were "no better than they should be," as certain vinegar faced ole ladies say. Yes, we have bicycles in Providence. I have seen them flitting dimly by at dusk, bestridden by a spectral Brown student, who feared derision by daylight.

We are having a jolly snowstorm today. . . . But I fear it is too late for any good sleighing. I haven't had my skates out this year. And oh! The ice! . . . I don't suppose the cares of housekeeping weigh heavily enough upon your shoulders for you to realize its value, but I do.

Yours affectionately,<br>Charlotte A. Perkins.

Providence<br>Aug 22nd. 1880.

Beloved Aunt,[12]

I believe mother has informed you of the change we propose to make if the Pitcherses will only move out.

Won't it be jolly!

You see you will sit down stairs, and when a swain cometh we can play whist, and if it is an eligible youth you can smuggle mother out of the way in fine style.

> At present you know
> She has no where to go,
> But she rocks as she sits,
> And she yawns and she knits,
> And she nods in her chair
> While the young men are there,
> And behaves in a way
> That will surely delay
> The most sanguine young man's
> Matrimonial plans.
> But if you take the reins
> There's an end to my pains;
> With your daughters they tell
> you have done very well
> And your labors won't cease
> Till you've paired off your niece
> Why if you're at the head
> I can see myself wed,

Inside of a year
From the time you appear.

Shan't we have good times! . . .
Why don't you write to me again O recreant aunt!
Here I am writing and writing to you, and you haven't answered but once.
Now be good. . . .

Charlotte A. Perkins

Providence<br>April 10th 1881.

Dear father,

As you have not answered mother's letter of March 6th, acknowledging yours with $15.00 enclosed, received on the 2nd, we conclude you did not get it, and being of importance I will repeat the substance of her letter.

We have taken that house of which we wrote to you last fall; in every respect superior to this and for the same rent that you pay here—$15.00 a month. I've had to decide rather suddenly, and the chance seemed too good to lose, so we took it, and are anxious to know if you will mind sending the rent to mother instead of Mr. Sayles. . . .

I am well now, reasonably happy, and as busy as I want to be. Have been at work since November on advertising cards. My cousin Robert Brown is the business partner of the firm of "Perkins & Co. Designers,"[13] furnishes ideas, go-ahead-itiveness, and everything else save the pencil part, and so far we have done well. We have turned out four sets this winter, and are working on the fifth. . . .

I am twenty one this 3rd of July, have outgrown sundry imbecilities of which I wrote you at the age of fifteen; and am rapidly turning into an unattractive strongminded old maid. It has been, and is, a very curious study with me to watch the growth and change of conflicting hereditary traits of character and the rapid crystallization and decided prominence of certain strongly marked peculiarities which I think I come by honestly. Life looks broad and pleasant, with much to do for the general good; and personal pain or pleasure not worth counting on. . . .

I know of old that you are too busy to write letters, even if you cared to, but I <u>should</u> like to know whether you wish me to write to you, for I am anything but desirous to intrude.

Do you know,—I think I should have liked you very much—as a casual acquaintance.

Yours truly,<br>C. A. Perkins.

Providence<br>July 22nd. 1881.[14]

[To Martha Luther]

O my pet and sweetheart! That I should be so busy I can't find time to write to my own little girl! . . .

I supposed you have already found out that I can't come to your Eden; worse for me than for you, my chicken. But I <u>will</u> go somewhere. For I rise at five, and sit laboriously in one chair all day, and feel as lame on rising as if I had walked 100 miles. . . .

I would don my bathing dress after breakfast, take some dinner with me, and spend whole days in sand and water! Oh my ducky! if only you—, I wish you to understand Miss Luther that the pleasantest part of this excursion is it's [*sic*] entire solitude! I hope I can do it, and if not this summer, next. (I have thought seriously of buying a wig, and going man fashion—young artist, etc.) . . .

Providence.<br>July 24th, 1881.

[To Martha Luther]

Little kitten, little kitten,

They are all "abed," and I love you this warm bright Sunday morning more than ever.

But you don't answer letters worth a cent. When I takes [*sic*] pains and writes lots of pwitty fings to 'moose my little girl, I like to have my little girl notice 'em.

Likes to have her 'stonished at my 'ventures, and pleased when I remember every word of some folk's conversation to tell her.

Hasn't said a word bout nuffin, I said, 'ny more 'n if you hadn't got 'em! Long, fat, <u>beautiful</u> letters! . . .

I wish I could come up for a call, but I can't my chick, it wouldn't give me half the absolute rest, change, and freedom, that I can get at some hole around here, and I want salt water <u>awfully</u>. . . .

I am really getting glad not to marry. For the mother side of me is strong enough to make an interminable war between plain duties & irrepressible instincts, I should rage as I do now at confinement and steady work, and spend all my force in pushing two way [*sic*] without getting anywhere. I be spiled [*sic*] like my pa most likely.

Whereas if I let that business alone, and go on in my own way; what I gain in individual strength and development of personal power of character, <u>myself as a self</u>, you know, not merely as a woman, or that useful animal a wife and mother, will I think make up, and more than make up in usefulness and effect, for the other happiness that part of me would so enjoy. If Avis[15] had looked at it so, she might have trodden on two hearts, and stood heaven high in her art in consequence. . . .

My little girl! Who lives in my heart, and gives me what no one else in the world ever knows I want!

I could spend hours in cuddling if I had you here. I can see all your manifold little dearnesses, and "I'd be willing to bet five cents, if I was in the habit of betting" that you will make up to me for husband and children and all that I shall miss. And if I can't do enough for mankind to earn myself a home in my old age, I don't deserve one. Oh! I am so grateful to the kind father or the just law that led us two together, and for that intrinsic perversity of character that led me to love you the more, the more I wasn't wanted to.

It isn't that I don't enjoy your letters dear, you know how much I do, and don't you dare to leave out a word of 'em! but I am a <u>talkin'</u> to yer! And taint "pillite" not to take any notice of my observations in your ir-relevant replies.

What a delicious little signature you have invented! Let me quote it—

Yours <u>in love</u>,
Charlotte A. Perkins

Providence
July 29th. 1881.

[To Martha Luther]
Dear Puss,

. . . I got your letter this morning, <u>my first</u>, and was pleased, though I think you misunderstood me a trifle. I don't want you to be the same kind of humbug that I am, not a bit of it. You are to be your own sweet lovely self, marry all you please, and be loved and cared for to your hearts content. But be your home as charming as it may, I am to have a night-key as it were, and shall enjoy in you and yours all that I don't have myself. Halicarnassus[16] will like me I know, and as for the children—look out for your laurels! You see I never said that I was to make up to you for all this, but you to me, and that without requiring the slightest sacrifice on your part. And if Halicarnassus doesn't like me, or if you should up and die, in short if I can't have it—why I'll go it alone and be as happy as a clam natheless.

I've dropped the heart business once and for all, it never was as strong as my head and the sooner I squelch it altogether the more firmly shall I progress.

Sam[17] was here last night, and nearer than I ever thought he could be again. He marched into my room and sat down, ignoring the occupants of the next apartment for some time. Aunt C. had a cold and retired, mother came in, talked frigidly a while, and retired, and I luxuriated in clear Sam. (as one might in clear Sam, you know.)

I launched at him all my "generalities & particulars" theory, changing the last illustration as you may imagine, and had the exquisite satisfaction of hearing him say with a most deeply interested expression that that was a new thought to him!

Now that is just what I want. To be the sort of woman, handsome, self-poised, well-read, keen-sighted, refreshing,—who men will delight to talk with, and always find meat. . . .

Well, I opened on Sammy, with great care, and many masked batteries beforehand; put the case before him—1st the frightful incompatibility between mother & myself, my rebellion and utter inefficiency in this runround sort of life, my gradually strengthening and now unconquerable desire for mental culture and exercise; my determination to drop my half-developed functional womanhood, and take the broad road of individuality apart from sex; and all the bother and uncertainty resulting from mother's inability to live without me, and my surviving relics of overdriven hereditary concience [*sic*]—showed him the state of the case as plainly and fairly as I could, and asked his honest advice as an unbiased observer and a man.

And what do you think he said?

In the first place he took it beautifully, was as respectful and as deeply interested as heart could wish; saw the whole seriousness of his position too, in giving the casting vote perhaps to a young girl standing with her well controlled nature in her hand, waiting to let it go one way or the other—admitted that, in almost as many words, said, he "saw that I was in a place where a very little urging would send me on in the way I was pointing," and reallizing [*sic*] his responsibility, and knowing what he did of mother's life and my life—his advice would be "<u>Go Ahead!</u>"

And I'm <u>going</u>. . . .

<u>I have decided</u>. I'm <u>not</u> domestic and don't want to be. Neither am I a genius in any especial sense, but a <u>strong-minded</u> woman I will be if I have to wade in blood as the ancient bravado hath it. I can work now to some purpose, wait with some patience, guard my health and strength with an end in view, and cultivate my beauty (don't laugh) to its utmost, as one strong weapon. Mind, I haven't let Ambition so much as squeak yet; just as I crush a haunting thought out of my mind and cooly walk on feelings (ever blessed be my education!) so do I keep that strong angel gagged and bound, pushing with articulate clamor from behind my outer brain and adding all his prisoned force to mine. . . .

What I want you see is to acquire sufficient <u>strength</u>, real literal <u>strength</u> of mind to be able to see clearly and <u>kill</u> swiftly any recalcitrance of the past of my heart in after years.

(Here I pause a bit to sit on Ambition. Let him kick, by all means, he does very well where he is, but once out I should lose the power that all <u>ungratified</u> longing gives, and have harder work in catching him than the Fisherman & the Afrite.)[18] . . .

Yours with the first free breath I ever drew<br>Charlotte Anna <u>Perkins</u>!

9–10 P.M. Providence<br>July 30th. 1881

[To Martha Luther]
Dear little girl,

A well-earned hour, and all for you. And I am rereading your dear comfortable little letter, and find room for comment. . . .

I am not sure that it is a blameworthy characteristic but as you may have learned by this time, I gather inspiration from outside sources, and can do great things while the fit lasts. And my present aim is to keep this exalted state of mind and work from it, till it gets to be the normal position. . . .

Remember my idea that what one can conceive one can do? . . . If I can comprehend a life like this, I can do it. Now I shall descend from my eminence with surpassing agility, and I shall continue to resemble other people in the most reassuring manner, so don't feel that I have fled to Parnassus[19] without a goodbye; but I shall be conscious all the time of how I <u>can</u> feel, and take every opportunity to read the books and get among the people who will wake me up. . . .

O my little love! I'd like to wind all round and round you and let you feel my heart.

What horrid stuff these letters would be for the Philistines! Lock 'em up, and some time we'll have a grand cremation. . . .

O I was tired yesterday. Two long letters for rest and recreation, and paint, paint, paint. I have written down and pasted up my labors for this winter. . . . I have boiled it all down, together with the imperative need to finish all I have in hand in order to get to more, into the one word <u>Work</u>! And "work!" I say when the bent head turns and the tired eyes stray out of the window; "Work"! when my senses fail and the unconscious hand drops the colorfilled brush right on the paper,— "Work!" when I drowsily open my eyes after 6 hours sleep and would give the world for more, and "<u>Work</u>!" this minute when I want to talk for hours to my little love, and must go and wash dishes <u>and</u> so forth. Good bye chick! I shan't stop even for you if you don't want to go. I could not love thee dear so much, <u>loved I not honor more</u>![20] <u>Good</u> bye. I love you more at any rate, and we'll have our pleasant wink, and be as happy as clams when I come down off the mountain. Yours ever, C. A. Perkins

Providence
Aug. 1st. 1881.

[To Martha Luther]
Dear Pussy,

Here I am again, writing to you half from personal love, and half because I must talk, and those here are deaf and dumb. Don't ever think that I look down on my relations, or despise and dislike them because they are not like me, it is only that we are not on the same road.

Their level may be higher than mine, but as our Sage hath it "if I am the devil's child, I will live then from the devil."[21] . . .

My pet! Fancy me strong and unassailable to all the world beside, and then coming down and truckling to you like a half-fed amiable kitten!

I have a pleasing scheme on hand now. Wouldn't it be nice if one had the means to start, I mean, to get Dr. Brooks to start, a class in the higher gymnastics for young ladies.[22] Just a few of us, a nice set and a hall with "facilities" where we could wear abbreviated garments and elevate the massive dumb bell at our leisure. And a lady physician to examine us and tell what course we should pursue. This for the future I fear, but wouldn't it be nice. Well puss, I'll write more bye and bye. "Work" now. Houp la! I see the Postman coming. I'll wait and see if I hear from you. . . .

10 a.m. Tuesday.

I'm disappointed. That mean owdacious postman stalked straight by, and I have no letter from Marfa!

Don't care. I shall viciously quote from the Sage, (who you may have divined is in my mind at present)—"It has seemed to me lately more possible than I knew, to carry a friendship greatly on one side, without due <u>correspondence</u> on the other."[23] Shall I go on? It grows viciouser.

"Why should I cumber myself with the poor fact that the receiver is not capacious?" You've read his "Friendship"? haven't you?

I am skimming just now for your benefit, and was ever anything more pat—"The scholar sits down to write, and all his years of meditation do not furnish him with one good thought or happy expression; but it is necessary to write a letter to a friend,—and, forthwith, troop of gentle thoughts invest themselves, on every hand, with chosen words." And see here pussy, "Friendship, like the immortality of the soul, is too good to be believed.(!) The lover, beholding his maiden, half knows that she is not verily that which he worships; <u>and in the golden hour of friendship, we are surprised with shades of suspicion and unbelief</u> (!)["] "In strictness, the soul does not respect men as it respects itself" (!)

And O Martha, just look here! <u>I was right</u>, I read Emersons incomprehensible conundrum! My mind was his for a moment! Here is the question you gave me, that we never could find, answered just as I answered it.

Right after my last quotation—"In strict science, <u>all persons underlie the same condition of infinite remoteness</u>."!!!!! . . .

Do you congratulate me? I feel as proud and glad as if I had discovered a country.

I shan't write an [*sic*] more Sage just now, this whole essay is alive, and I can't wait till you return to read it to you—just one more though, <u>for you</u>, really, this time.

"Let me be alone to the end of the world, rather than that my friend should overstep by a word or a look his real sympathy. . . ."

Now if you don't take some notice of my letters—I'll <u>stop writing</u>! CAP

Providence
Aug. 6th 1881.

[To Martha Luther]
Little Pet,

It has got to where I don't need the slightest excuse to write to you pussy, not the least incident, not a grain of news. Simply that I love you. I don't know that we ever refrain from calling on each other on account of a special topic of conversation lacking, and why should correspondence pale for a like reason?

I haven't got over basking in your last letter yet. It was so deliciously comforting, so exactly what I wanted!

Do you get tired of my everlasting ecstacies, sweetheart? Because they are only just beginning, and you had better protest now if you are going to.

You are slowly dawning on me "as it were," I am gradually reallizing [*sic*] what you are, and what you are to me. And I'm happy.

I have entered a new line of culture, chick—i.e. that bête-noir[24] of my aboriginally savage disposition, and natural laziness, a minute attention to personal cleanliness. I take a cold Ammonia bath every morning when I get up (won't that be fun in winter?) I tend my nails (all ten of 'em) with scrupulous care, and with many groans I have set myself to the Augean task of keeping my head clean. Object, merely additional perfection of character and that respectful love which you cannot but feel for a thing you at once revere and take care off [*sic*]. . . .

Truly my body shall be as much a fit dwelling place for my aspiring soul as hands can make it. . . .

A.M. 7th.

Yours just received.

O you dear bewitching lovely little Frotty!

You obtuse perversely-misunderstanding thickheaded little idiot!

What under the sun do I love you for, save that you are not like me!

Incoherent as they must have been, I don't see how you could so have misinterpreted my letters. . . .

Why the grand base of my towering pile, is the divine right of <u>each individual</u> to act out <u>his own nature</u>.

You can do the other thing and do it well. You can be all that is sweet and delicious as well as intellectual, but I can't, & you know it. . . .

I think I may be a help to you, and you are my greatest comfort now and ever, a loving sister soul, who will see the need of my ascending, and always have a nest for me when I come down. . . .

Understand once and for all that you are my one stay and support,—my other self, who makes up to me with tenfold sweetness for the barren places in my own uneven nature. If I can return it in any way, in virile force, or anything which I have & you haven't, so much happier I, and if I can't I shall remain the most ungrateful & contented beneficiary you ever saw.

Now is that plain?

Are you convinced of your indispensability?

<u>Will</u> you stop talking nonsense? . . .

With love that steadily increases, yours ever

Charlotte.

Aug. 8th, 1881

[To Martha Luther]

Sweet Puss,

. . . I have a cat.

Edward Brown b[r]ought it over to me last evening.

A delicate big-eared little beast, one of the celebrated "Chace[25] breed"—good ratters. . . .

[S]he manifested <u>every</u> symptom of dissatisfaction at having to spend the night in the cellar; and this morning when I go down to feed & cuddle her—Lo! she is not.

Some one hath taken away my cat, and I know not where they have laid it. "Umm [?] pooshy cat! Where you shpose um go qu?" . . .

What'll I name her?

I thought of "<u>Chick</u>" (!) but considered that when I called her all

Mr. Budlong's hens would scale the fence instanter, and reluctantly gave up the idea.

Help a feller.

CAP.

7–8 a.m.

An hour or two having elapsed since my last word I again incline to conversation. . . .

My only accession of news is that Grimalkin[26] has presented herself. She was discovered by mother and the washerwoman on careful search, crouching timorously in a coal hod. . . . A more thoroughly frightened pussy cat I never saw.

I went down and cuddled her, soothing her fears somewhat; gave her a bit of meat and some milk, and finally left her ebbing and flowing fitfully about the cellar, the image of nervous timidity.

I called at the Pub. Lib. [Public Library] yesterday afternoon, casually lost my card, and must wait 15 days for another one. I read a "Pop. Sci. [Popular Science]" with starved eagerness, and on my way home stopped at the Atheneaum and dipped into Punch, Harper's & The London Ill[ustrated].[27] I have determined to keep up with the literature and art of the day, and any designing person who covets my acquaintance this winter, may achieve the same by bearding me at either of the aforementioned places of amusement at regular hours.

Let's go together! Read and co-criticize! Houp la! What a deliciously private and mutual swear word that little objurgation is! Nobody else says "Houp la"! Nor will, soon, to my thinking. . . .

Private![28] I would like to put my hand under your chin, and look way down into your big eyes, ask questions, deposit kisses, recommend a nailbrush or a needle as the case might be, and generally enjoy myself. It's to be hoped that you will be quite strong when you get home!

2:30 P.M.

O my dear little girl! O my sweet little girl! Yours of Sunday last rec'd this morning. If you enjoy my letter half as much as I do yours, you must be a happy infant this summer. Why I hang around and wait for that postman. . . . I look forward to 'em from day to day, go back to my work in the most dispirited way when it don't come, and when it does I carry it in my pocket and gloat over it ever so long before reading and put it hurriedly aside after the first perusal to get some work done before the second.

I was a little dubious about writing the above, but even if the Philistines ever should see it, what care I!

If I am not ashamed of having sentiments I am not ashamed of admitting them, and why should I love my little comfort when I haven't anything else to love? . . .

I go through life "head-foremost" as one might say. I <u>am</u> certain of you pussy. Sure as death—for now. I'm not for ever, and I don't want to be. I should hardly care to turn my hand over if I thought I had such a friend as you for all time. No, I will keep you while I have you, and revel & luxuriate in the clear cool depths of your heart as I do in the sea, but if ever you grow, or I grow, in another path—, why there is bliss behind and hope before. It seems improbable to me that two souls <u>could</u> be so perfectly matched as ours seem now. There must be places in each that we don't either of us know about yet—undiscovered countries where we may go together, and may not.

I shouldn't much wonder if Halicarnassus after all might be the stream to divide us. Apply our pet poem dear, imagine our finding the young affection deep in your heart, walking hand in hand over the pretty thing—and then—and then—"And yet I know past all doubting, truly, a knowledge greater than death can stir, That as I loved she will love me, duly, And better, Aye better! than I love her."[29]

Believe it, pussy. Ever time that little cherub of ours sits down in that unsteady resting place, my heart, he is bigger than he was before. And able to keep his seat longer. . . .

Yours in a <u>calm ordinary wellbehaved</u> friendly (not intimate) <u>Masculine</u>! way, Charlotte A. Perkins

Providence.
August 13th, 1881.

[To Martha Luther]
O Marf<u>i</u>a! Dear Marf<u>i</u>a!

Your letter reaches me at the end of a day's pleasure, and caps the climax. My little chicken! I wonder if I ever shall love you less! What would we do. The freedom of it! The deliciousness! The utter absence of the "how will he take it?"! Never again will I admit that women are incapable of genuine friendship. . . .

I am wholly pleased to find that you have finally got some inkling of my idea of an answered letter. Doin' very well my dear! . . .

I didn't mean to tease—I am more than satisfied with your letters, and the wonder is how you can give me so much of your time and remember any one else. When I don't write it's because genius fails to burn, and concocted stuff I won't send you. And I <u>do</u> think you love me, pussy, indeed I know it, (this conviction and announcement must strike you as novel!) and I fancy my "little girl," "pussy," and "chicken" will be music in your ears for many years yet. . . .

I taste your letter all the way down—. . . .

Incidental thought, wouldn't these letters of mine be nuts for commentators! <u>If</u> & <u>if</u> of course, but how they would squabble over indistinct references and possible meanings! <u>Wouldn't it</u>! . . .

I went to see Retta Clark at the Diman's. Stayed to tea, and had a little tennis with her afterward. <u>Talked</u> to Retta. Like her deeply, and hope to know her more and long. . . .

Fri. I shortened the shoulder straps of my beloved bathing dress . . . and went and played tennis and <u>talked</u> again, with Retta. She is alive, & you will like her. We shall have a glorious company yet. . . .

Look here. Some sort of a club—a Society we must have. It is too hard for girls of this stamp not to know each other, and the meetings of ordinary society are at once impractble [*sic*] to some of us . . . and insufficient at the best of times.

In unity is strength, and many a girl would not be ashamed to mend her life if she were supported by others she knew. We as a class—girls, think our higher aspirations untrustworthy, we don't show them to parents, we don't show them to friends, they don't accord with ministers—with the Bible either, perhaps, but aspirations they are, and aspiration is the first step of ascent. Now I know that there is an element of reform and growth among lots of the girls I know, girls who have have [*sic*] no atmosphere to encourage it and who will lose it altogether in a few years. . . .

This may be wild. At any rate, it is an idea, and ideas are worth having. . . .

——Truly the manageress and reformer worketh within me! Shades of Aunt Catherine![30]

I love you—

Charlotte A. Perkins.

Providence
Aug. 16th. 1881.

Martha Luther!

Suppose you love that man[31] as I think you do—fear you will. Suppose he's cold and proud enough to suppress his own feelings forever. You see, I take it for granted he has 'em, a dishonorable flirt else.

Well now is that sort of thing going to satisfy you? Can you live and grow on an <u>uncertain</u> consciousness of a grand man's love? Can you wait for years without a word while he is trying to do something? My little girl! My little girl! If this thing comes to pass you will need me in good earnest.

If you can do it and be comfortable and happy go ahead. If you think it's good for you, pleasure aside, go ahead by all means.

If you can't help it—why I love you still. But you shall not have to mourn that you never considered the question. . . .

I could not love thee dear so much if I wasn't sure I could get along without it.

But it would be dreadful some twenty years hence to have you wishing that your heart had not carried you where you were no longer happy. . . .

A side of you likes a side of him, but Oh! the others! Now to retract and qualif[y] in my usual timid style. You <u>may</u> (!) see him differently. He <u>may</u> love you and all your little ways better than I do.

As a husband and father he would be virtuous in the extreme—his universality of home talent would figure well in a house of his own. He would let <u>you</u> have as large a library as he could afford I doubt not, and everything else that money could buy and love could give,—when he had it.

And you would probably love him enough to scale all chasms, surmount all hills, and smooth off the face of nature as it were, to suit yourself.

<u>But would you always suit</u>? . . .

Love you can do great things, but could all the love under God make Jim Simmons change those religious views of his? Do you want to be dragged into things; persuaded, convinced, and converted, before you come to it naturally: to have a neverending contention; or to have an unmentioned gulf lying quietly between you, to have him pray <u>for</u> you, and not <u>with</u> you?

Oh my kitten! my kitten! You may need me in good earnest yet.

Are you sufficiently scared? . . .

You <u>are</u> good this summer little girl. And so are your letters. You are in every way just what I want. (Of course you have no further ambition!) . . .

Yours ever,

Charlotte A. Perkins.

Providence

Aug. Tues. 23rd. 1881.

[To Martha Luther]

Little Pet, little Pet, . . .

I think about you lots, and love you more. . . .

. . . You are to marry, of course, you would never be satisfied if you didn't, and after a certain period of unmerited happiness, his, your young man is to drop off, die somehow, and lo! I will be all in all!

Now isn't that a charming plan? You can always have a tender melancholy about you, during special fits of which I will thoughtfully explain that "she is thinking of the old 'un," and then it's more than likely that there would be some little Halicarnassuses, which you would be too much occupied with grief to mind my experimenting on! Glorious. . . .

Wed. Eve. . . .

When <u>do</u> you come home Pussy? I am getting loneshomer & loneshomer [*sic*]. . . .

Yours always,

Charlotte.

Providence.

Sept. 1st. 1881.

[To Martha Luther]

My dear young child! . . .

Your delicious little tangles amuse this strongminded old maid immensely. You like to think about it, but you're not in love with him—no necessary connection there! He's devoted to you, but you don't care for him—just as it should be, my love! And you hope you showed it, but don't know whether you did or not—why you precious duckling what earthly difference does it make!

Just go right on and live your own life, do good and enjoy yourself, and <u>if</u>, in consequence of your being and doing certain things, diverse menfolks are affected in certain ways—why you should say "what difference does that make to me!" . . .

I wouldn't be cold and frigid to him unless from some convulsion of nature you should chance to feel so, if you are glad, why <u>be</u> glad, and if the gallant Lane[32] misunderstand you—why that's his lookout. <u>Don't you see</u>, he can misinterpret forced behavior as readily as natural, so that you save nothing anyway.

I think I know how you feel pussy, as well as an outside barbarian can, and I am certain that you share the feeling with every concientious [*sic*] woman under the same circumstances. But. These compunctions, to my mind, are more composed of a dread of subsequent reproach, fear of personal remorse, and timorous distrust of your own conduct when adversely commented on,—by you, him, or Mrs. Grundy;[33] then of real concern for "the other man." . . .

And as to that marauder's being pitifully unhappy—why so he ought to, to leave you. Wasn't <u>I</u> pitifully unhappy? And ain't I now? Pity 'bout him! . . .

I don't see why you should have been scared at his startling remarks. What if he was going to propose, that would have been funnier. Just open your big eyes, and tell him you are spoken for by a female in Providence, and can't marry just yet. . . .

It is about 11 P.M. on one of the hottest nights imaginable. Hot, hot, hot, all day, a brooding quiet <u>impressive</u> heat with a lurid haze that almost hid the sun. . . .

We are doing splendidly with our beggary—I have over $40.00 now!

You see Carrie Hazard[34] sent me ten and her aunt Mrs. Augusta H. $25.00!

Which mites count up. . . .

There puss, I'm sleepy and it's hot, and there's <u>mur</u>skeeters all over me. Goodnight.

Charlotte A. Perkins

Providence<br>Sept. 4th. 1881.

[To Martha Luther]

Little Pet, . . .

I have said full enough concerning your man I think. Still I will give you my benediction over again if you wish.

But—Ah! Remember clear and plain.
When strong his love is burning,
That it's the longest kind of Lane
That never knows a turning! . . .

You are my one comfort, Pussy, as I believe I've said before.
I love you. I love you. And O dear! dear! when do you come home?
Just you come and stay all night with me! O my eye!

Goodnight dovey.

Charlotte A. Perkins.

Providence<br>Sept. 14th. 1881

Dear Martha,

. . . Am going out with Aunt Mary this afternoon.

That good lady is greatly shocked and grieved at the independent stand I have taken in general, and my attitude towards mother in particular.

They all opened on me at breakfast yesterday, Mother silent and pathetic, Aunt Mary outspoken & exhortive [*sic*], and even Aunt C. chiming in with the crowd, as she always does. And I was fool enough to <u>cry</u>! O! I was mad.

There I was, as cool and unmoved as I ever was, certain of my own ground, and divinely indifferent to anybody's opinion, and yet my insufferable diaphraghm [*sic*] all afloat, so that I couldn't talk at all! O! I was mad. . . .

More later—CAP

7.30 P.M. . . .

Aunt Mary and I went out to make calls this afternoon, and I have seen the inside of our lovely little house on Charles Field st; O it is go-orgeous! I'll tell you 'bout it when you come home—if you ever do. Why it's <u>62</u> days—! <u>9 weeks</u> tomorrow since you deserted me!

<u>Isn't</u> you chummin' home pwitty shoon? . . .

Aunt M. stays till next Wed. So we can't coalesce till after that, but <u>then</u> you can come and spend a night with me, and I can go and spend a night with you, and we'll be as happy as clams.

It is so nice to think that you can love and trust all the while I am writhing, and hold me fast with faith in the final transfiguration.

Little pet!

Goodnight.

Charlotte A. Perkins.

8:30 P.M. Mon. Nov. 14. 1881.[35]

[To Sam Simmons]

Quiet.

Dead quiet; with the cat too fast asleep to purr, my watch, and the still lamp, for company.

. . . You see I have changed my mind about writing. It is just this way, I ask no more for help from you, but write as my only outlet for thoughts and feelings which crowd painfully. Like one who has safely passed through a serious amputation—cautery has stopped the <u>danger</u>, I complain no longer of the <u>pain</u>, but feel the <u>loss of the limb</u> as sensibly as ever. So I trespass still further on your kindness. And in very truth I had rather write to you than see you; in this I am free as air, candid, un-embarrassed, mistress of expression; but when you are with me it is all a blurr of what the old novellists called "conflicting emotions." I keep crossing my desire to speak with your "undesire" to hear, my wish for things with your probable attitude of reception if I asked, my string of ideas that want to come out with your quiet sufficiency that needs for no one—so there's "a little talking of outward things," and no help. . . .

To return to my surgical simile, there's no amount of ingenious ma-chinery, no cork, steel, iron, or wood, that can fill the place of the live warm living thing that is gone; but for all that they are grandly useful, and one would be a mere cripple without them. As I look at it now I think that in my first blind misery I must have actually expected you to step into the vacancy, to calmly hand over an arm of your own to fill my empty sleeve! . . .

You say that it would only bring you closer if your friend were en-gaged. True, but remember that she would be added to him, he would not go to her. "As the husband is the wife is—"

Then imagine if you can that you had filled to him in a thousand ways the place that she now would—, not that you covered all of her ground, but she all yours and acres more, and see how you would feel to have everything that you had given, <u>better</u> given by some one else. . . .

And then imagine you had noone else—that you lived in antago-nism to a greater or less degree with nearly every one else, and further-more that the whole business was an incredible surprise to you, and per-haps you may form some conception of this little tangle.

Excuse repitition [*sic*], this is not moan, this time, but explanation with a view to conviction; I have no tears tonight, nor pain. That only comes now under touch of sympathy.

I was at the Hazard's the other night, and talking to Carrie. There's a deal of kindness in those people, and much common ground between Carrie and me, so I told her some little, just to explain my dolorousness, and when she stroked my hand in her soft ones, and said "my poor stormy child!" I could have wilted down into my shoes. Just as you can cut yourself in cold weather, and never know it as long as your hands are numb, but warmth will revive the smart and start the blood with amazing speed.

Goodnight.

You are an immeasurable comfort as far as you go, and I only wish you went farther. . . .

And tell me please with that unmistakakable [*sic*] plainness you so well understand, if you object to being written at in <u>this</u> style.

Charlotte A. Perkins

Providence<br>Feb. 13th. 1882.

_____. [To Charles Walter Stetson][36]

I have no title to address you by. They don't satisfy me, any of them.

I got your letter of the postman, on Waterman St., as I was going over to have a tooth filled between lessons. There wasn't time to fill it, and I read that Letter—at my dentists!

And I could not have been quieter or more alone, either. Then I tucked it carefully in among the crackers in my coat pocket, and walked up to Bridgham st.—on air!

O my Friend! My Friend! What can I say to thank you for your noble confidence? How can I live purely and grandly enough to justify—God helping me to <u>glorify</u> your love! . . . I kneel to you!

*   *   *

You are the first man I have met whom I recognize as an equal; and that is saying a good deal for me.

I would call you grandly superior, but that I am fighting just now against a heart-touched woman's passion of abnegation.

You are the first man I ever saw beside whom I felt humble, the first man I ever saw who <u>I felt could help me to live</u>. The difference between our lives is this:

You have lived purely and grandly from an inward impulse, a noble spirit that would be heard.

I have seen certain characteristics to be good and desirable, and then beaten them into a nature where evil (of some sorts) was predominant.

You have struggled through blood and fire to be true to your own high instincts; I, working on my theories of malleable human nature and invincible human will, have stood on some misty middle ground, and—lifted my own weight, as it were.

\* \* \* \* \*

I am not fit to write to you tonight. Twelve hours of steady effort are no fair preparation for what I would like to say. My head is awake, and—my heart also, more's the pity! But my visible self is very tired. I shouldn't be if there was work to do! It is the warmth & quiet that put me to sleep. . . .

Providence
Feb. 20th. 1882.

[To: Charles Walter Stetson]
Dear Friend;

. . . I am very sorry that you could not stay with us last night, and appreciably sorrier that I could not really see you at all. But those things have to be expected sometimes, and we must learn to put up with it.

I have rescued your photograph from its ignominious hiding place, and laid it with your letters. Do I value it? Most highly.

\* \* \* \*

I am thinking deeply just now. And the more I think the more appalled I am at the gravity of the subject. I dare not let myself dwell for an instant on the sense of double responsibility; the fact of two lives being implicated. From all that I have read, seen, and heard, that is a fatal step; it instantly weighs on the conscience of the arbiter; and hopelessly complicates a case already confused. No sir! You and your life are not the subject of discussion just now. . . . But I am studying mine with breathless care, backward as far as I can see, and forward in two directions, with the formula that has been my dependence for years—"if I do this this will not happen, and if I do that" _____.

And the fruit of my meditation thus far is this conclusion: That it is an open question which life I can work best in.

That if I were to try the path you open to me I could not reconsider—I could never try my own; but if I first prove my own—if I find on fair trial that I cannot do as I think—perhaps—Therefore, that it is right for me to give a fair chance to feelings and instincts which are certainly well-founded; to risk the loss of a few years possible happiness, rather than to risk the endurance of a lifetime's possible pain.

I am not a tenderhearted child; neither am I an impulsive girl: but a clearheaded woman who is weighing a lifetime in her hand.

The question under any circumstances is a hard one (it weighed heavily on my lost friend,[37] though she had only to consider whether she loved or not, and had my best love and thought to help her) but situated as I am it is absolutely cruel.

If I were out and free, if I had my home to live in and my work to lean on, if I knew as I then should just what I was losing, (I <u>dare</u> not count the <u>gains</u>!) it would be much easier. . . .

Here is a force—the strongest known to human nature, which says "Yield!" and I stand quietly against it. The voice of all the ages sounds in my ears, saying that this is noble, natural, and right; that no woman yet has ever attempted to stand alone as I intend but that she had to submit or else repented in dust and ashes—too late! that needless suffering at the best, or miserable failure at the end is all that I can hope if I persevere and I have nothing to answer but the meek assertion that I am different from, if not better than all these, and that my life is mine in spite of a myriad [of] lost sisters before me. Cool, isn't it?

Providence
Feb. 21st. '82.

[To Charles Walter Stetson]
Dear Friend,

I have just spent 3/4 of an hour in writing to you, and written nothing.

It is not the first time either. You see I am not free. If you were the friend I wish you were I could write letters that keep you warm in winter. If you were such a friend as I have already I could write most amusing and graceful epistles.

If you were still what you are, and I were—what I <u>wish I was</u>—I could write like Sappho[38] herself.

But now——.

I am crushing my heart under foot, and the exercise is <u>not</u> conducive to a free and easy demeanor.

I was afraid of it, as you know, and thought to prevent it if possible.

It was not possible, but the foresight was some protection, and I was not taken unawares.

I know, of course, that the time would come when I must choose between two lives, but never did I dream that it would come so soon, and that the struggle would be so terrible.

It is well for me that my life has been what it has, that I have studied and practiced self-control til it is a second nature, that pleasure to me is always a thing to be . . . distrusted, and that my decisions are solely self supported.

Well also that the feelings you have for me & the feelings I have for you are so[39] pure and high, that through you I have found my God, and am praying as I never prayed before—for strength to turn my face from the Paradise that lies before me.

A paradise it is, for the life which I might have with you is precisely that of all others which I should most enjoy.

22nd.

[To Charles Walter Stetson]
Dear Friend,

Just look at the date of this letter! I have begun and begun and begun again, but have so far been unable to write.

Beside all the usual hindrances I am utterly forbidden by the unsettled nature of our relations. How can I write? Who am I writing too [sic].

How can I offer even the warmest friendliness to one who asks for love?

If only you <u>didn't</u>, if only you could help it—if only we might have given me what I wanted and not this—!

Forgive me. I ought not to complain of being offered the crown of womanhood, even if I may not wear it.

And in the bottom of my heart I do not regret it; it is only at times that I shrink from a trial which in very truth <u>does</u> try me like fire.

It is no more than fair that I should tell you this, for you must not think me higher than I am. . . .

I feel helpless, and dumb. The feeling of delighted companionship with which I met you so gladly at first fades to insignificance before the look in your eyes that asks for more than I dare give.

I knew it would come.

I feared it as you know, and vainly tried to prevent it. I was afraid, as well I might be, of the struggle and the pain; but little did I guess that the taste would be so bitter. . . .

Providence
March. 26th. 1882.

Dear Miss Charlotte [Hedge],[40]

What must you think of me for having left you all this time without a letter! . . .

But this dull, bleak Sunday is the last day of a week's delicious idleness and semi-invalidism, and it is a fitting celebration to have a little talk with you.

The way it is was this. I, the Strong and Impregnable; I, the budding athlete, and Chief Performer at the Prov. [Providence] Ladies Sanitary Gymnasium; I, the surefooted and steady eyed, ignominiously tumbled over a chair, and so injured myself. That I was laid up for four days, and must walk no more than is necessary for some time yet.

Now don't inquire like an anxious gentleman of my acquaintance, "was Miss Perkins injured in her <u>arms</u>? or her <u>limbs</u>?" for I will inform you in strict confidence that it was neither, but in the worst place you can imagine.[41] You see I came down with an antipodean stretch of leg, right <u>across</u> the back of a chair! Result, much black & blueness, and a horrid little cut, which I subsequently ascertained ought to have been sewed and wasn't. And O! I've had <u>such</u> a good time!

Time to read and time to write, time to sew, and time to knit, time to paint, and time to lie down and take naps at all hours of the day. Luxury! Kind of an expensive luxury, too, for mother had to dismiss her school in order to do the housework, and I had to make that up, pay the doctors who made an examination, lose three lessons (lucky t'wasn't more), and now am wasting my substance in riotous living in the horse-cars in a way that horrifies my pedestrian soul. (sole?)

However, the rest was worth it, and I don't really grumble. And also I have been blessed with more callers than I have had time for in all winter, and with bananas, <u>strawberries</u>, oranges, candy, ice, and flowers in abundance. Should like to do it again some time. . . .

But, I have, really, I have been sur-<u>priz</u>-ingly industrious, and accomplished a good deal. . . .

My principal cash this year has been my two girls whom I have been instructing in all the common branches, and as much else as I could give and they could hold. The effect of my labors has been good for the girls, as is generally admitted; and invaluable to myself, for such a drilling in the first part of education I never had before, and never should have had in any other way. . . .

I think I can call my first attempt at teaching school a success, and $40.00 every ten weeks has kept the market man in subjection.

Also I have given drawing lessons this winter to the extent of eight engagements a week, which has swelled my income to $8.50. Also I have done some little painting to order. Also I have read an hour a day of Egyptian history with much edification and enjoyment. . . .

Also I have steadily attended church and S[unday]. school this winter, and a weekly Bible Class, and the Saturday night "Boy's Room" at the Union for Christian Workers, and the Gymnasium twice a week. . . . And my regular weekly walking, just trotting about among my scholars every afternoon, has been over thirty miles. . . .

I have a Lover!

Yes'm. Not an "admirer" merely, but a real one.

He is a young artist of rising reputation, and a purest, scientist more or less, and well read man besides.

Charles Walt. Stetson by name.

He thinks me a queen among women, and I am rapidly giving him first place in my esteem. But the longer I live, and the more I know of myself, the more firmly I am convinced that I am not meant for that class of work (!) with all its utility and happiness.

I do not pretend to know just what I am going to do, but . . . [t]ime will show. Meanwhile I am willing to work and wait, and every year grow stronger and more earnest. . . .

This is our "secret" to be hidden forever, but I only tell <u>you</u> because I love you and know you love me, and if I could not trust you, I should not write.

Ever your friend,<br>Charlotte A. Perkins.

Providence<br>June 19th 1882

Dear father,

Yours of the 9th received, perused, and listened to. I am very much obliged to you.

I have wanted for very long to have some ones judgement set against my own which I could obey without feeling as if I was running on "sleepers." Now it dawns on my aspiring mind that you know more than I do! And it also occurs to me that if I were in your place and had a daughter, that I should like to have her follow my suggestion in a case like this....

If we ultimately marry we can readily make up for lost time, and if we do not it is certainly better to have no room for even small repentance.

But your rule binds heartily—there is much in my intercourse with my friend which I should <u>not</u> desire to have mother see.

Not that I am ashamed or afraid, there are other people wise and good whom I shouldn't object to as spectators, but somehow I can't show things to mother. I can't be easily myself in her company. She always used to read my letters, written and received, and I never knew what it was to write a letter till I was twenty-one, and rebelled. May I not take you for my invisible judge? ...

Providence<br>May 13th. 1883

Dear Brother,[42]

I learn from mother that Julia is ill again, or has been, for I hope she is well again.

I'm sorry she should be sick. Does she know, do you all about the laws and rules of common life that keep people well?

... You see I am so well myself, and lay it so wholly to observance of such laws as I have laid down for myself that I feel as if everyone else might do the same things and enjoy the same effects....

As for my "rules" it would puzzle me to particularize I fear. I guess they would amount to about this:

Good <u>air</u> and <u>plenty of</u> it.

Good food and plenty of it.

<u>Good</u> exercise and plenty of it.

Good sleep and plenty of it.

Good clothes and as few as possible....

Please don't think this "not funny but insulting," and that I'm an incipient Aunt Catherine Beecher, I don't mean to be invidious at all.

Guess I'll write to Julia and ask he[r] questions about her clothes and things. Do you think she'd resent it? ...

I always think of you much, am proud of you, and glad indeed for your happiness. But I seem to be singularly barren of natural affection. "Brother" brings no answering thrill to my heart. Perhaps because we had so little genuine loving intercourse when we were together. Fun we had in plenty, and a large fund of common intelligence; but I can never remember any companionship more [*sic*] beautiful ideas. . . .

As I grow and grow I care more and more for right living, not of a pious kind—I yoke myself with neither creed nor Bible, but such living as will most conduce to the progress and happiness of self and all self touches.

I have ideas and theories which time will develope [*sic*], and I work.

Bye and bye when I know much more and hold such place in society as I will hold, perhaps I might write you letters that would be of some use. . . .

"Speak what you think today in hard words, and tomorrow speak what tomorrow thinks in hard words again, though it contradict everything you have said today"; says Emerson.[43] Also "with consistency a great soul has simply nothing to do." Which I believe; but where rules may be followed it is safer to test well before promulgating. . . .

> Camp Walter. Upper Wilson Pond—
> Jumping Off Place. Maine
> 7 A.M. Thurs. Sept. 6th. 1883.

My dear little Martha,

I received your letter yesterday, it having been over night in the hotel box.

But hotel boxes are trivial conveniences now far removed from us; for yesterday morning at about an hour's notice, Dr. & Mrs. Jackson & Eddie, a Mr. & Mrs. Hopkins, & I, with sundry guides, set forth in two wagons and rode for several miles.[44] Then we changed about and we delicate females rode while the menfolk walked for about a mile further. . . .

Then a scramble through a shady zigzag woodland path, a "trail"; then more boat, and so here. "Here" is a <u>camp</u>, a <u>log cabin</u>, bare and genuine, where we disport ourselves for some days.

We sleep on cot beds, hay stuffed, comfortable, with soft coarse blankets. We have a rickety little stove with a long pipe going up through a hole in the roof. . . .

The men folks fish and hunt, the women folks knit and crochet and chatter, and I (neuter you observe!) Write & Draw & Read & Paint and make myself generally usefull [*sic*]. . . .

Bless your little heart Martha, you're a comfort. You and your good husband and little fat-legged baby[45]—I like to think of you. . . .

I'm glad you want to see me pussy, and so do I want to see you. But there is a man in Providence whom I would not stay away from for an extra minute even to see you! Now doesn't that show some change, some advance in my power of loving since I saw you last?

I tell you dear there is no question now except one of time and means. Not even to you can I show my heart now, but you know it well from your own. Happy? Happy beyond words. You know, little girl, you know.

I would like much to see that babling of yours. Bless his blue eyes! . . . Tell him confidentially that his Aunt Charlotte is very fond of him, and will come and see him sometime.

Allow me to explain with grief and shame that it is now the 16th of September; 9.40 or so, P.M.

You see I have very little time by myself; and I write to Walter every night before bed, retiring at 9 as I did in Providence. It is a fortunate habit, for it gives me an hour or two untouched.

What do you think shiger [*sic*]! I'm going to leave this interesting family.

And furthermore I am glad of it! Now lest you burst with wild conjecture let me tell you that the reason I go is because Mrs. J. suggests that she is afraid Eddie won't let me teach him this winter; and the reason I'm glad is because the people have grown highly obnoxious to me, and the boy in especial is abhorrent to my every—antenna.

If it perplexes you to reconcile this with my former buoyant content, remember that I am always apt to be pleased with my surroundings, and that character is a slow book to read. You know how fond I am of children & children of me; so you will believe it to be of no light matter that could cause me to heartily dislike a child.

Selfish. Rude. Lazy. Dishonorable. Weak. Timid. And more than I care to mention.

I have no wish to give him pain, but I do want to get away from him; and to have to be around all day and every day with a youth who has neither respect nor love for me is hard. . . .

Don't you think I'm naturally inclined to be obliging and patient? Well this boy taxes both. Always his will and never mine, unless one prefers sulky resistance. So I just bear his exactions as long as I can, and then baulk and let him think me as "horrid" as he pleases. Little fool! I know I could make his summer happy and useful if he would only let me, if he were only different.

I'll tell you all about it when I can; but take it on trust dear that the winter looked like Purgatory to me; to be endured with hope of the Paradise beyond, and because it seemed weak and selfish to back out. Wasn't I glad of release!

Mrs. J. suggested my keeping my room and board, and amusing Eddie evenings as an equivalent. Not much madame! If he were a little gentleman or even a lovable child, I would; but this little ruffian, who has told me I lied right to my face!—me! is more than I can bear willingly. I would have stayed for a sense of honor, but stay from my own will, I hardly think I shall. So goodbye to rich living and empty home—....

You see the hard part of it is having to bend my will and do what [Eddie] likes all the time, wholly regardless of my own feelings or convenience. He is seldom ever willing to do my way when there is any question; and if I compel him he is unhappy, cross, insulting.

I am here only to amuse him, and that I must do; but the worst of it is that he hurts me immensely for very slight pleasure on his part, pleasure that he might have had as much or more of by doing my way.

For instance. I am perfectly willing to get a big stone for anchor, and a long rope, and tie them together and drop and raise the same. But it's big and heavy, very, and when it comes to dropping and pulling right up again because he thought he'd fish in one place and then changed his mind, is aggravating. Even then it would be little if he were pleasant about it; but he snarls and storms and contradicts and insults at the slightest provocation.

F'instance again. We had chartered one of these little steamers for the day and were fishing. At least the men were, and Eddie. They had a boat and were out in it some of the time. I was loafing about aboard, reading I believe, when Mrs. J. thoughtfully asked me if I wouldn't like to take the boat and go off by myself a little while. There was a shady island close by; and I joyfully acquiesced. You know how I love to be alone, especially when my companions are unpleasant to me. But Master E.

beheld, and wanted to go. His mother demurred, but I smothered my selfishness and let him go. Off I set, meaning to row around the island. He desired to row of course as soon as in [*sic*], but that I would not permit, at first anyway. I was so glad to stretch my arms. Then he didn't want to go around the island so I came back. <u>Then</u> he proposed that I should row him over to the fishing place and he'd fish! Now firstly I <u>hate</u> fishing. Secondly it was so hot that he and his father had but a short while since come in because E. was unable to bear it. Thirdly, there was no need of my going at all, for he had his father who did like fishing. To give up not only my promised aloneness and shady trees, but the quiet haven of the steamboat where was shade and cleanliness, and row out there in that still heat, and sit, (which is hotter) in a dirty boat while he slaughtered fish under my eyes and expected me to sympathize, and all without <u>need</u>—I could not. I would not. I told him so, saying it was too hot, and that he could go with his father just as well. (Am not <u>sure</u> I mentioned that last.)

Said he, "Weren't you coming out here to row?" "Yes" said I. "Well then"! said he, and in words I do not just remember gave it as his opinion that a person who would go out to row in the heat and not be willing to sit still in it, was a fool! To which I said nothing. (He went back to the boat & I had nearly an hour on the island. And was happy there.) Now <u>isn't</u> that a lovely boy?

This is all you can have. Righteous indignation makes me garrulous. Goodnight dear. Love to the baby, bless him!

Charlotte A. Perkins.

11.10–15 p.m.<br>Tues. Jan. 1st 1884<br>Providence

[To Charles Walter Stetson]
My dear Love:

Did you see by the paper this morning that Conway Brown shot himself yesterday at Mrs. Maurans?[46]

And I saw him only Sunday, shook hands with him, and was glad of his bright face.

And now————————

He told me last summer of having times of deep depression; and of having often thought of shooting himself.

I can well sympathize with such feelings; can almost excuse his forgetting the parents whose only child he was. Well do I know that in such times the love of others seems as nothing; obligation nothing, duty nothing; nothing anywhere but misery that grows and grows till click!————and it is over forever.

If it is. If I were <u>sure</u> that death changed life for the better, changed personality and relation, I fear that even my sense of duty &c. would hardly save you from what you most dread.

And if my "times of depression" increase in intensity I really have serious doubts as to whether even that mistrust would withhold me. Suicide was nearer to me this last time than ever in my life.[47]

Poor Conway! Poor boy! He told me much of his life and character last summer; and I pity him in his young death.

Not that he <u>is</u> dead—O no!, but because I fear he is no happier. . . .

O why couldn't he think of the sorrow he would cause? Because in those black hours one <u>cannot</u> think, one only <u>feels</u>, and on every side feels only pain. . . .

I have a frail hope that our life together will have enough of joy to keep me sane.

Perhaps the children will do much. . . .

God send we marry soon.

Charlotte A. Perkins.

Figure 2. Charlotte Perkins Stetson, January
1899. Courtesy of Denise D. Knight.

## 2

# A Life in Transition

## "an artist of sufficient merit"

Within weeks after her May 2, 1884, marriage to Charles Walter Stetson, Charlotte Perkins Gilman was pregnant. On the morning of March 23, 1885, she gave birth to her only child, Katharine Beecher Stetson. When she resumed her correspondence some two weeks later, Gilman remarked that she had been forbidden to write—and even to "think"—following Katharine's birth, a restriction that she found manipulative and unnecessary, and one that she would famously ridicule some five years later in her best-known story, "The Yellow Wall-Paper." To her aunt Emily Hale she wrote, "I would have sent you word [of Katharine's birth] before, but they so impressed it on my mind that I wasn't to think of anything that I gave up—and didn't" (April 5, 1885). While the letter also expressed her hope that she would soon be up and about, the demands of motherhood left Gilman anxious and depressed. As she remarked her in memoir, "I, the ceaselessly industrious, could do no work of any kind. . . . I lay on that lounge and wept all day. The tears ran down into my ears on either side. I went to bed crying, woke in the night crying, sat on the edge of the bed in the morning and cried—from sheer continuous pain" (*Living* 91). Her diaries were even more grim; on August 28, 1885, Gilman reported feeling "highly excited, hysterical; seeming to myself wellnigh insane" (331), and two days later she wrote that Walter "cannot see how irrevocably bound I am, for life, for life. No, unless he die and the baby die, or he change or I change there is no way out" (332).

Temporary relief eventually came when, in October, at the invitation of Grace Ellery Channing and her family, Gilman left Katharine and Walter to travel to Pasadena, where she would spend the winter. Gilman thrived in California, though letter writing proved a struggle. To Martha Lane she wrote: "I have not written to you for so long because of—circumstances. The mere writing itself is still an effort; and then my mental condition has made me oblivious of even my best friends. In despair of ever getting well at home I suddenly undertook this journey. It has already done me an immense amount of good and I expect to return in the spring as well as I ever shall be" (January 4, 1886). Just two months later, Gilman confided to Martha that although she felt stronger, she feared a relapse once she returned east. "I look forward with both joy and dread to see my darlings again; and dread of further illness under family cares" (March 13, 1886).

In fact, Gilman suffered a major relapse shortly after she arrived home that spring. When she was forced to adhere to the cult of domesticity, she became despondent. Conversely, her activism on behalf of women's rights in the fall of 1886 left her feeling hopeful and alive. By the early spring of 1887, however, Gilman was again suffering from "hysteria" (*Diaries* 383). As her depression deepened, she investigated treatment options. Eventually, she decided to seek the "rest cure" in Philadelphia from Dr. Silas Weir Mitchell, the nation's leading nerve specialist.

Prior to her departure for Mitchell's sanitarium, Gilman wrote Mitchell a long letter, reprinted in its entirety in this chapter. Her purpose in writing, Gilman remarked, was to acquaint the doctor "with all the facts of the case" so that he might "form a deeper judgement" of her condition than would be possible "from mere casual examination" (April 19,

1887). Although Mitchell "scornfully" dismissed the letter as a product of Gilman's "self-conceit," it is nevertheless an enormously important document, both historically and biographically (*Living* 95). Not only does it corroborate Gilman's autobiographical account of her breakdown, but it also elucidates the identity that Gilman was forming of herself: "I am an artist of sufficient merit to earn an easy living when well. I am a writer, a poet, a philosopher, in little. I am a teacher by instinct and profession. I am a reader and thinker. I can do some good work for the world if I live. . . . I want to <u>work</u>, to help people, to do good. . . . Surely it is worth while to save a good worker, one who asks little and longs to give much!" Of special significance is Gilman's emphasis on "work," a word that is repeated three times in the paragraph and underlined, emphasizing its importance in her life.

The rest cure that Gilman underwent was designed to treat depression by focusing on its symptoms rather than its causes; as a result, it demanded enforced bed rest and removed all liberties and freedom from the patient. "I was put to bed and kept there," Gilman explained in her autobiography (*Living* 96). After a month's stay, Mitchell sent Gilman home and instructed her to "Live as domestic a life as possible. Have your child with you all the time. . . . Lie down an hour after each meal. Have but two hours' intellectual life a day. And never touch pen, brush or pencil as long as you live" (96).

Gilman left the sanitarium, "went home, followed those directions rigidly for months," and subsequently suffered a nervous breakdown (96). On June 30, 1887, Stetson reported in his diary that his wife "was in the depths of melancholia again, with talk of pistols & chloroform" (*Endure* 342). By early that fall it was apparent that she could no longer stay in the marriage. "It seemed plain that if I went crazy it would do my husband no good, and be a deadly injury to my child," she wrote in her autobiography (*Living* 96). Gilman made a conscious decision to craft a life that would accommodate her desire to contribute something meaningful to humankind.

Over the next year, Gilman raised enough money to move with Katharine back to California. In early October the two traveled with Grace Channing to Pasadena. Stetson followed in December, hoping for a reconciliation. As Gilman remarked in her memoir, however, "a dragging year followed, and . . . he finally left me, called suddenly to the bedside of his dying mother" (*Living* 109). Not coincidentally, Gilman's professional life began in earnest after Stetson's departure. To Martha she wrote that being unshackled from the constraints of marriage left her more certain "of usefulness and joy" than ever before (August 15, 1889). She also wrote about the rebirth that resulted from her freedom to work: "The girl you knew, the woman you loved died some years past, died in long slow unutterable pain. . . . I have good friends here; and plenty of work to do. . . . I look forward to doing great things" (January 20, 1890).

As the letters in this chapter attest, the California years marked one of the most productive periods of Gilman's life. Gilman became a proponent of Nationalism, a reform movement that advocated an end to capitalistic greed and class distinctions and promoted the progressive and democratic improvement of the human race. Her satirical poem "Similar Cases" was published in the *Nationalist* magazine, winning the attention of William Dean Howells, who wrote to praise its merits. "Howells . . . tell[s] me I'm the prophetess of a new religion!" she announced to her cousin Marian Parker Whitney (February 19, 1894). In fact, 1890 was a banner year for Gilman; she began lecturing, wrote her most famous work of fiction, and in a single month managed to produce fifteen separate works, including essays, poems, and lectures. To Whitney she bragged, "I have aquired [*sic*] in three month's space the great sum of Ten Dollars by my pen!!!" (May 30, 1890).

The sudden acceleration of Gilman's career, however, did not come without complications. As the demands for her services as a speaker increased, caring for Katharine became more difficult, particularly after Gilman entered a romantic friendship in 1891 with Adeline E. Knapp, a journalist for the *San Francisco Call*. Their tempestuous relationship has been well documented by Gilman's biographers. During this time, Gilman informed Walter, who was still back east, that her determination to end the marriage was unwavering. "Do not deceive yourself dear. My life is too precious to me to waste anymore of it like those seven years we spent together," she wrote on June 16, 1891. "Since you left I have done good work and lots of it—have made a reputation in one year. The difference is too great. Work I must, and when I live with you I can't. Therefore I shall never live with you again as a wife. I know it's hard for you but I can't help it. You must take the hard the [*sic*] truth and make the best of it."

Balancing motherhood with a burgeoning career became further complicated when Mary Perkins, terminally ill with cancer, arrived in California in 1891. Gilman assumed responsibility for her care, and as Mary's health declined, Gilman's anxieties rose. The following year, Gilman took over the management of a boardinghouse—a difficult endeavor under the best of circumstances—and her relationship with Knapp began to crumble. Through it all, however, Gilman continued to write. Clearly, her work was an escape from the painful realities of Mary's impending death, the collapse of her relationship with Knapp, and her growing concerns about Katharine's welfare. Even as she sat by Mary's deathbed in early March 1893, Gilman immersed herself in work: "Sit up till near 2 with mother. . . . Write short powerful paper—'The Sex Question Answered' for the World's Congress. Nothing seems to seriously affect my power to write" (*Diaries* 520). Early on the morning of Tuesday, March 7, 1893, Mary Perkins quietly passed away; four months later, Gilman's increasingly volatile relationship with Knapp ended. Gilman redoubled her efforts on behalf of both Nationalism and women's issues, and she was elected president of the Pacific Coast Woman's Press Association. She also began writing poems that would appear in her first volume of verse, *In This Our World*, published in the fall of 1893. The following summer, Gilman moved to San Francisco to assume the management of the *Impress*, a literary weekly newspaper. In June she received a letter from Walter, announcing his marriage to Grace Channing, with whom he had been romantically involved for years. By this time, Gilman had decided to send Katharine back east to live with Walter and Grace. To her cousin Mary D. Phelon, she explained her decision: "The child's father loves her dearly and wanted to see her—has wanted to these four years. . . . [H]e has some right as a father . . . and needed her society. . . . [T]he child herself needed to see her father and some other people beside me. . . . It's a good thing all round, for her, for him, for me. . . . And [Grace is] the noblest loveliest greatest woman I know. . . . Her influence will be lovely for Kate; and we all four love each other dearly" (June 18, 1894).

In the summer of 1895, Gilman left California after the *Impress* folded. In her memoir she blamed the paper's demise on her status as a divorcée and as an "unnatural" mother, stemming from her decision to temporarily relinquish custody of Katharine: "I had put in five years of most earnest work [in California] with voice and pen, and registered complete failure. . . . I had warm personal friends, to be sure, but the public verdict [of my work] was utter condemnation" (*Living* 176). She decided to head east.

At the invitation of Jane Addams, Gilman traveled to Chicago, where she spent several months at Hull House, the social settlement house founded by Addams and Ellen Gates Starr. To her friend Sarah Brown Ingersoll Cooper, Gilman wrote, "I spoke sixteen times in [the] course of the month; fine regular lectures at Hull House, several little talks to working girls clubs, mother's clubs, and one to a Trades Union" (November 10, 1895). In January 1896 Gilman attended the annual Women's Suffrage Convention in Washington, D.C., where she met the prominent sociologist and professor Lester F. Ward. Ward, the country's leading advocate of Reform Darwinism, a controversial movement whose proponents advocated stronger government-led policies, including support for eugenics, held a reception in Gilman's honor. Soon thereafter she began an extended lecture tour that would take her to dozens of U.S. cities, including Milwaukee, Detroit, Philadelphia, Boston, Kansas City, and Topeka. She also formed friendships with a number of leading women's rights activists; Susan B. Anthony, Carrie Chapman Catt, Anna Howard Shaw, and Elizabeth Cady Stanton were among them. Later that year, Gilman traveled to England, where she attended the International Socialist and Labor Congress and hit the British lecture circuit for a three-week tour.

Unquestionably, Gilman's most significant professional accomplishment during her transitional years was the publication of her major feminist polemic, *Women and Economics* (1898), which addressed the relationship between sexual oppression and women's economic dependence on men. Eventually translated into seven languages, the book won Gilman international acclaim. In November 1897 she returned to New York and renewed her acquaintance with her cousin George Houghton Gilman, whom she would marry in June 1900. In her relationship with Houghton, Gilman was finally able to achieve her long-held ambition for public service and to experience the love and support that had escaped her during her marriage to Walter.

Also included in this chapter are letters alluding to events or to people that played a significant role in Gilman's repudiation of the cult of domesticity. In still other letters, Gilman, who by now had firmly established a reputation as "an artist of sufficient merit," distanced herself from her earlier tolerance of traditional roles. In a letter that is both testy and humorous, Gilman responds to an invitation from her cousin Katharine Seymour Day: "It's very kind and nice of you to ask me but I cannot by the wildest stretch of the imagination see myself 'pouring' at a tea. I feel as I did when I was first asked to be a 'Patroness' at a ball" (May 21, 1909). Gilman's tea-pouring days were over.

1 Wayland St.
Providence R. I.
5th April, 1885

Dear Aunt Emily [Perkins Hale]:[1]

You have a grand niece, quite small for the adjective but rightful owner thereof.

She came Monday, 23d March, and seems quite at home.

If you'll please inform me where my grand mother is I'll write her about it.

I would have sent you word before, but they so impressed it on my mind that I wasn't to think of anything that I gave up—and didn't.

I'm "as comfortable as could be expected" and hope soon to be about.

Your happy niece
Charlotte Perkins Stetson
by C. W. S. [Charles Walter Stetson]

[January 4, 1886]
Care [of] Dr. Wm. F. Channing, Pasadena
Los Angeles C. California.

Dear Martha,

I thank you for the pretty kerchief received yesterday and still more for the picture of Chester. I wish he was near enough for me to see more of him, for I know he is just the child I should love and enjoy. Dear bright little face! It makes me homesick for my own baby.

I have not written to you for so long because of—circumstances. The mere writing itself is still an effort; and then my mental condition has made me oblivious of even my best friends.

In despair of ever getting well at home I suddenly undertook this journey. It has already done me an immense amount of good and I expect to return in the spring as well as I ever shall be. Perhaps that is not saying much.

I stayed a month with my brother and learned to know and love his wife. . . .

Then a week in San Francisco where I learned much and enjoyed more. Saw something of father, who made himself quite agreeable.

Then here by the second week in December; and here I am likely to remain for rest of the winter. They are all very kind to me; and I gain rapidly. Was actually able to paint a little for Xmas—three cards. But the holiday festivities have pretty well worn me out. . . .

Perhaps later I shall have more energy to write; but now I haven't.

I don't forget you dear.

Your old friend

Charlotte Perkins Stetson

Evening, Sat. March. 13th. 1886.

Pasadena, Cala.

Dear Martha,

I send with this [a play] which will give you some idea of what I have been doing. You can see I am not so sick as I was.

Please understand that Grace is co-author, did <u>just</u> as much of it as I did. . . .

O but twas fun! To write a play and give it ourselves, all in a real theatre, to a real audience, who laughed and clapped and enjoyed it. We enjoyed it more. . . .

My baby will be big enough to talk pretty soon! She does some now, and has got two teeth! So there!

My California winter is about done. Shall start for home in a week or two more. I look forward with both joy and dread to see my darlings again; and dread of further illness under family cares. Well. I have chosen. . . .

Your old friend

Charlotte Perkins Stetson.

<u>Tues. April 19th. 1887</u>.

<u>26 Humboldt Ave. Providence R. I.</u>

Dr. Weir Mitchell,[2]

Dear Sir;

I write this for you, fearing that I shall soon be unable to remember even this much. I am coming to Philadelphia next week, to see you, but a week does a great deal now. Excuse me if I write unnessary [*sic*] facts, it is through ignorance. My desire is to make you acquainted with all the facts of the case, that you may form a deeper judgement than from mere casual examination.

To cure disease says Dr. Holmes, we must begin with the grand-fathers.[3] Here are mine.

Maternal grandfather.[4]

A sturdy New Englander of strong domestic disposition, intensely loving and benevolent. Nervous and fretful over his family as he grew old. died of paralysis.

Maternal grandmother.[5]

Married at fifteen or sixteen, her husband being a widower of thirty-six. Had a child at seventeen. Died. Another at eighteen, my mother. Was a delicate woman always, suffered much, was bedridden ten years with a complication of diseases, died of I don't remember what in particular.

Mother.[6]

A sickly and delicate child, overdosed and petted. Abnormally affectionate and conscientious. Given up to die with consumption three times, but still lives. An intellect large in some directions but singularly limited in others. Highly talented in music but no perception of art or poetry. A deep thinker, but absolutely illogical. Is in every way an exaggerated type of the so called "feminine" qualities, love of husband home and children being almost manias. Highly religious.

Paternal Grandfather.[7]

Of a family of New England divines. Was a distinguished lawyer in his city. A good man and clearheaded. Died of Bright's disease I think.

Paternal grandmother.[8]

Of a very distinguished New England family; the Beechers. Hated matrimony. Had "nervous fevers" I am told, and was obliged to leave home at recurring intervals. Could not bear to see her husband at such times. Had four children, my father the oldest. One of her daughters has had nervous prostration. The other under pressure of great trouble lost her reason for a time, recovered, was ill again, and was out of her mind when she died I believe. One son a fine lawyer.

My father.[9]

Highly eccentric. Of a benevolent and reformatory disposition at first, but grew more solitary and morose with years. Brilliant intellect, an author, editor, librarian, etc. Also musical. Has not a superior in the county for general information. Had several love affairs but broke them off, one on the very eve of marriage. Finally married. Took separate rooms when the children came, "could not be broken of his rest." Left his family after three years and has since lived alone. Boarded with a well loved sister awhile, but could not bear even such restraint, and returned to his room. Has neglected his wife who procured divorce. Neglected his children. Would take money his family needed to buy some precious book. Fine physique as a young man, but delicate lungs. Large brain, susceptible nerves, small moral sense. Very reserved and proud. My self.

The youngest of three children born in three successive years. Mother in miserable health, the doctor saying if she had another child then it would kill her. As a baby and child, delicate; but receiving excellent care, out door life, exercise, etc. Reached womanhood in perfect health. At fifteen became impressed with the truths of physiology and hygiene, and adopted "reform dress," cold daily sponge bath, open window at night, gymnastics, etc; abjuring corsets, tea, coffee, late hours and all other known evils. (If one can abjure what one never has had.) On this regimen I improved yearly, growing stronger and developing in brain and muscle. Was never tired, did not know what the word meant, could walk indefinitely, wash, scrub, lift, row, run, do anything; and never know I had a body. As for nerves I denied their existence. Physically I was perfectly well up to my marriage at twenty-three—four.

The mental history is more important. A clever and precocious child. At eight my imagination was already at work and I regaled myself with visions of unattainable delights, not occasionally, but as a nightly solace before sleeping. (But even at that age conscience was predominant, and I limited my luxury in this wise. Once a week I would imagine things a little more impossible than the every day repast. Once a month things still more unusual and delightful. Once a year anything I chose!) This habit grew, making up for a thousand outside ills, till at thirteen it was a large part of my life, and so real that I actually believed it.

This powerful current of thought my mother suddenly checked, telling me it was dangerous and wrong, and I must never think of those things again. Conscience and will were equal to the task, and I shut back that lovely dream world out of my mind forever. No new channel was presented me however, and as a natural consequence I found one, worse than the other. Having always a taste for the morbid and ghostly I now launched upon a sea of Poe-like visions, carrying my dream life through a most wicked and unhealthy world. No one knew of this and no one stopped it; till I myself, growing in health and wisdom, saw the evil, and resolved that I would <u>think</u> no longer, but <u>do</u>. Was not <u>wholly</u> free from this till about twenty. Meanwhile, from the age of fifteen, I began to live a strong self poised, individual life; drawing help and companionship from books, scientific and philosophical. I developed a theory of self culture of my own; and practiced it; till will and reason were free to act, and mind and body were strong and willing servants, and here began the strain which brings me here today.

Those servants were so strong and so willing, and so severely disciplined withal; that they never complained under their burdens, and I overworked them steadily for eight years. They both fail me now.

The work was not so much, it was the constant self-supervision and restraint. I never <u>rested</u>. Besides this there was a constant strain on the nerves in this way. My mother and myself are utterly uncongenial—antagonistic. In all those years, since childhood, living with her has been a daily jar, a strain, a struggle for patience and endurance. The ingenious agony she unwittingly inflicts has never been equaled by any one else. There was no person in my immediate environment who <u>was</u> congenial,—to say the truth I inherit my father's solitary disposition. I lived alone among them, and was thought "queer" and "odd" in the last degree.

At twenty one I lost my one friend, a girl; a desperate grief to me.

Then came a lover, my only one, and after two years of terrible struggle and agony of mind I was weak enough to marry him.

I married in May. The next March I had a daughter. Was not specially sick in carrying her; and had an easy time enough at birth. Had terrible fits of remorse and depression all through the time, but thought nothing of them as I had had the same in the two years torture called courtship. Began to show "nervousness" in the months confinement. Had wild and dreadful ideas which I was powerless to check, times of excitement and times of tears. No one thought there was anything the matter. Nurse left in four weeks and I was alone with the baby for three weeks, getting scarcely any sleep. Then my mother came and took the baby, and I have been sick ever since. No <u>pain</u>, I never had a pain except having my teeth filled, having a sore finger, and having the baby; but a mental misery and an accompanying weakiness [*sic*] beyond description.

Before marriage I had a very cheerful disposition, notably so; I said <u>I could not imagine the combination of circumstance that would make me unhappy</u>. Since then I have scarce known a happy moment. There have been changes of course, but no real joy. Do not lay this to circumstances. My husband is devotion itself, my child well and good, I have a lovely home, and a perfect maidservant, there is no outside trouble but poverty, and that I always had and don't mind. Neither is their [*sic*] an inside trouble, of a physical nature. I have been examined twice since the child's birth by a competent physician, and there is nothing wrong.

This agony of mind set in with the child's coming. I nursed her in slow tears. All that summer I did nothing but cry, save for times when the pain was unbearable and I grew wild, hysterical, almost imbecile at times. Late in 1885 I made a wild determination, weaned the child, borrowed money, and started to visit friends in California. Spent the winter there, getting perfectly well I thought. Came home in March. Had bronchitis six weeks and before that was over relapsed into the previous years condition.

This lasted all summer. In August 1886 I began to take Dr. Bucklands Essence of Oats;[10] and became well apparently, but not strong. Painted and wrote of course, over-did of course, and was tired by Xmas. But I rested thereafter, and felt tolerably well till this March. Then I had a severe cold, the worst of my life, lasting in full fury for a week. As I began to recover the baby had it, and I had to nurse her day and night. Three days finished me, I broke down in helpless tears, and since then have grown steadily worse.

There is more physical prostration than ever before. And there are mental symptoms which alarm me seriously. These I can tell you better. But I beg of you not to laugh at me as every one else does, not to say it is "almost as bad as a disease" as one of my friends does, not to turn me off.

I am an artist of sufficient merit to earn an easy living when well. I am a writer, a poet, a philosopher, in little. I am a teacher by instinct and profession. I am a reader and thinker. I can do some good work for the world if I live. I cannot bear to die or go insane or linger on [in] this wretched invalid existence, and be a weight on this poor world which has so many now. I want to <u>work</u>, to help people, to do good. I did for years, and can again if I get well. Surely it is worth while to save a good worker, one who asks little and longs to give much! I have long wished I could see you, without hope of it; and now some kind friend has given me means to go away and stay awhile, to rest and try to get well.

I understand you are the first authority on nervous diseases. Are you on brain troubles too? There is something the matter with my head. No one here knows or believes or cares. Of course they can't care for what they don't believe. But you will know.

It is harder to write every day. I have given up my newspaper work little as it was. I can't think, I can't remember, I cant grasp an idea. But I could once. I shall have a fine night after writing this, but I fear every day to lose memory entirely. And maybe you can help me.

Forgive the length.

I know it isn't what I should have written but I can't do better now. Perhaps you can gather something of what I want you to see. I am all alone in the house or I couldn't write this. <u>People</u> tire me frightfully.

I'm running down like a clock—could go one [*sic*] scribbling now indefinitely—but the letters don't come right.[11]

Charlotte Perkins Stetson.

8:30 P.M.

Tues. Oct. 30th. 1888.

Pasadena.

Los Angeles Co.

Cala.

Care [of] Dr. Wm. F. Channing

Dear Mother [Rebecca Steere Stetson],[12]

I am sorry not to write you often, but between hard work and weariness I haven't been able. I arrived Wednesday, hired the house Thursday, selected papers Friday, had it papered & whitewashed Saturday, and moved in Monday....

I really can't remember whether I've written to you about it or not, so I'll go right ahead and explain that out of my nine big packing cases I've had a little kitchen made, whose total cost was about eleven dollars. My cottage now has five rooms, beside a cellar of some 6 x 8 feet. There are three great rose bushes on the cottage, and some ivy and scarlet passion flower [*sic*]. It is quite surrounded with orange trees, great handsome ones, but not looking their best now owing to temporary neglect on the part of the owner who lives in Los Angeles....

We are all wearing summer clothes, and spend a good part of our time on the piazza. Katharine luxuriates in it all and grows visibly.... The Channings have been kind as only they can, have helped in every possible way, and put me into the house bodily with all my goods. It's very cozy here. I have had it beautifully papered with paper at 12 cts and 7 ½ cts a roll, and the lovely familiar things look well in it. There is a pretty piazza in front with an orange tree at each end and two great rose vines in f[r]ont. The roof is dull red and house white washed or yellow washed some time since, a very nice color. There is a straight path to the front—hitching post, with lots of flowers on each side. The lemon verbenas of great size[,] one over six feet high, are on either side of the path. . . . The little girl seems perfectly contented with her new home, and enjoys the lovely sunshine and the flowers as much as I do. Such hosts of roses as the Channings have! And such beauties! I am told to help myself freely at any time. . . .

I get up at half past six and fly about at my work as briskly as you please. . . .

There seems to be a good market for my work here, of all kinds. . . . We'll get on swimmingly, I know. . . .

My love to you all.

Charlotte Perkins Stetson.

Sat. March 16th. 1889.<br>Pasadena, Cala.

Dear Martha,

I have a dim idea that I owe you a letter! With it I send a little dress of Kate's which may serve Margaret[13] for awhile, and the immortal poem you so patiently request. As for the parlor farces you speak of we may quite possibly send you some next Fall, in time to open the season with so to speak. . . . We have had an encouraging letter from Gillette[14] in which he speaks of coming here in May possibly, and bringing out our play in San Francisco with good company. . . .

Walter is very happy here, but has done little pecuniarily so far. Still we think the prospect is good, and he is painting steadily. He and Grace are great friends, which gives me sincere delight.

Katharine flourishes amazingly, like unto a "green baize tree" as it were.[15] . . .

I am running a "literature class." Some ten or twelve ladies, at five dollars a head, ten lessons. I deal with modern literature, its causes and effects. Very successful so far.

Am feeling pretty well along now, and consequently hopeful. . . .

Charlotte Perkins Stetson.

Wed. April 24th or 5th. 1889.

Pasadena. Cala.

Dear Mother [Stetson],

Just as I begin Kate interrupts me. She says "Are you writing to both my granmas?" I told her to her grandma Stetson.

"Tell her dear love and to come out here!"

That's what I would say to all my friends—dear love, and to come out here!

I am very sorry not to have written you oftener. I am very sorry for a great many things, and am only of late years learning to bear patiently the things I am sorry for. My own mother has fared no better. She has been put to the device of sending a message to Grace Channing to see if I were alive or dead.

You fare better, for a loving son keeps you well posted as to all our doings and happenings, and the lovely land we live in.

Dear Kate! It is truly a paradise for children. We spend all our days on the rose shaded piazza, and she is even now swinging there in a hammock while I sit in a wicker rocker and write. It has been a comfort and delight all winter (—to call it winter!) and is now a necessity. For our little plasterless house gets hot by noon, though we are thankful to say it cools as quickly at night. They tell us this is summer weather now, that it is scarcely even hotter, save for a few phenomenal days. . . .

Walter keeps well and enjoys his work. Kate is the picture of sturdy health, though we suspect she has whooping cough. It is a very mild form indeed.

She is good as gold, and bright enough to please any grandma. She often speaks of you all, and longs to see her various relatives. I fancy she will love her home more than I ever did. . . .

Yours with love

Charlotte Perkins Stetson.

Box 1844. Pasadena, Cala.

Thurs. Aug. 15th, 1889.

Dear Martha,

. . . I am long past apologizing for the lack of letters. To some I say "I can't," to the others nothing.

To you I will remark at some length that the weakness of brain which has so devastated my life for the past five years still holds very largely;

and while I can do considerable work of a kind which dominates me at the time, or which necessity demands, yet ordinary labor or obligation goes neglected.

The two things still almost impossible to me are sewing and the writing of letters.

I have written my half of two plays since March, planned a deal beside, and made a few poems, beside my regular week's work with my class in literature, etc., but letters I try simply to forget, in order that they may not haunt me. . . .

I look back with incredulous amazement to the time when writing was easier than talking and I sought correspondence for correspondence' sake.

Well. There are better things in store. I never had a larger hope than I have now at favorable moments, never more certainty of usefulness and joy. But to communicate with the individual though it be even you, is no longer an impulse, but an effort. And I have no strength for effort of any sort.

No one has ever taken your place, heart's dearest. No one has ever given me the happiness that you did, the peace the rest the everpresent joy. I do not forget.

Neither do I remember, for the immediate past is still so vital a horror, and all the antecedent years so lonely and drear, that I never look back if I can avoid it.

I felt in your yesterday's letter that the time might yet come when we should again be much to each other. If it be so how gladly will we hail it! . . .

Yours with love,
Charlotte Perkins Stetson.

Box 1844. Pasadena
Cala—
Tues. Oct. 22nd. 1889.

[To Martha Luther Lane]
Dear little girl,

It is a pity we can't have a real good talk—"like we useter!"

Some day we will.

If you are in earnest about a possible situation here I will look about a little. I know a man in a large canning business—making money fast.

Now it seems to me within the bounds of possibility that Mr. Lane's experience in similar lines might be of some service to this men [*sic*], that he might establish through him a larger eastern connection, or some such rosy cloud of chance. I'll furtively and non-committaly inquire.

Haven't you got over that Puritan conscience yet? You do need me, if you are still in the toils to that degree. . . .

I haven't seen Brownings' thing about Fitzgerald,[16] but I don't blame him, whatever it was. F. was dead, but what then? <u>She</u> was dead, when he wrote his contemptible remarks. If any man had so spoken of <u>my</u> dead wife, and she a queen-poet too; I would pillory him in any fashion that offered—cowardly vermin! . . .

<u>Dear</u> little girl! I am so sorry you are lonesome! It's a hard thing to bear as well I know.

And O if I could talk to you, how many new things I should have to say!

For I have lived and learned a great deal in these long dreary years of illness and melancholy. Now I am busy and full of interests old and new.

I am teaching a young girl, a housemaid at present, for three evenings a week. She is American, and has had a hard bitter life, with much fraud and meanness in it—a <u>bound child</u>. She is about eighteen, and hungry for the education Fate has denied her. . . .

Box 1844.
Pasadena, Cal., Mon. Jan. 20th 1890

Dear Martha,

A long and loving letter from you this morning; and now it is but quarter to eight, Kate is in bed, and there is nothing to prevent my answering you as you deserve except ability.

I will do my best.

I should no more dare to read old letters from you or even far less dear ones, than I should dare read Jean Ingelow's "Divided" to a sympathizing friend.

You knew and loved me once. You do not know me now, and I am not at all sure that you would love me if you did.

What you cling to so tenderly is a sweet memory, a lovely past; as many a man or woman cherishes a lost love.

Time and experiences make us grow and change, in varying degree, and while you have changed only in a calmer wisdom, a sweet maturity, grown only on the lovely lines marked out already in your character, an orderly wise kind loving woman, an ideal mother, a contenting wife, and with all literature and learning before you to rise in an[y] you choose and can—I have grown and changed wildly, darkly, strangely, beyond a mother's recognition, beyond my own. The girl you knew, the woman you loved died some years past, died in long slow unutterable pain.

I believe you had some knowledge of it at the time.

Whether she who now writes is a better woman or as good or worse is a matter of some scientific interest perhaps, but one which I consider seldom.

A change—a difference—a distance incalculable, an impassable gulph [*sic*], lies between me and your old friend.

We may be friends again, new ones, but I do not dare to hope for it.

So utterly unstable, rootless and windblown is my life, that all calm restful rooted things are my admiration and my dispair [*sic*] and they do not generally like me, which is selfprotecting natural instinct on their part.

But this I will say of my love for you.

Through the first year or two of my marriage, in every depth of pain and loss and loneliness, <u>yours</u> was the name my heart cried—not his. I loved you better than any one, in those days when I had a heart to love and ache.

And now always in the future of wealth and fame which I dangle before my own eyes as an incentive to life and effort, I always think first of you as a sort of haven; to gorgeously befriend you—(only audacious fancies!) and to beg some of your sweet family influence for Kate.

Grace Channing saved what there is of me. Grace Channing pulled me out of living death, set me on my staggering feet, helped me to get to work again, did more than I can say to make me live, and I love her, I think, as well as any one on earth.

But it is different. With you I <u>was happy</u>, and that is a word I have forgotten.

Those years with you, that blessed summer of eighty one—I don't doubt it most people have as much happiness in all their lives as I had then. I do not forget. But neither do I remember, because it hurts.

It is useless for me to write all this. I know enough of the human mind, the laws of brain structure and action, to know that the concept "Charlotte" which forms part of your life is in no way me; and yet that every word I say is taken by the helpless brain as coming from that concept. Even if by fresh incessant effort, you endeavor to background my words with an imaginary figure, a new concept, based on what I say, it is only imaginary, and distinctly forced and artificial. When your will releases the brain it slowly reacts from the new forced impression, and there is the old one again. That is why for one reason I write so little. You <u>cannot</u> understand. Unless we could live together again, or indeed if I wrote daily and vitalized each letter with my present self, we can come to no contact whatever. Write so I cannot, meet we cannot, now.

But time may turn the wheel to our old gladness again—"When you and I asked nothing of the world but room and one another!,"[17] or may turn it to something better. Can there be anything better? Different let me say. You ask me to "reassure you." This is but sad reply, and yet I have no better. . . .

Walter has gone East. He got a telegram last Saturday week, saying "come home at once quickest way. Mother is very low."

He started Sunday and I got a telegram yesterday saying "Arrived last night. Mother was buried Thursday." So there is trouble enough if one would grieve. The sad joyless old woman dying without one glimpse of her last born and best loved; and he not even seeing his mother's face! And no wife to comfort him.

Write him a line if you can and care to, I know it would please him. . . .

I think you are very right about your marriage and especially the children. I don't know any better blood on earth than that pure New England stock; so sane and steady and clever and true; so safely anchored and yet so open to all finer growth and influence.

That line of your letter is perhaps the sweetest of it all to me—"and your old enthusiasm has put new life into me today." I like to think that even the ghost of that girl is some good; and that I being another ghost, may be some good yet before I die.

And I don't seem at all prepared to die yet. The machinery runs as steady as ever; and I begin to hope I may yet catch and bind the loose walking-beam which has so long done destruction in hull and rigging. . . .

Don't imagine I am still a melancholiac. Out here they think me "so bright! So clever! So goodnatured!" and I am sent for to officiate at church socials and similar festivities. And I never had so much praise for beauty in my palmiest days as I have here. I am considered <u>beautiful</u>—really! That would have been a great pleasure nine years ago, wouldn't it!

And I have good friends here; and plenty of work to do. I like my work, I am getting <u>very</u> fond of Kate; I look forward as I always shall, to doing great things sometime. . . .

Good night dear. You were more <u>comfort</u> to me—more pure joy, than anyone else ever was. Good night.

Yes I did well to mourn when you left me; but it was to be. . . .

Yours tenderly,

Charlotte Perkins Stetson.

Box 1844 Pasadena Cala.
12 M. Sat. March 15th 1890.

Dear Martha,

It is high noon of a most delicious Saturday, not time to get dinner yet, and not time to write with a big W. So I unceremoniously put you into the chink. . . .

I've been scribbling a lot lately, a lot for me that is, and Grace and I are embarked on our third play. "A Pretty Idiot" is trembling on the verge of success, we have solid hope of it. . . . Do you see the Nationalist? I sent them a poem, funny, which I think they will take, as it was upon invitation from one of the editorial board. Named "Similar Cases." I know it will amuse you. . . .

Have you seen Grace's story, "A Strange Dinner Party" in The New England Mag? The illustrations <u>were</u> Walter's, but he disowns them now. Never was anything so mined or debased in purity. Actually I hardly know them.

I've sent a story there too, my one ghost story, which I think I read you once. It now figures as "The Giant Wistaria," and has a prelude.[18]

Grace is rapidly sailing into public recognition. The press is glibly passing her on as "a young writer of promise" etc., and she is printing pretty fast too.

"Kate Field's Washington" has had a poem of hers, and a translation; and the "Overland" a poem, a story, and an article.

I hope to follow soon in her wake, for reasons many and good.

Walter is working splendidly. If you chance to be in Providence don't fail to see his pictures, to say nothin' of him.

He has been writing stories too, much to our disgust. We (that's Grace & I) threaten to outpaint him if he persists. But he has not achieved print yet. . . .

"We are all well," and I am really quite happy. I ought to be. The great blue periwinkles crowd around my little piazza, the roses are coming out by the hundreds—(two great vines that shade and sweeten the whole front of the house); the Banksia rose flourishes from ground to ridgepole on the South, and is myriad budded now; the oranges hang ever ready and the orange blossoms make a dreamland all about me, and then there are mockingbirds and moonlight galore. . . .

Now I must get dinner, no great task for just Kate and myself. A tiny oil stove does it all.

Good bye dear

Charlotte Perkins Stetson.

Box 401 Pasadena, Cal.—

8.12 P.M. Fri. May 30th. 1890.

[To Marian Parker Whitney]
Most Charming Cousin![19]

. . . Now I am well aware that I undertook, in the subtle stimulus of your delightful society, to write to you; but as I remember, there was no time set for the accomplishment of that rash promise so that this belated epistle will answer as well as another.

You may well be puzzled however, as to why, not having written so long, I should write now, and this shall be circumstantially explained.

Time was, in the young exuberance of hereditary pen-power, that I sought about wildly for correspondents; pursued, discovered, created them; and could write more letters in a day, about nothing at all, than I can write now in a week on life death and money matters.

Time was again, in another young exuberance of opinion and idea, that I wrote letters not so numerous, but O so <u>long</u>! Voluminous, heavy, prospective, retrospective, introspective; a tax on the stationer the post-office and the recipient.

But then alas! came a time, and a long time, when I could write no letters at all—scarce read them! and that period is but just passing. Upon its heels comes my first genuine professional work in this line; with my slowly gaining strength I write and write and write; invariably overdoing and then having to rest a bit. . . .

And now, having made you sufficiently uncomfortable I hope! I will furthermore explain why this present affliction falleth upon you.

Firstly it is one of the very tired periods in which I stop "writing" for a day or two.

Secondly today has been a very pleasant and mildly exciting one, so that I have still sufficient energy to "take my pen in hand."

Thirdly Miss Delia Lyman[20] is here! And with Miss Lyman such a nice kind jolly seductive little note of introduction.

So here I am!

I live in a little house, a very little house with four corners, an orange tree at each corner, three orange trees behind each orange tree, and an orange tree on every orange tree's tail! . . .

Here I live, all alone with Kate. . . .

A large part of the time I fizzle out, and have to intersperse days of gloomy idleness. Gloomy because the illness of six years hovers gently in the background, and extra weariness brings melancholy in its train. Melancholia I should say—which is a different thing.

I like Miss Lyman. I am glad to have her here. I will talk to her as much as she can stand, and listen to her as much as she can talk.

. . . Lo! I have aquired [*sic*] in three month's space the great sum of Ten Dollars by my pen!!! And such fame as newspaper notices in which I figure as an addition to Miss Grace Ellery Channing, and which have not more than three errors to the inch.

To follow Miss Channing is a horror. <u>She</u> is a genius. It is barely possible that this unsupported assertion may not carry much weight to your sagacity, but just you wait! And remember I said so! Miss Channing and I are inseparable. We have worked together some two years, though now writing individually. Her house is near mine. We drop in in the morning. We occasionally dine together. We call or visit in the afternoon. We go to places together. We frequently stay to tea with one another. We very often spend long evenings together. And we find—at least <u>I</u> find, an everlasting never-fading charm in these rare meetings!

From which you may perhaps gather a faint idea of the perfection of Miss Grace Ellery Channing.

Now mademoiselle wherein further shall I expatiate? Shall I tell you how the mockingbirds sing and sing in these orange trees of mine? Or how Katharine Beecher Stetson, my young, waxeth steadily in the good graces of all who know her? Or how Mr. Stetson languisheth in Providence, a banished Pasadenian, and painteth mighty pictures for a Fall Exhibition in New York?[21] Get to see that if you can. About the last of Nov. I believe. Then he will go abroad. In the fullness of time I follow, and Kate likewise. O that ecstatic and aesthetic child! "I love you mama!" she exclaims in rapturous embrace; "I love you better than I love a stick!" Isn't that reassuring? "Mama—" she says, coming out of a brown study[22] as to her muscular power: "Mama! Couldn't I knock over any old lady?" "Of course I wouldn't!" is the hasty and diplomatic addition—but I doubt it. And as I was putting her to bed one night, clean and sweet from her bath, and just receiving the shimmering white nightdress, fresh and chilly from the drawer—she said with a profound air of scientific research "I suppose skunks would find this cool!"

Now why skunks?

There ma'am! If you want to know anything further about me, read Kate Fields Washington and The Woman's Journal and the New England Magazine! (let me humbly add that this last has not yet published a certain tale, though accepted.) Oh, and The Nationalist—the Boston one.

Good night fair cousin. I shall rejoice to hear from you at any time.

Yours affectionately

Charlotte Perkins Stetson.

Box 401, Pasadena Cal—
Tues June 17th. 1890

Dear Martha,

Here is a long neglected letters of yours—April 23rd, pricking me sore. You want to talk do you? (Or did, then!) Well, we'll do it sometime. . . .

I am glad you thought my poem ["Similar Cases"] funny. I herein boastfully enclose a copy of a letter showing it was thought rather more of by some! (You see this version—proving that your criticisms had weight.[)]

Here is the letter.

"184 Commonwealth Ave.
Boston, June 9th, 1890.

Dear Madam:

I have been wishing ever since I first read it—and I've read it many times with unfailing joy—to thank you for your poem in the April <u>Nationalist.</u> We have had nothing since the Biglow Papers half so good in a good cause as Similar Cases.

And just now I've read in the Woman's Journal your Women of Today. It is as good almost as the other, and <u>dreadfully</u> true!

Yours sincerely,<br>W. D. Howells"[23] . . .

I am so pleased too to find the man thinks well of Nationalism in spite of its "flabby apostle" (!)[24]

And even more pleased that he should be on the right side of the Woman Question too. That last is a long inference I admit—I wouldn't presume on it publicly, but it does seem so to me.

Look here dear; if I come East next Fall for a visit do you want me to count you in? Or may I humbly inquire if you will count <u>me</u> in for a little? Maybe I shan't come, but I want to very much, either in the Fall or Winter. . . .

Your old friend<br>Charlotte Perkins Stetson.

Box 401 Pasadena Cal.<br>Sun. July 27th, 1890.

Dear Martha,

I am sitting on the piazza of my small house, drying my hair, and otherwise enjoying myself. . . .

Here's a letter of yours way back in June somewhere. No, I haven't read "A Hazard of New Fortune[s],"[25] only parts of it. Howells never was a favorite of mine you know. His work is exquisite, painfully exquisite, but save for that Chinese delicacy of workmanship it seems to me of small artistic value.

As far as I have seen, the waste horrors of our high class life, which he so fearfully portrays, awake no other emotion in the class portrayed than a pleased surprise at their own reproduction. Like a child with a looking-glass. I may do him wrong, he may be accomplishing an immense deal somewhere, but I never heard him credited with what seems to me his real purpose—a biting moralism. . . .

Still for all this I know no higher authority in this country, and was correspondingly elated with his letter. Wasn't it nice of him. . . .

I'm glad you have seen the sense in equal suffrage. I never was a very ardent suffragist, it has long seemed such a foregone conclusion that I can't get all excited over it. But it is vitally essential. . . .

My latest departure is in public speaking.

I guess I told you of my first adventure in this line—with the local Nationalist Club. That was my first speech to a mixed audience, and they were so pleased they got me to <u>repeat</u> it, to a larger evening audience!

Certain grandees from Los Angeles were present (acquaintances) and they besought me to repeat the address at their house to a large invited party. Which I cheerfully did, being the lion of a ladies lunch first, and speaker afterward. Then the 1st Nationalist Club in Los Angeles, hearing of my prowess, invited me to give them an address, which I did, and they were tumultuous in their applause, and begged repitition [*sic*]. Also they sent me a most appreciative letter some time since, enclosing five dollars! Said they didn't often pay, but mine was the best address they had ever had, and should be paid for however inadequately!

Wasn't that fine! Now I am helping to organize a Social Purity[26] society here, with good success.

I may get to be a dangerous person to know, so you had better hedge a little, hadn't you?

When my awful story, "The Yellow Wallpaper" comes out, you must try & read it. Walter says he has read it <u>four</u> times, and thinks it the most ghastly tale he ever read. Says it beats Poe, and Doré! But that's only a husband's opinion.[27]

I read the thing to three women here however, and I never saw such squirms! Daylight too. It's a simple tale, but highly unpleasant.

I don't know yet where it will be. If none of the big things will take it I mean to try the New York Ledger. Have you that in its new form? Kipling and Stevenson etc. etc. write for that now, so I guess I can.

Goodbye, ma'am!

Charlotte Perkins Stetson.

Sat. Sept. 4th. 1890.

Pasadena—Cal.

Dear Martha,

. . . Grace has left me on a tour of visits north and eastward, ending by a jump to Florence where she will settle down with a Miss Senter[28] of this place, and write.

I miss her rather more than I do most people. But I never really

<u>missed</u> anybody but you. Still you went, and now you are not there! Those were good days.

But like everything else taken out of my life I do not regret it—it all leaves me stronger and more independant [*sic*], better able to do world's work.

I am writing now almost exclusively—a little teaching here and there thrown in.

If you know anybody that takes Kate Fields Washington, she has a lot of my things.

Walter tells me they are widely copied—there was a story in the "Globe" the other day.

When I have anything big out you will probably know it as soon as I shall. . . .

Cheerfully<br>Charlotte Perkins Stetson.

Sun. Sept. 28th 1890.<br>Pasadena, Cal.

My Dear [Cousin] Marian,

I am still in time to reach you before Oct. 15th—before you leave the house described in your most welcome letter of Aug. 17th. Oh! Indeed it is more like <u>Ow</u>!—how <u>homesick</u> that letter made me! . . .

As a rule people weary me, irritate me, enrage me, or cause me to writhe in sympathy.

I suppose you might say as Grimm's cat says to his partner the mouse—"That comes of always sitting at home in your little gray frock and hairy tale and never seeing the world!"[29] . . .

My experience in general society is like that of the hapless scientist standing dumb before a newly introduced fair enslaver, and finally busting out—"If you have no more facts to communicate I will bid you good evening!" and fleeing in despair.

I have but one resource—to be funny. And you can't be funny forever and ever nor with all kinds of people.

You ask with gentle irony where my great works are published.

Fair cousin, I have only been writing, professionally, since <u>March 1st of this year</u>! . . .

I have written one powerful story, "The Yellow Wall-paper," but that is not out yet.

When I do get anything out worth hearing of, you will probably hear of it without me telling you—see? . . .

Now your work fills me with envy and despair. To understand "grammar" is to me like being an astronomer, and when it comes to "furrin tongues" my forehead is in the dust.[30]

So we will be a mutual admiration society. . . .

Did you chance to see Miss Channing's story in the August Scribner? And her poem in the September?

They tell me she is receiving more newspaper notice than any young writer now.

She is now on her way to Florence, with intermediate visits, and from thence will come a stream of literature which will astonish the world. . . .

> Goodbye.
>
> Charlotte Perkins Stetson.

> June 16th. 1891.
> Pasadena Cal.

Dear Walter,[31]

It seems to me possible that from my continued friendliness and perhaps tenderness in some past letters, you may have misunderstood my position—have had some hope that I would some day be yours again. Do not deceive yourself dear. My life is too precious to me to waste anymore of it like those seven years we spent together.

Not wasted in some ways & [I] grant full of deep experience and that pain that means growth. But you will know how it unfitted me for any work and how since you left I have done good work and lots of it— have made a reputation in one year. The difference is too great. Work I must, and when I live with you I can't. Therefore I shall never live with you again as a wife. I know it's hard for you but I can't help it. You must take the hard the [sic] truth and make the best of it.

Kate is well and happy and very glad to be at home after our trip. I'll write more soon, but this was on my mind to-day.

> Sincerely,
>
> Charlotte Perkins Stetson

> Near 4 P.M. 4th of July 1891, Pasadena.

Dear Walter,[32]

I am delighted to hear of your excellent health. I too am feeling well and improving steadily, and Kate is superb. I have been working hard this week cleaning house for Miss Knapp's coming and have thriven upon the exercise.

I am sorry you did not find my last letter plain enough—it is hard for us both. But since you ask so specifically, I will answer specifically. I have told you these things for years past you know—you would never believe me—now you must. No. I will not live with you again—not even in the same house. I know too well what that would amount to. Not as your wife in any case. How can you ask me again when you know! Nor will I come to Providence on any terms. You have to live there? Well, I don't. And I will not go abroad with you. As you know I have been planning and hoping these years past to have you go—alone. I will not accompany you on any terms. And for my work—that is my life and I shall pursue it as long as I live, whether you consent or not[,] approve or not. I had my work to do before ever I knew you, you know.

I am sorry very sorry to have to put these things so plainly, but you would have it. I hope you will not ever need to ask again. We two must part—and then [*sic*] is an end to it.

All goes well here and you need to be under no concern about my health, it is fast becoming established.

Regretfully but sincerely,
Charlotte.

1258 Webster St. Oakland
Mon. Feb. 19th 1894.

Dear [Cousin] Marian,

. . . I'm glad you liked my book [In This Our World] and not at all displeased at your disagreeing with some of it. You see it is not literature, merely teaching, some ideas "with verses on," and I'm not a bit sensitive about it as a piece of work.

But it does gladden my heart to have Howells write across the continent and tell me I'm the prophetess of the new religion! He says very encouraging things; and I value them immensely in view of his recent work in The Cosmopolitan. Have you read his Traveller from Altruria?[33] There's socialism for you. . . .

[Gilman resumed the letter on March 14, 1894]

Your letter speaks, a little hesitatingly, of my having "seen trouble" as it were.

To which I reply drily, I have. . . .

In unconfidential superficial facts I have had hard times always, and of late years the most ingenious combination of patent miseries and af-flictions. These play back and forth over a varying background of nervous weakness, which shades all the way from depression of spirits to devouring melancholia; and which gives to my visible conduct a graduated scale of merit. At times I don't do as well as a person of my "parts" might be expected to, but at other times to do anything at all becomes so heroic that the consciousness thereof almost offsets the misery within. . . .

If I gain in health a little I can do better in all ways. My head is what fails you know—or rather the nerve force—brain power—whatever it is you write letters with.

Sincerely,

Charlotte Perkins Stetson

1004 Powell St. S. F. [San Francisco]

Mon. June 18th 1894.

Dear Cousin Mary,[34]

Your distracted little letter amuses me much. I'll tell you "what it all means" as well as I can.[35] But first let me say how glad I am you had Kate there and liked her. She is a good little person. . . .

Now it "all means" only this; that the child's father loves her dearly and wanted to see her—has wanted to these four years. That he has some right as a father—(I don't admit much, but some,) and needed her society.

That the child herself needed to see her father and some other people beside me.

(You know I don't believe in the "divine right of mothers.")

That I had carried her four years, as it were, and it was his turn.

That my health and general work and progress will be the better for a years vacation from the constant care of a child.

And that I borrowed some money, took advantage of my father's trip east, and sent the darling off.

It hurt, awfully, and does yet—but what of that?

It's a good thing all round, for her, for him, for me.

You know Walter and I are dear and tender friends though I proved inequal to matrimony. (You know I always maintained I wasn't fit for it.)

And now I hear from Walter today that he is married to Grace Channing and my cup of happiness is full.[36] I am safe, free, out of it all;

and yet he has a wife! And that wife [is] the noblest loveliest greatest woman I know. I am so glad! Her influence will be lovely for Kate; and we all four love each other dearly. Is that clear? I suppose it does look rather queer from the outside. . . .

Now as to me, I have a lovely little home here, and am more comfortable than I ever was in my life. Really. . . .

I've been off lecturing once already, and shall again.

My Impress office is here in the home and I have a large parlor I let to the W. P. A. [Women's Press Association] and intend to to other clubs of women, classes, etc.[37]

Then in September Helen Campbell[38] comes out to join me on the paper; we are making it a weekly and make it go. After a few years steady work I shall have—think of it!—money enough to live on and maybe more.

It is really a very good business venture, as we have no other such paper here at all. . . .

With the paper on my hands and lecturing and writing besides I have need of all my time and strength, and am glad to have Kate gone for a while in spite of the hole in my heart.

And best of all my health is improving in leaps and bounds; all my troubles seem ended, and I begin to feel a very very little like what I was fifteen years ago! Aren't you glad? . . .

Affectionately yours—

Charlotte Perkins Stetson.

Will you write me how Kate struck you—as to behavior etc.? I'm anxious to know. Walter thinks her perfect of course, but I want a mother's opinion.

Hull House Chicago Ills.

Sunday Sept. 1st. 1895.

Dear Mrs. Cooper,[39]

Your letter of Aug. 8th was another touch of comfort. I am glad indeed to have some friends behind me—not glad to leave them, but glad they are friends.

And I particularly value your loving kindness because I know your opinion is formed of long practical knowledge, and takes cognizance of my numerous failings as well as the good things. I am very glad you care for me.

Here things go well. Dear Mrs. Campbell has been staying with me here the past week; to my great joy and advantage.

From the 22nd to the 29th was held a School of Economics at Chicago Commons[40]—another social settlement not far away. . . . Mrs. Campbell and I held forth on one evening devoted to Women Workers. . . . People were asking widely for my book [In This Our World]—I shall sell a lot here. Several have ordered.

I have spoken before the Radical Club . . . am to speak before the Ethical Society next Sunday morning, and before the Lasalle Club— one of this neighborhood's products—a Socialist Club of Russian Jews, a little later.

Last night Mrs. Campbell, Miss Addams and I were among those who responded to toasts at a banquet given to Keir Hardie[41] by the Labor Congress here. . . . It was a very calm and pleasant occasion. We all like Mr. Hardie. . . .

It is a great pleasure to see Mrs. Campbell so recognized, honored, and loved as she is here.

When she was introduced to Mr. Hardie last night he instantly said, "Author of 'Prisoner's Poverty?'" and was so glad to see her.

It reflects rather hardly [*sic*] I think on many of our San Franciscans, who either did not know the name at all or did not know enough to value it. What a comfort you always were to her, you dear wise woman. I love you the more for that.

With best love to you and Hattie [Howe],[42] and remembrance to all real friends—

Charlotte Perkins Stetson

80 Elm st. Chicago Ills.
Nov. 10th. 1895.

Dear Mrs. Cooper:

. . . All October has been brimful of work and the pleasure that comes of work which seems to be wanted. I spoke sixteen times in [the] course of the month; five regular lectures at Hull House, several little talks to working girls clubs, mother's clubs, etc. etc, and one to a Trades Union, one in public for a charity, one in Mrs. Washburne's home to a picked audience, and one to a study class of The Woman's Club. . . .

Since Nov. 1st I have spoken four times already, these being paid for. One was an address at the South Side Club; a big rich fashionable audience. The mayor addressed them also. I was sent for in great state in a carriage with [a] pair of prancing greys—an elegant private carriage; sent home thereafter in the same way, and paid ten dollars which I had not asked for at all! . . .

Last Monday I spoke in Evanston, on "The Royal Road To Learning," in a course given for the benefit of the North Western University Settlement Kindergarten. . . . John Vance Cheney preceded me, and Eugene Field was to have followed, the next week, but he died.[43] . . .

Wednesday I went to Grand Rapids on the early train. I was entertained at the house of Dr. Rutherford, the leading woman physician there; and had a delightful time. . . . Hothouse roses waited for me; a reception was given me in the afternoon at the house of one of the ladies of the town; and in the evening I attended the big reception of the Federation in the Morton House. . . .

Ever so many of them knew me through my book, and were delighted to see me. Dear old Lucinda Stone[44] "the mother of clubs" in Michigan said it was worth while to come, just to see me. I was glad enough to see her, splendid woman that she is!

Thursday evening I spoke, and it was really a great success. Two ladies that very night and one the next morning came to see about my lecturing otherwhere in Michigan; so they must have been favorably impressed. You see they were tired of two days of stultifying self praise in club "papers"; and I simply stood up and talked.

"Just let me see you smile!" said one eager handshaker afterward; "it was your smile that captured them!"

For all of this pleasure I was paid—actually paid! when I would cheerfully pay for the privilege could I afford it. Twenty five dollars and expenses. Fifty five dollars inside of a week! Isn't that fine! And fifty of it goes back to California tomorrow, as six and a half went a little while back—the first beginning of relief from my pile of debt. O it feels so good! So very good!

Dear Mrs. Fitch that helped me out of my last month's rent on Powell st, she's all paid back now; and some to Hattie, and some to my good Oakland grocer and most of all to my mother's nurse. I want to begin on Delle Knapp as soon as I can, for she must need it.

If things go well this winter I hope to clear off a good many of the smaller ones and perhaps begin on the larger. Some day——!

Now please dear friend don't read these bragging letters of mine to the W. P. A. or anybody—I wouldn't write so freely for them. I write it all to you because I know it gives you pleasure, even the details about flowers and carriages; but I would not write such a string of self glorification except to you.

Tell about it all you want to—that's all right.

And in especial, where you have a chance, say that I am <u>paying my debts</u>. . . .

Work here has begun very auspiciously. . . .

I feel so grateful to God for my rich life. I've had so much—so very much!

There are people who die and call themselves wealthy, without ever having a hundredth part of what I've had.

I can just feel myself grow. Dear Mrs. Cooper—I remember your kindness so gratefully! You were good to me when I needed it sorely. . . .

Don't worry about my health—I don't mind physical hardships, but I do mind being hated. I'd rather live in these slums in this atmosphere of social friendliness and appreciation than to have all California's glorious climate and Century Club women going to my doctor to say I wasn't fit to be in her house!

My love to Hattie and to other friends.

And very much to you, from yours faithfully.

Charlotte Perkins Stetson.

House of Mrs. Alvin James
4716 Winsor Ave. W. Phila. Penn.
Sat. Feb. 1st. 1896.

My dear Mrs. Cooper:

The [Women's Suffrage] Convention [in Washington, D.C.] is all over . . . and I start back to Little Hell[45] this afternoon. . . .

I started in fine feather, very happy and proud on Wed. Jan. 22nd at 10:30 P.M., with my little new steamer trunk and brown bag. Had a pleasant day's journey and two good meals. Wrote letters and had a good time generally.

Slept almost none however; and was violently sea-sick—<u>carsick</u> in the morning. . . . I reached Hotel Arno at Washington about 2. P.M. . . .

That very afternoon there called to see me Prof. Lester F. Ward.[46] Now here is the difference between east and west. California was afraid of me on account of my "views," took no account of my work, and damned me because of my personal misfortunes. Here I am constantly astonished at the reputation I have made by a few verses; my "views" are considered far-seeing and wise, and the personal history does not count at all apparently.

Prof. Ward is a botanist, geologist, sociologist, of great reputation. His Dynamic Sociology is a text book in Stanford University. His Psychic Factors of Civilization[47] is one of the deepest and newest contributions to sociologic science.

He has admired my work for years, wrote for my book as soon as he knew my address; and when he found that I was coming to Washington—moreover that I was a friend of Helen Campbell's—he wrote most cordially to make me welcome. . . .

Well he called on Thursday; was most warmly kind, came with his wife to hear me preach Sunday morning; called for me, took me home to supper with them Sunday evening, spent the evening talking with me, and "saw me home"; gave a reception in my honor Tuesday evening . . . and called again Wed. P.M. and again that evening at a a [*sic*] friends where I was dining, and came home with me. Has ordered twenty copies of "In This Our World."

And at the reception the friends there assembled knew my work and valued it. This means the beginning of an assured place among the best kind of people as an original thinker—and is a great joy to my heart. . . .

After he had called I went to Miss Anthony's room and Miss Shaw's and was warmly greeted.[48] Miss Anthony set me at her table, by her side, and was uniformly kind and tender to me all through the week. . . .

Everybody spoke of my book, and I sold all that I had with me in no time.

Sunday I preached in the morning at The People's Church, on "The Ethics & Economics of The Women's Movement"; and in the afternoon I . . . preached on . . . "The Spiritual Significance of Democracy and Woman's Relation to it." . . . It was an impressive and successful sermon, and after my evening with the Ward's [*sic*] I went to bed feeling very proud and happy.

Aunt Susan[49] told me I should be all right if I didn't get the "big head"! I told her my experience in California would keep me humble for a long time yet! I'm not at all sorry for those bitter years. They have made a wiser and stronger woman of me.

Well as I was saying I went to bed Sunday night feeling very proud and happy.

Monday morning I woke up <u>with the mumps</u>!!!

Actually, I had them lightly as I always do have things; kept up, and never missed a session where I was needed. . . . [I spoke] before the Judiciary Committee of the House Tues. morning. Miss Anthony presided.

I did well that time—really made an impression on the members—I could see it. And that afternoon I helped Aunt Susan fight the "Woman's Bible" resolution—in vain.[50]

It carried by a small majority, and the dear soul is much grieved over it. . . .

Thursday morning I really felt better; and took the five-five train for Philadelphia with dear Aunt Susan, coming straight to this niece of hers, who is a dear quiet little body and makes us very welcome.

Yesterday I spoke in the afternoon and evening and again made an impression. This afternoon I start back again, by no means well yet, but well content. . . .

And from Kansas to Mass. and Mass. to South Carolina I am now wanted to come and lecture. . . .

People have opened their hearts to me. . . .

As to my coming this year [to San Francisco]—no dear, I do not think it would be wise. . . . I do not wish to appear publicly in San Francisco again till I can stand up free—with my debts paid.

I simply shiver as I think of the pressure of condemnation I lived under while there; and these months of kind appreciation will not make it easy to go back. No. I shall keep. I shall be more worth your while every year—God willing!

Bye and bye I will come to California to live—in my dear Southland, and then I can always be on hand to work with you. . . .

Think of me always as loving you, and remembering you with the tenderest gratitude. . . .

> Most truly yours,
> Charlotte Perkins Stetson.

> The Elm Settlement,
> 80 Elm Street,
> Chicago, Feb. 5th 1896.

Mr. Dear Uncle Edward [Everett Hale],[51]

Some good women with whom I lunched yesterday were speaking of you and what good your work had done.

I was thinking deep inside of the great help you had been to me. And it struck me as a harmless thing to write and tell you so. It is but one among many thousand whom your life has helped, but each one belongs.

Certain specific truths were were [*sic*] given me by you; large lovely truths, light giving always; certain views and habits of life I got from you—good ones all; and the direct influence of the large loving wisdom of your life—the personal touch which is best of all—that alone has made my life richer, sweeter, stronger to help.

If I live to do all that I hope to it will be one more voice to carry on some part of the beautiful work you have done. . . .

Most gratefully and sincerely—
Charlotte Perkins Stetson

361 W. 57th St. New York
April 23rd. 1896—

Dear Walter,[52]

I was very sorry to hear such ill news of the San Francisco show—but to say truth, expected nothing better of that "city of dogs".

They buy good pictures? Never. I'd have written you long since but have been "low" for awhile—had to leave the settlement etc.—all of which I wrote the fair Kate. Now I feel quite like myself again, but it is thin—I have no strength to spare. All summer, I shall trot about and visit, loafing and working by turns; and I have a misty hope that I may get over to London for a little—but that's vague. The Internationalist Socialist Reunion or Convention or whatever is there the last week in July, and I'd like to be in it. Meanwhile, I am here in New York, at my stepmothers.[53] She is a dear little lady and I like her much.

Also she likes me.

With her I inherit stepsisters, not ugly and haughty, but sweet little blond damsels, twins, very like, and looking sixteen though twenty two. Father writes me quite affectionately—is pleased that I like the new mother.

I am making this journey on the strength of an engagement in Boston and return—from Chicago. Then I scratched together some other things to do, and here I am. Monday I attended a grand Woman's Club Lunch—annual affair, at a gorgeous Club House in Brooklyn. Was a guest of honor as it were, and made a little speech with great applause—also poems.

The next day I attended a woman suffrage meeting over there, and spoke further. Tonight I lecture, for half the profits, under W. S. auspices. I could have wished it other, but this opening was here and I took it.

Also from it came another—Mrs. Catt,[54] a very prominent suffragist, had an engagement in Providence for the 22nd and didn't want to go. Would I go in her stead? Yes, truly.

So I went on Tuesday night, and came back last night. Eight years in October next since I was there!

How little and pretty it is! So hard-and-fast, so clean, so dead and buried.

And yet the houses spring up to the eastward, and the cove is filled at last! I . . . ran about town profusely, addressed the Committee on Special Legislation in the Senate Chamber, had four meals and a nap, attended a reception and banquet in the evening and speechified thereat.

And I went about all day on a broad grin. It did seem so like getting into my child's doll house again! Sidney Burleigh[55] and his mother were at the W. S. Banquet. He seemed very glad to see me. But how insignificant he is getting to look! . . .

I've got a lot of nice visits in hand—enough to last months. And everybody seemed glad to see me. How pleasant it is. I had no idea they'd be so glad.

I hope to build up solid this summer and write a lot. Already I'm lots better.

As ever

Charlotte.

20 West 32nd st.
New York City.
Jan. 11th. '97

[To Cousin Marian Whitney]

You are forgiven [for not writing sooner], O erring one, the more joyfully in that I remember mountainous sins of that nature on my own record, and hope by magnanimity to wipe out some of them!

And what do I find to do? Well, well! Don't you know that I am that perpetual motion engine a Reformer. When one undertakes to repair the world, there is never any lack of employment. Also I have a large job on hand in mending myself—being so seriously damaged in past years.

I had another bad time while in England—was shockingly low for awhile—Reason "drunk and incapable" on her throne; or perhaps mostly trailing off it. Now however I am feeling very well—have been since I landed, and blandly forget all previous incapacity. . . .

Also I write, a little.

Also I "speak," "read," etc. when occasion offers; winning golden opinions thereby.

Just at present I am on my way West for a Lecture Trip.—It's principal object is the Annual W. S. Convention at Des Moines Iowa. Incidental to this are many lectures on the way, to pay for going.

And the ultimate purpose is to lay out lines of popularity and general acquaintance with a view to future lecture trips of deeper import. I expect to traverse all America as the years pass, poking it up in all its peaceful corners. How heartily I shall be disliked—and also adored. . . .

I looked in the directory for Houghton—and found him not, alas!

O, you ask also how do I amuse myself. Bless you! "I don't have to" as we say out West. The whole world conspires to amuse me.

I find life increasingly delicious and entertaining. And as to the wolf—I <u>let him in</u> long ago! He don't bite! More prosaically, I pick up what I can lecturing, writing, and from the sale of my books. That's all. But if I wax in public esteem I think another year and a half will see the California debts lifted and then enough to have Katharine with me for a while. I get along somehow. It doesn't matter.

As to seeing me—I hope by next May to be able to "visit" some more. . . . But come now, or rather "go to!" is there not some woman's club in New Haven that I could entertain, instruct, and horrify some time? If so here I am. . . .

Your errant cousin—

Charlotte Perkins Stetson.

Harrisburg Pa—

April 23rd. 1897.

Dear Walter,

. . . Thank you very much for the proofs. I looked at them before I read the letter, and did not recognize Katharine at all! Not till I saw the large side view—sitting, did I suspect. What a beautiful damsel she makes in the one with her hand to her chin! . . . I should like some of them very much. . . . You needn't even ask me—any picture of her that is good enough to print will always be warmly welcomed by me. . . . And Grace looks as well and strong! I shall have one some day too. But as to being strong—I'm getting almost as well as I used to be. Walked six miles Sunday and rowed half an hour beside. Can carry a 150 lb. man. Can put up a twenty pound dumbbell with either hand, even lying flat on my back & doing it with the arm laid straight overhead. I begin to think that I have almost got back to twenty three—fourteen years! And if strength holds it now remains to be seen what I can do. . . .

I am unceasingly grateful to Grace for being what she is—have been ever since I knew her.

Surely I have often said before that there is no person on earth I would rather have my child with. . . .

And your father is 78! Mine is but 68, and quite broken now. I bade him goodbye last Saturday—for the summer. I've seen a good deal of him this winter—more than I ever did before. He speaks very tenderly of Katharine. . . .

Serenely—<br>Charlotte.

743 Orchard st. Chicago<br>May 24th 1897.

Dear Aunt Emily [Hale],

. . . It seems good to hear from you—brings back the happy times I had in your house in my not too happy girlhood. And then I've always felt a keen sympathy with you during the years when I no longer saw you, and the years when my head was no good at all. Yes, it is getting better now, markedly so. I shall be thirtyseven this July, and am just beginning to get back to something of the brainpower I had at twenty three.

Please God I shall do good work yet, and make up in general service for my lamentable failure in the personal kind!

Being tolerably well, growing steadily in my work, and perfectly at ease about my child, I make no complaint; though life is rather baldheaded from a purely personal standpoint!

I miss Katharine more every year, and it will be some time yet before

I feel that it will be for her advantage to share my lot again; but she is very happy, very well, and growing in all good ways under the wise and loving care of her other mother—so I am content.

If I were a queen—and could secure the best educators on earth for my child—I would ask no better than that noble woman—always my dear friend. And then I did not wish my child to grow up fatherless.

My summer arranges very pleasantly in lecturing and visiting. Kansas—Wisconsin—Michigan—New York state—Maine—New Hampshire—back to New York in Sept. or Oct. Two weeks at Summerbrook and one or two at Greenacre-on-the-Piscataqua are the best part of it all.[56]

I am writing very freely now—good work too—poems, essays, stories—and hope the ensuing year will find me well on my feet in literature.

With love to Uncle Edward and Nellie—[57]

Your affectionate niece
Charlotte Perkins Stetson.

11-11-'05
Charlotte Perkins Gilman
179 West 76th Street, New York

Dear Cousin Alice,[58]

Your coals of fire are heaped upon my head, wherefore my too-long smouldering ire should rightfully be dead.

The moral measure of an act is surely the intent, and whatsoe'er the harm in fact I'm sure that not was meant.

We differed in our social code, as many people do; and Luncheon Laws are not the load to me they were to you. Were I the hostess in such case I'm sure that I would say "Better a crowded extra place—or service on a tray—better another table small—better a cousin in the hall—than a cousin turned away!["]

But all conventions have their weight—by different lives' position; and I'm a little lame and late in making this admission.

Your flowers in colors warm and sweet are round my rooms disposed; and we'll consider when we meet the incident as closed.

Yours amiably—
Charlotte Perkins Gilman.

Bellport L.I.
New York.
5-21-'09

Dear Cousin Katharine—[59]

Please excuse . . . me—it's very kind and nice of you to ask me but I cannot by the wildest stretch of the imagination see myself "pouring" at a tea.

I feel as I did when I was first asked to be a "Patroness" at a ball.

"Me that 'ave been where I've been!

Me!"[60] . . .

Your disagreeable cousin
Charlotte Perkins Gilman

313 W. 82. New York.
June 13th. 1909.

Dear Aunt Emily [Hale]—

In the beautiful June weather, on the eve of our 9th wedding anniversary, we got the news of our great loss.[61]

It brought to both of us a warm remembrance of your kindness to us then; you were the first of the family to receive us—and you were so good!

Uncle Edward was more my uncle than Uncle Charles somehow—kinder to me—more loving and helpful. One of the steady griefs of life is the inability to see as much as we want to of the people we love. Perhaps bearing that makes us better able to bear the last loss of all.

I have so often wished that I were near enough to you to come in and sit—and bring my sewing; be a sort of extra partial daughter—though dear Nellie doesn't require any substitutes! Now I wish it more than ever. You—and Aunt Katie too—have been so good to me! And in all my youth, Uncle Edward was to me—as to so many thousands of people—a strength and comfort.

A life like that is never ended; and to have lived with it, to have helped it—your joy has been so great that it will help to carry sorrow. . . .

Your loving niece—
Charlotte Perkins Gilman

224 Riverside Drive
New York City
7-23-'11

Dear Nellie [Hale],

. . . Have you seen the notice of Mr. Stetson's death?[62] On the 20th—in Rome.

He has been a pretty sick man for some years back.

Katharine was there, for which she will always be thankful.

Poor Grace! She loved him all absorbingly! . . .

I'm coming back and forth through Boston presently and will try to see you and dear Aunt Emily.

Your affectionate cousin
Charlotte.

Figure 3. Charlotte with Grace Ellery
Channing Stetson, ca. 1910. Courtesy of
Denise D. Knight.

# 3
# Letters to Grace
## "how deeply and reverently grateful I am"

In her late teens, Gilman became friendly with the Channing family of
Providence, Rhode Island, descendants of William Ellery Channing, one
of the founders of the Unitarian Church in the United States. The Channings, particularly daughter Grace, would prove vital friends and supporters throughout Gilman's life. "Here I found broad free-thinking, scientific
talk, earnest promotion of great causes—life," Gilman would later report
of their household. "There were two beautiful daughters, lifelong friends,
one closer than a sister to this day" (*Living* 49). In many ways, it was the
Channings, and more so Grace herself, who enabled Gilman to depart so
successfully from her expected social role. "Dear—do you not know how

deeply and reverently grateful I am for all you have done for my child and for me?" wrote Gilman to Grace on October 13, 1898. Gilman's initial flight from marriage and motherhood during her first major breakdown, her rejection of the rest cure's domestic ideology, her budding literary career and intellectual life, her eventual divorce and delegation of maternal responsibilities—all of these were facilitated in some way by Grace specifically or her family more generally. Gilman's life and Grace's were irrevocably intertwined, and though they experienced tensions and rivalries, their friendship, like their correspondence, was lifelong.

Gilman's early letters to Grace reveal her ambition and naïveté and are prophetic of the first major life crisis in which Gilman would call upon the Channings. Of her approaching marriage to Charles Walter Stetson, she wrote: "If health should fail then trouble would come of course, but I see no reason to fear it." She confessed that she did fear "some sorrow . . . lest my other occupations rob my love of time and interest he may feel should be his and ours" (February 28, 1884). When all of these things did come to pass, with Gilman suffering a nervous breakdown after her marriage and the birth of her daughter, she "did not simply seek out but fled in desperation to the Channing family," who had moved to Pasadena, California (A. J. Lane 138). While at the Channings', Gilman escaped pressing domestic demands and immersed herself in what she saw as the healing landscape of the West. No less significantly, she and Grace wrote their first play together and enjoyed a variety of creative and intellectual pursuits. All of this led to a temporary recovery from her ills. It is not surprising, then, that after her unsuccessful rest cure and her decision to separate from Walter, Gilman would enjoy similar healing experiences with Grace, first in Bristol, Rhode Island, in the summer of 1888, where they avidly continued their playwriting, and then in Pasadena, where Gilman and Katharine moved in the fall of that year, living in a cottage the Channings found for them.

The intellectual stimulation and creative camaraderie Grace offered were clearly a balm to Gilman, providing her with an alternative to the dreary fate she had contemplated before her marital separation as well as to Weir Mitchell's prescription that she devote herself exclusively to marriage and motherhood. She confessed to Grace that "What pleases me most is when I leave Walter entirely out of my calculations, and make no attempt to fulfill my wifely duties toward him." In short, she had "decided to cast off Dr. Mitchell bodily, and do exactly what I pleased" (November 21, 1887). In this letter she lays out her plans for herself and Grace, with an enthusiasm that is only partly exaggerated: "We will be the leading dramatists of the age! We will create a new school! . . . Our names shall be long in the land. Dr. Mitchell be ——————!" Although their playwriting did not garner critical acclaim, the collaboration with Grace provided Gilman with the kind of creative and intellectual outlet that Mitchell's prescription denied. Gilman would later credit Grace with "sav[ing] what there is of me. . . . [She] pulled me out of living death, set me on my staggering feet, helped me to get work again, did more than I can say to make me live, and I love her, I think, as well as any one on earth" (Gilman to Martha Luther Lane, January 20, 1890).

A few months after Gilman and Katharine moved to Pasadena, Walter came to live with them, hoping for reconciliation. He settled in with his family, using a room at the Channing home as his studio, while Gilman and Grace continued their playwriting and acting with great enthusiasm. An unexpected benefit of this arrangement was the blossoming relationship between Walter and Grace, which gradually improved the tense emotional atmosphere by diverting Walter's attentions from Gilman, who found them increasingly unwelcome. In March 1889, Gilman indicated to Martha that Grace and Walter "are great friends, which gives me sincere delight" (March 16, 1889). By the beginning of 1890, when Walter returned to the East, the budding romance was confirmed: Grace and Walter would eventually marry, after Gilman and Walter's divorce was finally granted, in 1894. While Gilman was intensely relieved to have escaped her own unsatisfying marriage, she came to realize that this new relationship had stolen from her not Walter but Grace.

In her autobiography, Gilman claims that she greeted Walter's second marriage with "gladness" and "relief" (*Living* 167). However, in a letter to Grace she laments that "that dreadful angel has come and swallowed you and I am nowhere! It is awful to be a man inside and not able to marry the women you love! When Martha married it cracked my heart a good deal—your loss will finish it. . . . I think of you with a great howlin' selfish heartache—I want you—I love you—I need you myself!" (December 3, 1890). Similarly, her diary confirms that the year 1890, while professionally productive, was "cruelly hard since Grace went" (*Diaries* 428). It appears, then, that Grace was one of several women whom Gilman would love intensely throughout the course of her life—whom she would love as if she were "a man inside." In this case, it also appears that such feelings of romantic attachment were not reciprocated by Grace. In a letter to Grace, Gilman would later refer to this incident as her "trespass" (January 22, 1893).

Between 1890 and 1894, Gilman nursed her wounds, slogged through divorce proceedings (all the while pretending publicly that she and Walter were still happily married), and threw herself into her career, writing to Grace of her growing fame, her lectures, invitations, publications, and earnings. She also struggled to care for Katharine as a single parent, finally resolving to send her daughter to live with Walter and Grace. Thus did Katharine become their "three[-]ply daughter" (Gilman to Grace, July 4, 1895). Less overtly ambitious than Gilman, Grace would continue to write throughout her life, but with Walter's meager support and her own less lofty ambitions, she was better prepared (and more willing) than Gilman to devote herself to "maintaining a home and caring for a child" (A. J. Lane 316). All of this freed Gilman to pursue her work with full force.

This arrangement was, however, not without its costs. "People blame me violently for sending Kate away," she confessed to Grace (January 9, 1895). Even more poignant than the considerable public scandal, however, was Gilman's "enormous longing to see my baby" (Gilman to Grace, June 26, 1895), a longing she continually repressed. She described the pain to Grace: "I opened the door a little and looked in. [Might] As well pluck at an amputation! It began to bleed and ache and I hasted to shut it again" (May 3, 1896). As Ann J. Lane has pointed out, Gilman's references in her letters to "missing Katharine are often followed by words describing her own triumph, as if the separation was somehow justified thereby" (309). While Gilman claimed both publicly and privately that the separation was indeed so justified, and while she knew Katharine loved Grace "as another mother" (*Living* 162), Gilman's letters to Grace from this period reveal the tensions, misunderstandings, and hurts that roiled behind the mask of familial harmony and career success.

In contrast, Gilman's later correspondence with Grace is much less fraught with emotion. Having evolved from co-mothers to co-grandmothers, Gilman and Grace could put the difficulties of the 1890s behind them, and the tone of Gilman's letters illustrates the depth of their relationship. Gilman still worried over Grace and often sent her money if she could, with Grace doing likewise on occasion—particularly in the lean years of the Depression. But much of their late correspondence gives voice to Gilman's assessment of her life and career, her concern for her legacy, and her desire to have Grace with her as she ended her life. Referring to old friend Augusta Senter, Gilman urged Grace to move to the West, which she would do in June 1935: "I'd like K. [Katharine] to have her <u>three</u> mothers together before we all die on her!" she writes (April 17, 1935). "It's been an honor to be your friend, dear Grace," she proclaimed just five months before her death. "And I have loved you a long time!" (March 3, 1935).

P.M. 7.30 about. Thursday.
Feb. 28th. 1884—
Providence

Dear Grace;[1]

I was very glad to get your letter. It is always a pleasure to me to find myself in some degree liked and respected by those whom I like and respect.

As I do you.

Walter likes you too, which is agreeable, and you like Walter which is balm to my soul. . . .

Why were you surprised at the news of my marriage? I told you I meant to marry as soon as possible. . . . I'm sure I thought you knew.

Yes, I'm really going to do it, on Friday the second of May I believe. Month and day unlucky you see, which horrifies many.[2]

As to being <u>very</u> happy, as you hope, that is not my constant expectation. There will be happy times I am sure, unhappy ones too, unless marriage alters my character much. . . .

My "plans" are simple. To take a few rooms—we have a lovely little tenement in mind now, as yet undecided—to live as cheaply as possible; to work. . . .

If health should fail then trouble would come of course; but I see no reason to fear it.

The whole thing seems to me far different from what it is to most women.

Instead of being a goal—a duty—a hope, a long expected fate, a bewildering delight; it is a concession, a digression, a thing good and necessary perhaps as matters stand, but still a means, not an end.

I look through it, beyond it, over it. It is a happiness no doubt, a duty no doubt; but a happiness to result in new strength for other things; a duty only one of others.

It fills my mind much; but plans for teaching and writing, for studying <u>living</u> and helping, are more prominent and active.

And that is where I fear some sorrow; lest my other occupations rob my love of time and interest he may feel should be his and ours.

Well, he knows what to expect; and I must try not to neglect home duties for the wider ones. . . .

I am glad you feel as I do about the Y. W. C. T. U. [Young Woman's Christian Temperance Union].[3] If we could <u>obliterate</u> Alcohol once and for all, I think the good would be far greater than the harm. But we cannot, it is here, man is man, and we have no right to say "<u>you shall not do wrong</u>!" I guess we agree. With each other and with Mill, whose "Liberty" I have just been reading at your suggestion.[4] How cool and clear and reasonable he is! . . .

What do I read? All manner of books concerning the Greeks, their history, manners, everything about them. To a student of Life, as I mean to be, so typical a people are worth much study. Just at present I'm in Symond's [*sic*] "Essays on the Greek Poets." [*sic*] . . .

If you haven't read it, and if you care at all for that sort of information, do add this to your store of knowledge. It is a wonderfully good book.

Did you see the "pome" [*sic*] in the Alpha?[5] Don't it look fine! . . .

Charlotte A. Perkins.

26 Humboldt Ave.
Providence, R. I.
Mon. Nov. 21st. 1887.

Dear Grace;

. . . O I <u>am</u> so much better! First there was the great lift of my Western plan. Then I decided to cast off Dr. Mitchell bodily, and do exactly what I pleased. . . .

What underlies the change is this decision: I have giving [*sic*] up trying to assimilate with Walter; have accepted my life as I did that with mother, as a thing to be endured and resisted, not a thing I must agree with; have determined to be myself as far as I can in spite of circumstances.

It is astonishing how my whole nature responds. The other life is impossible, that's all. What pleases me most is that when I leave Walter entirely out of my calculations, and make no attempt to fulfill my wifely duties toward him; why straitway his various excellencies become visible again and he becomes a loved companion instead of a nightmare husband.

And under that arrangement a certain approximation to Alpha doctrines[6] becomes possible, as my health improves and conscience does not gnaw increasingly.

I feel really hopeful. . . .

By next summer I shall be ready to aid you in taking the world by storm. Hm! We will be the leading dramatists of the age! We will create a new school! We will combine the most literal realism with the highest art, and cover both with the loftiest morality!!! . . .

O what life it will give me if I become able to have a home in California and help my friends! I mean to make money when I get there! My dear girl a good play is a paying thing. If we can write one we can write two. If we can write one in one year we can write another in another year. Yea verily. Our names shall be long in the land. Dr. Mitchell be ——————!

Yours hopefully,
Charlotte Perkins Stetson

Stone Lea[7] [Narragansett, R.I.]
Tues. Oct. 2nd. 1888.

Dear Grace,

Your note asking about the house received last night.[8] You do well to remind me of the trifling matter. I know no more of it than you do. I wrote your father definitely to hire a house within certain restrictions, and if he could not do that to have the tent ready. But I have nothing from him. Your mother wrote me at length about the four-room cottage, and I haven't even answered it. I thought the definite letter to your father would do, and afterward, I forgot it. Dear me! If I can only get started without losing my head! Am not feeling very well today.

Read Gillette's novel "A Legal Wreck"[9] and see what you think of it.

Yours with love,
Charlotte Perkins Stetson.

9.10. Wed. Dec. 3rd. 1890
Pasadena Cal.

Dear Grace,

... O it seems an <u>age</u> since I have heard from you—really heard from you!

You say in this of Nov. 3rd, at sea, that I am haunting your dreams, etc. and you feel as if I was in trouble.

Perhaps this pre[s]cience may mean my local ailments. . . .

Well it appears that I have but two good reasons for my woes and weaknesses.

There is retroversion <u>and</u> retroflexing of the uterus, with chronic congestion and catarrh.

She said it had been so for a long time, that the uterus in fact had never been small enough since Kate's birth—had not fully shrunk.

My explanation is, that in those years of prostrate weeping—supine mostly, the congestion was quiet but steady; and that my start out here with the worry and housework while it did me good mentally, pulled on those heavy things and upset 'em. Don't you think that's reasonable?

Dr. Follansbec is "treating" me. I swim in hot water, and entertain myself the whilst with pills of a tonic nature and a sleeping arrangement to make my rest more restful—more actual and effective. On which treatment I wax daily. . . .

Do you know I think I suffer more in giving you up than in Walter—for you were all joy to me. And it was not till things were well underway that that side of the arrangement dawned upon me.

I know I was gradually getting very near to you, and now that dreadful angel has come and swallowed you and I am nowhere!

It is awful to be a man inside and not able to marry the women you love! When Martha married it cracked my heart a good deal—your loss will finish it.

Never mind, I will divide the pieces among people in general and continue to "contemplate my virtues." I think of Walter with some pain, more pleasure, and a glorious sense of <u>rightness</u>—escape—triumph.

I think of you with a great howlin' selfish heartache—<u>I</u> want you—<u>I</u> love you—<u>I</u> need you <u>myself</u>! . . .

So your clairvoyance has seen through my mask of joy has it? I don't care a bit, because I can gladly assert that Walter <u>hasn't</u>! . . .

I haven't said a word to him about the new internal discoveries—I fear it would worry him seriously, and there is no need.

It is only a temporary matter.

But I am thinking now that if I get no better footing pecuniarily, and do not get over these things rapidly enough, that after the divorce is granted I will go to Dr. Gleasons Sanitarium for repairs, and lie over till I am sound and strong again.

In which case I should ask Walter to take Kate abroad with him, and it would have no worse affect than to hasten your marriage a little perhaps!

But if I am well and flourishing I will keep her a while yet that your honeymoon be undisturbed. . . .

Walter writes almost daily, bravely, affectionately, lonesomely.

You two are rapidly <u>deserving</u> each other I think!

But I miss you most.

With great love, and no intention of failure!

> 9.10 P.M. Mon. Feb. 16th. 1891.
> Pasadena Cal.

Dear Grace,

Your sister has come and gone, and is, they say, doing finely. . . . It seemed very strange to have her in the house—I never feel <u>near</u> to Mary at all, never feel that I know her.[10] . . .

Dorothy is lovely.[11] . . . It would rejoice your heart to see how Katharine treats her. She has lent her both her music-box and harmonica to take to the other house, only solemnly commissioning the nurse "not to let her drop it on the floor!" She has gracefully yielded up to her, high chair, table tray, and silver cup; she plays with her tenderly and softly—I am proud of her really. She is worthy of her father, and it makes my heart glad to think how much they will one day be to each other. He seems to love her constantly more and more, and writes her the sweetest letters!

She says I am the best mama in the world. I tell her perhaps—next to Grace—that Grace is never cross. She says well—next to Grace—she loves me next best. That is well. However I entertain a treacherous hope that someday you may be cross or something, and then she will love me the best! Do be a little wicked dear, can't you?

My lectures thrive apace.

This Sunday it was rainy and yet I had a good audience—a real good audience, and mostly women. . . . Tuesday evening I speak briefly at an entertainment in honor of Susan B. Anthony's birthday, in town; and Wednesday afternoon my third address to the Woman's Club—on "Who Owns The Children." . . .

And what do you think! Mrs. Parkhurst—Emilie Tracy[12] . . . —has invited me to come to San Francisco to the convention of the Woman's Press Association—three days—she to furnish transportation and entertain me—and Kate!!! Is this friendship? Or is it Fame? The latter I expect. Anyhow I mean to go, it will do me lots of good. And I mean to arrange to do some speaking while there, just as I spoke of last summer you know. Here I have a dozen lectures all written—why not deliver them here and there and make a little pile thereby? I'll do it if I can, and thereby bring home a little money.

I guess I haven't written you since Life [magazine] took my butterfly, have I—"A Conservative" you know.[13] They "pay on acceptance," as does the Century, a good habit and worthy of encouragement. Scribner does too—pity the little ones can't follow suit!

Do you chance to have seen the February Nationalist? I guess not. They have an [*sic*] eulogistic notice of "The Author of Similar Cases," and also have my name down among the distinguished contributors, with Bellamy, E.E. Hale, etc. That is the first time I have been so mentioned, and it pleases me. Things seem to be coming on, don't they? . . .

I earned nearly $40.00 in January, and this month about $60.00—think of that! . . . It all goes into bills of course, but the bills are lightening fast. The grocer is paid—clean paid, and the rent is up to three months now. Long before this year is out I may pay you—and even your father!

But I must not brag—I am not far enough out of the woods to whistle. . . .

You should have seen that sister of yours keep me up o' nights and ask questions! Not about you or Walter—O no, but about me, and just what caused my trouble. . . . I told her the "plain facts only"—that I wasn't fit for matrimony and had to give it up. . . . But you should have seen the artless way in which I praised Walter, and indicated that his virtues were such as deserved a better fate! She seems to think I don't know anything about it; or else she don't, or else she is most duplicitous. Well, so are we all. . . .

I know this is a shallow letter. . . . I hope it will be better after this long strain is over. . . .

I really love you. . . .

Charlotte.

A little after 9. P.M. Sun. Jan. 22nd. 1893
1258 Webster St. Oakland Cal.

Dear Grace, Dear Sister—Noble woman whom I revere!—I have just read your new year's letter. Apropos of which I too will make a confession, namely that I have let it wait some thirty six hours in pure fear. Lest you might therein express as Walter did a feeling that what the papers said I said would ruin the case. His letter was heavy to bear and I dreaded yours still more; for I had enough real sense of remorse to make it hurt. I ought not to have seen the reporter, but I know how they talk when denied and had a dire sense of standing in front and covering the thing a little longer.[14] My head is very shaky now. I was afraid it was going to hurt, and it did seem to me I could not carry any more. It came yesterday morning, and I hid it in my bosom till I had the housework done—for I could not afford to take any strength from that. Then I wrote—and wanted all the poor wits I had. Then I could ill afford to spoil my dinner; I put it in my little drawer. "I'll wait till just before I go to bed," said I; "I'll take an assocfetida [*sic*] pill—(mild nerve quieters) and then read it. I'll be so tired I shall sleep, and the next morning it will be only one more Past."

Then, as there were folks here, and it was very late, and my head is very weak—I forgot it. But tonight I collected my recreant forces and read it, only to find more comfort than I have had from another hand this many a day. . . .

We all undertook to do and bear, at any cost, what we thought right—and more than that no mortal soul can do. We know more now. Dense souls must they be who could not learn in such three years as these. I should hardly have thought it that long—so whirling full have been these years of mine. And you are thirty! I am soon thirty-three. Walter soon thirty-five. . . .

Did I write you of my socialists in "the late unpleasantness["]? . . . I had engaded [*sic*] to speak for them in S. F. on "Socialism as it Concerns The Social Evil," and the first blast of the astonished press came out the day before.

On the day of the address the Examiner reeked of me; and I must say it daunted me for a second or two—to face a San Francisco audience on such a subject, at such a time.

They sent over their chairman that evening—a thing never done before—to delicately inquire if anything would prevent my speaking—? No, I told him, I always kept engagements unless absolutely prevented.

And when I stood before them you should have heard them clap! . . .

For inside life, as I said, I am bigger, wiser, stronger. So it is no bad record after all. For health—it is pretty bad. A sort of eczema between the shoulders, and weird movable little lumps under the skin of neck— what is it? I ask the doctor, and she says calmly "scrofula."[15] The same blood as mother's it appears, and the nursing and confinement in her room brought it out. . . .

Mother sinks wavering downward, like a tin plate in dark water; sinks, and yet fights every step of the way.[16]

She has no opiate-demanding pain, but suffers much. . . .

Her being here has served me well—made me seem a live human creature to the others, and so made my words better weighed.

I have three boarders yet, Delle, Mrs. Howe, Miss Sherman.[17] . . .

I am at present doing the cooking, some dishwashing, and hiring a woman once a week. . . .

A little longer—there is an end—I shall someday have room and time and strength—this cannot last. When you and Walter are so that you can take Kate—when I can at least stagger out into the open and stretch glad hands abroad and not strike any wall—well then in a year or two I shall be so glad to have the little girl who loves me again! She does love me, dearly.

For "pain and soreness" dear, the only hurts you ever gave me (that I recall), were reactionary—the inevitable result of my trespass.

You never offended in the initiative—how could you!

I think you may feel surely glad about me in all that speaks of our soul love and work. . . .

In love and honor[—]yours—
Charlotte Perkins Stetson.

[San Francisco]
Wed. Jan. 9th. 1895.

Dearest Grace,

I rejoice in a tiny moment when heart and pen can combine to tell you again how much you are to [me] and have always been—Wisdom—Purity—Truth.

Also how utterly glad I am to have my darling with you and your dear people. It is also a tender comfort to me to have her a joy to her father, having had always the wish to give him joy though not the power.

That the fair child thrives and is a pleasure and a pride to you, is pleasure and pride to me. Some day I shall be with her again—God knows when. . . .

I work more regularly now than I ever did, and very enjoyably. The story work in especial is doing me much good. But I work too hard, and am too much worried and driven to make any gain except in the training itself.

Mrs. Campbell is a world of comfort to me, and Mr. Tyner[18] proves companionable and pleasant!

But things in general go hard. . . .

People blame me violently for sending Kate away. Of course. . . .

Most lovingly—

Charlotte Perkins Stetson

San Francisco, June 15th 1895

My dearest Grace—

Another dear letter from you today. . . .

You dear great woman! I know you think I don't know and don't care. Some day we shall be largely together again, and you will like me better than you ever did Before. I grow and grow and grow, and Oh!—Life is so good, so great, so real and sweet and joyous! I am happier now, freer, stronger, braver, wiser, <u>gladder</u> than in twelve long years.

Open sea is before me—the great wide see [*sic*], storms and calms and dangers of the deep no doubt, but no more danger of the shallows.

Tomorrow I go to Los Gatos. . . . Then . . . a Southern lecture trip, which if it matures will bring me to Los Angeles and perhaps Pasadena.

Now if so I want to see you and Kate, and I don't want to see Walter. If he particularly wished it I wouldn't mind, but I have no desire to see him. I would rather have what I remember than any new strained touch.

Things being so perhaps I had better not come to Pasadena after all. You know how crassly stupid I am about those things, yet "well-intentioned"—which is but mild reproach.

But I will let you know when I'm to be in L. A., and you will come in with Kate, won't you? ...

Lovingly—<br>Charlotte

They say Olive Schreiner[19] has had a baby—and it died!

Noon Wed. June 26th [1895]<br>on train near—Castroville?—

Dear Grace,

I am to speak in Santa Maria tomorrow night and shall come to Los Angeles thereafter—being half way and having just money enough and feeling an enormous longing to see my baby—a longing which I haven't looked at or measured but which brings the tears to my eyes even while I distantly speak of it. . . . I shall come unless definite engagement prevents.

I continue to be well, real well, and happy—real happy. . . .

A letter from Mrs. Campbell today makes me very happy—She has been talking to Jane Addams, and she said I was "her one bright spot in San Francisco and she loved me." Invited me to spend three months at Hull House. . . .

Hoping soon to see you dear girl, and my own dear girl—lovingly—

Charlotte.

[San Francisco]<br>July 4th 1895

My dearest Grace—

I'm very glad I stayed; and only hope that none of you are sorry. I'm glad all ways, more especially because it makes a plain sweet reality of a sort of cloud, ghost of possible hurt—makes all pleasant daylight instead of mist. Yes, he [Walter] is changed, but not as I thought. I am very glad to see him instead of the photograph.

It makes me feel a sort of big hovering motherly lovingness—a wish to be good to him somehow—that sort of large world-embracing affection which I always had and which he never yet understood or wanted. I fear I shall never escape his personal remembrance, and that means separation.

Well—we're different.

But the main impression I get of you all three is solid comfortable growth and gain; and I feel easy in my mind concerning you. My little darling—our three[-]ply daughter! is all the motherliest mother could desire; and though I confess to a very hollow feeling when I went off in the car and left all my people behind—yet I soon drowned it in proof reading, and forgot it in the cordial greeting of a whilom disciple who was rejoiced to see me again. . . .

So, dearest, I'm glad to have seen you—have seen you all . . . and glad especially for the glimpse of Walter—inasmuch as the quiet present quite obliterates the waner past and makes it recede still further into the fading distance.

Very lovingly your<br>
Charlotte

Hull House Chicago Ills.<br>
Sept. 16th. 1895—

My dear Grace,

. . . I send with this a Hull House circular of classes and clubs—last winters, for the new one is not out yet; and a little booklet giving a brief account of the place and its purposes. . . .

Now for my view.

Jane Addams[20] might be President of the United States, to the great advantage of the country. She is a woman of tremendous will, sad eyes, sweet delicate mouth, and a manner so still as to seem negative—which it isn't. She "steadies on even keel" through all the stress of this mixed living; saying the most society-splitting things with that gentle unmoved voice and placid manner that defies amazement. The neighbors and the residents love and follow her, and friends of wealth and station put money and power into her hands unquestioningly. She is a quiet queen in Chicago. Miss Starr,[21] her companion from the first, is a small frail creature in "artistic" dresses, having large slant-wise ears, good teeth in frequent view, and carefully arranged loose hair which she lifts gingerly to wipe her brow—in this hot weather. . . . Nearly all [residents] . . . come here because there [*sic*] own lives are broken and gone or of a lagging unfulfillment. . . .

Miss Addams thought, as I get it, is largely this: That "the social spirit" should rise among the people themselves. They have no mechanical conveniences for social life—not even for its physical accommodation. Hull House offers a local vehicle for the natural development of the <u>social</u> spirit. . . .

You ask "What Hull House is standing for and how effectively." It stands first for common humanity and <u>social</u> democracy. Second for such help as may be possible from the stronger neighbor to the weaker. Third for scientific study of such sociological problems as present themselves. And it is effective in all three ways. It is healthy. It grows. It has set the neighborhood to sprouting with clubs and classes. . . .

To me as a resident the place and work are good. It is meat and drink to me to be among people who <u>care</u>; who are in any way living for humanity. It is the kind of home I am most at home in, and I slip into usefulness very easily.

The sociological library I am browsing in, the great folks who come and go I delight to meet, and it is for my souls good to be for the first time in my life a small fish in a large pond—well stocked with bigger ones! . . .

I shall creep into pulpit and platform very reasonably soon I think, and so far have made a good impression. For writing—I did three good poems—yes and more, on the cars coming out; and have made a lot of "Labor songs" and the like of that, here. More will come. . . .

My "plans" are made for five years. Here till next summer, then east and visit round awhile among old friends. Then settle in New York or Boston for the winter—(with Mrs. Campbell all this) and root a little (not pig-wise but plant-wise!) in the literary world. (Come to think of it both senses will serve!) Then to London and stay a year drinking deep, and rooting (2nd sense) in the world life. Then to Paris, and get back my pencil power. So home and build me a home in Pasadena. Then—life all over—lecture and write and teach and preach; mostly at large. . . .

Did you see—(no its not in print I guess) what Lester Ward has done with "Similar Cases?" He used it in a lecture, adding a fourth part of his own, as a weapon against Kidd's Social Evolution, and The New York Nation.[22] These things delight my very soul, because I disagree with Kidd and loathe The Nation. I am so delighted over it. As though the stone in David's sling had had a secret grudge against the giant and chuckled as it flew! . . .

I[t] gladdens my heart to have the steady good news of Katharine. I find I grow more sensitive about her, rather than less. Sometimes it aches. But I try to hold the right attidude [*sic*] unflinchingly. Sometime she will be with me again.

Tell her I got her little letter today, of the 8th, and will answer soon. . . .

Has she had Water Babies yet? And Phantastes?[23] O dear—I want to do it too!

Never mind. I had fine lovely years when I could read to her, and I did. . . .

Did I ever tell you of the one time when she began to fret and grieve over the pending divorce? Some neighbor had no doubt been enlightening and alarming her. She said "Then I won't have any father!" I told her how that would be, but she still objected. "And he may marry again and then I'll have a stepmother!" she said, and began to cry. Then I thought it right to tell her what was coming. "Dear" said I—"If papa does marry again it will be only to marry our dear Grace," and, dear sister—it would have been a great joy to you I know to have seen the tears change to smiles, and the little face light up with perfect contentment. She seemed to feel exactly as I would have her, that she lost no one and gained you. Some day she will count it as one of her chiefest blessings. And as I count my dreadful years well spent for her sake, looking for great things from that strangely blended life, so I think one day you will be glad to have had so large a hand in the training.

I think the world has had few lives so rich as hers will be. She seems to have inherited the best "points" in her ancestors; and her babyhood and childhood have been rarely free and healthful. Some things are already flourishing in her which do not show a meager sprout till much later in most of us. . . .

Always yours with love and gratitude—

Charlotte—

80 Elm st. Chicago Ill.
Feb. 25th. 1896.

Dear Grace,

. . . My sweetest letter lately is that one from Kate, with a green sunny[?] bill at the bottom and "I love you for tow [*sic*] raisins"—<u>with the raisins enclosed!</u>—

Yes I went to Washington as you hoped. . . . But between the duties I was there for, and the mumps[,] I saw little of the real city and all it means.

My best pleasure there was the cordial reception I had from Prof. Lester F. Ward. . . . [A]ppreciative recognition from men like that is a surprise and a delight. . . . I was glad also of the historic opportunity of being with "Aunt Susan" [B. Anthony]; and found her very kind and wise as well as brave and strong. She was good to me too.

Out of the convention speaking have arisen other opportunities, and I seem in a fair way to lecture a good deal. Pleasanter work I would not ask, not more suited to my powers—and limitations. The travel of it is delightful to me; the meeting of nice people everywhere—I always seem to be "entertained" by delightful people, so that I wonder at their multitude on earth. . . .

I have learned sufficient skill in the art to attract more than I repel; and leave behind me a divided wake—half hating and half loving. . . .

I am engaged in the last week of May, in Boston—Suffrage thing,— they to pay my expenses; and I hope to do lecturing enough to make quite a little stay, and run about diversely. I shall visit Martha Lane, see Providence folks a little, and circulate generally. But O how I shall enjoy some quiet days in the country, in New England Spring! . . .

With love always—dear mother of my child—

Charlotte.

214. W. Logan Sq. Phil.

Sun. May 3rd. 1896.

My dearest Grace,

. . . Here is enclosed five dollars. Mrs. Cresson gave me four when I went to call on her the other day—said it was "car-money["]— affectionately stuffed it down my neck when I would not take it—so I put one more with it and send it to fill some chink for the girlie.

I said to myself the other night—"Now why not think about her— just think of her beauty and sweetness and all the lovely things that you can remember of her." And I opened the door a little and looked in. [Might] As well pluck at an amputation!

It began to bleed and ache and I hasted and shut it again. Sometime when I have her in my arms—asleep perhaps—and know there are months of it ahead—then I will open the door and let the past join the present. But as it is I do not think of her much. . . .

When you get to where things make it imperative for you two to go where she would hinder I will take her whether I can or not. Otherwise I will take her when I can, which looks to me still about four years off. But one cannot say. I might take her with me to London in two years or so, and to Paris thereafter. . . .

Lately I have had a return of the intense nervous weakness and depression, enough to make me feel that I can not live so for any length of time. . . .

Health comes at once as I take the field again. I shall always have to keep moving I fancy. . . .

Good bye, dear.<br>Charlotte.

Mon. June. 8th. 1896.<br>Topeka Kansas.

My dear Grace,

I am very comfortable and happy. I haven't made any more debts since the paper [Impress] failed; and have paid some. I see my way to pay some more pretty soon, thanks to this new found trade of lecturing.

Such an easy business! Around and about I go; travelling luxuriously, eating of the fat—(I hate fat!) and drinking of the strong—(I like mine weak!) as it were; staying with nice people of astounding variety, and doing nothing at all but say things. My fame waxeth, and I see no reason why I should not clear myself entirely in the course of a few years. . . .

Dear—will you tell me what sort of letter [Katharine] likes best? I write mostly of what I do, etc, partly that you may all know; and because incident is dear to the young—also because I wish carefully to avoid such emotional touches as might make her grieve a little. Now tell me either from her words and acts, or in various subtle ways, can you judge if she tires of the mere itinerary and would like more specialized scenes and events—more of the dramatic as it were and less mere history; and also if she seems to want more lovingness—to miss it in the letters. . . .

No, I did not see Mrs. Stanton in New York, though I had promised myself to do so. I hope to in the fall. I wrote to her awhile back, praising the <u>Woman's Bible</u>[24] as it were, and she wrote me very warmly. She was much hurt at the paltry meanness of the W. S. Convention towards it last winter.

And yes, I really am going to London. I have bought my ticket—$50.00—Str. Mongolian, Allan Line, from Montreal. I go there from Chicago, down the St. Lawrence—through the Thousand Islands—such a lovely long voyage! It will do me world's of good I know. It is to me most wonderful—most beautiful—most awe-inspiring and yet tender—to see how my life unrolls now step by step along the lines I trod so in the dark in those black San Francisco years. . . .

June seems to be full here in Kansas; and the people and the papers ire with each other in being nice. When I read the papers I exclaim with Whitman "O I am wonderful"—"I did not know I contained so much goodness!"[25]

That dear old edition of '67[26] you people gave me travels with me. I love him more and more. . . .

My London address will be at my Publishers—(!!!—doesn't that taste good!) T. Fisher Unwin[,] Paternoster Square.

Goodbye for now dear friend,<br>Charlotte.

20 West 32nd st.<br>New York City.<br>Jan. 11th. '97

My dearest Grace,

I do not quite know why I should sit here holding Katharine's letter to my heart and sobbing. It came following yours this morning, and they were both so loving, so sort of real and near—perhaps you can tell as well as I.

I sent you a word Saturday—just to say I knew and cared; but your letter makes it all realer and closer.[27]

Is not cremation a genuine blessing! I felt so grateful to my mother for having it so—I should not have expected it of her. Such a clean sweet natural redistribution of things! Do you know I am exceedingly glad that our little one should have twice seen "death coming as friend" and met as such. We had no undertaker either—the child knows only the true side of it. It is wealth early acquired, and will last—must last.

This letter of hers is somehow the most personal I have ever had from her. It makes me feel as if she knew me. Perhaps this seems absurd to you, but child years are so long and full—so full of forgetting too; and it has been so unbelievably difficult for me to write letters until perhaps within his last year—I have felt so unutterably far away and out of touch with all that is mine on earth—just calling in the dark—and this letter really seems as if she heard. . . .

I <u>know</u> that she is in all ways better off with you than with me now. But sometimes it gets out . . . just pure selfish longing. . . . and I ache a thousand ways at once.

This won't do. I can't afford to ache. Dear, I think if you could see how patiently I try to carry my patched and cracked and leaky vessel of life—how I pray endlessly for strength to do my work!—only that—how I use what strength I have, when I have any, to hold the attitude and do the things which to me seem right, how I have truly and fully accepted the <u>not-having</u>—O well, there!—We all do what we can. . . .

Dined with the Stanton's last night.[28] Afterward we played games. Mrs. Stanton playing Dumb Crambo—fancy! And enjoying it as much as any of us. . . .

Lovingly—<br>Charlotte.

20 West 32nd st.<br>New York<br>March 21. 1897

My dear Grace,

I was at Mrs. Stanton's to dinner last Monday, and learned through them that you are thinking of going abroad. Do you take Katharine? And if so please let me know as far in advance as you can when you come so that I may not miss her. . . .

Yes, I had a very good time in Washington—very indeed; and like the city. I went to a White House reception and shook hands with Mrs. [Grover] Cleveland—a warm soft kind hand.[29] . . .

I've not done much since returning to New York—spoken a few times, gathered a few dollars, and rested somewhat. But last night I had a great pleasure.

I lectured for the Manhattan Single Tax Club,[30] and William Dean Howells came to hear me! He was introduced, and said he was coming to see me.

"I can't tell you how delighted I have been" he said of the lecture—as simply as a child. And he looks such a <u>good</u> little man! I was made very happy to really see him at last—and to have his approval again. . . .

Always lovingly yours—

Charlotte Perkins Stetson.

C. B. & Q. train, about 3 p.m.

Sat. May 1st. '97.

Dearest Grace,

I have come down this morning from Savanna, Ill[inoi]s where the plum trees are in bud, to Rock Island, where they are in bloom.

The Mississippi rolls beside me like a sea—sea-colored, absolutely, it is so blue and so purple dark. . . .

I am writing again. Just the beginnings of what I hope to be a year of fruitful work. Ah but it feels good! I can, as yesterday, write eight letters and five cards in the morning, travel four hours, in which I wrote two letters and two poems, and speak in the evening—and do not feel tired today! . . .

To be able to work! Really able to work again!

Did I write Katharine this week of my Kansas offer?

A position in the State Agricultural College for $1400.00 a year! Wouldn't it be fine if I could take such a chance as that. That would pay all debts and make possible a home such as would not mean to[o] great a loss to Katharine.

But I'm not trained for such work—they suggested Cooking & Hygiene—and couldn't honestly undertake it.

I felt greatly pleased though with the offer. . . .

I heard some one speak the other day with intense appreciation of your "House on The Hill Top"—of the subtle delicacy of its rendering of the spirit of the people and place.[31]

I was pleased. . . .

Always lovingly yours—

Charlotte.

c/o The Woman's Journal

3 Park st. Boston Mass.

Oct. 13th 1898.

Dear Grace,

Your letter of Oct. 2nd is welcome . . . but somehow there seems to be a note of pain in it. I grieve to feel any sort of misunderstanding creep between us; and all this summer I have felt as if it was so creeping. Dear—do you not know how deeply and reverently grateful I am for all you have done for my child and for me? Do you think I do not honor the motive, admire the method, appreciate the skill, and recognize the power?

I do. One cannot keep saying that sort of thing. But you know I do. I know it has not been easy. I know that there are few women on earth who could do what you have done. But you are you; and I have always loved and honored you.

And when you speak in this sort of explanatory way of your work with the child it seems as if you thought I was doubting or blaming you. Poor as my own surroundings have been for the child I should have kept her with me if I had not known that you were heavenly-wise with children; and must love Walter's child—be fond of mine—and as won by the darling herself. Be well assured that I shall never ascribe any shortcoming of hers to lack of yours; and that I shall be grateful always for the beautiful fruit of her life with you.

I sought to institute no new regime—I did urge her to learn to read my writing if she could, for the reason you naturally anticipated and similarly urged. If she makes a difference it is from observation and her own will.

What I did beg of her was to be as good as she could in going back to you—lest you who have done so much might think her harmed by being with me who have been so long away from her; a nervous fear, but natural. I felt the same anxiety about your opinion when you first saw her as a child. . . .

It is of course a strain on a child to have two parents who widely differ; but in casting her lot with you two who are alike for most of her youth, I had hoped, still hope, that the strain will not be severe. If she does not easily and naturally like me and my life when she sees more of it, I shall never demand a forced association from her. But our happiness together this summer made me feel at ease about that. . . .

Affectionately,<br>Charlotte.

7-21—'11

My Dear————

I think that sudden little burst of loving thought which made me send a mere word the other day, must have been very near the hour of your grief.[32]

I was ploughing through a heap of as always neglected letters, and suddenly felt how much I loved you and how little use or comfort I had been. . . .

I've just written Katharine to cable "yes" if there is a pinch, and we will send on a hundred dollars. . . .

Will you come to me, when you return? We should love to have you.

I do not attempt to offer you words of consolation; much less to dwell on the measureless pain. . . .

Sympathy—and Love—and Honor—these I offer—knowing well how uselessly.

At least He Has Done Great Work.

And you, at least, Have Had———some never have!

Yours as always—<br>Charlotte.

6-26-14—<br>Portage Wis.

My dear Grace—

Salem burned![33] Salem!————

Are we Americans never going to learn "Safety First"? But Salem———! . . .

Our motor trip from Evanston to Madison—150 miles, was a long day's delight. From Madison to Portage—scant 40 miles, took us 8–9 hours. Mud, sticky mud, and a lost wheel-chain. Twice we were reduced to horses. It was a sight to see. Lucy Fitch Perkins, our hostess, Zona Gale, Margaret Wilson, and C. P. Gilman, pushing a muddy motor, ankle-deep.[34] Mr. Perkins had us all autograph one of his headlights, with a diamond. But it was a pleasant trip none the less. . . .

Yours—Charlotte

near 6 p.m.<br>Fri, Feb. 17—1922.<br>Pasadena—

Dear Grace—

This is just a word to tell you that I am here safe and sound, after an unusually pleasant journey—good weather, warm and bright, every day.

Katharine looks well, has color, but tires easily. Frank looks splendidly.[35] He is heavier, and looks calm and strong, much improved. The babies are simply charming. You've got to come and see 'em—quick! . . .

The little house is charming, very comfortable and convenient. I have the S.E. front room, quiet and sunny, most luxurious. The excellent colored girl is again on the job, to Katharine's joy. . . .

I have lectures enough to cover the trip, so I am feeling quite independent as to any more. . . . I do not know yet if any of the brilliant literary prospects are to materialize. But just now I'm barking in pure delight to be here again! . . .

Love to you dear, lots and always,
Charlotte

10-27-22

Dear Grace—

I never better appreciated the use of a tonic. I've been taking my old favorite, <u>Eskay's Neuro-Phosphate</u> since coming here. It means better appetite, better digestion, better sleep, and—best of all—<u>better work</u>!!! . . .

I've done an outline of chapters [for <u>His Religion and Hers</u>], a tentative preface, and begin to <u>see</u> the book, and to feel that it will be a powerful usefull [*sic*] illuminating thing.[36] Religion and feminism are surely popular topics—the time is roaring ripe for such a book—I have Hopes! . . .

I get on very nicely indeed with this Brother & Sister.[37] She has splendid qualities—he is "a dear." Houghton is but a weekender till May, when we hope to absorb him for keeps. . . .

Please feel thoroughly happy about me—I've not been so gay and hopeful for years. It is so lovely here!

Yours lovingly, Charlotte.

[August 8, 1923]

Dear Grace,

I was glad of your little birthday note—glad to hear from you any time. I worry over you more or less—would more, only what's the use? . . .

I continue to enjoy living here. To step out of doors into beauty and peace—to see the moon as a moon should be seen—just sky & tree tops—and the long sweeping shadow, of great elms across the meadows! The quiet, the fragrance, the still lov[e]liness—it delights me daily—& nightly. . . .

The decision still hangs fire; but we have privately decided—(quite privately) to stay [in Norwich Town, Connecticut] anyway. I will not go back to New York. . . . And I truly think that if Houghton builds up a small business here, he will soon be "at the head of the bar" in his old home, and enjoy it; really enjoy it, and the friends so long known, and the old home. You see he inherits a half-interest in the home & furniture from Aunt Emily.

My book [His Religion and Hers] comes out in late September, Mr. Black's[38] article about me in the Oct. Century—wasn't it lovely of him to do that! And he's done it beautifully, I think even you will say.

Always your loving friend—<br>
Charlotte

380 Washington St.<br>
Norwich Town, Conn.<br>
Sept 4th, 1923

Dear Grace,

. . . Now I'm taking a liberty which please excuse if unnecessary—I thought that this might strike you in a period of shortage, and demand some small outlay, so I'm sticking in a little extra check. If not necessary you can send it back,—or keep till it is. . . .

I see my way through to January—carrying [my brother] Thomas and all—so things look easy. . . .

Did I write since your little birthday note? Perhaps I didn't, being always a sinner. But I love you, all the same, and am continually anxious about you—when I think of it! . . .

Your loving friend,<br>
Charlotte P. Gilman

380 Washington Street<br>
Norwich Town, Conn.<br>
1-5-'24

Dear Grace—

Do you feel strong enough to put me up four nights—May 12–13–14–15?

The P.E.N. Club[39] has an international meeting—beginning with a dinner on the 13th, and I'd like to come the day before so as not to be too tired.

If you don't feel up to it you'll say so—won't you; I'll only be there nights, and my breakfast is only fruit bread & coffee.

I feel quite dashing to make a trip to N. Y. just for a thing like that! Shall try to work in some editor-seeing besides, and so on.

Your loving friend—<br>
Charlotte.

380 Washington Street
Norwich Town, Conn.
May 26. '24

My Dearest Grace—

. . . I'm worried stiff about you now—just plain worried. Will you forgive me dear if I stick in this little wee [check]—for an anchor to windward—in case of an absolute shortage you know! . . .

Dear girl—I feel so clumsy and stupid, fearing always to hurt you; but I do love you, dearly, and carry you in my heart. We have seen much Life—we two. . . .

I hear from my Mormon friend that Rebecca West[40] says that I, forsooth, am "the greatest woman in the world today"!!!! Now if I only thought more of Rebecca's opinion! . . .

380 Washington Street
Norwich Town, Conn.
10-13-'25

Dear Grace,

I did have such a nice time with you! Always I feel guilty, interrupting and making more work, but I do love to come. . . .

Looking for an old article Mr. Wells wanted to see I found a lot of letters saved for biographical use. One from Lilian Whiting— profound admiration for "The Yellow Wallpaper"—its "art"! Poor me—that never thought of having any art in it! Howell's [*sic*] lovely letter about <u>Similar Cases</u>; Uncle Edward Hale's—& Edward Bellamy![41] I was quite cheered to read them. How <u>gone</u> a thing is after its written & printed! Only the work ahead is interesting; what one is doing and to do—not ancient history. . . .

<u>Charlotte</u>.

Salt Lake City, Utah.
Sun. July 10, 1927.

Dearest Grace,

Here I am, foregathering with the Mormons. . . .

Here all goes well. The course of six [lectures] at the Univ. of Utah was most successful—great enthusiasm. This is a very <u>vital</u> people. Their religious enthusiasm is fresh and real; and under the guidance of that great man Brigham Young they learned to make their religion <u>work</u>. . . . Today at 2 p.m.—(horrid hour!) I speak in the Tabernacle. Not as big, nor as holy as the Temple—but a huge auditorium— And alas!—broadcasting! But I'll do my best. I am at present visiting with Mrs. Widtsoe, one of Mrs. Gates' daughters. He, Mr. W. [Widtsoe], was president of State Agricultural College at Logan . . . and of the University here. Took <u>summa cum laude</u> at Harvard. Quite a man. And they have a lovely well appointed house. . . . Yesterday p.m., there was a trip up into a canyon, and along the face of the Wasatch, with a geologist who discoursed on the formation and history thereof. Interesting. . . . If you write here address c/o Susa Young Gates,[42] E. S. Temple st. . . .

> Love to you, dear girl, love and honor—
> C. P. Gilman

> 380 Washington Street
> Norwichtown, Conn.
> Sept. 2nd. 1927.

My dearest Grace,

We got home last night—found your letter. By all means stop over—as long as you can. . . .

Katharine is far better than I expected to see her, in spite of the whooping cough. She doesn't look any more tired than she did last winter—that I see. The children are pale and thin—but not more than is to be expected. Dorothy[43] (where can she have got it!) is extremely "cocky"—thinks she can do everything. . . . They are charming children, and Houghton lost his heart to them as I knew he would. . . .

> Charlotte.

> 380 Washington Street
> Norwichtown, Conn.
> Nov. 15. '27

Dear Grace—

I'm coming to the city—under special urging—to attend the dinner to Eva Le-Gallienne[44] on Sun. 20th. . . . Would you like to have me in for Mon. & Tues. nights? & have you seen Uncle Tom's Cabin yet?[45] If it doesn't cost too awful much I'd like to see it with you. . . .

> Hastily but lovingly,
> C. P. Gilman

380 Washington Street
Norwich Town, Conn.
Feb. 15th, 1928

You dear Girl—

Seems forever since I've written, or heard. You aren't dead or anything are you? . . .

As for me I plow about in a vast field of ethics. I sent on some first draft work for Miss Watkins to see—wishing to get "points" as to treatment. She found it too heavy, and I'm having to do a lot of it over. This was a set back, discouraging. It is not literary criticism I was after, but "salability"—I want to have this book go, and her judgment on that line is necessarily good. My neuritis is "yielding to treatment." Iodex and methyl-salycilate[46]—a black salve—which utterly disappears when rubbed in! . . .

This letter is an extra—written before breakfast. Because I love you.

Charlotte. . . .

May 28th. '29

Dearest Grace,

. . . My "corruption" [article] has not been offered as yet. I wouldn't have believed that I should have so sunk as to think it a possibility.

But when my nice agent—Miss Charlotte Barbour, with the Putnams on W. 45th—said she had submitted it to Good Housekeeping I disgracefully held my tongue. Whoso looketh on a Hearst paper to deal with it, hathe [*sic*] sinned already.[47]

It is a sad fact, my friend, that I'm nothing like as "noble" as I was once. Living in this degrading family atmosphere is a major cause.

I hate to think of your sending me a cheque! It doesn't seem at all right. . . .

Love always,
Charlotte.

380 Washington Street
Norwichtown, Conn.
July 6th. '29

Dear Grace—

. . . I have thought of you much—in that long "hot spell." O how <u>glad</u> I shall be when you get clean away!

'Cause I love you.

I've written three little articles, one is taken by The Outlook.[48] They only pay a pittance, but I'm getting desperate to have something printed.

Now I'm trying to hew out some short stories. Hard sledding. But the market is so large and steady that if I can strike it at all it ought to carry my "western branch." . . .

Charlotte.

July 9th.'29

Dear Grace—

. . . I sent Oliver Herford word of a nice cat book; and he returned a most cordial letter, with this pleasing P.S., "Speaking of <u>you</u> in relation to women in general—Howells whom at one time I used to see every day (I <u>almost</u> had a latch key) was constantly quoting you, & was the first who read "Similar Cases" to me—& he asserted in my presence that you had the best brains <u>and</u> the best profile of any woman in America—and Mrs. Howells added "or any where else"![49]

Wasn't it nice of him to remember and tell me that! I'm getting to feel so very much of a has been that such memories are very pleasant.

Lots of love to you, as always<br>Charlotte.

380 Washington Street<br>Norwichtown, Conn.<br>Aug. 21st. 1929.

Dearest Grace—

. . . The garden flourishes, and we revel in its products.

Yesterday I showed it to The Lord Mayor of Norwich. . . . My Scotch friend, John Howie of Buffalo, was escorting the visitor and insisted that [he] must see "America's leading feminist"—I abominate being called a feminist. . . .

With love—<br>Charlotte.

Thurs. April 24th 1930.

Dear Grace—

A bit of news. My un-esteemed sister-in-law [Emily Gilman], despite having long blamed me for not being willing to do my share of the house-keeping, is so furious with me for having taken it in charge; (I well knew she would be!) and so violently critical as to the way I am doing it, that she and F. [Francis] once more demanded that we divide the house. Houghton very rightly refuses. . . . I'm so sorry for Francis. She torments him with talking about it all the time.

Present status: I run the house, have guests as I like, and so on. Separate breakfasts, separate lunch, dinner together. Francis does his best to be polite and conversational at said dinner. E. [Emily] does not speak! . . .

I am no longer hurt, angry, or worried; it is comic-grotesque. She fairly hates us, not only me, for which there is some reason in our hopelessly discordant temperaments; but <u>Houghton</u>! . . .

If she should die first we'd be very glad to have Francis back. But she won't. Meanwhile the house is large. I hope you are well again dear—and will come soon.

Charlotte.

380 Washington St.<br>Norwich Town. Conn.<br>April 18th. 1932.

Dear Grace,

. . . So Katharine is a Professional Genealogist! Funny, that she she [*sic*] should have taken to that, seems to me. But I'm glad she is getting on well with it. If only it will "pay"—I'm getting sordid. What a degrading thing poverty is. Never before in my life have I felt poor, but I do now. . . .

For that matter we are "in straightened circumstances" ourselves. Houghton will add the lawn mowing etc. to his gardening, and that was enough for him. I think he feels quite as old as I do, if not more. He never did like physical labor, hasn't a working hand, at all. . . .

As to the Lindberg [*sic*] atrocity, I simply do not read or think about it—so far as it can be helped.[50] It simply piles up my shame for my country, that we are so crime-ridden that such things can happen. That it should happen to those people makes me wish slow tortures for the criminals, but again, what good would that do! To inflict such anguish on any father and mother is bad enough, but hurt millions besides. The moral corruption which could do it is a hideous thing. . . .

I don't do anything but gardening, and trying to write letters. Head bad, fuzzy and depressed. . . . Nuisance. . . .

Your most unsatisfactory old friend<br>Sophronia[51]

July 21. 1932.

[Dear Grace,]

. . . as I sit at my west window . . . with a honeysuckle scented breeze flowing softly over me, and look down on a melody of var-colored holly-hocks and those tall lemon-yellow primroses, with garden meadow and massed trees beyond—it is heavenly. What a dear earth it is! And how much dearer it is going to be, when we get civilized. . . .

Have you read those two nice Cape Cod Murder stories, with "Asey Mayo" in them? The last one is called "Death Lights a Candle," I forget the other, and, alas! the author.[52] . . .

As for me I am going carefully through Human Work,[53] to make such corrections as seem best, with a view to its republishing. I think I'll have a "litcrary executor.["] There might be a flash of interest when I pop off. I feel sure that the new poems, with the old ones, would sell somewhat. Also I want to re-write my Ethics. There is great stuff in it.

My cousin Emily Perkins has lent me a book about Catharine Beecher.[54] What a prodigious worker, and what a Beechery Beecher!

I'm also planning to write a convincing article on the complete jus-tifiability of suicide under some circumstances. . . . Of course I do not mean mere cowardly escape from a painful position, so long as one is still capable of service or any comfort to any one, like one I read of re-cently where the man said he could not bear to see his wife suffer pov-erty! So he left her to suffer it alone.

My good Mr. Abbott[55] here speaks of the noble virtues developed by bearing pain. I ask him what good those virtues do when the sufferer is helplessly dying; whether he assumes the immortal soul takes those vir-tues with it: whether the virtue of bearing pain is what he expects to use in heaven: and what virtues are developed in the loving family who have to see the pain borne! . . .

Love always, dear.<br>Charlotte

380 Washington st.
Norwich Town. Conn.
March. 13. 1933.

Dearest Grace,

. . . I wish, Oh how I wish! I could lift any of the load from your long over-burdened shoulders. But this is an exquisitely selected moment for further misfortunes, when even what little we have is tied up in the bank! We were caught with seventeen dollars between us, which is better than most. Incidentally the weather seized on the same happy moment to blow off some of our roofing. Francis of course contributes nothing. . . .

Houghton has been appointed a judge, a small one, assistant in a minor court. Doesn't begin till July. Salary <u>very</u> small, but more than welcome. And the work practically nothing. We are planning somehow to step out from under next winter. Make them [Francis and Emily] but [buy] their coal or leave. Not one word of apology or gratitude, coldness and insolence instead, just "I haven't got any money." The motto being as usual "Let George do it."[56] He has aged, dear boy, dreadfully, these last years. For that matter so have I, not perhaps so markedly, but suitable to my years. . . .

Did you get a chance to see Kate Hepburn in The Bill of Divorcement?[57] She was better that John Barrymore [was] in it. . . .

Me, I'm writing some articles. Got to do something even if I get nothing out.

Love dear, lots, and useless sympathy.
C. P. Gilman

Washington st.
Norwich Town, Conn.
Nov. 10th. 1933.

Dear Grace,

. . . That angel Houghton has no[w] either sciatica or neuritis in one leg—hurts so he can't sleep well—and I'm inclined to attribute it to coming from a warm office to a cold house. It's dreadful. Also, we only got coal for a month. You speak of using almost a ton a month—our furnace takes, Houghton says, almost a ton a week! Our fuel bill is about $300. a year! Why we could live in Pasadena—rent, light, heat and water—for $350! We "figured" [our finances] last Sunday; but what H. earns is a little more than what we would save by moving. His "income," like everyone else's, is painfully reduced. . . .

As to this wonderful new generation—I can see <u>no</u> contribution as yet, nothing to mark any superiority for their boasted 20th Century. Of course its evils they blame on the preceding one; but its advances—inventions—discoveries give no credit to those who so indubitably began, or promoted them, in the magnificent <u>19th</u>.

Well ma'am—I must get at the Ethics. If I can get that out—I'll die happy.

Always your loving<br>Charlotte.

Dec. 14th. '33

Dear Grace,

Such a nice letter you sent—and such a measly scrap I belatedly return! I'm pleased that you agree with my high opinion of Katharine Hepburn. If that "Bill of Divorcement" turns up anywhere go miles to see it—she's a wonder in that. And in Little Women——![58] It is a delight to have some one like that to count on.

. . . I still love you.

C. P. G.

380 Washington St.<br>Norwich Town. Conn.<br>April 25th. 1934.

Dearest Grace,

. . . As to the biography, it was not expected that Lyman [Beecher Stowe] was to write it while I was alive, but that he should get what information, or at least impression, he could from two intimate contemporaries, while they were. You see there aren't so many contemporaries left, and never any who knew me so well as you, and in a lesser way, Martha Luther Lane. . . .

Mr. Farrar has refused the [Ethics] book, suggests W. W. Norton Co, 70 Fifth Ave. I never heard of them, but that's nothing. I'll have to have an agent again—and they don't do much. . . .

The garden very slowly getting into shape, not much strength between us. I find the housework takes care of itself very well. A colored retainer who once worked here does the washing and cleans half the rooms each week. All I have to do is get our little meals.

Come along and sample them my dear!

Your loving Old Friend—<br>Charlotte.

Thurs. May 3rd. '34

Thanks again, Dear,

. . . I <u>have</u> been having rather a time with this "cold." Houghton is long since over his, but I still cough, night & morning—a spot low down in the "Bronx."[59] Still its nearly over, and I begin to feel some strength. Guess it was grippe, or what have you! And if I was Jane Addams I'd a' been in bed, attended by a physician. It's a fortnight—which I believe is the time it takes <u>if</u> one has the best of care! It does dawn on me occasionally that I'm not as young as I used to be. . . .

Houghton went on to see Cousin Eliz. Gilman in Baltimore—he belongs to a "Christian Social Justice" thing she promotes & they pay expenses. It appears that These [Francis and Emily] have been visiting her also, and she agrees that Francis is sub-normal. What a wretched pair! Poor Emily a cripple & F. almost a dwarf and moron. He's so clever too—would have made an ideal King's Jester! Just the type.

Well dear, I love you.<br>Charlotte.

May 22. 1934

Dear Grace—

. . . The doctor gives a good report. It appears these treatments—a bunch of them, cost $60 or $75.[60] I've no money to spend on useless prolongation. I asked how long it would be—probably—without any more treatments, and he said—not as a definite statement but a loose estimate—a year or perhaps two.

It's little I care.

If I can get the Ethics going—! You see I'm no good to Katharine, there's nobody to miss me but you—and my brother—and that's not for long. If I find work in California, I shall hang on as long as I can, of course. . . .

Dear—it was heavenly of you to come. And such a help! The letters still pile up. . . .

With long love—
Charlotte.

Norwich, Conn. June 12th. '34

Dear Grace—

Nice paper, in his [Houghton's] desk in my room.[61] I'm so thankful for every little convenience I did provide for him,—so remorseful for all that I might have and didn't—now looming enormous. Mustn't think of it. . . .

When I get away from here I shan't "miss" so much; that is it will not be such an incessant haunting. Every inch of the garden, now orphaned—the uncut grass. . . .

Yours as always—
Charlotte—

June 25th. 1934.

Yes, dear girl—

Come as soon as you wish and can; & stay as long. Always glad to see you. . . .

I'm getting along lazily, selfishly, trying to enjoy the sun and air and clean quiet, my food and bed—whatever remains; and planning valiantly for work ahead. If I live to do it. The doctors seem to think I am doing pretty well.

So—love to you dear.

I'll make up the bed—and lay in some beer!

With love—
Charlotte.

Hotel Constance
Pasadena, California
Sat. Sept. 1st. 1934.

Well, dear girl,

I sent you a wire and follow with a bit of a letter. Our 35 minute delay increased to two hours or more, but we made it up, mostly, and arrived at 7.45 instead of 7.[62] . . .

Now as to air travel—: as to height, houses were plainly visible, and automobiles. Didn't seem a greight [*sic*] height at all.

As to speed—there <u>wasn't any</u>! I really did expect to feel <u>some</u> thing, at 200 miles an hour; but the impression—judging from our progress over the country, was of a slow steady advance only. Not till I could see a parallel road, with moving autos, and note our gradual overtaking of them, did I get any sense of speed, and not much then.

As for noise, I didn't mind it at all. It is smooth and steady. You'd love it—you can hear so well. Unfortunately there was fog or mist till dark—no very distant range of vision. I wish now I had taken the other line—I'd have seen the great lakes, the Sierras by sunrise, and all down California. . . . All northern Ohio & Indiana sparkling with close sprinkled cities—lovely. And Chicago, by night, seen from above is worth the trip. So was a thunder storm we ran into afterward—lightening [*sic*] everywhere. At Kansas City I had to change to a rear seat, and promptly became car-sick! Very. No sleep, miserable time for seven hours or so. . . .

O—the "dinner" was a box lunch, plenty for me, but naught for a hungry man; 3 tiny half-sandwiches, one small cake, two olives, a little carton of canned fruit—mixed—a few grapes, and a cup of coffee; I ate every scrap.

The lavatory—with which I became intimately acquainted, is evidently treated with chemicals, and "air conditioned" to perfection. It was fresh and sweet, even to one in my condition! . . .

I was too sea sick to appreciate our entrance over the Arizona hills and deserts; and this city, seen from above, appeared mainly dirt! The time of year.

Katharine does look a good deal older—and worn. I didn't see much of Frank, who departed when we reached the hotel. My brother & young Thomas were here, and had breakfast together, more or less. He looks dreadfull [*sic*] my brother—a shadowy wreck. I'm glad to see him again anyhow. . . .

Yours always—

Charlotte.

127 N. Madison st.

Pasadena, Cal.

Wed. Sept. 5th. 1934.

My dear Amelia,[63]

Yours is the first letter from my new home, rented on the 5th. . . . The location is just what I wanted. It is six blocks west of Catalina, and (by number) about three north of her. . . . My brother is about a mile northeast. The library is just around the corner, so to speak, two or three minutes. Colorado,[64] a block & a bit south of me, offers a cheap movie place close by, others farther; Sears & Roebuck for "just every-thing." . . . Perfect. The street is dignified, established, beautiful houses, not bungalows, immensely tall palms, big camphor trees, and such. . . . It is definitely a "rooming house," run by an indefatigable little Swedish woman—Caroline Johnson. She <u>works</u>. Everything clean, quiet, busi-ness like—so <u>much</u> better than in a private house!

I'm on the third floor—which I delight in. A window, wide but not high, opens on the mountains. Right over the roofs & tree tops—save for a few tall palms, close shaven to the top-knot, above the level of the other trees. . . . A good bed, a couch, small bureau, two tables, 3 chairs. The water closet to the west, and space enough to store several trunks. . . . There are three windows in the hall eastward. So I have air on three sides—with my door open—which it mostly is. I've little to lose and shan't bother to lock up much. . . .

So everything looks promising; and I hope to get to work by next week.

I <u>could</u> live on $30.00 a month—really. With more leeway, carfares, amusements, & clothes, very comfortably on $40.00. Now I'll keep ac-counts and see if I do need to save for X rays etc; to say nothing of something over for Katharine. . . .

Meanwhile, as far as all immediate necessities and comforts go, con-sider me as a contented

Sophronia.

127 Madison st.
Pasadena. Cal.
[n.d.; postmarked September 14, 1934]

Dearest Grace,

. . . Grace—I sympathize <u>intensely</u> with his [son-in-law Frank's] pa-tient suffering in that disorderly cluttered house! Of course a lot of it just now is due to my stuff—all the picture puzzle cartons are in there and so on; but—Oh, dear! And that pale frail lovely Katharine—so brave, so patient—. . . . O, WOW! Let us slay some unnecessary mil-lionaire and get some of his useless gold!

Well. Personally I am <u>very</u> comfortable, as near happy as I have any right to expect. But "personally" is so <u>little</u> compared to all you people I love—and can't help! Maybe I can presently earn something!

Yours always, Charlotte.

Near 11. a.m. Tues. Sept. 18th 1934.
127 N. Madison st. Pasadena, Cal.

My dear Grace—

Katharine has wired—; I can't say I'm sorry—though we all wish it might have been Clarence first![65] . . .

Surely now, as soon as some arrangement can be made about the pictures, you will come to us here.

K. put a notice in the paper about me—and I've had a nibble already, from the College Club. <u>Won't</u> it be a joy if I can be earning again! Then I can help all around.

Dear Girl—I want you. I want [to] be some little use and comfort, and have you near. . . .

Love to you—and sympathy—and more love.

Charlotte.

127 N. Madison st.
Pasadena Cal.
Oct. 14th. 1934.

Dear Grace—

. . . You ask about [my doctor]—yes, I have a good one, two for that matter. First I went to one Augusta[66] recommended, but found him so pious that I doubted his intelligence. He seemed to think nothing need be done at present, but said I should call every month for examination. I didn't push matters till I had those boxes & trunks attended to and was fairly settled here, and then, as my left arm began to swell, I wrote to him to please see about the Xray man at once. Then he referred me to an excellent one, <u>the</u> one I fancy, has the Xray department at the Pasadena Hospital, Dr. Chapman. He is fine, frank, rational, and humorous. . . . He recommended me to a Dr. Sanford, in a delightful group of buildings nearly opposite pink bungalows—"medical court"; also an attractive man, and evidently expensive—though he gave me a 2/3 reduction—I suspect Dr. C. suggested it; as he had already told me he was going to reduce the Xray charges. Sort of professional courtesy, I fancy. . . . This man gave me a careful examination and pursuant thereto I've had sixteen days of treatment! . . .

The arm is somewhat better, though still puffy—it varies.

I marvel that Katharine's measuring eyes have not noted the difference in wrists. Must see to it that my sleeves are voluminous!

You see it's a long process. But I have no pain at all, and am able to get about as usual, and am not fussing. . . .

Augusta is exhausted again—heart. If you want to see her—to say nothing of me! again you just better get out here! . . .

Always lovingly yours,<br>Charlotte.

127 N. Madison st.<br>Pasadena. Cal.<br>[n.d.; postmarked November 18, 1934]

Dear Grace:

I was so absent minded (a fairly permanent condition!) as to show Katharine your last letter; forgetting your remarks about my "treatment."

"What is this 'treatment?'" she naturally inquired. I did not turn a hair but casually replied, "That's some of my doin's." As I seem perfectly well I don't believe she'll worry over it. But it was horribly careless of me. She is pathetically worn, but makes little of it. Says her head is all she is concerned about. A real good fortune would revive her I think—as with so many. . . .

Frank's many disappointments have not improved his disposition—nor has that added to his popularity. It looks pretty dark all around. So I'm only too happy to be of immediate assistance. This is just a scrap to say I love you.

Charlotte.

125 N. Madison st.<br>Pasadena. Cal.<br>Dec. 7th. 1934.

Dear Grace;

I am beginning to understand how women spend their lives, contentedly, without doing anything! It is incredible to my once violently active conscience that I can sit here in comfort and peace and luxury—you see it is luxury to me, my tastes being so limited—to do so little.

Up late—breakfast often at <u>nine</u> or after! . . . You see I have no "push" to write, no inner urge; and I never could produce even my kind of literature without it.

Afternoons I rest a bit (!) and deliberately go for walks; ride as far north as a car line goes and then walk home, now one way now another. . . . I continue to love the place and delight in it.

My "stepping out of doors" is the balcony. . . . I bring my little rocker out here and sit by that door—wide open; the suitcase which serves as my writing desk on a chair before me; my solitaire board in my lap. . . . But first thing in the morning or last at night I can walk right out and see the whole sky! I <u>do</u> enjoy it. . . . I'm so glad to end my days in sunlight and moonlight too. As to which ending I think Katharine feels quite at ease about me. If I did not know of this lurking enemy, I should say I was perfectly well! I feel so, I act so; and I do not think about the enemy at all! That last dose of Xray was most successful. . . .

I am thoroughly enjoying my Sunday morning engagement. It is only a "chapel class," most old folks of negligible importance; but there was a "church dinner" Wed. evening, which I also addressed, and there were some young folks. I reached 'em! . . .

Also I addressed a club of colored young people! Invited on the ground of being a niece of H. B. S. [Harriet Beecher Stowe].[67] They seemed to enjoy it!

Xmas coming! How long it is since that was welcome! I have to hand out so much to meet K's necessities that I can't spend much on extras, even for the children.

Did I tell you that I've got my food expenses down to about $7.00 a month? . . .

Always your loving C.P.G.

127 N. Madison st.
Pasadena, Cal.
Fri. Dec. 21st. 1934.

Dear Grace—

. . . I'm sitting out in the sun, on my beloved balcony. . . . As I sit this minute I lift my eyes and O I'm so <u>thankful</u>! It is <u>still</u>; beautifully still. And sweet aired. I just <u>ache</u> to have you here too. . . .

The [grand]children are well. I fell upon them both one evening when [we] were alone, told them flatly that to save their mother as well as themselves from deserved blame, they ought at the least to keep the bathroom clean! I touched Walter in the right spot by suggesting that men were as good cleaners as women—look at sailors! . . . Last night I had occasion to visit their place—and lo! tub, basin, and hopper were clean!!! I cannot conceive how they have lived so indifferently in <u>dirt</u>—real dirt. One would think that sheer shame would reach Dorothy. Bye and bye I'll push a little more. Katharine is sensitive, resents "criticism," is painfully aware of her shortcomings. Poor dear! . . .

Yours always lovingly—<br>Charlotte.

127 N. Madison Ave.<br>Pasadena, Cal.<br>Feb. 20th. '35

Dear Grace,

Are you dead? I am. The grasshopper is getting to be a burden.[68] You never mention any of your pains and disabilities—so I will not dilate unduly; but my time—and strength—gets shorter. No harm. Only I do so hate to pile it on dear Katharine. I've told my brother, who is wholly of one mind with me. How nice it is to have folks understanding and reasonable. My nice doctor approves. He did not like being sole confidant.

My "Class" goes on.[69] (I'm still able to talk an hour or so!) They are interested. Of course it amounts to nothing—a dozen or so of nice "intelligent" women. But it is a pleasure to me, and no harm to any one. . . .

I take Katharine—and the children—to the movies. Am not walking much any more.

Have begun to arrange the poems for the second volume—tentative effort.[70] . . .

I'm endeavoring to incite Dorothy to take a personal interest in the house; to be ashamed of the dirt, to begin to enforce order. . . . Katharine is a shadowy wreck—she does all she can and more. D. is the only hope.

Well dear girl—I love you as always.

And can keep on telling you so for a while yet.

Charlotte.

Sun. Mch. 3rd. 1935.<br>127 N. Madison Ave.<br>Pasadena. Cal.

Dear Grace—

Yes, I'd better tell her.[71] I do hate to, she is so pale and frail and overburdened. I don't doubt she loves him and wants to save him all she can, but Frank is—apparently—a dead weight. No "lift," no stimulating current. Of course nothing is said, by anybody, even by me, who would like to if it would do any good.

Apparently Katharine has largely supported them for some years by borrowing money! My poor little scrap—the most she can get will be, say $4,000.00—will be lost in the shuffle. . . . On top of this I've got to tell her that [I'm] going to leave her soon.

You and I and Augusta—the three of us—can't last very long. . . . One woman in eight [is diagnosed with breast cancer] I've understood. But claiming the right to shorten the unpleasantness its [*sic*] not so much worse than other things. So far as I think I've told you, I've had no pain whatever. But I'm sub-nauseated—no appetite—can eat very little—and am getting weaker. . . . When I can't take care of myself any longer, off I go!

My very nice Xray doctor has been treating the upper part of the lungs, and that choking clutch is much eased. But cough? O my! There now I've told you all of my sorrows, which are no sorrow to me—only I hate it so for Katharine. The most awful thing was to tell Houghton [. . .]

Its been an honor to be your friend, dear Grace. And I have loved you a long time!—Some 56 or 7 years isn't it?

> As ever, yours,
> Charlotte.

> Wed. Mch. 20. 1935
> 127 N. Madison Ave.
> Pasadena. Cal.

Dearest Grace;

. . . Well I've told Katharine; and she has told Tolles & Anna.[72] . . . Tolles walked home with me the last time I was there—Sun. evening. And Grace—I don't wonder Katharine is worried about his mind! . . . (The dear brave child took it as quietly as I [k]new she would. . . .

Well, beyond a word or two about that house . . . he talked, as usual, of nothing but his own disappointments and dislikes! It would be funny if it was not so alarming. He has sat alone in his studio and chewed the cud of repeated failures till he can think of nothing else. . . .

The trouble is not in the facts, though, they are difficult, but in his inability to bear his own troubles. O—I have a bit of good news for "her mother's books." Zona Gale has consented—warmly & affectionately, to take my autobiography as a base and write a—something—on my life.[73] I am not bragging yet—shan't feel sure tell [*sic*] I see it in print. (I fear I wont, for that matter; my nice doctor says "6 months" now—and I imagine that means with nursing.) . . .

Charlotte.

127 N. Madison Ave.
Pasadena Cal.
Mch. 29th. 1935

Dear Grace—

I forgot when I wrote (and most other things!) . . .

Katharine, brave, patient, sweet, is eager to get me over there, and I'm getting quite ready to go—to get into bed and stay there—for a little while. If it wasn't for her I should not wait any longer—I'm so tired of coughing!

You see the critter is in the lungs now—making heaps of trouble. No "pain," not a bit from first to last, but I'm <u>tired</u>.

Lyman Stowe[74] approves of my "get away." Says he thinks it fine that my last act should be to help establish a principle for the good of humanity. I think it will promote discussion and help change an already changing opinion. I'm hoping to stick [it] out another month at least; but there's no knowing. I love you dear Grace.

Charlotte Perkins Gilman.

My New House!
Sat. April 17th 1935

Dearest Grace,

Here I am in comfort and luxury, wishing with all my heart that you were in the front bedroom!

It is a big lot, 15 ft. wider than K's, and with pleasant houses & quiet people on both sides. All green and lovely & full of flowers. Mrs. Harris has lent me a chaise longue (?) [*sic*] which is placed under a blossoming orange tree—a tall old one. Birds, bees, and blossoms, with an occasional haughty wandering cat—I'm enjoying being an invalid. It's part of the beneficent process of departure doubtless, my amiable and cheerful submission to being nursed and tended would surprise you. Katharine seems no worse for her added cares, at present, and it won't last over long. . . .

I'm pretty feeble, but still without pain, and not kicking against the chokes! <u>What</u> a difference it makes to have an assured peaceful end to look forward too [*sic*] when things get too unpleasant! . . .

Love to you—and hurry up! I'd like K. to have her <u>three</u> mothers together before we all die on her![75]

C. P. G.

223 S. Catalina Ave.<br>Pasadena Cal.<br>April 25th. 1935

Dearest Grace;

Here I am, in Anna Wallers nice little house, at her writing table in the pleasant front room, doors and windows open wide—flowers inside and out. At about 8:30 I phone over to Katharine, who comes bounding over and gives me my luxurious breakfast in bed. Thereafter I loll awhile, and then dress and come in here, trying to get all my letters "answered up." . . .

Just at present I'm feeling quite markedly better—to Katharine's triumph. She does like to take care of people! . . .

Amy Wellington[76] is at The Wyndham. . . . If in the vicinity why not go and see her? . . . I'm sure she'd love to see you. I've sent her the verses, she'll have to get them typed—Lyman cheerfully undertook to pay for it and anything else necessary! He is standing by beautifully!

I only got half an hour of Zona Gale; but anything she does in the biography line will be beneficial. I feel so fortunate—so grateful—so blessed in my friends.

It's too bad about your telephone—and the poor ears![77] When you get out here—as I am now confidently assuming you will!—we shall have to "correspond." I can't talk much, to any one, and you couldn't hear me if I did. But you could talk and I'd scribble! So come ahead. I don't want Agusta [*sic*] to give us the slip yet—awhile—we need that reunion!

Love as ever, dear.<br>Charlotte

Figure 4. *Evening—Mother & Child,* 1886–87. Oil painting of Charlotte with Katharine by Charles Walter Stetson. Courtesy of the private collection of Christopher and Melinda Ratcliffe.

# 4
# A Mother's Love
## "to the best of daughters"

In her memoir, Charlotte Perkins Gilman describes her highly controversial and much-criticized decision to send her daughter, Katharine, to the East, when she was nine, to live with Walter Stetson and his new wife, Grace Channing: "To hear what was said and read what was printed one would think I had handed over a baby in a basket. In the years that followed she divided her time fairly equally between us. . . . I lived without her, temporarily, but why did they think I liked it? She was all I had" (*Living* 163). Katharine's departure, however, had its benefits; it eased the economic burden of raising a young child and gave Gilman the freedom to embark on lengthy U.S. lecture tours and to travel abroad, unimpeded by the demands of child care.

While there is little question that Gilman loved her daughter, the extant correspondence reveals a sometimes prickly, at times awkward, and often strained relationship. The presence of didacticism in the early letters—those written in the years immediately after Gilman relinquished custody—is particularly noteworthy. When Katharine was nine, for example, Gilman attempted to instill a lesson about capitalistic greed, philanthropy, and socialism, invoking a comparison between the cupidity of John D. Rockfeller of Standard Oil and the generosity of socialist John Burns of England (January 18, 1895). She also tried to educate Katharine about the purpose of Chicago's Hull House, where Gilman worked for awhile after her departure from California in 1895, and to teach her about the adulteration of food, which was an issue before consumer protection legislation regulating food safety was enacted: "They are having a dreadful time here in the city about milk. The milkmen are being arrested for selling bad milk, and it is making lots of trouble for them. It ought to. A man that will poison babies to make money ought to be arrested—don't you think so?" Sensing perhaps that her lessons in social awareness might not strike a chord with her ten-year-old daughter, she asked, "Do you like this kind of a letter little one, or does it bore you?" (September 15, 1895). Moreover, when Katharine was fourteen, Gilman seemed anxious to determine whether her daughter shared her penchant for public service: "I am intensely interested in finding out your own lines of work and liking" (May 26, 1899).

As much as Gilman desired to educate her daughter, she also sought Katharine's approval. In one letter she crowed about her newly acquired fame: "Today I have answered letters, many letters from . . . admirers, mostly women, one of whom burst forth rapturously, 'Thank God there is such a woman as you on earth!'—this although she had but begun [reading] the mighty work [*Women and Economics*]! . . . Another lady wrote to say that she and five others had been reading studying and discussing it, and would I answer [some] questions. . . . I wrote back politely that to answer her questions would require time and labor worth one or two hundred dollars, and I could not afford it!" (September 16, 1899). Even as late as 1928, Gilman longed for Katharine's respect: "Did I repeat that lovely compliment Oliver Herford just sent me—that he remembered Mr. Howells saying that I had 'the best brains and the best profile of any

woman in America'—? And Mrs. Howells added, 'Or anywhere else'"
(July 25, 1928).

When Katharine became a young adult, it was clear that she would
follow in her father's footsteps rather than her mother's. She had a knack
for art rather than for activism. After her marriage in 1918 to Frank Tolles
Chamberlin, who was himself an artist, Katharine embraced the traditional roles of wife and mother, though she continued to paint and sculpt
as time permitted. Because an artist's life is often a lean one, the Cham-
berlins lived a financially precarious existence. To her credit, Gilman,
whose own financial standing was shaky at best, bailed out Katharine repeatedly. In the first six months of 1920 alone she sent Katharine $2,500;
thereafter, her assistance dwindled as the Great Depression loomed and
the market for Gilman's work declined.

While she was generous in addressing Katharine's financial shortfalls,
as the letters in this chapter attest, Gilman was nevertheless sometimes
insensitive about other matters. After giving birth to her second child,
son Walter, in 1920, Katharine sought information from her mother about
the particulars of her own infancy. Gilman responded, "I'm sorry, but I do
not remember any details about your early babyhood, as to ey[e]brows etc;
only that you were very lovely and very good" (July 12, 1920). She was also
quick to disparage Katharine's housekeeping skills. On July 18, 1922, for
example, following a visit to Katharine in Pasadena, Gilman wrote, "I'm
particularly pleased that you are able . . . to have the kitchen more orderly,
because I know it was a constant strain on Frank. He was wonderfully
good about it, but that kind of visual chaos is trying. What I minded most
was my inability to help. I had hoped that I could at least wash dishes for
you, but I confess that when I went in there I was floored—couldn't seem
to get a foothold—just backed out in despair."

Gilman also needled Katharine about her spelling errors on occasion
and continued her quest to educate her daughter about various social issues, including venereal disease: "We now know that 98% or so [of sur-
geries] when performed on young married women are due to gonorrhea.
You see that is [a] very common disease among men—about 75% even in
America; it often seems to do them no harm—though sometimes resulting in sterility; but the germ remains in the blood, and when it has access to the larger field of the woman's interior it increases with fresh ardor
and results in all manner of ovarian[,] fallopian, and uterine disorders"
(November 16, 1923). She also dismissed an article that Katharine wrote

for *Art and Architecture* magazine as "gratuitous," implying that Katharine had better things to do with her time (July 21, 1931).

Gilman, however, was also capable of sympathizing with Katharine during times of trouble. On May 2, 1933, she wrote to her forty-eight-year-old daughter: "I wish—O how I wish!—you and I were 'near' enough for me to comfort you.... How children suffer from those who love them most! I did try so carefully not to hurt you, and to love and pet you as I so longed to be loved and petted and never was. But I suppose you were hurt in ways I never knew." In a letter some three and a half months later, she confessed to feeling helpless: "These hard times make it more and more difficult for me to write to the people I love. I know your distress and cannot alleviate it. If I plead poverty as preventing my doing anything[—] that seems only adding to your worries. If I dilate on my own happiness and health and all the charms of this lovely old place—that sounds like gloating. If I ask anxiously after your troubles you hate to tell them to me. And if I congratulate you on the good things you have—that's small comfort" (August 26, 1933).

While Gilman had always hoped to end her days in California, Houghton's sudden death in May 1934 forced the issue. She decided to spend what remained of her life in Pasadena, where Katharine had lived for many years. "I shall break up as soon as I can, and come to Pasadena," she wrote. "There will be enough to maintain an economical old lady I think" (May 5, 1934). She also tried to persuade Grace Channing, who had been widowed in 1911, to join her. "Wouldn't it be lovely if we two could end our lives together out there!" she exclaimed to Katharine on May 19, 1934. Grace, she acknowledged, would "be an enormous comfort to" Katharine (Gilman to Lyman Beecher Stowe, April 23, 1935). "She has been more of a mother to her than I have, in many ways; has influenced her character more, I think" (Gilman to Lyman Beecher Stowe, May 27, 1935).

Shortly after Gilman's death by suicide on August 17, 1935, Katharine wrote to Lyman Beecher Stowe that "the first few whiffs [of chloroform] must have carried her off.... So there was an air of peaceful triumph in her quiet figure—she had carried out her plan in all details as she had wished." According to Katharine, Gilman "had failed very fast" during her last week and was so "feeble" and "weary" that she welcomed death. "She was happy in the thought—she just longed for it," Katharine wrote, "so we feel that it was better—far[—]for her to go" (August 20, 1935).

San Francisco, Cal.[1]
January 30th. 1895.

My dear little girl-child,

Your last pictures are so surprising that I [must] write you a special letter at once to tell you how pleased I am with them.

I could not begin to do such work, not when I was twelve or thirteen years old. . . .

The portrait of Grace shows careful study. I can see how closely you looked and how carefully you drew and colored. . . . That wild sunset scene with the two murderers in it and blood everywhere is awfully funny—makes me think of the dear old Nonsense Book. But I like best of all the scene with "A Woman Getting"—something, she being finely planted on a large brown rock, with a stout horse tethered in the foreground and an alert fish in the waters beneath; and the other sketch marked "Kate 24th Jan. '95" and having such suggestion of peace and beauty and power in it.

You are doing splendidly my darling. Keep on being good and be as wise as you can, and in time you ought to be able to bring great beauty to the world.

Are you big enough to care to think of this—

Mr. Rockefeller of the Standard Oil Co. has an income of $15,000,000.00 a year. He does nothing but handle other people's work.

John Burns[2] gives to England by his work the same sum—$15,000,000.00 a year. He has an income of $1200.00.

John Burns gives the people all that money and gets hardly anything for it.

Mr. Rockefeller gets all that money from the people and gives hardly anything for it. Which would you rather be?

Your loving mother
Charlotte Perkins Stetson

Hull House. Chicago, Ill.
Aug. 20th. 1895

My own dearest little daughter;

. . . I have such lovely little letters from you, dear. They make me very happy. . . .

I didn't leave any new address dear heart because I had none. The old one would have done all right enough though—letters were forwarded till I knew where I was. . . .

Do you ever make pin-dolls out of little flowers? Take a sweet pea or some such blossom and put a pin down though so it will stand up; and they make lovely ladies. Any little flower will do. My brother and I used to play with them. . . .

I am getting along very nicely here. I have a southwest room in the third story, a very comfortable little room indeed, with two windows, a closet, a steam-heater, and various other conveniences.

This house is a large beautiful one, with pictures, busts, and casts of lovely things about. The inmates are folks who want to come here to study the life of the poor people about them and help them if they can; for the house is in a very poor quarter of the city. It is largely a foreign quarter also, Italians, Hungarians, Polish Jews, all sorts of immigrants. . . .

I am glad to be here for a while and study the movement. Tonight I am to go with a Russian girl to meet some members of a Socialist Club of Polish Jews. Next Tuesday I speak for the Radical Club. So already I begin to find out some things.

Write when you like to, dear little one.

Your loving mother<br>Charlotte Perkins Stetson

Love to Papa and Grace and all.

Hull House Chicago Ill.<br>Sun. Sept. 15th 1895.

My own dear little girl—

Here it is Sunday again, and here I am to talk to you. . . . Miss [Jane] Addams has been quite ill all the week, but is getting better now, and the house has been very quiet. Little Stanley, with whom I went to the circus last Saturday, has not come this week, on account of his aunt's being ill; which is I think a sore disappointment to him. There is a little niece here now, a daughter of Miss Addams sister, a small blue-eyed child who is very particular about her food I notice. . . .

Thursday I went to the North-Western Settlement and addressed a Mother's Club there; mostly German women, but they could talk English.

Do you understand what these Settlements are, dear?

Some people who have money and education and culture, and who feel badly because so many other people have none of these things, come to live among these other people in order to be frends with them and help them live.

It is not to help them by giving money, nor by preaching, nor by teaching, but to be friends and help in all sorts of ways as it happens; and to give the poor people a large beautiful place to meet in and do things for themselves. You see people have to get together to do much and poor people have no place to meet in however much they want to. This particular Settlement, Hull House, is the largest and best known in the country, and has spread into many kinds of work. There is a crèche or day-nursery where women who have to work out by the day can leave their babies and feel safe about it. They pay five cents. There is a kindergarten of course, with three teachers. There is a gymnasium which has both male and female classes. There is a men's club room, with billiard tables; and the women's and girl's and boy's and mixed clubs meet all over the place, in various rooms and halls.

It is big and busy, and there's lots to do. Each "resident"—that is what they call the people who live here and help,—each resident has some kind of a club or class or department to attend to. I am supposed mostly to hold my self free for lecturing, to all kinds of clubs, etc. Then I help about in the house, wait on the door, see visitors, and "tote." That is what they call it when there are visitors who want to see the whole place and we residents take them about—tote them. I make a splendid "toter" for I rejoice to talk in a glib and cheerful manner about the place and its purposes and achievements. We all get our breakfast in the Hull House restaurant—a public eating house they maintain—and lunch and dinner in our capacious dining hall. . . . The cooking is all done in the big kitchen, the one that feeds the restaurant. Last night I washed my hair—and wow! but it was dirty!

You see this is a soft coal city, full of mills and railroads and all manner of chimneys, and the air is pretty damp.

Hence a fine black smear settles all over you as you go about. After you walk down town, wipe your face with your handkerchief and it is all smutty, as if you were on the cars.

It's lucky my hair is pretty black anyway! Weekly washing wouldn't keep it clean. . . .

Last night there was a meeting in the gymnasium—which also is theatre and lecture hall, holding five hundred when full—on the "Adulteration of Food." They are having a dreadful time here in the city about milk. The milkmen are being arrested for selling bad milk, and it is making lots of trouble for them. It ought to. A man that will poison babies to make money ought to be arrested—don't you think so? ...

Do you like this kind of a letter little one, or does it bore you?

Your loving mother,

Charlotte Perkins Stetson

[n.d.; ca. February 1897]
In My Room. Fourth floor
Back 20 West 32nd. St.
New York City.

My Small Beloved—

Your mama is that thick-headed and weary after her five weeks career of late, that she cannot remember whether she wrote to her daughter last week or not. I'm <u>afraid</u> not—but oft times I do a thing and forget it. . . .

Anyhow, I am back in New York again, and installed in the funniest little room! It is only 5 ft. 6 in. wide! About 12 or 13 long, and seven high. . . .

Now if I <u>didn't</u> write you from Washington I should say that I . . . spent four days with pleasure and profit. I lectured the night I came and then attended the National Congress of Mothers—of which I enclose [the] program—a little one. It was interesting. Some day we shall learn to do right by our children.

I feel so glad for you, my darling, that these years of your life are being passed with the best person I ever saw to guide a child—dear Grace. . . .

You will be pleased to learn that I made some money off this last trip; so that I have paid $54.25 of debts. That's good, and there's some left. How I would like to see you and Grace and Papa. . . .

Papa writes me that you are doing finely in all ways—to my much satisfaction.

You're a comfort, you are.

Your loving Mother.

20 West 32nd st.
New York.
March 14th 1897.

My darling Daughter:

This letter ought to reach you for your birthday—also the Astonishing present I am mailing with it. And by this time you should have had from Mr. Lummis[3] the small sum I promised you from . . . the little poems. The poem is in the last "Sunshine," and you are to have the proceeds—perhaps a dollar and a half—perhaps two dollars—for another birthday present.

All of which I would gladly multiply by a thousand—if I could! . . .

And what are you doing all these glorious Pasadena days? I think of you . . . picking flowers—and am glad from my heart that you are a California child. . . .

It will be a deep sweet background of joy to you always, as my New England country life was to me. Some day you must have the skating and coasting too. But flowerland is the place to grow up in. . . .

And all the time grows in my heart the love of you and the hope for the time when I can make your acquaintance personally again. You will be so different a person from my little Gold hair of '94.

And I shall be a different person too from the sick feeble mother you had then, poor and shabby and struggling to keep the roof overhead and the table well covered.

I think—I truly think—that we shall have happy years together.

Twelve years old! When I was twelve I was living in a wonderland of my own mostly. . . .

I used to spend lots of time in the woods, picking flowers, climbing the tall soft-boughed pine trees and swinging in their tops, wading in brooks, swimming in the little river, dreaming always of lovely things beyond. . . .

Last week I made a delightful discovery! Found a cousin! Cousins are real nice. They are better than brothers. . . . This cousin is Houghton Gilman—George H. Gilman. He is now a grown man—nearly thirty; but when I remember him he was just your age. . . .

There is a younger brother—Francis Gilman, who is almost a dwarf, but also a very agreeable fellow. They are sons of my father's sister, Aunt Katy.

I went to see Grandpa the other day. He has moved to Morristown, N.J. care [of] Dr. J. E. Wright, 26 High st. . . . He was real jolly and nice.

I am writing notices to clubs and things preparatory to setting forth on another lecture tour. . . .

Maybe—<u>maybe</u>—I might run across the desert to see you!! Wouldn't that be fine!

I think I could get a lecture or so in Southern Cal. that would cover the trip.

But I can't tell at all at all [*sic*], and you mustn't count on it; or, what's more to the purpose, I mustn't. . . .

Your loving Mother.

About 7.55 in my room at 35 West 32nd st.,<br>New York City. Sept. 16th. 1899.

Dear Daughter—

. . . Today I have answered letters, many letters from similar admirers, mostly women, one of whom burst forth rapturously, "Thank God there is such a woman as you on earth!"—this although she had but begun the mighty work [<u>Women and Economics</u>]! Dear knows what she'll say when she is through with it. Another lady wrote to say that she and five others had been reading studying and discussing it, and would I answer these questions:—"1st, what is your definition of life?" etc. I wrote back politely that to answer her questions would require time and labor worth one or two hundred dollars, and I could not afford it!

Some of these days you will be amused to see some of my letters.

Do you remember the only time you cried at Cold Spring? Because you spilled the ink, you dear thing—as if it mattered in the least! Well today I spilled mine, knocked it helter-skelter off the table, into my lap, and onto the floor.

Up I rose calm and determined, and scrubbed things for the next half hour.

My dress, being pure wool, I just held under the cold water faucet until the ink all washed off. Not a sign remains. . . .

I've got my check for the article[4] in this month's Ainslee's Magazine—guess how much? 125.00. Isn't that fine! 'Twasn't much of an article either. And forthwith I paid 50.00 of debts. . . .

It is lots of fun paying people, especially when they thought I wouldn't. A woman wrote me a letter the other day—used to be on "Town Talk" in San Francisco and said her husband was dead, she had moved to—Indianapolis I think 'twas—and did I remember that I owed them something. Course I do. I've got a list of all of 'em. But she'll be surprised to see it nonetheless. . . .

Am feeling ever and ever so much better.

O my little sweetheart—if only I keep well what good times we are going to have!

Your loving<br>Mother.

Sept. 23. 1911[5]

Dearest Daughter,

. . . [T]he pretty room will be ready for you and Grace—plus the bed in my study—when you come—I am hoping to get here by Sun the 17th Dec. at latest and want very much to be on the Dock to greet you.[6] Houghton will anyway. . . .

From Mrs. Campbell I hear . . . rather gloomy reports. I mean to go see her before starting west—as I fear me much I won't get another chance. A dear brave sweet woman: leaving good work behind her. That is a tremendous record—your father's. You dear child! You mustn't mind being overweighted with parents. Yours being rather exceptional does not necessitate your keeping up with both—or with either, for that matter.

You have your own life to live on its own merits and will do your own good work I won't doubt. You are a slow grower, that's all. So was I. I never did anything to speak of till after I was 30. Anyhow I love you dearly.

Mother

Aug 5th. 1913

Dearest Daughter,

This is a hasty word to acknowledge your nice letters. . . . Further I wish to give you the very latest news as to me. Dr. Shelby sent me to another Xray man, who took three pictures—$30.00!!!—I don't care, it is worth it; for Dr. S. phones me just now that he has found the cause of all the trouble—an abscess in the jaw bone—upper jaw—discharging into the back of the throat! Must have been there a long time he says. Of course the teeth were part of the trouble but this was the big thing. So now there's a chance of getting well at last. I don't know how they propose to get at the thing—and don't care. Give me ether enough and they can explore at leisure. . . .

I can't write much—being still "limp," and hard at work when able; but I know you'll be pleased to know we have tracked the villain to his lair.

Dr. Edward Ross[7] the Sociologist was here to dinner last night—we are always so glad to see him. . . .

Your loving Mother.

4-25-18

Dearest Daughter—
. . . Mrs. Campbell's funeral today—I'm not going. What's the use?
Your loving Mother.

Friendship, Me.<br>Aug. 23, 1918

Dear Daughter,
. . . This is a lovely place. A comfortable little farm house with an "ell" built on, with five bedrooms more. . . . Cousin Charles [Stowe] has a sailboat and a row boat. He takes us out more or less every day, which is excellent for the hayfever. . . .

The house sits high on a green slope, a point running out into the bay. Blue water, long points, and wooded islands lie before us. Still, clean, and lovely everywhere. . . .

I'm so glad you are well, dear child, and happy. It is a heavenly thing—to love that little Life inside, and to feel it coming, coming, coming, to be a Real Person—your very own.[8] I am so glad for you, Dearest Girl.

Your loving Mother.

Mon April 6th. [1919?]

Well, darling daughter,
. . . We had done very little in the garden—March was cold. . . . [B]y the 24th we got in one row of peas.

This I did, digging and all, (very slowly, & resting in between—took me two days) for dear H. was down with the grip. I began to have a sore throat myself. . . . Wed. night I began to cough, awfully, tearing, continuous, no sleep whatever, and this morning I looked so grey and awful that H. was scared. But I knew the grip took you all sorts of ways and it didn't worry me. "Dr. Diet, Dr. Quiet, & Dr. Merryman."[9] So I loafed around down stairs, dressed on in [*sic*] my nice pink wrapper, and rejoiced in the lovely music. I was coughing and spitting all the time more or less, and the nights were really dreadful. I had a low fever at night—I could tell because I was mildly delirious. . . . No sleep—constant tearing cough. Didn't hurt any. No pain of any kind. And I wasn't worried. . . . Monday, H. came home early, it was a warm bright day. . . . Then he had to leave for New York Wed. night, and I was still so weak we concluded to have the doctor. . . . Thur. a.m. the doctor appears. And <u>what</u> do you think your aged parent had been playing with?—Pneumonia!!! Yessir! The crisis had passed & I was on the road to recovery; but there was a consolidation in the lower left lung & no heart complication as yet. It appears that the pneumonia deathrate is next to tuberculosis; and that after 65 it is over 80%! Further that the way the old folks pass out is from the strain on the heart. And here's your pigheaded old mother, (deceived by the grip) just having pneumonia without knowing it. And getting past the danger at that! . . .

So I'm not ashamed at all, and bragging as usual. . . . I just sit there in that huge bed and eat—and read—& play solitaire—& do crossword puzzles—and look out of four windows . . . And it's the heavenly time of year—grass getting green, treetops all dim & misty with lovely colors—"March peepers" making Spring music. . . .

All I have to do now is to bask and be lazy and get strength for my garden! & <u>don't</u> you think its a joke—having the pneumonia without knowing it?

Your loving Mother.

627 W. 136. [New York City]<br>Feb. 23, 1920

Dear Child—

. . . Here is $150. for March and $250. for April. Don't cash that please before the middle of March or later. I shall be off on that trip from March 1st to near the end of the month, but will send you the rest for April by the first week or so—this will start you. I'm a bit depleted just now by my income tax—think of me paying an income tax! But this is all right, and there'll be more. . . . I'm writing at night, which I seldom do, and am a bit "woozy," but I wanted to send these off before it was any later. Am planning to start early tomorrow and look at some embroidered jersey dresses advertised by Oppenheim & Collins in Brooklyn for $14.00. If they are any good I'll have one; always wanted one.

We had the Blacks to dinner last Thursday and went to the movies—Charles Ray in "Red Hot Dollars." Houghton & I "blew ourselves" last week—going to see Lionel Barrymore in "The Copperhead," at the Rialto.[10] That was magnificent acting. We both cried! . . .

I hope you are still doing well, dear. I think I have a nice letter of yours, here in this heap somewhere, but cannot look for it now.

Your loving mother

Thurs. March 24, 1920.
Home Again!

Dearest Daughter,

I reached the house about 11 this morning. It does feel good to be at home once more. Everything is so clean and quiet and sunny! I have been looking over the letters and find that astonishing check from Providence![11] Isn't that splendid for you! I'm so delighted! I mean to hand mine right over to Houghton—I still owe him that much, on the Forerunner, and he is running very low this year. It quite takes you off my mind, for a while, too. Now if I can only get my brother self-supporting—then I'll begin to have a bank account!!! . . .

I'm delighted to hear that you have such a good nurse engaged.[12] Keep her <u>four weeks</u>—of course. Do have some sense, its not too late to develop it. The <u>Most Important Thing</u> is for you to get strong. There's money enough. You see I'll have a little ahead now, and you can draw on me ahead when you need to. I judge you won't need another check from me at present—how about it? . . .

Your loving Mother.

Mon. June 14, 1920

Dear Katharine—

. . . Our new landlord, J. Schlinger—German Jew—atrocious combination[,] has raised us the limit—25%. He had it a little more but Ho. called him down.

Guess we'll stay—we couldn't do better anywhere else, except in heat.

Your loving mother.

627 W. 136
6-26-'20

Dear Katharine . . .

I didn't tell Grace of that last $500. Thought perhaps you might like
to have a bit of money all to yourself! But that's $2500.00 this year—
and ought to make a big difference to you. My heart smites me to have
stopped sending to Thomas, but summer is the best time, and he ought
to be able to do <u>something</u>. . . . I have cleared off a special debt I had, of
500—that I never told Houghton about—it was an "extra" for Thomas
when he was in a bad hole once; and paid Ho. all I owed him for Forerunner money—$1500.00. That, with a $244. dentists bill, has not left
me rich—but at least I'm out of debt. There was a hundred I'd owed
<u>since 1891</u>—I wrote to find that kind creditors address—and she was
dead. Wasn't that too bad! But I sent it to the niece who had nursed her,
and she was mighty glad of it. . . .

I've had a letter from a Japanese admirer who wants to subscribe for
[*sic*] the <u>Forerunner</u>! He's read W. & E. [<u>Women and Economics</u>] in
Japanese, and The Man Made World in English. I'm sending him two
sets of F. [<u>Forerunner</u>] & am going to ask him to send me a copy of
W. & E. to put with my collection.

Your loving Mother.

July 10th. 1920.

Dearest Daughter:

It is so good to hear of all your happiness.

To have the husband of your choice, two perfect children—both
kinds, <u>and</u> a house in Pasadena—seems to me pretty near heaven. See
to it that your health builds up & that's the main thing now.

Also of course the work, for both of you. . . .

How I want to see my grandson! To say nothing of my grand-
daughter. I hope we shall get there before they grow up! . . .

Your loving Mother.

627 W. 136.<br>July 12—1920

Dearest Daughter—

. . . I told you how glad I was of your birthday letter—it was <u>so</u> pleasant to get it. . . .

I'm sorry, but I do not remember any details about your early baby-hood, as to ey[e]brows etc; only that you were very lovely and very good. Also most astonishingly intelligent—a wise cheerful quiet baby. . . .

I made another little call on Dr. Dunning-Barringer[13] lately. . . . As an experiment in bettering my general health and mental power she prescribed thyroid tablets—made from sheep's thyroid gland. She says some people lack a little of this or a little of that in their systems. It is doing wonders. No perceptible result as a stimulant, but a steady rising average of mental power. I am delighted I am able to work more and better than for long. It seems a simple dose, and is, thank goodness, cheap, 30 cents for a little bottle of 100!. . .

Love to you all,<br>Mother.

Mon. Aug. 9th. 1920.

Dearest Daughter:

. . . This year I remembered Houghtons birthday and am immensely proud of it. I got him a new brief-case, a splendid one, strong and hand-some.

Your loving Mother.

627 W. 136. New York.<br>Mch. 6th 1921.

Dearest Daughter;

Yours of the 26.th reached me Friday P.M. about 3—that was when I saw it, poked through the crack. I looked at the clock, phoned the bank to make sure they were open until 4—and then scooted down there & deposited $200. to your account. . . .

Did I tell you that I must haul in my horns a little as to the $1500.? The income tax & dentist will make a big hole in the five. But there'll be about $1000 you can draw on—800 now. You are more than welcome, precious child. <u>Don't try to save on labor!</u> It is more important that you should have competent help than almost anything. Of course you'll be doing better soon—these have been terrible years, as you say, for artists. Also for professionals. "Labor" and "the rich" have profitted. . . .

O me! O my! How I do long for a Real House, in California—with everything fixed the way I want it! . . .

Tonight we are going to hear Sir Phillip Gibbs[14] (unless the audience prevents it!) on "The Irish Situation." Last time he tried it the Paddies howled him down—or tried to. Contemptible people. We are rather looking forward to a fracas! . . .

Mother.

627 W. 136th st.

New York City.

March 21st. 1921.

Dearest Daughter,

. . . I am so homesick for those babies! . . . I am so glad for you, dear—to have all this joy and triumph. These are the <u>real</u> things, money matters can be managed somehow. You don't have to pay back any of this "mother money," you know. It is the lovingest of free gifts. And who knows? I may come down on you in my old age, and "board it out." . . .

Your loving Mother.

627 W. 136.

New York

April 28th 1921.

Yes, my Dearest—

I [will] skip down town this afternoon and send you another hundred, glad to. Of <u>course</u> it takes you people some time to get started in a new place. I think Frank is doing wonderfully well to become so "well and favorably" known so soon. Everybody likes him, I hear on all sides. I'm proud of you both, and only too glad to be useful. There has been so much, so very much, that I I [*sic*] failed in giving you, dear child. It is a joy to my heart to be of some use now. And I beg you not to feel it as a debt—it is not even a gift—it is mother-due, long over due! So there. (and Grace was in a [financial] hole—temporarily—don't mention it!)

Poor Thomas had to ask another driblet—he's had an awful year. . . . But you can be sure of $<u>400</u>. more, anyhow, when needed. And I'm feeling quite gay and hopeful over my prospects. The Century only paid $125.00 for a 3000 wd. article—paltry, but I'm glad to be there.[15] . . .

Mrs. M. [Mumford] had taken me to see two of her pictures . . . & I sat dumb—thought they were horrid. I showed her my flowers—and she magnanimously raved over them. Then she pounced on that little thing I did of the asylum wall & afterglow—do you remember? This she lavished such wild encomiums upon that I gave it to her—it seemed the least I could do. She declares I'm a great artist!!!!! Well! Well! . . .

627 W. 136. New York
Mon. May 9, 1921

Dear Daughter,

The money $200 was deposited Saturday, as I wired. That leaves me $343. & the dentist yet to pay! Looks as if there wasn't but $100. more for you to be sure of, <u>perhaps</u> 200—when I earn some more. Met Hamilton Holt[16] of the <u>Independent</u> the other night, and he was cordial, wanted more stuff. So I guess I can wring 200 out of him during the summer. And probably more from the Century later.

What are you going to do if I give out, dear child? There's not more than 2 or 300 more from Prov[idence]. And that wholly uncertain as to date. I hate to go back on you, my dear child, but it looks as if I'd be of small use for a while. Are you strong enough now to care for your two chicks alone? . . .

I am getting quite friendly with Leonora Speyer, the poet.[17] As her father was a Prussian and her husband a Jew (Baron Speyer)—it seems a bit odd for me. But her mother was, is, a New England woman; she also writes I think. The Lady Speyer is a beautiful woman. She has a married daughter of 25—by a previous husband, and three children by this one—but she looks about 35. They live at 22 Washington Sq. N.—a fine old house, gorgeously furnished with the fruits of travel, taste, and money—he's very rich I understand. . . .

Yours with love always—

Mother.

Mon. June 13th. 1921.
627 W. 136. New York.

Well, Daughter——!

. . . I forgot our anniversary as I always do, and when Houghton was giving me some extra kisses I said—"This isn't a birthday!" What a woman! We celebrated yesterday by taking a lovely walk and finishing up at the movies. Mary Pickford in <u>Through the Back Door</u>. Not very good. Her face—and hair—are now too old to play a ten-year-old child.[18]

Last Sunday the Bruère's[19] asked us to "weekend" with them, at

Sneeden's Landing, where they have rented a house this summer. . . .
Love to all of you—

Mother.

627 W. 136.
New York
July 28th. '21

Dear Daughter,
. . . Mr. Frank and Mr. Aley,[20] of The Century, asked me to lunch at
the Nat'l Arts Club, and discussed further work. Mr. F. has taken <u>all</u> the
<u>Forerunners</u> to look over, and Human Work. It really seems as if I had
a good prospect before me. If he is sufficiently impressed perhaps he'll
bring out all the books—the Century C., that is. . . .

Much love to all my family from
Mother

627 W. 136.
New York.
August 5th. '21

Bless your hearts!—
. . . I've accepted a most cordial invitation for a two week's visit with
Inez Haynes Irwin, Scituate, Mass. and Houghton the same from
Chester Lane—on their little island in Penobscot Bay—Maine.[21] Then
he joins me in Scituate—(it is between Boston & Plymouth) and we
board another fortnight. I'm trying to persuade Grace to go there too.
She is in great need of a rest. This has been a very hot summer, but I
have stood it pretty well. Am a bit "low" now—absent minded and forgetful. . . . Perhaps I can manage somehow to get to you this winter. . . .

Lots of love,
Mother.

Scituate, Mass.
Aug. 18, 1921

Well, Daughter—
You are neglected. I got rather run down the last week or two. Four
days of shopping—I only had mornings you see, used me up a good
deal. Guess it was time I had a vacation. . . . The Browns say there is
a little more of that money coming,—perhaps twice more. I'm glad to

hear it. Just think, Robert, leaving half a million, left his sisters only two thousand each—I think it was that. . . .

I go over and spend the mornings with Grace. We're already starting on a play—to her great delight. We go down to the beach and she bathes. The water is very cold. I don't seem to want to bother with it.

But I'm eating and sleeping and resting, and enjoying it all very much. . . .

Your loving mother.

627 W. 136.<br>New York<br>Sept. 8th, 1921

Dearest Daughter,

We are at home again, and Harold[22] has phoned that he expects Grace tomorrow. . . . I am delighted at the effect of the three week bathing etc. on Grace—she looks a lot better. The work went well, and she had a big additional idea on next to the last day—she was immensely pleased, and she certainly needed a rest & change. . . .

Dear Child—<u>don't</u> fatigue yourself writing me letters—just send a post card once a week. <u>I</u> know, none better, how impossible letters are!! You two certainly are crowded just at present. . . .

Love to you all, you dear Family!<br>Mother.

(You should see how black I am—burned to an African complexion.)

Sat. Oct. 15, 1921.

My dear Daughter,

. . . I went to the Life Extension Institute again, and they report improvement since last time. My nice examiner—Dr. Dunning—says mine are the best feet she ever saw—(meaning for my age of course) and that she has examined 16000 cases! (I wrote you that Houghton is well and as nice as always, bless him!)

Grace you've heard from. If this play succeeds I shall feel it a life saver to her. I've never known her so near breaking as these last two years. . . . And even if she does most of the work on the play, I still feel as if it was mine, because of fairly making her do it—as it were. And it comes on well, I think. . . .

Mr. Aley tells me that Mr. Frank was "much impressed" by looking over the Forerunners, and that they are going to "feature" me next year. First time I've ever been "featured"! The thing on "Dressing to Please Men" I did with Mr. Black comes out in Jan. and they've just sent me a check for $150. for it. For the first one—3,000 wds. They only gave $125.00 and this was a bare 2000, so evidently my stock is rising. Goody! Now if they'll only bring out the books!!!! . . .

Your loving Mother.

627 W. 136. New York<br>Jan. 16, 1922.

Dear Katharine,

<u>Did</u> I answer that telegram or not? I cant be sure, so I'm writing again to say that I will not speak for these women's clubs—no matter how enthusiastic, for less than my regular rate of $100.00. Why should I? I've just turned [down] the Chicago Woman's Club, who wanted me at $75. Forums, and educational or religious affairs I'm willing to do for 75. or even 50. But generally speaking it's a flat $100.00.

I thought you knew that long since. . . . Don't <u>worry</u> about lectures dear child—I have enough now to more than half cover the trip, and some more prospects—<u>en route</u>.

Love to you and the darlings,<br>Mother.

Sun. 3-19-'22<br>c/o Mrs. Mary H. Page<br>1604 Chapin Ave.<br>Burlingame, Cal.

Dear Katharine—

. . . Had a <u>lovely</u> trip up from S. B. [Santa Barbara]——Oh this country!——I do so glory in it. . . . Broke a piece of the inside off a "bicuspid" on the way here, <u>tied it on</u>—it hadn't dropped, but waggled and pucked[?] the gum—with dental floss. Went to my old dentist in S. F. Dr. Leander Van Orden, and he built on more amalgam in place of the bit of shell so the tooth is really better than before. Only $6.00.

Dear child—you made me very happy; made me feel really welcome. I think we shall have good times living near together; and I shall never be contented not to see those darling children growing up. . . . I miss those blessed darlings—want 'em! So I'll work to get to Pasadena or thereabouts, as fast as I can.

Your loving Mother.

627 W. 136. New York
Mon. March 27, 1922

Well, Darling Daughter:

Here I am safe at home, sitting in my snug parlor, drying my hair. . . .

I had a very nice easy journey, and feel all right, but notice by the vagaries of handwriting that I'm not "focusing" very sharply. I wrote Houghton & wired, but, by our usual hoodoo he didn't get the wire, wasn't sure of the hour from the letter—and had gone to Glen Ridge, N. J. to spend the night with the Chester Lanes! So, arriving at 125th st. at 7.45—and being but just dressed—had to pop out with no toilet whatever—(you know I descend from my berth with my hat on!) I found no husband awaiting. I brushed my teeth etc. in the station— very empty and clean that early Sunday morning; and phoned him, first—to no purpose. Undisturbed I rode calmly to 136, marched down the hill with . . . the two grips, taking my time & resting occasionally, and then found that my key wouldn't open the house door! So I went down in the basement, & the worthy Mr. Hartman carried the bags up stairs for me and let me in. I proceeded to unpack and put things in order, and Houghton arrived about noon. There was a table full of stuff to look over and we had a lovely time. . . .

Your loving Mother

627 W. 136. New York
Tues. April 3rd. 1922

Dearest Daughter,

Houghton's father died last Thursday. As you know it was what they used to call "a blessed release" for him, and I know Aunt Louise is unselfishly glad that she survived him. Over his bed he had long kept Durer's "Death Cometh as a Friend"—it is Durer, isn't it?[23] And as they all believe he will be with his reassembled family—of all ages—and as she [Aunt Louise], poor dear, doubtless hopes soon to join him, there is no cause for grief. He left no money, and precious little in the way of "effects," but Houghton is the richer by two heavy overcoats, which can be cut down somewhat for him, and several pairs of old shoes.

Ho. & Francis went over the stuff & I made the inventory. Ho. went down Wed. with Emily, Francis had gone to the home with them & stayed; they had great difficulty in getting the poor old man off the train . . . and at last up stairs and to bed. He spoke to the dog—spoke to the doctor Wed a.m. I believe—& did not regain consciousness. I went down Sat. to the funeral; 10 a.m. train was to take [me to] a 1.15 train from New London, we were late & missed [it]—other relatives took an auto, but I missed them too—got a car, which was late also—and arrived as they were coming out of the church! I was very sorry indeed to have it happen so, but it couldn't be helped, and of course was no real harm to any one.

Aunt Louise spoke very cordially of your coming down to the train with the children and the fine fudge! That was just like you—you are always so thoughtful of others. I wish I was. I mean kindly, and am more than willing, but things don't occur to me. . . .

That large and glittering prospect I spoke of has vanished quite— Mr. Aley's friend is no longer on that magazine. Also he is not at all sure about the books.[24] However—I am full of plans and shall accomplish something. . . .

Love to all of you—& specially to my babies!
Mother

380 Washington st.
Norwich Town Conn.
Wed. June 1st. '22

Dear Katharine:
. . . We came here last Friday afternoon for the Week-End. . . . Good for Houghton (not so good for me!)

Still I am enjoying this visit more than I ever did before. Aunt Louise is rather fond of me; and, she being at present in bed, we younger ones have the dining room to ourselves, and I get "what I want when I want it." . . . Aunt Louise is still weak from the shingles, naturally tired from the journey and the sorrow and strain of Uncle William's death and funeral, etc. . . .

Ho and I feel that we must lay hold of young friends, as far as may be, for the old ones "die on us"—so fast. Until we do ourselves. . . .

Home. June 2nd.

Well dear, here I am at my desk again. . . . That was the pleasantest visit I ever had there, because I was useful, & was liked. . . .

Now if I can just get to work and earn something!

Your loving Mother.

627 W. 136.
July 5th. 1922.
New York.

Dear Katharine,

Here I am at my desk, having my moving picture taken! You see the "Twelve Greatest Women" discussion has reached such dimensions that they are giving pictures of 'em in the Pathe News.[25] . . .

It is all very amusing. The <u>Tribune</u> was the best, said we had not twelve great men in the country, nor women, but "There are, if a guess may be hazarded, four American women now living, who, with all allowance for the enlargement due to close perspective, have claims to the name of "Great"; and they gave Jane Addams, Edith Wharton, M. Carey Thomas, and C. P. G.—"whose books prepared the way for a new era in women's economic life—these are persons 'born for the universe' who have fulfilled their callings.["] The Herald you saw. Mrs. Vanderlip put me in fourth of twelve, and one "Sara M'Pike"— who wanted Maud Nathan & Florence put in to take the place of any Mrs. Catt named—"with the possible exception of Mrs. Gilman. Mrs. Gilman is a woman of genius and should be included with the artists who are great by the Grace of God. Nevertheless, Mrs. Gilman's gifts have been expended so generously on behalf of the emancipation of women that Mrs. Catt naturally places her on the list of great women!——["]

So I'm feeling quite cocky! . . .

I'm 115 [lbs.], and am feeling particularly well just now. . . .

We had a very pleasant visit with Aunt Louise. Elizabeth G. [Gilman] from Baltimore is there for July, bringing with her a friends car, & chauffer—a nice colored man, quite black, but having clean cut delicately modeled lips—must be some special tribe. He is boarded down town somewhere with others of his race. . . .

You will be amused to here [*sic*] that [Aunt Louise] was pleased with my rendering of one of those "negro spirituals"—we have four records thereof—fancy me winning approval as a vocalist!!! So we borrowed a phonograph from a friend who was just leaving home, and as soon as we got back we sent down the records—& a lot more, and she can have some music. . . .

My birthday was announced in the local paper—boiler plate stuff— "Notables of the day" or some like. . . .

We took a long motor ride—on Lizzie, & found a cherry tree—with a girl picking. The folks said we could have some—& I went up the ladder and helped myself! Gorgeous! I haven't done that in fifty years I guess! . . .

> Love to you dearest girl—and all the rest of you, from Mother.

> 627 W. 136.
> New York
> July 18, 1922

Dear Daughter,

. . . No, I didn't read about the 133 yr. old man. Should want to see his birth certificate!!! And a 7 year old son—at that age! Alas and alas but I suspect the ladies morals! . . .

I'm particularly pleased that you are able to keep the housework behind you—to have the kitchen more orderly, because I know it was a constant strain on Frank. He was wonderfully good about it, but that kind of visual chaos _is_ trying. What I minded most was my inability to help. I had hoped that I could <u>at least</u> wash dishes for you, but I confess that when I went in there I was floored—couldn't seem to get a foothold—just backed out in despair. I know perfectly well, dear, how hard it all was for you, and greatly admire the cheerful patience with which you did the most necessary things, regularly and well, and wisely ignored the rest. But now that you are able to do better it will be far easier for all of you. . . .

I continue to long to buy all the pretty things I see in the windows, for them [my grandchildren], but refrain. I'm getting sordid, positively sordid. Avarice is the vice of old age, and I'm succumbing to it. Ho. & I are planning as to how soon we can save enough to come to California & live.

How much, or rather how little, should you think we could live on, just renting a little house—with a garden & a few chicks perhaps? Give us an estimate. (This is in case I realize none of my golden dreams of building the fine big house!)

I am about to lose my biographer!

Poor little Amy Wellington, all alone in her tiny apartment on Sun. July 9th, was taken with one of those terrible "attacks" of hers.[26] . . .

Sat. eve. she lost all patience with Dr. Shelby—got in another doctor—they wrapped the child in a blanket and trundled her off to the Presbyterian hospital and operated—giving no real hope at that. . . .

There was a fibroid tumorous growth on one of the ovaries and some gut had hooked around loops of the intestine and strangled it as it were. This having gone on for about a week it was pretty awful—he said the worst operation he had ever seen! She survived it—which astonished them, and is still lingering. They said she might hold out perhaps four days—this is the third. . . .

It's a case where surgery was needed, and might have been perfectly efficacious—in time. Poor little girl! She leaves no one dependent on her, and her mother is such a—horrid old person that I don't mind her missing her—hope she will! She was Amy's heaviest burden, for years—just meanness, not illness. . . .

Love to all of you dear ones from Mother.

627 W. 136. New York
July 27, 1922.

Dear Daughter,

Just a word to keep you posted. Amy Wellington is still living and says she means to get well. Aunt Louise is still living—a matter of days, they say. . . .

I have hopes for Amy. Aunt Louise couldn't have lived long anyhow, but still———. Its hard on Houghton, dear boy—she's the last. . . .

Your loving Mother.

627 W. 136. New York
Aug 5. 1922.

Dear Katharine,

Thank you so much for that lovely picture of the darlings. O dear! I want 'em so!—However, they are there, at least and I'll see them again inside of 6 or 7 months! No word for some time as to your health, dear child—and weight. I do hope you are gaining a little—or a lot. I am pretty well, but somewhat distracted among invalids. Aunt Louise lin-

gers indefinitely, may, for weeks. We are not going down this week-
end. You see it costs us $20. a trip! I am hoping, since it must come,
that it be before we are confronted with another year's lease; for lo!—
(This is a Great Secret; trusted to your well known reserve!) We are seriously thinking of going there to live!!! You see Houghton inherits the
place—and it is an elephant—far from white—on our hands. It is not
an outright ownership either, but followed by Francis, and then by a
mixture, we do not feel sure of till we see the will. . . .

This plan of ours wholly depends on Francis & Emily living with us
and her managing the house; which they seem well inclined to do. . . .

There are many advantages in the plan. I should escape, forever, this
hideous city—and its Jews. The nerve-wearing noise—the dirt—the
ugliness, the steaming masses in the subway—and have the loveliness
of New England at its best to live in.

There is a house full of books and a good library, clean & quiet—(I
hate 'em here, on account of the people.) I can be outdoors, work in
the garden, have a cat!!!—plant hone[y]suckle, play croquet and maybe
badminton—walk for miles around. Then, as Francis proudly says—
we'll have a Ford—and go to California! You see if Ho. gets used to "retiring" there, it won't come so hard to do it out our way!

I think it will be a joy to him, to feel that he is living in his own house,
his boyhood's home. . . . I shall miss nothing here but the shops and the
movies—and there are two or three movie houses in Norwich—only
not so convenient. . . .

New York has never been of any advantage to me that I know of, and
has been a large and serious injury to my health and character. . . .

Oliver Herford, no[w] asst. editor of "Life" is getting out a book of
poems therein published, and asked me if I had any beside "The Conservative" and, if not, if I could give them some, quickly, so that he
could run them in! I did. . . .

Your loving Mother.

380 Washington st.<br>
Norwich Town. Conn.<br>
Aug. 9th. 1922

Well Dear Daughter,
    . . . Aunt Louise died last Monday, the 7th.[27] We arrived Tues. Fu-
neral Wed.—& [her] will read to group of nephews & nieces, deco-
rous but eager. . . . [H]er estate (we don't know how much it is exactly

but its over 100,000) she gave devised and bequeathed outright to her three executors—"<u>to distribute as they saw fit</u>." These three executors are that old lady who was out there with them, Caroline, who has the house up the hill opposite—, and who has no fortune, and—Houghton & Francis!!! Now you can see the confusion we are in. Francis & Emily would like nothing better than to grab a third outright. . . .

Some [friends and relatives] want F. & H. to go there and live—as I think I wrote you we might do. I'd like it for a few years well enough, coming to see you every year. If our share as ultimately decided is enough to live on we may come out next year to stay. . . . But you may feel cheerfully certain that by this & by that we shall total enough to have a large easy feeling for the rest of our lives! He got 6,000 when his father died you see.

Meanwhile you will be glad to hear that I had a talk with both my Century editors lately; they've taken the Santa Claus article for Dec.[28] . . . and have ordered two for next year. Also Mr. Frank—indeed both of them—is much interested in the next book which <u>I</u> think will be best to write; not on Feminist stuff, but on religion—with a Feminist side to it. . . .

Your very uncertain but cheerful
Mother.

Sept. 4th. 1922.
380 Washington st.
Norwich Town. Conn.

Well, Daughter,

The die is cast, we four are going to live here, for a while anyway. . . .

We have the big bedroom over the library—some 15 x 20 or more; and a small room, for Ho., besides. We're going to have croquet, tetherball, ring toss, get a lot of outdoor exercise; and, next summer, the garden. Meanwhile Ho. is going to have a room in N.Y., room & bath if possible, for this coming year; so as to wind up his business. . . .

Love to all of you, from
Mother.

627 W. 136. N.Y.
9-7-22

Dear Daughter,

. . . Your ideas as to Houghton's inheritance soar too high. He is one of 3 executors, I said—that does not mean one of 3 heirs! There are <u>8</u> legal heirs if they break the will, and they are trying to. . . . [A]t any rate, there will be something. Meanwhile we'll have a year in the old house, all together; . . . what I meant by its costing more in Norwich is the expensive old house—coal & light very high, must have two servants—(three heretofore) and food expensive, much higher than here. . . .

Love to you all from Mother.

380 Washington St.<br>Norwich Town Conn.<br>9-24-'22

Dear Daughter,

A very tired old mother is sitting in a rather small sized and very comfortable Morris chair[29] in the east window of her new bed chamber. It is so big, that "library bedroom," that my huge desk makes no impression on it. . . .

My last weeks in New York were a sort of nightmare—the endless sorting and packing, and every afternoon going to see poor little Amy Wellington. She is out of danger now, gaining strength, will probably do better than ever before. She had a big ovarian tumor, poor thing. . . .

There is a family row over the will, as I think I said, going to be litigation, and much hard feeling. At the worst however, Ho. & F. [Francis] will get the respective 7ths—or 8ths—to which they would have been entitled if there had been no will. Not very much, but at least we'll be that much better off than before. . . .

I think the burst of heavy work will be a useful "shakeup"—and that I shall presently settle into peace and quiet here and get to work on my new book.[30] If that goes well it will be a new life to me—a fresh beginning.

There dear—O, I forgot what I meant most to tell you. I never before so deeply appreciated your lovely pictures! Their soft rich colors light up the room. . . . Emily begs for some in her room—& shall have a few. . . . I have eleven of them! and am thankful my dear daughter is a painter. . . .

Love to you, dear child. Mother.

Oct. 2nd. 1922.

Dear Daughter,

. . . Yes, I was pretty well exhausted, but am picking up fast; taking "Eskay's Neurophosphates" (with meals), and "Nujol" night & morning.[31] The Nujol is one of these petroleum products, the other an agreeable tonic, so I prosper finely. . . .

It was a barren summer for me, as far as work went. Just now came the Century check for the Dec. article, and next day a letter from Maggie—two months shy on rent and would lose the place if they didn't pay.[32] It was only $30.—so I sent fifty. I don't know what they will do this winter. . . .

Your loving Mother—

380 Washington St.<br>Norwich Town Conn.<br>Oct. 26, 1922

Dear Katharine,

. . . My health and spirits seem well on the upgrade. I have written one small article and one really big one—"His Religion and Hers"—an important chapter in the coming book. I think it will make a real stir, and facilitate the chance of publication.

If the power to work comes back as it seems to be, I shall soon be earning heaps!! . . .

Think of me as better and more hopeful, & far happier, than I've been in many years.

Your loving Mother.

380 Washington st.<br>Norwich Town Conn.<br>11-7—22

Dear Daughter,

. . . I sympathize very deeply with your own difficulties, my dearest girl—but I know you are willing to give up much for husband home & children—very wisely. Your time will come later. . . .

I laughed out loud at your "wripen"-ing figs. Ripe has no w, dear child. . . .

I keep well, and am working merrily on my book. . . .

Love to you both and all four,<br>from Mother.

Sat. Dec. 16. 1922

Yes, Daughter dear—

. . . I'm sending you a little extra for Xmas, not for lumber![33] The Century is to pay me more for these two articles than for earlier ones, so

I'm feeling quite easy. And Santa Barbara is to have a [Gilman] week—and that makes the trip all right. So just you buy those babies something from Grandma! . . .

Wishing you all a very merry Xmas!!!

Your loving Mother

1-17-'23

Dear Katharine:

Here is a definite proposition. I am going to borrow a thousand dollars from Houghton—I can pay him 5% on it as well as that bank can!

I'm going to rent a place in or close to Pasadena, while I'm with you, & furnish as necessary—maybe we can get one that is furnished. . . . Then I'll bring down my Idaho family—& see them started. The proposition is to have a room for Harold [Channing]—or let him have a tent house or something if he prefers—and what his sisters can pay for him—or he can earn perhaps—a nominal sum such as $6.00 a week—will help pay the grocer etc.

The garden should furnish almost all the fruit & vegetables.

There are to be hens—such as your neighbors do so well with; and they ought to give 'em eggs, meat, & enough profit to cover other meat & milk also, I should think.

Then I'll have rent, fuel & light—& water. . . .

All this will appear to be done in the name of Mr. T. A. Perkins of Hailey Idaho—he'll pay the landlord etc.

In Thomase's [*sic*] recent letter he, for the first time, speaks of a willingness to go there. My! <u>What</u> a load it will be off my mind! With the garden and the hills they won't starve! They won't have to spend so much on fuel, or heavy clothes. Good schools etc. for Thomas Jr. And Maggie could make an honest living off a boarder or two. . . .

Love to you all, dear daughter—
Mother.

C. P. Gilman c/o Mr. J. K. Hamilton
2317 Scottwood Ave.
Toledo, O.
Feb. 6. 1923.

Dear Daughter,

. . . I'm having a much needed rest, here in this quiet home. . . . Am still rather feeble & thick headed, I guess it was a touch of flu I had. But its wearing off. . . .

Did I write you how well things are going, with my work? The Century paid me $250, each for those March & April articles, and they are going to take the book [His Religion and Hers].[34] Comes out next Oct. . . . And . . . Alexander Black is going to write an article about me—in the Century! That will help enormously. After the book comes out I'll have all the lectures I want[,] you may be sure. . . .

Love to you dear—see you soon.<br>Mother.

Fri. March 2nd. '23<br>1616 Grand Ave.<br>Sta. Barbara Cal.

Dearest Daughter;

I arrive in Los Angeles about 6 P.M. Sunday, and shall probably come out on the same car and then ride up Colorado, as I went down. So I'll come toddling along Catalina about 6.45–7. I judge. Mebbe sooner.

The lectures are going successfully. Who you do think turned up at the first one—Maria Pease—who was my nurse when you were born.

Everybody is very nice to me. . . .

Your loving Mother.

3-22-23

Dear Daughter;

My last personal touch in P. [Pasadena] was Harold on the porch waving to the train—it did seem friendly![35] . . .

The lower berth, under me, was taken by two negroes, grandmother & g-son—about 10 I guess. I got transferred to upper 8—one old lady under. She is a Prussian! All well & happy—supper excellent. Got a glass of milk at San B [Santa Barbara]. Love to all my dear family—Mother.

Tues. Mch. 27. 1923. . . .

My own dear Daughter—

. . . So far all has gone well. Thanks to Veronal[36] I've stood the five nights on a sleeper pretty well. Last night a luxurious clean bed—af[t]er a good hot bath—lovely. . . .

It was a great pleasure to be with you dear. And those lovely darlings!

If only I hadn't had so much care and work—I would have been out in the yard with them—would have got closer. . . .

Also as I said before I'm getting fond of Frank. There is something very—appealing, about him, something tender and good. And I admire the strong courage with which he does his work. . . .

. . . I am certain that as soon as Frank feels properly placed—with the <u>strain</u> off him, that he will do big work, clear off debts, and become a power in the art life of the Coast—of the country.

He's <u>young enough</u>! Just remind him of the splendid things artists have done when they were really old! . . .

Love and love to you, dearest child—
Mother.

Sun. Mch. 31st. '23.
At Home—!

Dear Daughter,

. . . They kindly changed my berth to one over a single lady—white—and on the shady side.

To have sat in the sun, opposite those coons and their baggage—& their lunch—the boy squirming about and making all manner of noises—would have used me up pretty badly. . . .

Saw Dr. Dunning-Barringer, who says I appear entirely healed of a slight abrasion around the neck of the uterus she has been keeping an eye on for quite a number of years—(always a chance of those things developing into a morbid growth); then lunched with Grace and had a good talk, and then down town to shop a little. . . .

Your loving Mother.

380 Washington st.
Norwich Town Conn.
April 18. 1923

My dear Daughter—

. . . Poor Thomas, Maggie has been "carrying on" again—return of menstruation which she thought all over—hysteria and general horrors. Too bad! She certainly is a failure in all kinds of ways. I dare say she is kind of crazy—poor child.

As to Grace . . . she is far from strong. I want her to come here and have a rest—but she won't. . . .

Your loving Mother.

380 Washington st.
Norwich Town, Conn.
7-8-'23

Deaughter, (That set out to be Dear Daughter!)

. . . I chuckle over your "wippened." I suppose it was meant for <u>wrip-pened</u>; and that stood in your wonderful mind for "<u>ripened</u>"! You dear funny child! . . .

Our [inheritance] case is not yet decided. We probably shall not hear, now, until October! It is hard on all of 'em but me. . . .

I think we'll stay in Norwich in any case. Houghton would far rather live here than in Pasadena. He has been "approached," tentatively, by an old friend, a lawyer, here. Nothing may come of it, but I think he could manage to get enough to eke out what he'd have in any case. So we live on hopes, anyhow.

Johan Bojer,[37] the "de Maupassant of the North" has written me & sent me his novel "The Great Hunger." . . . A dismal story! Those Scandinavians are so gloomy!

Love to all of you from Mother.

7-21-'23

Dear Katharine,

Don't give Thomas <u>a cent</u>! Not a cent! He had $407. in March—& rent paid for 2 months. . . . Since then I've sent $220.—(just sent another 20 today—can't do more till Aug.) 627 dollars should have been <u>ample</u>. They had to lay out about 40. I believe on further furnishings, but if they're out of money its pure carelessness. Remember—don't give them <u>anything</u>. Let Maggie go to work again! I'm really angry—because I'm doing my best for 'em. . . . T. won't work (poor dear—I suppose he really can't, now!) and they don't seem to know how to live within their means. . . .

Your loving Mother.

380 Washington Street
Norwich Town, Conn.
Sept. 5th '23

Dear Daughter,

. . . Thomas writes that he can't keep Harold. Oct. 1st the latest. I wrote to Grace. I'm awfully sorry. It looked so pleasant, at first. Maggie is hopeless I fear—unreliable—Irish.

Well—I can't help it. I hope I can put the boy in a good boarding school later on; that will be the best thing for him. . . .

I see my way through the year, for Thomas I mean. They'll take a cheaper place next year, they think. . . .

Lots of love dear, from Mother.

Fri. 9-28-'23

Dear Daughter—

I have neglected you shamefully. . . . I've been busy with letters and mss.—have succeeded in doing one regular article & one little one. . . .

The book [His Religion and Hers] is out, I learn from Mr. [Lyman B.] Sturgiss, the head of the publishing dept [at Century Co.]. I am to have 6 copies, of which one will go to you, one to Thomas, one to Houghton, one to Emily, one to Mrs. Black; one for me! Here's hoping it "goes."

Thomas writes. . . . I can see how hideously difficult it was for him—having to do the cooking and all—Maggie is pretty nearly crazy I think. Poor old man! He certainly made an awful mistake in that marriage. . . .

Mother.

380 Washington Street<br>Norwich, Conn.<br>Oct. 6. '23

Hurrah!

Case decided—in our favor! Houghton was here, brought in the evening paper. Paragraph with big heading "Will of Norwich Woman." He read it, solemnly—"the executors to inherit free of any trust"—and, owing to his reputation [for jokes] we all thought he was lying! Thought he made it up as he went along! But he arose and kissed us all—bless his loving heart! . . .

. . . The old Judge is pleased, because it was the biggest case he'd had since he left the Bench; and all his confreres here had thought the other side would win.

We are all delighted on Houghton's account because he has established a new view of the law as to executors inheriting. . . . It really is a feather in Houghton's cap, and will add to his prestige when he begins to practice here. I think he will be happier if he does, though now he doesn't have to. So all I earn—over what Thomas needs—and you if you do need any—I can save for the Californian home!

Mr. Black has made me a splendid circular—I've only seen the proof—; J. B. Pond[38] has undertaken the "exclusive management"; engagements are dribbling in to me, in the meanwhile. . . .

Love to the Darlings—and their parents
from Mother.

Evanston Ill.
Nov. 15th. 1923

My dear Child—

Here's a check—today's lecture—which may help out for the moment. . . .

But as to asking Houghton for more—at this moment—I somehow can't. You see I borrowed a 1000 last winter, and he has advanced further since then—about 500. That's mostly on Thomas' acct. But royalties will be coming soon—a first "statement," amounting to about a hundred dollars has come in, this trip nets me 200. at least and there's a net 70.00 or so in Dec.—I <u>think</u> I can manage to send you another 100 before Xmas—and more later. . . .

Your loving Mother.

Hotel Radisson
Minneapolis, Minn.
about noon
Nov. 16, 1923.

Now dear Child,

. . . My lecture for the Drama League yesterday was a great success; they were delighted—most enthusiastic—want me again. The check for $100. I promptly endorsed and enclosed in a letter I had ready in my bag . . . and mailed. . . .

Those "operations" such as Delia has undergone used to be considered due to "diseases peculiar to women."[39] We now know that 98% or so—(well over 90) when performed on young married women are due to gonorrhea. You see that is [a] <u>very</u> common disease among men—about 75% even in America; it often seems to do them no harm—though sometimes resulting in sterility; but the germ remains in the blood, and when it has access to the larger field of the woman's interior it increases with fresh ardor and results in all manner of ovarian[,] fallopian, and uterine disorders.

It does not mean that all men are grossly wicked—but that very few are absolutely chaste before marriage, and one "misstep"—some college boys, drunken escapade or any momentary lapse, allows the nimble gonococcus to enter upon a fresh career! It is so universal that boys used to call an attack "getting burnt" and thought it—Heaven save the mark—a sign of manliness! . . .

Now here is your very tired and distressed letter of Nov. 10th. How I wish I could send you $1000.00 forthwith! But one now and one in Dec. will help some (and I think one in Jan. too!) Anyhow I feel that next year will be more prosperous for me. Pond will charge more for my lectures, and I guess get more of them than I did. Judging by yesterday's success I have not lost my ability as a speaker! . . .

Your loving Mother.

Dec. 28. '23

Dear Daughter,

. . . Last Saturday I went to Providence to Cousin Ray Phelon's funeral. It should have been a year ago! Senile dementia & cancer of the bowels—<u>awful</u>. It is wicked to let a good man die like that—the long horror obscuring all his goodness—everybody glad he's gone—pleasantest funeral I ever attended! . . .

Forgive brevity—you'll understand.
Your loving Mother.

2415 Pioneer Rd.<br>Evanston, Ill—<br>Feb. 9th. 1924.

Dear Daughter,

. . . I start for Salt Lake City tonight. . . . Expect to spend a few days with the Stowes, toward the end of my visit—say around March 8 to 12. . . .

As to health I'm all right, but not very "peppy." Expect to brace up when I reach you. . . .

Love to all<br>Mother.

5-6-24

Dear Daughter—

Are you dead or anything? Yours to Houghton—April 16—is the last I have heard—and then you were pretty tired. . . .

I did a little scratch article for <u>The Nation</u> for $25!—and am going to blow in that large sum on a trip to N. Y. to attend the Annual International Convention Representing The Writers of The World—!—a P.E.N. Club affair.[40] There's a big dinner at the Penn. Hotel, (I don't know if they chose it for the name or not)—a garden party at Garden City.—Doubleday Page & Co., a theatrical benefit—and so on. I thought I'd better go. . . .

I reached home astonishingly fresh—had no period of exhaustion, and am getting along very well. Ho. and I walked twelve miles a week ago Sunday—and I was neither tired nor stiff next day. . . .

Your loving Mother.

Dr. Shelby's office, 11.40 a.m.
Tues. May 13, '24.

Well Daughter Dear,

. . . Grace seems to me a shade better. I shall try not to tire her—and I think she really enjoys having me. It seems very quiet and lovely there, and the streets are clean after several days of rain. But it was <u>cold</u>! No heat on—and no sun—for four days—but this morning glorious.

I've trotted down here to see the doctor, mainly about the bow-wows[41]—see if something can't be done to set that difficulty straight. I <u>ought</u> to be perfectly well now, and do some more work, but that keeps me inwardly "pizened,"[42] injures sleep—and worries me. . . .

Last Fri. Ho. & I went to Providence. . . . Walter [Daboll] drove us out to Rehoboth, to revisit the scenes of my childhood.

But the house had long ago burned down—the succeeding house looked old, barn also, and only the stump left of the giant locust tree I used to climb. There remained a well, one side of the house & a pump on the other—which I remembered. And the pine grove, alas! only old stumps and scraggly second growth!

In the city I took Houghton to see the four houses I had lived in, and two of them were clean gone! Gives me a sense of extreme age; I hadn't noticed it while it was happening but when I say "55 years ago"—it seems quite a stretch. . . .

Your loving Mother.

5-31-'24

Dear Daughter,

. . . As to the genealogy you ask about—I shall have to make inquiries. I remember nothing save that Grandfather Westcott was a descendent of Stukely Westcott, who came with Roger Williams to settle R. I.[43] Being a Baptist was a daring thing in those days, and grandpa was a Unitarian—when that took courage too. It is through the Perkinses & Pitkins that we go back to all creation! See if your Library has "American Families of Royal Descent," you'll fine a lot of interesting matter there....

My various doctors found nothing particular the matter. . . . Dr. Dunning-Barringer says [I have] "a chronic toxemia (poisoning) from a delayed digestion" which is reasonable enough, and common enough. Guess I'll survive awhile yet. The trouble is it keeps me below par all the time, not able to do my best work. Which is bad for all of us....

Your loving Mother.

6-23-'24

Dearest Daughter,

Thank you for your nice letter of June 13th. [and] for the lovely pictures....

How those babies grow! The fiercest one, of Dorothy, looks a little like me I think. I love the group with my baby in it—very lovely of you, dear. I am so glad for you, that you very imprudently amassed this family; I was from the first. Economic issues don't matter compared with the real achievement, and your children will have to be fine!...

Our garden is dreadfully behind; partly weather and partly neglect. . . . Ho. & I are working hard, hoeing and pulling weeds, putting in second crops and so on; also he cuts grass industriously. I'm delighted for it will prepare him for our final settlement in California—with nothing to do but garden!...

My mother's father was Henry Westcott. (You'll find his bookplate in some of the old books.) His mother was a Greene—his first wife a Dana. My mother's mother was Clarissa Fitch Perkins—her mother was a Fitch; her father Edward Perkins. He was the son of Nathan (?) Perkins; and our cousin to my father's father, Thomas C. Perkins of Hartford; so Clarissa was second cousin to her son-in-law! (And you and I are cousins, too!) I can't remember any dates at all, but I was born in 1860 the third of three in three years—& so mother was probably married in 1857 or thereabouts. I will ask Cousin Mary Phelon, who is now visiting us, for some more data....

Mother.

July 10, 1924.

Dearest of Daughters,

. . . As to Thomas—my heart aches for him—but, what can I do more? I begin to think the thing to do is to get Maggie—shall we say better placed? . . . I think any psychiatrist would agree with my opinion of her case. . . .

I feel calm in my mind about the year's earnings. If things go as now apparently settled I see my way through to next February—and enough engaged on the trip to cover it! . . .

Here's Hoping!

Love to those blessed babies, and parents,

From Mother.

Aug. 1st. '24

Dear Daughter,

. . . Did I tell you that I have discontinued the Life Extension service? I can't bother to go to the city for it—and seem to be all right anyhow.

My gardening is doing wonders for me. You should see your aged parent, in her denim kneebreeches and green smock, hammering away with the hoe by the hour.—Does me heaps of good. . . .

Any how I love you—

C. P. Gilman

(Otherwise Mother.)

9-16-'24

Daughter Dear,

. . . Except for that engrossing garden I seem to have done practically nothing this summer. And I had expected to do so much! . . .

Our principal trouble is in the matter of servants. The attic accommodations are very poor, to my mind shamefully so; the kitchen large—lots of walking; the house pretty big to keep clean. And, in my judgement, Emily doesn't go at it in the right way. She takes up with makeshifts—instead of spending time and money to secure the right person. But then Norwich is a hard place for getting servants. At present we are cookless, but have a nice little Irish second maid who does very well. . . .

Your loving Mother.

10-18-24

Dearest of Daughters;

I have some bad news. . . . Your poor Uncle Thomas is in a bad way—and has to go to a hospital and have an operation! Trouble with the prostate gland—not uncommon at this age. Comes on to me, of course, to pay for; but I'm worrying over what'll happen if he dies; as is likely enough. Still, he stood that rupture operation finely, and perhaps he will this one. You see Maggie will be the legal guardian of the boy— and Houghton is so desperately legal-minded that he won't act without her consent.

I don't want it to come on you, but if my brother dies I will ask you to try to keep Maggie going until I get there in Feb. about the 20th I guess. I should send you the money I think—$110.00 would do perhaps—and she could work out a little perhaps—or do those rugs.[44]

You know it is quite possible she may pull herself together with T. gone! Anyhow—there it is. I hope the father will survive—he is needed! . . .

Your loving Mother.

New London, Conn.
11-26-'24

Dear Daughter;

I'm on my last lap homeward from a particularly jerky little trip.

Grace probably wrote you that I stopped two nights with her, on my way. I came two days ahead, as to have some more pictures taken by that Miss Ulman, urged upon me by Oliver Herford. The P.E.N. Club dinner was Tues. evening. . . . Mr. Herford had said he hoped to see something of me while I was in town, and I wrote that between 4 and 7, I should be "all dressed up and nowhere to go." So Mrs. H. asked me there to tea. Beatrice Herford was there also; we had a very pleasant time. . . . Then to the dinner, at the Brevoort. . . . Small round tables, crowded—8 people. I was stuck in a corner between Ellis Parker Butler's[45] wife, and a Jew. . . .

Spoke to Forum, in High School on His Religion & Hers. Next morning back to Boston, lunched with Martha [Luther Lane] and returned with her to Hingham. She has been to Manilla [*sic*], for her firm—Ginn & Co.,[46] via Yokonawa etc.—and is improved by the experience—is more of a Person. She was setting off for N.Y. very early next morning, so I was joyfully entertained by a Mrs. Swift—an ardent admirer of my line of work. . . . This morning [took the] 9.39 train for home. . . .

Your loving Mother—

Dec. 7th. 1924.

Dear Katharine,

I do not know if Thomas has gone to the hospital or not. In case he has, I'm sending the check to you—the extra $10. is for Xmas. . . . If my brother is at home just make it over to him to cash. If he's gone I wish you would give Maggie the 10. to spend for Xmas; pay the rent, ($40.00) and then give M. [Maggie] the rest in weekly 20s. I hate to trouble you—or Frank; but I'm so afraid she'll take the boy and clear out!—if she has any money beyond expenses. Wow! These families!——

Houghton is going with me to Providence Mon; tomorrow, for a day or two. . . . I speak in Boston Wed. 10th (for Jew) & Sunday 14th in Watertown, and again in Boston, Sunday evening, for Jews—on "<u>Americans and Non-Americans</u>"! There will be ructions I imagine. . . .

Houghton says he thinks well of the Federal Usurpation book—he's a democrat you know—that's their side. But he voted for LaFollette[47] because now-a-days there is so little difference between the two big parties; and Ho. is genuinely "progressive." . . .

Love—and a Merry Xmas, dear, from Mother.

Stoneleigh Court<br>Wed. 2-11-25

Dear Daughter;

. . . I am, uppermost, so sorry to have had to add this care to your other burdens—but, <u>what</u> else could I do! And I'm so <u>thankful</u> to you, dear child, as for my poor brother—save for the boy's sake I could wish him gone!—He is <u>so</u> unhappy and his misery no less for having made most of it himself. I am sending you two little checks. . . .

Salt Lake has been heard from—and I can't turn down another hundred or two—at this moment I doubt if I could reach Pasadena in time to see him [Thomas before he dies]—if you wire—but of course I wish to know. I[n] case of death cannot the undertaker manage to postpone ceremonies until I get there? Personally I advise cremation—there is a crematory in L. A. The ashes can be planted in the garden—or scattered. . . .

I'm trying to think straight and do what is right, and I do not see that I should break engagements and give up what may total $250.00 (—minus extra traveling expenses!) just for a funeral. And if he is "in extremis" I couldn't possibly get there in time to see him. Could you ask Dr. Sherk about the Crematory? He would know I should think of some man who would "undertake" that job—take the body there and bring back the ashes. But you must have free hand to arrange whatever is most convenient. . . .

I suppose my poor brother kept putting this off hoping to see me again! . . .

Mother.

2-14-'25

Dear Girl—

I keep thinking how good you were to send me that encouraging telegram—on the 12th.[48]

Do you remember hearing about an old friend of mine named Kate Bucklin—whom I whimsically included with your great great aunt—or is it "great-grand-aunt" Catharine Beecher, in naming you? Well, I tried to call on her when in Boston—she's kind of half crazy I think. I wrote her a nice grateful letter about how much she did for me when I was a girl. And <u>what</u> do you think she did? Sent me a book for Xmas, and later a most loving letter enclosing $200.00!!!! Yessir! Which helps on this trip! Need it too—it cost me about $165 <u>already</u>. . . . See you soon—love to my brother—to you—to all of the dear people.

Mother.

Salt Lake City. Utah.
Tues. Feb. 17th, 1925

Dearest Daughter—

I reached here at 8.35 or so this morning and was met at the car door almost by the friendly Gateses, both of em. . . . They are really fond of me, besides—well some collateral feelings! . . .

Well. I am all alone with good Mrs. G's house—and larder—at my service. Blessed peaceful aloneness. I'm fairly tired—as is to be expected, with all this extra worry. . . . I'm much relieved at continued good news. No doubt he will be better with this all over. I'll tell him about the [$200] present I had and it will ease his mind. Here is another check in case you need it before I come. I sent 50 & 35 before, here is 65—$150 in all. That ought to cover immediate needs. And he should have had most of what I sent for the purpose before—300 and something. Easy come easy go! Isn't it lovely that I can be paid for what is so easy and pleasant to do! Well, ma'am, I leave here 2.35 Friday P.M. and reach Pasadena—if on time—3.45 P.M. Saturday the 21st—thank goodness. And I'll try and not be a burden to you dearest child.

Love to all—

Mother.

4.15 P.M. Sun. Mch. 14. [1925]

Nevada

You Darling Daughter—

Every year I admire you more and love you better:—yessir! And as for those children, I can't imagine nicer ones, beautiful, good intelligent, <u>and</u> amusing. Bewitching, I should say. Bless 'em!

I made a modest supper on crackers and oranges—too tired to eat. Had a good night. The lights in my berth wouldn't burn, Coon couldn't fix 'em either. No harm—I went to sleep. . . .

Your loving Mother

May 4th. 1925

Hollins, Va.

Dearest of Daughters,

If I don't try to answer yours of April 21st before I get home goodness knows when 'twill be answered. The garden yawns before me. . . . Never did I so begrudge the time given away from home—right in the middle of the planting!!! Also, I have five small kittens waiting for me to see—all kinds & colors. I get home tomorrow about seven—and by Wednesday—we [reach] for the fork, spade, hoe, rake, <u>and</u> seeds! . . .

As to my auto-biography—I shall really make a better start if I wait till next week! Ahem! Then I'll have got some of the garden off my mind.

Thereafter I shall write mornings, & work afternoons. And evenings I must begin to go and see people—or I never will! . . .

Your loving Mother.

380 Washington st.
Norwich Town, Conn.
June 17th. 1925

Dearest Daughter,

... We had a lovely silver wedding [anniversary]. Houghton gave me a Hamilton wrist watch! ... Emily gave me a dollar in shining dimes—and Houghton had a box of chocolate "buds"—done up in silver foil you know. I gave him a long handled silver spoon with his initials on it—for a strawberry jam bottle. . . . I stopped gardening for a day, and walked down town with Houghton. There we happened to see "The Last Laugh"[49]—and that was the last day of it, too! . . . It is not a particularly pleasing story, but splendid acting—no captions at all—and an interesting commentary on the German character. . . .

The Abbots—he's that nice liberal minister we're so fond of—have asked us to visit them in August—at Ogunquit Maine. She knows "Charlotte Perkins' Leap"[50] up there, and I am curious to see if I can leap it now! . . .

Your loving Mother.

7-22-'25

Dear Daughter,

... Did you see my article in the June Century? Or did I tell you about it? I called it "Service, Social & Domestic." Look what they called it![51] An outrage. Editors have no write [*sic*] to cheapen and belittle a serious piece of work that way. . . .

The Century did finally send the $250. for the last article.[52] So now, with some Fall lectures and a Forum article coming, I should be able to see T. [Thomas] through February, and have something for Xmas. But I've got to have something over for Ho's interest—I owe him about $1600. now. . . .

Your loving Mother.

8-20-'25

Dearest Daughter,

It seems a long time since I've written to or heard from you. Is the summer too hot—using you up? . . . Seems to me I wrote just before going to Ogunquit—Aug. 5th. We were most warmly received. The Abbotts met us in Boston and we rolled smoothly northward in their big Cadillac. . . . We felt really honored to be invited, for they do not have any summer visitors except his mother & her father. . . . I had one morning's berrying, and enjoyed that. . . .

The garden is now feeding us plentifully. . . . I have on my list 40 vegetables planted . . . not counting asparagus! . . .

I only weigh 105! . . .

Your loving Mother.

Sept. 8. 1925

My dear Daughter,

Your nice letter of Aug. 24th should have been answered sooner—and I have no good excuse as you do. It is sad to admit, but I fear long years of trying [to] conserve strength have made me lazy! . . .

<u>Don't</u> feel that you have to write a letter a week, dear; but drop a card now and then. . . .

We're going to see "The Ten Commandments"[53] tomorrow—just for fun—so Ho. can join in my jeers. . . .

Mother.

9-25-'25

Goodmorning, Dear Daughter.

. . . I kept well; have got back to 110 [lbs.], which is my average. I take a glass of milk with each meal and eat all I'm able.

The Autobiography grows slowly; 8 chapters now—about 30,000 wds. I'm going in town next week, to give a little address and see editors, etc. Shall stay with Grace if she wants me.

I've got a little non-paying class—just three or four, to whom I'm reading "Human Work"—& we talk. . . .

We went to see <u>The Pony Express</u>—splendid. This P.M. we're going to see The Wizard of Oz.[54]

Are you well and happy, dear child? Do the children go to school yet? I shall be very glad to see you all.

Your loving Mother.

On train, near 1 P.M.
Fri. Oct. 9th '25

Dearest Daughter,

I'm on my way home after a very strenuous five days—not wasted I hope. There seems to be a keen interest in the forthcoming Autobiography—[Arthur T.] Vance wants to see it—(Pict[orial]. Review); Mr. [Hewitt H.] Howland, the new editor of the Century is looking at the piece I have done, Mr. [Thomas B.] Wells of Harpers thought he'd like bits of it; and Mr. [Maxfield] Aley says that if Vance takes it I ought to get $10,000.00!!!

So if—and if—and if!—I may get it in somewhere. . . .

Grace tells me this is Dorothy's birthday—as ever I had forgotten it. I get worse and worse. . . .

Much love, dear child, from Mother.

11-23-'25

Dear Daughter;

. . . Did I tell you that Amy Wellington is doing a book on The Literature of Feminism—and climaxes it with a chapter on me?[55] If she ever gets it out (—delayed by her illness you see—) it will be a good "opener" for the Autobi[ography]. . . .

Your loving Mother.

1926. on train. Sun. Jan. 3rd. . . .

Dearest Child—

. . . Dr. Ross invited me to the A. S. S. [American Sociological Society] dinner at the Faculty Club, and made me sit by him at the Speakers table. At the end they asked me to speak—I recited "Twigs"— warmly received.[56] . . . Dr. R. [Ross] & I came to Norwich on the 1.03— (met by Houghton in the square) & spent New Year's day with us. . . . I let the big man have my room. You see my bed is 7 ft. 6 in. from tip to tip, 6 ft. 6 wide; and as Dr. Ross is 6 ft. 5-1/2 inches he seldom finds a bed he can sleep <u>straight</u> in. He was delighted with it. He's a simple cordial soul, like a big country boy—as he is. Knows a lot and loves to tell about it; South America—Russia—China—India—Africa—he goes everywhere & then writes a book about it. . . .

Your loving Mother.

June 28th. 1926.

Dearest Daughter,

This is just a word of sympathy over the pressure you suffered in writing that last letter to Houghton. It carried me back to those years when you were little, when I had no money, when I had to borrow again and again—from strangers often—. I know the desperate feeling, the swimming round and round, like a rat in a rain barrel, with no way out—I desperately wish I could do more for you—instead of having to pour my small earnings on Thomas. If that boy [Thomas's son] amounts to anything it will be worthwhile—if not it's a dead loss. But that can't be helped.

I'm plugging along in a futile manner with my autobiography—have just got a new grip on it. If I can condense it into 12 chapters and sell it as a serial it would pay much better; I'm trying to do that now.

If that succeeds there will be more funds next year and I can be more useful. Meanwhile you had to have this right <u>now</u>—and I'm thankful Houghton could do it promptly. . . .

Your loving Mother.

380 Washington Street
Norwichtown, Conn.
Aug. 4th. '26

Dearest of Daughters—and Best of Confectioners!

On returning home from a week with the Websters in Byrdcliffe,[57] I found your lovely presents—all in good order and perfectly delicious.

To think of your adding to all your ceaseless labors by this extra work! Don't you do it any more, you dear child!—successful as it is. I'm keeping the apricot up stairs and eating it privily—There is so little I care for in the way of sweets. . . .

I poke along with the book—slow work. Have just got to a chapter about you!—Going to call it "Mother-Work." Little—O so little and poor compared to what it would have been if I'd been well! . . .

Love to you all from your inadequate
Mother.

Dec. 16. 1926

Well daughter dear,

This is just a word with my miserable little check for Christmas. I've just been off—Sun. to Wed., lecturing in Malden, Mass., near Boston, and in Providence. I stayed with Mrs. Walter Peck, and in her dining room is the big portrait your father painted of her daughter. . . . My time grows short now, and I find it very hard indeed to keep at that job of typing 90000 words again. But I must leave it in the hands of an agent—or publisher.[58] . . .

Speaking generally I'm well and happy, and wish I could send you a million dollars! . . .

Mother

Norwich Town. Conn.<br>Fri. April 1st. 1927.

Dear Daughter,

Here I am safe at home. I reached N. Y. Sunday P.M. and was met by Houghton. We went up to Grace's together, and she had a banquet for us—a nice little roast chicken from her favorite delicatessen, and some excellent near-beer—among other things. . . .

Mr. Aley says my Autobi. is with the Bobbs-Merrill readers—and that I am too pessimistic about it. I wish to goodness it would "go"—we need the money. . . .

Your loving Mother

672 North 1st West st.<br>Salt Lake City, Utah.<br>June 28th. '27

My very dear Daughter—

Since Grace told me Walter had the whooping cough I've been trying not to worry. There's nothing I can do—but send my anxious love—and that don't do any good!

But if you can find time to send a post card—I'll put one in, by way of encouragement!—do let me know how things are going. I hope you don't get [it]!!! Maybe you have, and are not able to write! But I mustn't get to imagining things; [. . .]

Here all goes well. . . . It is a great pleasure to me me [*sic*] to feel the same power and fire in speaking that I've always had. . . .

Good Mrs. Gates and I are warm friends regardless of our bridge-less differences; and I like her family. They give me the house as it were, and go about their business. Tonight Frank, one of her sons, has taken her to the movies. . . . She was perturbed—reluctant—concerned about the supper dishes. "Go ahead," I urged, "I'll wash the dishes." So off they piled, and I'm all by myself, cozy as can be, with cards, cross-word puzzles, and fine novels on the table. Also I can go to bed if I get sleepy. . . .

If everything goes well with you dear we shall reach you about Aug. 2nd or 3rd. . . .

Your loving Mother.

c/o Mrs. Susa Young Gates
47 E. South Temple St.
Salt Lake City, Utah.
July 17th. 1927.

Well, dear Daughter;

Houghton is here in good health and spirits. Arrived Fri. at 11.30 a.m. At present we are occupying the house of Mrs. Gates' operatic daughter Mrs. Bowen[59]—that fair singer being in the east, with her husband, and due back again about the 24th or 25th.

It's a nice house, pleasantly situated, with a hired girl thrown in! But we leave it tomorrow night—and take the Southern Utah trip—seeing all the high lights. . . .

I think maybe we can stay [in Pasadena] four weeks! . . .

Love to all my dear folks!

Sept. 23rd. 1927.

Dearest Daughter,

. . . Got the check for <u>Times Current History</u> mag.[60] Today, only $90.00 but every little [bit] helps. . . . North American Review orders an article on Birth Control—I've sent it, don't know what they pay—not much probably.

Now I'm going to begin on my Ethics.[61] . . . I'm going to N. Y. a few days . . . to see Grace and shop a bit. We are gradually subduing the wilderness in the garden. . . .

Love to all of you. Mother.

Nov. 27. '27

My dear Daughter,

. . . You've had word from Grace doubtless about your Aunt Carrie.[62] I can but hope the end is near for both of them—brave patient endurers!

"Endure" used to be your father's motto. I was very glad to have had a little visit with dear Grace just before this happened—she is so alone. And afterward, surely then she can be somehow induced to go to California for a rest! . . .

That neuritis in the left arm continues, and Dr. Shelby thinks its [caused by] my teeth. No wonder—such a graveyard as I have in my mouth! . . .

Grace and I went to a movie Mon. P.M. . . . Tues. I shopped a very little, lunched with Martha Bruère, saw Uncle Tom's Cabin,[63] p.m. I think it is fairly good, though a better one would have been just a series of scenes from the events as they happened, instead of trying to weave a "story" of the ordinary sort out of that great man. . . .

Lots of love for all of you from
Mother.

380 Washington Street
Norwichtown, Conn.
Jan. 5th. '28.

Dearest of Daughters;

. . . Houghton has a cold but got over it. As for me I've got a real Disease!—neuritis. Left arm. It hurts to do my hair. It hurts to button my petticoat, so I swing it around front, to fasten.

And it hurts off and on, variously, and extends both into the neck and hands—so I'm going to a doctor. Sooo—he'll doubtless prescribe "treatments," elective, and that'll cost money. And I haven't any. However its a small matter. It doesn't hurt enough to keep me awake, or interfere with two or three hours' typing a day. And I'm amused to see how trifling a thing is physical pain compared with the kind I've had so much of!

Meanwhile our prospects are good. Houghton sees his way to carry Thomas through this year. . . .

Grace had a hard trip, of course, but it had to be, and when that heroic Jane[64] is gone—there will be one less burden on her. . . .

Love to you best of dear daughters,
Mother.

380 Washington Street
Norwichtown, Conn.
Mch. 20th. '28

Dearest Daughter,

All at once I remembered three birthdays! Too late, but still within the month.[65] Please give Walter one dollar and keep two—only a scraplet, but as you know I'm short this year.

Two nice lectures on the 27th, in Wilmington, Del, and Newark, close by. The latter is at Delaware University—co-educational; the former to a Jewish group called "The Kallah"—whatever that may mean.[66] One is a hundred and the other is fifty; so I ought to get a month's funds for Thomas, and may [get] five or ten dollars above the trip—depends on whether I have to pay hotel bills or am "entertained." ...

Your loving Mother.

380 Washington Street<br>Norwichtown, Conn.<br>April 30th. 1928.

My dear Daughter,

... I'm amused that you sent your [genealogy] chart to Mrs. Gates—she is delighted to have it. No, you didn't mention the Gov. Dudley line.[67] I guess most well-descended New Englanders connect pretty closely.

Those Mormons are daffy on genealogy you know—always digging up more ancestors to "seal," their names I mean, not bones! ...

Ho. has to go to Hartford tomorrow, about a case. He gets almost no business—to his great dissatisfaction. But his health is good, and he takes more and more interest in the garden. I'm particularly glad of that, because it is an endless resource. ...

Mother.

10 a.m. July 25th. 1928.

Daughter Dearest;

Here I am at my big desk in the N. W. corner of this big, low, dark room, putting in a letter to you before I try to "write." ...

I've always been proud of you, you darling. You have been exceptionally intelligent, resourceful, reliable, capable in many ways. You weren't brilliant in school. Neither was I. Thats nothing. You are masterfully efficient in so many ways, even with a heavy handicap in health and strength; that such deficiencies as there are leave you still far ahead of most people. And as a mother you are wonderfully competent—everyone who knows you sees that. As far as I can see you are also a strong wise tender wife. On top of all this is your beautiful work—your professional work—itself a thing to be proud of even if you weren't so lovely otherwise. <u>So there</u>!!! ...

<u>What</u> a piece of work you have undertaken [to trace the family's genealogy]! . . . There is nothing to be ashamed of, behind us, that <u>I know</u> of. . . .

I'm all for Hoover—Houghton is—ordinarily—a democrat. He thinks well of Smith.[68] Yes. Mr. Hoover is <u>fine</u>. . . .

Yes, Mormon genealogy has an "animus." They want to prove their religious views. <u>Of course</u> Adam is "our first father"—if you believe it. And if you hook on to the Jews—there you are, straight back.

But I never heard of dragging in the Virgin Mary! They think Jesus was married to Mary & Martha, I believe. But I guess they are reliable on modern stuff. Amusing that they should leave out Cain! I guess Seth was a later son of Adam—yes, Genesis IV. 25. Doesn't say who he married—the Lord must have made a few more. Seth lived to be 912 yrs. old!

O, yes, they drag in a Jewish ancestry for the English and all good people. . . . Your father said that "Staetsan" was "stepson" in the Norse, or Swedish, & that's where it came from. . . .

Lots of love dear child, to you and yours,
Mother.

380 Washington Street
Norwichtown, Conn.
Nov. 11th. 1928

Dear Katharine;

. . . That was fine that you should hear Lucy Gates, and see my old friend, her mother. I'm glad you both like her. She's a good woman and an able one. Of course she exaggerates about me, but she's genuinely fond of me apart from that.

It's the <u>simplicity</u> of Lucy G. that always delighted. When she was first back from Germany, ready for Opera work, she'd sing "Juanita" for me as willing as could be. . . .

That was fine that you remembered about the 5000 converts in Germany. Myself I am suspicious that one cause was Germany's need of emigration! They are willing to come here on any terms! And often make good citizens. . . .

Yes, Houghton is a Democrat and thought Smith the best man. We went peaceably to the polls together and nullified each other's vote. Same with Emily and Francis. However that's all well over—thank goodness. . . . Wasn't it fun that Hoover did carry N.Y. state—as you hoped! . . .

You are the dearest girl that ever was. And I love you.

Mother.

Dec. 6th. [1928]

Dearest of Daughters—

At last Annie Westcott has sent me her precious Westcott book. You will be pleased to see that the Stukelys go back, to "the gentry" in England. Thomas Beers[69] in some of his delightful stories refers to the "Rhode Island Stukelys" as something very special.

I think I'll do a most immoral thing—and forward you the book to look at. She didn't say I might, I didn't ask her—she was so precious of it. But I shall acknowledge her kindness, and promise that "It shall be taken care of"—and that I will return it in January, after the holiday rush is over. I can leave another loophole and say—"I'm very forgetful sometimes—if it does not appear in January just drop me a post card."

It seems to me a real treat for you to see it, and by no means wicked—so I'll risk it. Please make your notes as quickly as you can, and return it right after Xmas—as soon as the rush is over that is—registered. . . .

No I had not seen Mr. Lummis' death. It was about time I suppose. . . .

I'm ploughing slowly along trying to write fiction. I never was anxious about being poor myself—but the sense of responsibility for those ill-advised folks of mine weighs on me. I feel that I must earn money. Well, I'd better get at it! . . .

Your loving Mother.

380 Washington Street<br>Norwichtown, Conn.<br>Jan. 30. 1929

Dearest of Daughters;

. . . Yesterday was very cold—about 10° above I think, with a piercing north wind. But I'm sitting before a wood fire, and between that, a radiator and a register, with plenty of woolens about me, do very well. A week ago today Houghton and I, marching townwards as usual, were exulting in our good health. "We're so well," said Houghton, "that

I'm afraid." Later in the day my nose ran water—and that night—whoop!—the flu! High fever—nausea—headache. . . . I just stayed in bed, and it made no difference to anybody. Fasted a few days—save for lemonade; then "resumed payment" on hot milk & toast. Yesterday was up, and dressed all day, and this a.m. down to breakfast—So now, except for the continuing weakness, am all right again. . . . A brief, peaceful, agreeable little illness, and very little trouble to anybody.

Houghton and I are castle-building. This book I'm on—the fiction thing—we fondly believe will sell.[70] And we regale ourselves with visions of down chickens—dozens of them! Using said chickens as a base, and our growing dislike for the behavior of the rest of the family (—how <u>awful</u> an unreasonable person is!—) we are planning a very modest little Utopia in the way of a clear $1500 a year. With this, one roseate plan is to come out to California, from say mid-Dec. to mid-March—every year!!! Both of us. . . .

Publishers still averse to my Ethics! I don't care—it's a great book all the same. . . .

Mother.

380 Washington st.<br>Norwich Town. Conn.<br>April 2nd. 1929.

Dear Daughter,

. . . I've just sent off the book I've been working on for nearly a year. Mr. [Edgar] Wallace,[71] the detective story factory, takes a <u>fortnight</u> to write one!!! Less, if driven. . . .

Not unnaturally I've "slumped" a bit. It's been a long pull, of uncongenial work. But I'm planning another—a prize competition thing. Not at all likely to get it, but I've got to do <u>something</u>. . . .

Love to all of you from your somewhat debilitated Mother.

April 20th 1929.

Daughter Dear!

. . . I most earnestly wish the book may "go"—but there's no knowing. The agent I have now, (Charlotte A. Barbour, with Putnam's) writes, "It interested me decidedly. . . . it seemed an original plot situation." It is. Houghton has read millions of detective stories—so to speak—and has never seen one like it. So I have hopes. . . .

I'd have to do a lot of hunting to find the date of that first marriage. When do you have to have to [*sic*] have it? I just looked in the "Autobiography"—but it only says "May 1884." <u>Somewhere</u> is the wedding ring—unless I gave it to you. And somewhere is an old diary I think. . . .

Love to you dear child, and all your dear ones.<br>Mother.

May 13th. 1929

Dearest Daughter;

. . . I cannot remember my father's death date either. . . . Seems to me it was in Dec. '99. I had a little stone "marker" made for him—he is buried in Hartford, and one of the cousins there will know. . . .

I certainly have been very rich in friends. Thomas was much amused by the "Magna Charter <u>Dames</u>."[72] Will you mark our illustrious progenitor and return? I'd really like to join one of those [genealogy organizations]—the Runnymede, or this one. I suppose the little "d." means "dead." I should say so! But I've no hundred dollars lying around loose at present.

I'm very happy in the garden—my sanitarium.

Your loving Mother.

May 18th. 1929.

Dear Katharine;

I've had a totally unexpected little fragment of money, which I can temporarily call mine. Since Houghton is carrying Thomas—and I am increasingly in debt to him, I don't feel as I owned a cent. Its amusing. All my life I've been poor, often entirely "penniless" as they call it, and for many years in debt, but I have never <u>felt</u> it. . . .

You certainly have conjured up a flock of ancestors. How about slaves, pirates, criminals generally? There must have been plenty of ignoble strains. . . .

Your loving Mother.

June 29th. 1929.

Dearest Daughter,

. . . My books still go begging. Wrote three good articles—agent sent 'em right back—said they had "too much dynamite"! I am sending them around, without much hope. And no lectures. Looks as if your mama was being considered a back number. . . .

I've just read a very pleasing story called "The Dower House Mystery" by Patricia Wentworth.[73] She writes well, very well. Try her "The Adventures of Jane Smith" some time. . . .

I'm scrabbling to remove a pile of letters, and then shall try to make a saleable story. <u>Got</u> to sell something!

Your loving Mother.

Aug. 5th 1929.

My dear Daughter;

I find an envelope addressed and stamped—and your letter of July 3rd; but I do not remember whether I answered that letter or not. A foggy-headed parent, you have! . . .

If I did write you—did I repeat that lovely compliment Oliver Herford just sent me—that he remembered Mr. Howells saying that I had "the best brains and the best profile of any woman in America"—? And Mrs. Howells added, "Or anywhere else." I think it was very nice of Mr. Herford. . . .

Love to all of you from Mother.

Fri. Sept. 19th. 1929

Dear Katharine—

. . . As soon as I feel a flicker of hope about the book, I fall to "figuring" as to possible sales, & royalties. A modest estimate provides me with a net sum of say,

$15,000.00

Then I promptly divide it thus:

| | |
|---|---|
| K. [Katherine] for year abroad— | 5,000.00 |
| G. [Grace] for year abroad— | 3,000.00 |
| (If not acceptable otherwise I'll buy a picture!) | |
| T. [Thomas] for three more years, +, | 5,000.00 |
| Oil burner furnace | <u>1,000.00</u> |
| | $14,000.00 |

And thus a thousand over for emergencies!
Wow! Wouldn't it be fine.

I think it would do you all wonderful good to go to Italy for a year. . . .

Love to everyone, from Mother.

Sept. 23rd. '29

Dear Katharine,

. . . Did I tell you that Martha Bruère brought to meet me a Mr. Tapley[74] of McMillans? He has read my Autobiography "with the keenest interest" he says, and is tackling the Ethics. Has asked me to dinner when I go to N.Y. Oct. 29th to speak for the Gamut Club.[75] . . . The agent who had the detective story wants me to "tighten up . . . the front part," so I'm facing that uncongenial task. If the Autobi. goes at all two thirds of that will have to be done over. So I have enough work before me. But I'll do <u>anything</u> that I possibly can to push those books!

One lecture, in Pittsburgh, Nov. 19th, is the only engagement I have ahead—& 75. net. . . .

Your loving Mother.

Nov. 12th. 29.

Dearest of Daughters,

. . . I was pleased and proud to read of your exhibits in S. F. [San Francisco]. Proud of both of you. And impressed anew with the d[r]eadful handicap of the Arts—used, perforce, as a means of livelihood. The same weight is on the ministry, and the sciences, largely, but most heavily on the arts, and sculpture most of all. That's fine about Frank's picture in the Hatfield Gallery.[76] I do hope they will sell it. . . . He has been so brave and patient. It takes real heroism for an artist to "carry on" as he has done. As for you, you splendid woman—I admire profoundly the beautiful work you do, for him, for the children, and with your own deferred and set aside so much. . . .

Your at-present useless Mother.

<u>Dec. 15. 1929</u>.

Dearest Girl,

. . . Houghton says he has seen my father's paper on the Perkins family. He was a very eminent scholar, your grandfather. Do you remember him at all clearly?—that trip across the continent? There's one thing I shall never forget—that is the dreadful pain in my heart when your little golden head moved farther and farther away as the train left Oakland. I can feel it yet [. . .]

Of course I hope I can come to see you this year. But it seems to me that even [if] I could I'd much better send you the money. . . .

Love to you, dear child.<br>Mother.

Feb. 14th. 1930.

Well Darling Daughter,

Here is your neglectful parent, way behind as usual. . . . [W]e sent the money[77] as quick as we could—"we" being dear Houghton—I have none now. But, except for staving off tradesmen I don't see that you are any better off! I'm worried about you—and apparently helpless. . . .

If I could divert say 20 a month to you, that would pay the milk bill! You say Frank's people aren't able to help. I should think his sister might lend him something. I know he'd hate to ask her—but why not? . . .

Now I will write you my own news, which is fine. Emily and Francis have gone off on a two month's trip—N.Y. to San. Fran. by st[eame]r. Feb. 5 to April 8th. I am running the house with one maid, an amiable Irish woman. Furthermore, I'm going to keep on running it!

Our last definite break was before Xmas, some disagreement as to what I said to the woman who was to have cleaned my room. She believed the woman's version and disbelieved mine, saying, "I have not found you to be truthful Charlotte." I replied, "I know you think so. I have known you take the word of a colored cook against mine."

She replied "I prefer to believe my servants are truthful and honest." I have not spoken to her since. Hereafter she will, so to speak, board here as I have done. Wow! It is such a comfort to have them gone!

My health is good, better and better. I am thoroughly enjoying the ordering food to suit my own tastes. And I am proving the needless extravagance I have always felt was there. Houghton and I have different methods. We are going to run the house our way; and if they can't stand they can leave—Ho. will buy out Francis' quarter of the place. . . .

Emily is so mean spirited that before leaving she <u>sent to the bank</u> all the teaspoons but <u>6</u>! Some of that silver was her own, but some must have belonged to the estate. I think she did it so I could not "entertain." I have bought 6 tin ones at Woolworths! And she took up various rugs that were hers and sent them to Hartford to be cleaned—leaving bare patches. And packed away a good set of china which F. [Francis] had given her.

Nice woman, Emily! . . .

You see Ho. and I have stood everything and never said a word, but this latest quarrel has been patent to the servants and is doubtless all over town. . . .

I hate to have Francis lose his home, but she is impossible. . . .

Your loving Mother.

April 16. 1930

Dearest Girl;

. . . Emily, it appears, has been spreading her views of me, representing for instance that I am a hypocrite!!!

"You may charge me with murder, or want of sense
    —We are all of us week [*sic*] at times,
But the slighted approach to a false pretense
    Was never among my crimes."[78]

Shows what a stupid person she is.

They arrived last Tuesday—that is Tuesday the 8th. She is behaving just as I knew she would. Now trying to mutilate the house, so as to have a separate establishment. An expensive, uncomfortable impractical performance. Mixture of babbling servants, and E. [Emily] gossiping with both of them. . . .

April 22nd.

. . . I've just sent T. [Thomas] 80—and to you this 40. Its only a scrap, but scraps help. Dear knows I'd do more—but absolutely haven't a cent. . . .

Well dear—good fortune to all of you, and love from Mother.

April 24th. 1930.

Dear Daughter;

. . . Good news here. F. [Francis] & E. [Emily] demanded a divided home. H. [Houghton] would not agree, so they are going away!!! Hurrah. Not before Sept. I fear, still we have it to look forward to. They speak of leaving the town even. All the better. . . .

Had a little talk with Francis yesterday. E. being out to lunch. . . . He spoke of E. as "having a chip on her shoulder"; said that I had been considerate and patient; that E. "had it in for" Houghton as much as for me almost, but that as for me she couldn't bear the sight of me or the sound of my voice!!!!

So it's about time all that hatred was removed. . . .

Your loving Mother.

May 21st. 1930.

Dearest Child,

. . . This afternoon the dentist. He tells me [I] have about a dozen teeth of my own. The rest are sewed on. (Perhaps he said "live teeth.") Anyhow they never ache, look decent, and serve my purpose well. There's a false corner on a front upper incisor—but its just as good as the other. . . .

Love to all of you . . .<br>Mother.

Wed. May 21. 1930.

Dearest Daughter,

. . . Our "other half" now denies that it said it would leave. Present policy is to stick tight and be as disagreeable as possible. But as perhaps I said, E. [Emily] in adopting a policy of excommunication, has cut herself off from the satisfaction of making disagreeable remarks three times a day. Good thing. We simply don't see them—as they won't eat with us. . . .

Your loving Mother.

Aug. 11th. [1930]

Dearest Daughter;

I "have you on my mind" as the saying goes; the more so as we're unable to do anything more to help. H. [Houghton] has arrange[d] for that $120 a month—and beyond that is up against it. . . .

Those years in California when I had you—and my mother came to "die on me"—and I took boarders & lodgers begged borrowed, everything but stole! Wow! I never got out of debt till a good while after I married Houghton. But, I was held up by all those tremendous convictions of mine—and by the one dear child to care for [. . .] Well, what can't be cured must be endured, that's all there is of it. I just want you to feel how much I care. . . .

Your loving mother.

Oct. 11. 1930.

Dearest Daughter,

... Dear child—we know you and Frank are doing everything you possibly can, and we know how you hate to be "done for"—but bless me! What else can we do. There are the children. My only comfort is that with the house, and a little bit coming regularly you won't starve or freeze! I had it for years—alone, with you to care for—in debt—no prospects—I know all about it. I expect your hardest part is keeping up Frank's spirits! He'll surely get something now the winter comes on. . . .

If I keep on feeling well I may yet write something that will sell. But I've an awful lot of discouragements piled up—three books and heaps of short things. I was amazed at the amount I've done, even in these last years—looking them over while I hunted for Isadora.[79] . . .

With love from both of us—
Mother.

Wed. Nov. 12th. 1930
at Grace's.

Dear Daughter,

Grace having got in a few dollars, insists on handing me over a fifty—here it is. Call it a Christmas present, (really from her,) and use as needed. . . .

I'm staying till Thursday when there is a luncheon at Sherry's,[80] for Mrs. C. C. [Carrie Chapman] Catt, who got the 5000 award this year. . . .

I've been to see my agent about books. Nothing doing. She seems to have done her part in sending the mss. about. "Hard times" of course. It hits us all. Dear—when any amelioration happens you'll tell me, won't you. As it is I just hate to think about it—having no way to help matters. . . .

Love to all of you from Mother.

June 19th. 1931

Dearest of Daughters,

Here is your nice letter dated "Apr. 29th" . . . and your neglectful parent not answering as she should. You see I carry a heartache about you, and dodge it all I can! When I think about your difficulties and my incapacities it gives me such a bitter feeling of failure, of shameful ability to take care of my beloved ones—a feeling which produces no results whatever, merely an ache. . . .

Then, on top of my mortification and grief at not being able to help you, I am so piggishly happy myself that it seems wicked. Here I sit with Houghton, served by a loving though stupid maid, well fed, with a constant supply of story books that H. [Houghton] brings from the library, and with our beloved garden to work in afternoons. Evenings of music and a sort of dual solitaire—we sit on a sofa together and he overlooks the game.

Pure sweet air, beautiful surroundings, a few pleasant friends—and an accumulation of pretty dresses dating back thirty years and more. Well and happy I am—except for being anxious over you, and in less degree over Thomas. . . .

Mother.

June 25th. 1931

Dear Daughter,

I was reading over some of your letters, and came to the one referring to Walter's birthday. Will you once more send me all the birthdays—I am putting them on cards in my card catalogue! That is the only permanent "filing system" I have. I've got Houghtons pretty well in mind; and I know yours by a bit of mnemonic test. Your father, I remember was "24 on the 25th of March"—and you came on the 23rd. The 23rd & 25th would have long since been hopelessly confused, but that "24" keep[s] them in place.[81]

I forget my own, mostly; forget our wedding day—forget most things. But I'm really well again, and quite shamefully happy & contented. . . .

With love always, Mother.

Tues. July 21st. 31

Dearest Daughter,

. . . I have your loving birthday letter, and the dear childrens. Tell them Grandmama was much pleased and will answer soon. . . .

. . . Why on earth should you write that gratuitous article for Art and Architecture? Do you like to?—Or will it serve somewhat as an advertisement? Madam Severance[82] is a good subject for local interest, but as you say, hard to look up back in Ohio. Such a lot of work! You know, I have kept that amazing letter she wrote to Aunt Isabella Hooker[83]— telling of my helpless condition and urging that the family bring me back to the east! Aunt I. sent it to Uncle Edward Hale & he sent it to your father—& he to me! It said that I had no capacity for earning a living—etc. . . .

Yes, dear, I deeply wish I could get out to see the children—and you, my own child. But it is out of the question. I desperately wanted Grace to go—but she wouldn't. . . .

Love for all of you, Mother.

Block Island, R. I.<br>Aug. 19th. 1931

Dear Daughter;

. . . Aren't you glad that women's garments again have "flow" and movement? I take great satisfaction in the changes. . . . Being of a vicious temper I also delight to see these proud superior contemptuous "modern" women unresistingly slipping back into the despised corsets of their grandmothers!—etc. Their improved dress was no credit to them, they did not reasoningly adopt it, and the next fashion overwhelms all their improvements. Of course the athletic gain is great, and solid gain. But the mass of women are "the same old fools they always were."

What an ill tempered old lady I'm getting to be.

But I love you, and yours.

Mother.

Sept. 10th. 1931.

Dearest of Daughters—

. . . As to this "time of life" performance I'm sure I hope so. It is a definite relief in many ways. Mine had no "symptoms" that I remember, but I keenly remember what a blow it was to me—for I was hoping with all my heart for a baby for Houghton. To expect a child and then find it is the end of all hope—it hurt.

I guess that is one reason you have been so "wuzzy" in the head—on top of all the other troubles. Congratulations. . . .

Had a lovely visit with Grace. . . .

What a marvelous woman she is. Noble is the word for her. Good-for-nothing is at present the word for your once achieving Mother.

Oct. 25th. 1931.<br>New York—

Dearest Child—

. . . I was a guest at the H. B. [*sic*] Wells[84] $10.00 dinner, new Waldorf-Astoria, (mine was an invitation) and they put me at the speaker's table right next to Mr. W., which I enjoyed. Wouldn't let me speak though which was an error! I could have wound up the exercises and left them all thrilled—in ten minutes. Instead of which they had a liberal minister who was long, and futile. . . .

I have really earned $50.00! To my great delight. Lecture. It was 45. net. And so I can manage a Xmas & birthday check to you, a bit for Thomas, a tiny bit for Ho. and even some for myself! . . .

Love, Mother.

Dec. 19th. 1931.

Dearest Daughter,

By [way] of a Christmas present Houghton sends one more check, and alas!—no more! His income has shrunk and shrunk; we've cut down our good Mary by $15.00 a month. . . . If it gets worse we'll have to drop Mary—but I hate to do that until we have the house to ourselves. Which will not be until Francis has more money. They are worse off than we are. . . .

Mary does all our work, including housecleaning. And she took her cut like a lamb—said "Everybody's being laid off—or have their wages cut—why shouldn't I?" I told her if she could get a place at her previous rate to go to it, and she said she'd rather work for us at less. She's what they call "devoted," thinks I'm wonderful, likes us both. Which makes a very easy comfortable life for me. . . .

The splendid work Frank does will surely give him a settled income soon. . . . I think the position of artists—music—acting—painting—all of them is simply wrong. To have to push and peddle ones work, to have no national contact with an eager market—well I won't argue about it. When [Theodore] Dreiser was on "The Delineator" he said to me "You should consider what the editors want."[85]

I told him that was not my job. . . .

No I didn't see the article you mention on Laws and Women. Women are not as able as men to work for changed laws. I have small patience with them—painted, powdered, high-heeled, cigaret smoking idiots. To deliberately take up an extra vice—or bad habit—just to show off—<u>imbecile</u>! . . .

Wish I could send you all a Gorgeous Christmas box——but can only send love.

Mother.

Feb. 5th. '32

Dearest Daughter,

. . . I've just made two trips to N.Y. to speak for the league of nations assn.—Expenses paid, no more. First a 15 minutes address by radio—my first attempt at a real radio speech. Some who heard it said the voice came over clear and strong, as if it was in the room. So that's all right. They were so pleased with the stuff they had it printed for distribution.

The second time was an evening address, to a handful of people, at an "exhibition" they are holding in an empty store at 746 5th Ave.— bet[ween]. 57 & 58th sts. Same sort of talk only more of it. Well received. I'm so pleased to have a chance to speak, in some "cause" I care for that payment doesnt' matter. They have no money to speak of—or to pay any one to speak of! I saw Grace both times. She is not well—but won't admit anything as usual. . . .

We ourselves, with careful economy . . . are scraping through, but it is scraping. A little while ago I made a careful estimate of what I cost Houghton a year, outside of food and shelter; . . . all my personal expenses, including allowance for doctor, dentist, amusement, stationery, stamps, all clothing, everything amounts to about $150. All together abt 420. Something like $8.40 a week for everything. It made me feel quite virtuous; and I need some comfort now I'm earning nothing. . . .

As for me I'm very well indeed. Getting fat!!! Weigh <u>123</u>! . . .

Your loving but ineffectual<br>Mother

April 1st. 1932

Dearest Daughter:

. . . You <u>are</u> busy! And now your [*sic*] entering on my pressures, and "speaking." I hope you'll soon find it easy. All I ever knew of the business was this[:] "Address the farthest person in the room." If that one hears, they all do. As for the audience—I don't look at them at all—as persons. If I have friends there I forget them. I talk to "It"—and it is helpless and dumb, nothing to mind in the least. And you remember my three rules for public speaking—that I made? 1st. Be heard. 2nd. Say something. 3rd. Stop. They are good rules.

Of course my speaking is pure heredity. The result of generations of ministers. You ought to have some of it, too. Being a preacher makes it easy. . . . I never had that feeling in the pit of the stomach—not once, even when I was asked to take a church service—the whole of it—in Oakland, and I'd never been in the pulpit before. Must be heredity. I never felt more at home anywhere. . . .

I'm amused to hear of that Miss Clark's remembering my addressing her college and the mothers being shocked. They were very easily shocked in those days. . . . If Miss Buchanan meant that my W. & E. was superior to Olive Schreiner's "Women & Labor," I think she was right.[86] But that was only on[e] reconstructed from a great book on women O. S. had been years in writing & which the British soldiers destroyed. I think Olive Schreiner's "<u>Dreams</u>" incomparably great. Such vast reach of thought with such perfect, beautiful, and exquisitely concentrated expression I know of nowhere else. . . .

Still, with apologies—your loving Mother.

June 24th. 1932.

Dear Daughter,

. . . I read the "interview" in the A. & A. [Art and Architecture] magazine with interest and approval. It is well done, good sense, well expressed. Do you know it is an effort for me, even yet, to realize that you are wholly grown up. Yet in three more years you'll be fifty!!! Preposterous!

I went to Hartford last week to take part in a Pageant they had to raise money for The Mark Twain memorial. Katharine Day was its instigator and asked me to take the part of Aunt Harriet Stowe, which I delighted to do.[87] . . . Miss Temple, who was the "whole show" arrangement, research, costume making, scene-painting, etc. etc., sent me this note [enclosed]—needn't keep.[88] You see it was dead easy for me—I just arranged my hair with a chignon, a broad black fillet, & loose bandeaux down over my ears, and "acted natural."

I've been looking over your [genealogy] article again. . . . I have urged that for many years, to show how traits blend, strengthen, or "breed out" assume a long fringe, each tassell [*sic*] of many different colored threads.[89] Then knot them into a network, and some special color might angle down in different combination till some descendant was solid red, so to speak, or other color—concentrated tendency. Or a thick bunch of red at the top, spread & weaken out.

It is really impressive, the way you have made a place for yourself in this genealogy line. You'll get orders when "the depression" is over. . . .

Your loving Mother.

Nov. 25th. '32

Dear Daughter,

You and I are certainly poor correspondents! You have every excuse. I have none, except my addle-headedness. . . .

I think I said that if I should go up in smoke as it were, it was possible H. [Houghton] might come out to Pasadena to live. Possible. I'm sure he could be more comfortable there, on less, than anywhere else. . . .

I'm working on my Ethics—rewriting it, bettering it I think. Lyman Stowe is coming presently to look over my stuff. Did I tell you he is to be my Literary Executor? I'm really hoping that after I'm gone there may be a new interest in my work, and perhaps some profit for you and the children. . . .

We are thankful that we are not in any physical pain—and that we have each other. That's a lot.

Poor dear Grace has gone hurrying on to see Mary again—who fails perceptibly. Dear me! I don't see why people mind dying! It always give me a sort of "School's Out!" feeling! . . .

Mother.

April 14th. '33

Dearest Daughter—

Its hard to write when I've a steady heartache over you. I hate to write emptyhanded. Then to explain why I'm emptyhanded is only the same tale we hear everywhere. Houghton is hanging on by "the skin of his teeth." . . .

By August H. [Houghton] will begin to draw a meager salary as Asst. Judge. Did I write you he was so appointed? Its only $900. a year, but O!—how big that looks. . . .

I'm forgetting birthdays as usual—wrote Walter a silly rhyme about it. Grace is a far better grandmother than I am. She spoke of your—48[th]—and Houghton and I were positively amazed! 48—8 years older than when I married him. It doesn't seem <u>possible</u>. I think of you—brave—patient—toiling away there—overstrained—weary—and I just ache. Then I tell myself that you have the man you love and two splendid children, that you live in a lovely place and have many friends—and then I just squirm away and stop thinking about it!

I've been writing several articles lately.—If—<u>IF</u> I can place one of them it will help a little. . . .

Your loving but inadequate

Mother

May 2nd. 1933.

My darling daughter—

What a peck of trouble! I wish—O how I wish!—you and I were "near" enough for me to comfort you. . . .

I'd no idea you were having it so hard, dear. I suppose you hate to tell me, knowing that I can no longer be of practical service. . . .

I don't feel able to advise you at all as to practical matters. There's no present way out of our pressing difficulties. I'm going to make another effort to write something salable, but—you see I'm "dated"—what I offer is "old stuff" and ten years of almost unbroken repeated failure have dampened my enthusiasm. . . .

How children suffer from those who love them most! I did try so carefully not to hurt you, and to love and pet you as I so longed to be loved and petted and never was. But I suppose you were hurt in ways I never knew.

I've got a bit of verse you wrote me when you were about twelve, appreciative of the way I had brought you up. I can tell you I prize it. Also your father wrote me, when you went to him in 94, that he was wholly satisfied with your rearing. But that's because you were wise and good yourself, amazingly so. Well daughter dear I can send you nothing but love and sympathy—quite useless. Yes, I can too! I can send honor and admiration for a brave strong life, for splendid talents, for magnificent motherhood, and wifehood, and friendship. For duty done as far as you could reach. For a husband to your heart's desire, for two incredibly fine children. For the admiring love of many many friends.

You are a very noble woman Katharine my dear.

It is hard that such as you should be harrassed by these cares and anxieties—but that we share with many millions.

Mother—

Aug. 26th. 33

Well, Daughter dear,

It is a long time since I've written to you or heard from you.

These hard times make it more and more difficult for me to write to the people I love. I know your distress and cannot alleviate it. If I plead poverty as preventing my doing anything[—]that seems only adding to your worries. If I dilate on my own happiness and health and all the charms of this lovely old place—that sounds like gloating. If I ask anxiously after your troubles you hate to tell them to me. And if I congratulate you on the good things you have—that's small comfort. . . .

The World Fellowship of Faiths, meeting in Chicago has asked me to speak. I am so desperate for opportunities, and this is so directly in my line, that I was really anxious to go. It seemed possible that I <u>might</u> get a real engagement out of it, (this one pays nothing!) or an article to write. And, failing that, it will rouse and stimulate my neglected powers and I'll be able to do better work afterward. So dear Houghton, who hasn't paid his taxes—nor the last dentist bill—is arranging for me to go. There are amazingly cheap rates. . . .

Then with a little visiting, and economy in meals, I can stay a week or more, & see what I want to of the Fair, and, including boat to N.Y. and back, keep inside of $60.00. . . .

I think Houghton enjoys being a judge, albeit a little one. Paltry cases—police court stuff. As for your Mama she is visibly an old lady. I hope—and hope—and hope—I shall see you again. . . .

Your loving Mother.

Sept. 21st. 1933.

My dear Daughter,

I hear from Mrs. Park[90] that you had a hope of getting some lecture engagements for me in Cal., in connection with my little Chicago trip. . . .

It was an immense pleasure to me to make that one engagement. Not a cent of pay—not even expenses, but Houghton said he regarded it as good business; if I got one real engagement it would cover it; and even if I didn't it would "set me up" for more work this winter. And it did.

My address was so warmly received that after I sat down and been duly applauded, they asked me to go on—give them some more! Mrs. P. [Perkins] said I have not lost in anyway—voice—delivery—fire—anything.

So I feel quite reassured and hope for more work. . . .

I'm really hoping to do something this season. Anyhow I love you, all of you.

Mother.

[P.S.] O, as to terms for lectures—most anything! Only I couldn't come out there unless the aggregate covered all expenses. Regular fee $100.00, half price frequently, & quarter if necessary!

Sept. 26. '33

Dear K.—

Did I tell you that the Golden Book for October has my "Yellow Wallpaper"? Good advertising—if some more people would read it. . . . Has Dorothy ever read it?

Hastily,<br>C.P.G.

Nov. 3rd. 1933.

Dearest Daughter—

Did I send a miserable dollar for Dorothy's birthday? I have a vague memory that I did, and don't want to be sorry for forgetting if after all I remembered. I think I answered yours of Sept. 23rd. . . .

I have an engagement in New York Feb. 4th—John Haynes Holmes[91] Church. Expenses & maybe something over. Visit Lyman Stowe, & may stay a few days. Then stop in Chicago—pick up something there maybe. Ought to get to Pasadena by the 15th—or before. . . . And do you know any rich women who'd like to give a parlor talk or reading—I'm planning to use The Yellow Wallpaper as a monolog!—raise their hair!

Well—our news is that on Oct. 31st a little money came in and we bought coal. Awfully chilly in October without any. And "These" circulating the story that we refused to get it to freeze them out as it were! As if we didn't freeze too! . . .

Houghton has aged under care and worry, shame and disappointment as to Francis and so on. He is less and less able to do heavy work, all the snow shoveling for instance. F. can't do much, and won't do anything.

So if things go on as they are I think he'd be willing to pull out. Tell me again the least you think we could live on. . . .

Love to all of you.<br>Mother.

Dec. 1st. 1933.

Dearest Daughter,

. . . I'm plowing along in the last revision of my ethics, Dearie! I did it first in The Forerunner—about 1914. Then the big one of several years back—then last year's, which was not really finished—and this final effort. It does improve, anyhow. If—O if! it would "go." It ought to. It is certainly needed, and its really a readable book. My health seems continuously good. Houghton's is not so good. Three times in [a] year he's had something to see a doctor about. And he never used to have anything the matter with him. . . .

Do you like horror stories? Gertrude Atherton's[92] "The Fog Horn," in a recent Good Housekeeping, is the worst I ever saw.

Drop me a postcard now & then.

Your loving Mother.

The Wauregan<br>Norwich, Conn.<br>Jan. 6th. 1934.

Dearest Daughter,

. . . I sent you a postcard of this Hotel yesterday, forgetting the stamp! . . . We have moved down here for three months to save paying for coal and everything else in that cold old house, while I worked in the frigid kitchen with Francis and their servant! It does not seem to us reasonable that I should do this while H. pays $450.00 a year—their half the cost of house & fuel etc—in order that they may keep a maid! That house calls for a ton of coal a week! $15.00 a ton I think now—

Here we have two rooms & a bath, top floor, west side, three windows, and a view over the roof to the surrounding hills. . . . We get our own breakfast—electric stove and toaster, also a sterno—but that requires to be replenished often, and it counts up. Our little stove cost a dollar, and is very hot, works beautifully.

I also lunch here; on such viands as I like, and we dine out, variously. They have a "counter dinner" in the restaurant below for 50 cts.—excellent, too. I can see the "5 & 10" [store]—(now alas! up to 25!) on the corner diagonally opposite. The Public library two or three hundred feet north of us, and the City Hall—we can see the clock. "Movies" all accessible. And we actually <u>save</u> by being here! No more than a few dollars; but it will enable us to go to said movies now and then! We didn't spend <u>one cent</u> for Christmas, except postage. I just scraped up what I could find in my bureau drawers. This is the third year I've done that—and there won't be any next year. . . .

Is Edwin Markham[93] still "showing"! We think him a good deal of a windbag. I knew him—(& you did too) before he was a poet at all—just an Oakland schoolteacher. . . .

Your loving mother.

The Wauregan<br>Norwich, Conn.<br>Jan. 27th. 1934.

Well, Darling Daughter,

. . . My Washington trip did not allow for a stopover in New York except the last afternoon, when Mrs. Hepburn took me to see her wonderful daughter again.[94] It is a <u>paltry</u> play; paltry; and its like putting a quart measure in a pint cup to see her try to crawl into a namby-pamby girl like that, but she does it.

As to "what happens to Ho" in my absence—he's exactly as well off. Gets his breakfast (laborious!) goes to walk—and office or court; lunches as usual; dines as usual—we get fine dinners in the restaurant "counter dinner 50 cts." <u>We</u> don't mind sitting at the counter! . . . One night I had "Fresh broiled mushrooms on toast"—delightful. . . . We enjoy it immensely, and mean to come next winter! . . . Why should we stay there, work hard, be cold most of the time, poor H. shovelling snow and emptying ashes & garbage, when we can be so comfortable here! . . .

Your loving Mother

Sun. Feb. 11th. 1934
The Wauregan.

Dear Katharine,

I got home last night, and found your letter. . . . That L. A. Bureau agreed to [pay me] 25!—if I got enough of 'em I wouldn't mind.[95] I'll come at once if wanted, and should love to <u>fly</u>! did I say so in the letter? The noise wouldn't kill me, and I'd have the trip to remember. I can stay all March, later if necessary, only the garden calls for April. . . .

If the lectures pay enough get me [a] room near you—I can see just as much of you dear people and not crowd you. You'd better do that <u>anyway</u> my dear. . . . I think I'd rest better too, not feeling that I added to your difficulties.

Dear me! How <u>good</u> it will be to see you! . . .

Your loving Mother.

The Wauregan.
Norwich, Conn.
Mch. 11th. 1934.

Well, Darling,

I guess we can dismiss from our minds that spring lecture trip. You see I have no "pull" any more. If the Ethics comes out and makes the noise I hope it will, next year might give a better chance. <u>If</u> it is published next fall, I might come out in the spring and pick out a house for us.

Anyhow, I do sincerely hope to arrive with Houghton in the summer of '35. . . .

Mother.

1934.
Sun. April 15.

Dear Daughter,

Here I am at cousin Lyman's, persuaded to stay over for two days, just to see them. I hated to miss an industrious Sunday at home, but wanted to talk to Lyman about my biography—which there is still a prospect of his doing. . . .

Grace did not look as badly as I have seen her, but she is far from well. What she lives on I do not know. She has done everything possible to find buyers for pictures, or for her furniture and things, but this is no time for such sales. Oh me, oh my! Isn't it awful to have <u>all</u> ones beloved people so hardly [*sic*] off! But no worse for us than for millions more and we haven't been hungry, yet. . . .

We have moved back into the house. The others are still away, which makes it possible for us to be comfortable in the kitchen by the gas stove. We have no coal, and the change from the hotel temperature of 76° to about 40° was rather sudden. The <u>beds</u> were so cold! But we slept in our wrappers, had the hot water bottle, and neither of us caught cold. We have the peas in now and did some spinach. Not as large a garden this year. . . . I've seen dear Dr. Shelby—who keeps tabs on my state of health. My "blood pressure" is if anything less than normal—none of that to consider. He always takes me to lunch, and now to a nice little place called Steuben's Tavern, where we have beer!

I sometimes go to stay with other people instead of Grace for various reasons. For one, she has to turn out of her bedroom for me—taking elaborate pains to clear drawers & closet—which I do not need. Then I know she is desperately hard up—and even one boarder counts and from my own point of view I'm not fond of those 72 stairs—with my suit case; and it is important for me to keep in touch with other friends—to be seen and met—not be extinct in N.Y.! Personally I think Grace would have been wiser if she had accepted our earnest and loving invitation, year after year, to come and stay with us a long quiet time, and write. . . . She's like Casibianca![96] She says now that she might really have earned more if she had done that—but she was always desperately hoping to sell something. . . .

With lots of love to all of you
Mother.

380 Washington St.
Norwich Town. Conn.
May 3rd. 1934.

My Darling Daughter,

I feel as if I had failed to answer some of your nice letters, sorry. I have one here asking about our "fire." It was no fire at all. A man banged on the door, about 6 a.m., saying "Better get dressed—there's a fire. You needn't hurry." We arose calmly, and dressed. Another man banged, "You'd better get up!" "We are getting up!" I replied calmly. We were both of us unmoved. I arranged to take my mss. etc. Always easy to put clothes in a sheet, tie 'em up and throw out the window. Especially my precious shoes . . . and presently we were told that there was no further danger. We had looked out the window, hoping for some excitement. There was the fire engines, hose going into the house. There was the hook-&-ladder wagon. There was the Chief's little red car, and that's all! No surging crowd, no police-guarded lines. No eager heads staring out of opposite windows. Nothing. 6 a.m. in Norwich is no time for excitement. We felt defrauded. It was a real fire all right, down in engine room or some such cellar, and working up through the walls. . . . If it had been in the night, undiscovered, the tale would have been different. . . .

We're going to see "Spitfire" this p.m. I see Miss Hepburn is getting divorced.[97] Almost inevitable that she should have married young— and the wrong man. . . .

Well dear, here's love for all of you from your

Aged Parent!

May 5th '34

Dear Daughter,

Here is bad news for you. Houghton died suddenly last night. Fell in the street—cerebral hemorhage, a very good way to go.

Cremation Monday—way up in Springfield, Mass. None nearer. Kind friends are taking me in their car.

Of course I shall break up as soon as I can, and come to Pasadena. There will be enough to maintain an economical old lady I think. And I may be able to do some work yet. We'll see. He'd been playing bridge at the Arcaium Club, & started home—about 10:30 I was sent for, but he was dead before they picked him up I believe.

Have to write several notes—

Your loving mother.

May 19th. 1934

Dear Daughter,

Thanks for your loving letter. I hate to think of having an added grief and care piled on you, you have enough to carry—too much.

Be sure dear that I will not be another! There may be a meager liv[e]lihood to be scraped up from what Houghton had left—it was very little and all complicated with loans and notes and things. Also I confidently expect to get enough lecturing on "The Coast" to make me very comfortable. . . .

Grace—dear Heart!—has been here since the 10th. Left this morning. I am trying to persuade her to come west with me—& bring Mary [Channing] if possible.

Wouldn't it be lovely if we two could end our lives together out there! . . .

My present plan is to take a furnished room rather near you; and "meal out"—with some use of my electric stove. Then I could look around, see what the prospects of work were, decide on further steps.

At present I'm plowing through letters; then face the long and, to me, dreadfully difficult job of going through things. So far I'm holding out very well. It's a clean pain. You see there's no one to be sorry for but me—and I'm not going to make much of that? All my Human life is untouched; only the personal life is injured; and I live mostly outside personality. But my head's pretty thick.

Your loving Mother

June 4th. 1934.

Dear Daughter,

It was sweet of you to even think of coming to me. I never thought of such a thing. There is nothing you could have done, dear, or any one, for that matter. Grace of course <u>knows</u> and her grief is greater than man [mine]—and [she has had] far longer time to bear it. And I was thankful for Lyman to have a member of the family, and a man—for Mr. Higgins to talk to. You see I am pitifully thickheaded in business matters, at my best, and am not at my best just now!

Yes, it was a beautiful way to die; and I would far rather have the shock of it than the long agonizing strain you and Grace had! Also I would rather bear the loneliness than have him bear it.

Except for me he was not a happy man. His unfortunate investment (which would have been a good one but for the "depression") the sense of responsibility for his brother's loss and that brothers abominable behavior to him—his suffering under this had aged him. He was not successful here, which was a disappointment. Yes, he would have been glad to go, save for leaving me. So, I have nothing to be sorry for but myself—and that is not a large part of my life.

Mr. Higgins, Houghton's closest friend and a good lawyer, is in charge of affairs and finds little enough to take charge of. . . .

I own a quarter of this place and half of its furnishings. Am going to try to induce "the family"—Cousin Elizabeth Gilman of Baltimore, who was very fond of Houghton; and Cousin Julia Bristol of New Haven, who has some money—to buy me out for $2,500.00. It would be a good bargain for them, for the place would sell better later on. But if they won't I'm going to force a sale—horrid business, lawsuit, auction—small returns. But I must have all I can scrape together. With that I can come out to you comfortably and live awhile—to see if I get work to do. If I don't, I tell you frankly that I do not intend to grow much older, with no work and no income! . . .

Don't make any large plans for me, dear child. I cannot arrive before August probably—I want to make some goodbye visits among friends here. . . .

Your loving Mother.

1934.
June 15th.

Dear Katharine,

. . . I've made a will leaving everything to you—and appointing you executrix—"without bond." . . . There will be little enough to attend to, but it will be a nuisance, and you do not need any more troubles. Of course I'm always hoping the books will be on the market again, & Lyman will attend to those.

To go back to the "room." You see I'm bringing no furniture and do not want to buy any. All I need room for is a couple of trunks and a few boxes of books & mss.

The picture, bedding, etc., I shall unload on you. I wouldn't destroy one of them. Your pictures. And I want to leave you the one Nellie Hale painted of me at seventeen.[98] . . .

Don't be too much concerned about me dear. It is just another "going without," and I've had lots of practice in that. So have most people. . . .

Your loving mother.

1934.
July 17th.

Dear Daughter;

If you have not definitely engaged a room with Miss Mills, don't.[99] The more I think of it the wiser it seems to go to a hotel first; and do my own looking. I will get me a map of Pasadena. . . . Having a "dignified base" with a view to lectures is wise of course; but having a comfortable base for the business of living 365 days in the year is wiser. Evenings I shall hope to see something of you and the children. . . .

Thanks for your kind efforts in my behalf, dear overworked woman!

As to those carfares & taxies you speak of so lightly—I may not get any lectures, and my income may be about $400. a year. Carfares count up—I'd rather have it for movies! Well dear, it will be good to see you all, any how.

Your loving Mother.

Stockbridge Mass.<br>Aug. 13, 1934.

Dear Child—

Yours of Aug. 5th received. I'm here [visiting Lyman and Hilda Stowe] till the 20th. Then Grace for three days. Then to Mrs. M. B. Bruère, Palisades, Rockland Co. . . . to the end of Aug. Then my dear I intend to fly to Cal. Yes, fly. It hurts my conscience a little, for I feel that you ought to have every cent I do not absolutely need; but the expense is not <u>greatly</u> over a one way trip by rail; and I think it will be a stimulating experience, even if tiring. They tell me the noise is not so great in a closed plane. . . .

Yes, those last weeks were pretty awful, but I stood, and am gaining strength here, and even, weight a little. Here is beauty, stillness, pure air, excellent food, and affection. . . .

I have a vast capacity for forgetting. Norwich and all its complications is rapidly receding. And am looking forward eagerly to my pleasantly limited and peaceful life in Pasadena. . . .

Your loving Mother.

With Grace.<br>Aug. 22. '34

Dear Daughter;

I have bought my ticket, <u>not</u> United Air Lines but Lindbergline— T.W.A.—Airport at Glendale, bus <u>at the port</u>, to Pasadena. <u>Much</u> easier. It comes direct, so I shall miss the Sierras by sunrise & coming down the coast from S. F.—but the convenience in landing settled it. I have a front seat to Chicago so I can see ahead—no wing to interfere; and a rear seat to sleep in, (if I do sleep) and also to see down, clear of the wing again. Air-conditioned, temperature at 70°—all lovely. I'm going to take out traveller's insurance—$2.00 for $5,000.00—so if we crash you will be immediately better off! I leave at 4 P.M. Fri. Aug 31st and arrive at 7 A.M. Sat. Sept. 1st. . . .

I'm writing to [my brother] T. [Thomas] & [nephew] T. [Thomas] to meet the bus in Pasadena, as I think you'll be wiser to do; and we'll all have breakfast together. Or, when you've engaged the room (make it a cheap one, dear!) they could be there to meet me—just drop a card to T. to say where it is. . . .

Your loving Mother.

Figure 5. Charlotte Perkins Gilman, ca. 1919. Courtesy of the Schlesinger Library, Radcliffe Institute, Harvard University.

# 5
# Work, Reform, and Activism
## "I love to preach better than anything"

As the twentieth century dawned, Gilman rose to the height of her career. In 1898, *Women and Economics* catapulted her to international fame, and she basked in its glow for several years. To one of her mentors, E. A. Ross, she joyfully cited a review of the volume that had proclaimed it "the best book on the subject since John Stuart Mill's Subjection of Women!!!" (June 23, 1899); Ross would later say in his autobiography that Gilman was "the most brilliant woman I have known" (qtd. in Hill, *Gilman* 244). Already prolific, within two years of *Women and Economics* she would publish *Concerning Children* (1900), followed quickly by *The Home: Its Work and Influence* (1903) and *Human Work* (1904). In 1904 she would also undertake contributing editorship of the *Woman's Journal*, which provided her with a venue for shorter pieces of various kinds, "the little things that flock so thickly" (Gilman to Caroline Severance, January 24, 1904).

Gilman employed a variety of methods to accomplish her goals. Upon her departure from California in 1895, she signed the Friday Morning Club's visitor's book "Charlotte Perkins Stetson. At large" (*Living* 181); while this phrase refers to her having no fixed address, it is also an apt metaphor for the life she led while riding the crest of her fame. "I'm a 'glossopod,'" she would later write to William Haslam Mills. "I travel on my tongue!" (December 28, 1923). A lecturer, writer, reformer, activist, and preacher, Gilman worked on behalf of numerous causes, and her work addressed a variety of subjects and constituencies. Over her career she would publish hundreds of poems, nearly two hundred works of short fiction, eight novels and novellas, seven nonfiction books, and hundreds of essays, in venues ranging from mainstream periodicals to politically oriented publications to her own journal, the *Forerunner*. Her lecture dates numbered nearly one thousand.

Though she was a vocal part of so many conversations and debates, Gilman had a secure home in no single movement or community. This was partly because her worldview exceeded that of any one theoretical stance: she refused fully to embrace Marxism because of her commitment to gender issues; she resisted a complete embrace of feminism in favor of "humanism." She also suffered from a "scandalous lack of education," which led her to use "most unscientific methods of work" (Gilman to Ross, November 28, 1900) and to compose her works largely in isolation from existing scholarship. (On November 28, 1900, she wrote to both E. A. Ross and Lester Ward asking for their help assembling a retroactive bibliography for *Women and Economics:* "who would have been my authorities if I'd read 'em?" she asked Ross.) At heart Gilman was a social philosopher—not an academic, not a journalist, not even (in the traditional sense) a novelist. "Such merit as I have is in the power of original thought, or seeing connections and relations. . . . But when I have to load up with a lot of arbitrarily gathered fresh material, and then as arbitrarily stick it together, the result is not good," she confessed to Arthur Vance, editor of the *Pictorial Review* (May 9, 1919). Gilman was not a part of the intellectual establishment, but her work was widely influential and recognized as such.

Gilman's personal life in the first two decades of the twentieth century, in contrast to previous years, enabled her to participate on the world stage, where she would work for reform as both a philosopher and an activist. Two years before their marriage in 1900, she had written to Houghton: "You understand to the full that I am a world-worker and must be—that I simply give you the part that stays home and that I shall go right along thinking, writing, lecturing and traveling when I must" (May 22, 1898; qtd. in A. J. Lane 212–13). With a spouse who supported her career and a daughter less needful of her immediate care (the teenaged Katharine did, however, live with Gilman and Houghton for more than a year during this time), she was free to pursue her lofty goals—and did so. Beyond her considerable output of writing, she continued her lecturing apace and involved herself in all sorts of clubs and organizations whose aims coincided with her own. For example, along with other writers and critics, she helped to form the Intercollegiate Socialist Society in 1905; in 1907 she served as an officer in the newly founded Equality League of Self-Supporting Women (later the Women's Political Union); with twenty-five others she created the Heterodoxy Club in 1912; she served on the Advisory Council for the National Woman's Party in the late 1910s—and the list goes on. Her letters were another forum for activism, containing references to topics such as women's suffrage, kitchenless houses, standardizing towns, her support of U.S. involvement in World War I, and her concurrent commitment to peace. Likewise, her letters give voice to the now well-documented nativism and racism that informed her reform activities, from her aversion to New York's "swarms of jostling aliens" (Gilman to Alice Stone Blackwell, 1923) to her assertion to Ross that the Turks were "an injury to the world" (July 6, 1925). Through all of this, what she apparently sought was the "fulfillment of true service" (Gilman to James Barry, December 23, 1920).

While her "world-work" took many forms, and while her print output was substantial, Gilman supported herself financially mainly through lecturing (with rare exceptions, such as her salaried position writing columns for the *New York Tribune* syndicate in 1919 and 1920). She admitted that she was "incapable of 'selling myself,' always was" (Gilman to Lyman Beecher Stowe, September 11, 1928), greeting the necessity with "great distaste" (Gilman to Lula Roantree, September 15, 1920). Nonetheless, her attempts to do so form a refrain that runs throughout her correspondence. Though she did use booking agents and national lecture agencies, she never had "a good lecture agent or manager for any length of time. Such a person, to succeed, must have a strong conviction of the value of my work, <u>and</u> business ability. These do not coexist" (*Living* 306). Instead, Gilman often secured and publicized speaking engagements (and publicized her written work) through the help of friends, family, and other supporters. Aware that her work—both the lecturing and the writing—was of value, and needing a livelihood, she wanted to be paid fairly; beyond this, however, she desired to spread her ideas and to promote change, and she would frequently travel to give lectures that were remunerated for little more than expenses incurred.

During these heady years, Gilman's commitment to spreading her message through writing was as unwavering as her drive to lecture. She began to find, however, that "if one writes to express important truths, needed yet unpopular, the market is necessarily limited" (*Living* 304). Having formed with Houghton the Charlton Company in 1905 to publish some of her own books, she launched her magazine, the *Forerunner,* in 1909 when she began to find it harder and harder to place her work. She single-handedly wrote and edited the diverse content, and published the magazine, each month for seven years. While the *Forerunner* was never self-sustaining, it did garner subscribers from all over the United States and abroad. Gilman subsidized it, predictably, through lectures and publishing her work elsewhere. A letter to Mabel Hay Barrows encapsulates what her life was like during these productive years, when her frenetic activity was both exhausting and exhilarating: "I've been . . . a'lecturing. A very hard trip. Had to write Forerunner stuff on the way. Cold weather. Heavy snow. Coal famine. Railroad strike. Trains late. Meals all upset. Sleep out of the question. Old lady pretty rocky. But speechifying to beat the band!" (January 16, 1910).

Having said much of what she needed to say, Gilman ended the *Forerunner* in 1916. As interest in her lectures and her published writing waned after World War I, she continued to see the need for her ideas. "Here's all this mass of young people," she complained to her cousin Lyman Beecher Stowe, "repudiating old standards and finding no new ones" (September 11, 1928). She began to look back upon her career and assess her contributions, continuing to write, publish, and lecture, and contemplating a uniform collection of her greatest works. While she would never again have the audience she did in the first years of the twentieth century, her commitment never wavered. "I love to preach better than anything," she wrote in response to an invitation to speak to a women's group in 1920 (Gilman to Roantree, September 15, 1920). This line also sums up the essence of her long career. Her power as a lecturer was well documented; so, too, was her desire to use her voice—in print, on the platform, in clubs and organizations, even in her letters—to effect change in the world.

Tues. Dec. 16th. 1890.
Pasadena Cal.

Mr. S. J. Barrows[1]
Dear Sir,

I am pleased that you like my articles, amused that you confess yourself afraid to publish one of them, and willing that you should have "The Divine Right of Mothers" and "Living from Day to Day" for five dollars each.

But, since you pay more when articles are specially ordered, and since mine please you, why not specially order some?

Try a few topics—do you order by topics, or by signatures?—and see if I suit.

I remember the [Christian] Register with interest, not to say affection, and shall be pleased to meet its large circle of readers.

May I make you a present of a stray idea? What in Shelley is called "A Fragment."[2]

"How dare you call one thing <u>above</u> another?
—There is no top or bottom to the universe!"

Stick it in at the bottom of a column; it is a good idea as far as it goes.

Sincerely—
Charlotte Perkins Stetson.

1258 Webster St., Oakland, Cal.
Wed. Oct. 19th 1892

Mr. Brander Matthews:[3]

Will you excuse a very earnest woman for appealing to you as a <u>critic</u> of high standing, and a gentleman, to know if there is not some literary tribunal before which a writer of peculiarly scurrilous and evil habits may be brought, exposed, and punished?

The faults I allude to are not those of a personal character, but of a professional character; and the more blamable that the writer is a powerful one.

As a soldier may be a good fighter, and yet conduct himself in a manner "unworthy of an officer and a gentleman," so may a man be a good writer and yet commit insufferable offense with his pen.

The person against whom I make this charge is Mr. Ambrose Bierce of San Francisco.

I have recently read your notice of his book in "More American Stories" in a recent magazine; and while I would like to take issue with you on the artistic merits of that mechanical chamber of horrors I will let it stand merely as a proof that the man is a writer of ability.

Being such, and so presumably able to maintain himself by honest productive work, he consents to write for the S. F. Examiner at a high salary, and to write for it such unmanly gossip and slander as no city but San Francisco would tolerate I think.

I speak generally, but am willing to produce evidence in plenty if it will be really of use.

Mr. Bierce has an outspoken contempt for women. "Lovely woman" he says "has no thinker." The domestic woman he treats gently, but let her touch the pen and he uses his to flay her.

Do you chance to know my father—Fred. B. Perkins, formerly of New York?

You have mentioned one of his stories "The Devil Puzzler" as one of the ten best short stories—in your Pen & Ink Sketches. I wrote and asked him if any good thing could be said of Ambrose Bierce?—I had heard naught but evil.

He answered that nothing good could be said of him—that he was the meanest hound that wrote—that "he thinks nothing of blackguarding women publicly, by name"; and more of as strong nature. . . .

He never strikes at large game—well known writers or women with lively and pugilistic "protectors," only at the weak women, the defenseless, the easily discouraged; women who are struggling and climbing, generally for the very lack of the husband or brother whose presence would close the sneering mouth.

What he dare not say directly he insinuates; as for instance he once spoke of me as "allowing herself to be lunched and feted by the ladies of Oakland, who delight to so honor any impostor who comes along."

Then hastily adding "Not that this lady is an impostor. For aught I know she is a most estimable woman and writer"—etc. etc. I enclose the most recent specimen I have of his delicate touch.

Miss Coolbrith is a poet of real merit—, a "lone woman" not well to do, and liable to real injury from such usage.[4] . . .

The point is that an able writer constantly attacks and insults defenseless women; regarding neither truth, honor, nor common decency; this all our reading public know.

The Examiner stands here as an example of the corrupt and does not stand at all elsewhere! Sensational and venal press, and Mr. Bierce's "Prattle" is a most juicy column in the Sunday edition.

It is difficult to reach a man of such nature in any sensitive place; but surely there must be <u>some</u> way of getting at him, some tribunal whose judgement he would feel.

It's not an indictable offense to ridicule and covertly slander the weaker works in one's own line; but it is an offense against common decency; and a crying shame on the noble art of letters.

I wish I could claim perfect immunity for myself, and so perfect disinterestedness; but there are few women writers of this coast who could—he scorns us all.

But I can honestly say that my personal offense never moved me to action—is more than a year old; and that this laborious and far-sent effort is due to purely impersonal resentment based on a widening knowledge of his immeasurable, ingenious, baseness.

Somebody ought to do something—can you advise any possible measures? Attacks from the local press are meat and drink to him—he has plenty, and minds them not a whit.

Is there no way by which his literary conscience could be reached?

Sincerely—somewhat apologetically,

Charlotte Perkins Stetson

1258 Webster St. Oakland Cal.

Nov. 18th, 1893.

Dear Mother,[5]

Here is a specimen mailed with this of my first—1500 is too many to call a litter, isn't it.[6]

Well, first-birth at any rate, and a fine promising child it seems to the fond mother.

Will you see about putting them in a book store for me? Send me word where to send them, and how many copies. They sell for 25 cts. Twenty per cent commission to dealers.

Please give one of these to the <u>Pasadena Star</u>—if still going. . . .

All doing well here.

With love,

Charlotte Perkins Stetson.

20 West 32nd st.

New York City.

Dec. 10th. '96.

Dear Mr. Garrison,[7]

Presently I shall have a lecture list printed—a new one—and will send you some. My California ones don't do now, and I have none other.

I do not have cut and dried "lectures," but talk with unceasing vigor on various large and vital themes.

In England and Scotland I've been doing mostly reform work. The splendid Single Tax[8] Campaign in Delaware I found well known there.

I have three lectures on the woman question which I think most valuably suggestive—

Woman and Man

Woman and Work

Woman and Child . . .

Then I have various ones on economic points of view, notably one [*sic*] the basic error in our present system and its coming change—called "Why We Work."

Also several ethical ones—preaching is my strong point. One of these is of the widest import—and interesting too. I call it Body and Soul.

I didn't mean to beseech you [to] become a lecture agent. But thought you were in the way of hearing of opportunities, and knew <u>how</u> I spoke—so you might be able to suggest my name somewhere.

But truly I don't want you to bother about it.

I am settling in very comfortably here, and things begin to open up already. But I always have something of a yearning Bostonwards.

Sincerely—

Charlotte Perkins Stetson.

20 W. 32. New York—
April 6th. '97

Dear Mrs. Howells—⁹

I am abased before you!

I don't know why, in that frenzied moment when the stormy African maidservant confronted me with your note—which gave me great delight—and the pink ticket of the messenger—which, as do all such printed forms, instantly took from me the knowledge of my own name—why, in that hour I should take for granted that it was your daughter who wrote, and not you. Thereafter I marveled, saying "Why should the damsel speak of her father as 'Mr. Howells'?" And my mind misgave me.

But after all, isn't it a compliment to a mother "to be taken for her daughter!"—there's something in that.

Anyway I will come on Wednesday at one o'clock, and trust you will forgive me my stupidity.

Sincerely—
Charlotte Perkins Stetson. . . .

18 West 32nd Street,
New York, Jan. 5th 1898.

[To William Lloyd Garrison]

Just to say that I am coming on again to Boston to lecture for the W. E. & I. U. [Women's Educational and Industrial Union] on Thurs. Jan. 20th.

Subject "Modern Myth."

Shall hope this time to be able to call on you and Mrs. Garrison.

You'll be mightily interested—I think—in the book I'm getting out—"Sex in Social Economics"¹⁰ Small, Maynard & Co. They're doing a new edition of the poems too.

Sincerely—
Charlotte Perkins Stetson

Camforth Lodge
Hammersmith W.
June 23rd. '99.

Dear Mr. Ross;¹¹

Now I am coming down on you hard! But don't you do it unless you really want to—I shan't mind a bit if you decline.

I am planning, for my fall lecture trip in America, to give a three night course on the Women & Economics theory—

1. Work & Women. 2. The Home. 3. The Child;

with a special descriptive circular to itself containing book notices etc. You spoke of writing me one—would you be willing to for such a circular? Don't hesitate to say no—but if you are willing it would count. . . .

I think it is worth while to take advantage off the public interest in the book [Women and Economics] and its theory. The New York Nation & Evening Post have—(or has)—given it a long and fine review. Says it's the best book on the subject since John Stuart Mill's Subjection of Women!!!¹² . . .

Yours cordially—
Charlotte Perkins Stetson . . .

Las Casitas Villa
Box 152. Pasadena, Cal.
Feb. 1st. 1900.

Dear Prof. Ross—

Veblun¹³ [*sic*] goes back to you with this, with sincere thanks and as sincere apologies for keeping it so long. . . .

It's a most interesting and suggestive book. I should have so liked to speak to you on various points that came up in reading. . . .

I see one way to cut under the springs of all the "invidious comparison" on which Veblun's theory rests—by an improved education of the little child. We can alter the set of the brain cells,—and then all of that colossal folly will die of itself. But that's a long story too. . . .

Warm regards to Mrs. Ross. . . .

Lots to you from your friend,
Charlotte Perkins Stetson.

Chicago Ill. Nov. 28th. 1900.

Dear Prof. Ross—

Shall I congratulate you—or comisserate [*sic*] you?¹⁴ Anyhow I hope you will be settled nearer my end of the country!

I've been staying here a bit, on a lecture trip, and have met Prof. Veblen, and found him very interesting. I'm still endeavoring to "promote" his amazing book.¹⁵

An Italian translation of Women & Economics is being made by the Contessa Pirouti of Naples; through the good offices of "Vernon Lee";[16] and the latter begs of me a "bibliography" of the authorities on whom I found my arguments.

Now that I have told you of my scandalous lack of education and most unscientific methods of work—behold me stranded groveling— unable to refer to anything but Lester F. Ward & Geddes & Thompson [*sic*]![17] Can you not, without taking much time of it, jot me down a little bit of Standard Authors on Scientific Subjects who would have been my authorities <u>if I'd read 'em</u>?

You know the book. The main theory is my own—the facts I have gathered "all over." But give me a few of the big progressive sociologists whose work bears out mine—or mine theirs[?]. . . .

Cordially your friend<br>Charlotte Perkins Gilman

Lockland [Road], Geneva, [New York]<br>May 28th, 1903.

Dear Mrs. Sweet:[18]

I have no definite engagement for next winter; and can come to you at any time if we agree on arrangements.[19]

But my feeling about payment has come to be settled in this way: if my reputation in a place is not good enough to draw a good pay- ing crowd, so that the club may make money from my services, I do not like to go. To feel that the club has to tax its slender resources to pay me a small sum is mortifying to me professionally. Next fall—in September—I have a new book coming out, on The Home—and I think you will find a general interest in the subject and the writer. Now if you can arrange a big public lecture, a pay lecture—admission 25 cts, reserved seats 50 cts; I will come on these terms.

My expenses to be paid (almost $18.00).

The lecture expenses to be paid.

Then I will divide the remaining proceeds with the club up to $50.00—and anything further will be the club's.

Now 300 people—100 "reserved" and 200 "admission"—would give you $100.00 and that ought to pay all expenses and a little over.

Suppose I gave a lecture on "The Home and The Ballot"—or some such thing.

I think you would find it popular—especially after this book. . . .

I would rather do this and make nothing over my expenses than to be paid by an effort of the club and lecture in a small way.

Sincerely yours

Charlotte Perkins Gilman.

1-25-'04

179 West 76th Street, New York

My Dear Mrs. Severance,[20]

I am very glad you take such an interest in my work.

You have noticed perhaps what I have undertaken in <u>The Woman's Journal</u>. I give my work for a year—with the purpose of ascertaining if enough people care for it to make the paper at least self-sustaining. (It never has been you know.) Then, if it pays, I am to have a share in it and help make it a broader more representative paper—embracing the whole woman movement and bringing it into relation with the world's movement—at last!

Isn't that worth trying for? So if you can corral some subscribers they will get 52 installments of original work by C.P.G.—poems and all. Some of it is consecutive and may be reprinted later as a booklet.

I am enjoying the work immensely—as a change from big books. <u>Human Work</u> is done at last and I am free to let out the little things that flock so thickly. No, I do not believe in the action of the Socialist Party—so far.

I am a socialist, of a sort, but not of the "orthodox."

Socialism is to be gained gradually, in steps, and the labor vote could bring gradual concessions from one party after another, if they were solid. But they are not. . . .

My dear daughter, nineteen in March coming, and bigger than I now, is studying art in Rome with her father and dear Grace. That is her chosen profession and she is doing well in it. I shall see her next summer—for I'm going over to speak at the International Congress.

Yours Cordially—

Charlotte Perkins Gilman

179 W. 76th Street, New York

9-20-05

Dear Mrs. Fenyes—[21]

I am at home at last considerably the worse for wear. Here are the autographs—two extra for good measure, with apologies for delay. I was so used up by my long traveling that all letters have been put off for weeks. . . .

The poems were largely written in the little cottage—now no more—on the corner of Orange Grove Ave. and Arroyo Drive.[22] Human Work was begun at Las Casitas—1899–1900. The theory of Woman [*sic*] & Economics occurred to me on the banks of the Arroyo—talking to Miss Senter. So you see I have many associations with Pasadena.

I was glad to see you, and will try to see more of you when I come again. . . .

Cordially—

Charlotte Perkins Gilman

179 West 76th Street, New York

11-12-05

Dr. Gould—[23]

Dear Sir—

. . . I had an article in The Independent on "Kitchen Dirt and Civic Health"[24] which you might find sense in . . . sorry I can't find it to send you. Showing how, in the slum problem, if they had good & cheap food provided by scientific kitchens you strike a double blow at disease; first by proper nourishment of the body; second by eliminating all the kitchen dirt—ashes, grease, smoke, garbage, and the noise and dirt of the street peddlers besides. . . .

Hastily—

C.P. Gilman.

3-15-'06

179 West 76th Street, New York.

Dear Prof. Ross;

I've been a goodfornothing invalid all winter; couldn't answer letters or do any work at all. Hence my dumb ingratitude for your book—Foundations of Sociology. I find it valuable and interesting and am obliged to you for it. Also I find why you think so little of "Human Work," and want to have a fine row with you some day!

I'm so pleased to have Prof. Ward's theory come out in the Independent! Mr. Holt tells me there are to be "three withering replies." I doubt if they wither. And the thing ought to be discussed thoroughly—it is of such tremendous importance. . . .

Cordially—

Charlotte Perkins Gilman

2-14-'08[25]

Ed. New York Times—

Dear Sir;

Will you give space to an appeal to your readers on the subject of a National Health Board?

By every reason that necessitates a City Board of Health are we also shown the need of a National Organization of that nature. The waste to the nation from preventable death, preventable sickness, and the preventable weakness and criminality arising from unhygienic surroundings and gross ignorance, is so enormous that a practical nation like ours should rouse itself to take action. . . .

The City can do much, and the state can do much, but when one state gets its typhoid supply from another or sends its consumptives to another, we need a broader authority for regulation.

When we realize that if the average life-span of our current population could be raised from 40 to 45 years, that the economic gain to the country would be $800,000,000. per annum, it seems worthwhile to undertake definite measures to that end. . . .

Trusting that a matter of such pressing public concern will seem to you worth the wholesouled assistance of the press.

I remain

Yours truly

C. P. Gilman

313 West 82d Street, New York

4-26-'08

Dr. E. R. L. Gould—

Dear Sir;

Thank you for sending us the account of your recent success in the C. & S. H. [City and Suburban Homes] Co. If I had money to invest this is exactly the kind of thing I should wish to invest in; but just at present there is no surplus. Meanwhile I will keep the matter in mind, and may be able to interest others.

Some day I'm going to have some model homes <u>without kitchens</u> built!—in the mean time all improvements are welcome!

Cordially—

Charlotte Perkins Gilman.

313 West 82d Street, New York

3-24-'09

Dear Sister Mabel [Hay Barrows Mussey]—[26]

It sounds deliciously attractive, but we can't make it. You see we haven't any leeway at all—these years; and every cent I can rake and scrape is going into the New Baby![27] . . .

I don't even feel sure of the time—not knowing just what this business will demand of me. I may only get a week here and a week there—and that nearer home! So I shall not be able to swim in the maple syrup, row up and down mountains, sleep in the blueberries and pick gallons of tents and cabins this year—alas!

On top of which nonsense I am sending you ten little folders; assailing you as I am all my friends now—they being my only capital. Will you keep one, and from time to time get confiding persons to sign the ten name list. . . . You see my little game is to get as many "promised subscribers" as I can (to say nothing of paid ones!) and on the strength of this list of names to get my advertisements. It is a "cheeky" business, but an honest one. I can promise them they'll get their money's worth!

Love to you dear. I'm sorry I can't come up and play with you among the firry hills!

Charlotte Perkins Gilman . . .

5-23-09

Dear Mrs. Dawson;[28]

I sent you an article early in February, called "<u>How To Make Better Men</u>," in accordance with hurry order in yours of Jan. 26th.

This article appeared on May 9th, in <u>The Sunday American</u> of New York, under the title "<u>When She Feels She's Falling In Love</u>." No credit is given.

Will you please advise me if this article was sold or given to them; or if they merely stole it. I particularly wish to know—on account of previous knowledge of the Hearst Papers.

Yours sincerely—

Charlotte Perkins Gilman

on train. Minnesota.

1-16-'10

Dear Sister [Mabel Hay Barrows Mussey]—

... We passed a very sulky Xmas. No money, over-worked, "didn't do a thing" to anybody.

Since then I've been as far as Fargo, N.D.—a'lecturing. A very hard trip. Had to write Forerunner stuff on the way. Cold weather. Heavy snow. Coal famine. Railroad strike. Trains late. Meals all upset. Sleep out of the question. Old lady pretty rocky. But speechifying to beat the band! Have made some new friends, some subscribers, some calls for next winter, and a little money—very little! ...

Yours with love—

Charlotte Perkins Gilman.

5-17-'15

My dear Miss Williams;[29]

As to that lecture agent work—will you please write to, or see, Mrs. Robert Evans first. She talked of doing it—that is, I talked with her about doing it. She was interested, but no definite plan settled on. ...

As a matter of fact I do not think she is in a position to do it as well as you, being so far out of town and so forth; so I shall be glad if she concludes not to; in which case I cheerfully accept your offer.

The work consists of, a., in communicating with various clubs, societies, or other organizations possibly wanting to engage single lectures; b. in "working up" a single lecture, through securing subscribers beforehand and selling tickets to the public; and c., in this new plan of mine for a "Gilman Week."

That involves securing a sufficient number of subscriptions to the course to warrant the undertaking; renting a hotel parlor or some such suitable place; and then, in the time left free, engaging single lectures by either of the other processes. ...

For a "week" I should want a bed-rock minimum of $300.00 net. ...

Also, if there were a number of single lectures on the side, afternoons or evenings, we could afford a less paying class. My general lecture rate now is $100.00; though for suffrage or socialist work I speak for less—sometimes for $50.00.

I really hope Mrs. Evans will not go on with it—I think you would be more successful. Thank you for asking.

Most cordially—

Charlotte Perkins Gilman.

Peterboro, N.H.

8-9-'15

[To William Haslam Mills][30]

My dear friend—

I have brought with, for "holiday work,["] 58 letters to answer! Among them yours of March 18th.

In spite of my sins in such delay I am always glad to hear from you. . . . I have pleasant memories of your house and garden and studio; and proudly exhibit my peacock pin to invariably admiring eyes.

All our hearts are with England today.[31] The "balance of power" for the world is in process of decision; and I firmly believe you will hold it. . . .

Also I hope to come myself [to England], when the sea is safe again and Europe at least resting!

Love to you.

Charlotte Perkins [*sic*]

10-2-15

Dear Dr. Ross,

The article on "Standardizing Towns" in the February Forerunner, of which I am sending you an extra copy, treat of the subject I wanted to see you about.[32] . . .

What I thought might have a "business end" to it was this. Suppose some authoritative source, like Wis. Univ. [Wisconsin University]— your own department in particular—should work up a little book— cheap—paper—25¢ say; perhaps .50; with the visible outlines of a standardized town; and its score card. The Thing should be done so that the average woman could see it. . . .

Then a special study should be made of some one town—same as the soil experts study counties—and that town rated—by the score card.

Then some sociological expert should be prepared to go, on request, and "take the measurements" of any town—filling in its card and issuing the books or sale in it.

I believe this would rouse enormous interest. . . . Civic pride and emulation are strong forces. . . .

Of its larger implications I will speak when I see you. . . .

Charlotte Perkins Gilman.

627 W. 136
New York
5-1-'17

My dear Mrs. Solomon;[33]

I can, of course, come again to your Forum if you want me; but I have adopted an absolute minimum of $50.00[.] That is half my regular rate, and I will no longer go lower than that. . . .

Yours sincerely,
Charlotte Perkins Gilman.

Aug. 28. '17.

My dear Mrs. Karsten;[34]

I have resigned from the Woman's Peace Party; and I suppose that automatically cuts me off from the I. C. W. P. P. [International Committee of Women for Permanent Peace]—does it not?[35] You see, I approve of our entering the war, think it necessary and right and believe that Germany must be not only conquered but punished.

While still profoundly interested in the establishment and maintenance of Peace, my judgement is that the immediate steps toward it require a successful prosecution of the war we have undertaken and that much of the present activity of the pacificists [*sic*] in our country—and in others—both prolong the struggle and tend to discredit the movement for Permanent Peace.

Now if I have thus excommunicated myself from you I'm sorry—but that is my position.

If, as an individual, deeply concerned to establish permanent peace, I can remain, I gladly do so.

Cordially your friend in any case—
Charlotte Perkins Gilman

627 West 136
New York City
June 9th 1918

Hon. Thomas W. Gregory,
Atty. General U. S. Govt.
Washington, D. C.
Dear Sir,

While in no way justifying the unwisdom of Mrs. Rose Pastor Stokes in the utterances upon which her trial was based, I find on every side the same strong feeling which rises in me—that her punishment is heavily disproportionate.[36] In the face of so many and so much worse offences on the part of others, notably in the mischievous and powerful work of W. R. Hearst, this peculiar weight of sentence on one ill-advised woman who used her tongue unwisely, seems almost Prussian in its ruthlessness.

Our Government needs to be strong and stern against all pro-German pacificism [*sic*] Bolshevism, and untimely demands for privileges or even rights not allowable in time of war, but any punishment savoring of cruelty or injustice arouses widespread protest, and tends to promote the very spirit it endeavors to suppress.

It is to be sincerely hoped that for the sake of our country's success in war and honor in peace we may maintain even-handed justice in spite of the fierce spirit of the hour.

Yours, not in extenuation of the offender,
but in protest against a dangerously severe sentence,
Charlotte Perkins Gilman

627 W. 136th st.
New York City.
Jan. 17th. 1919.

Mr. Norman White
Small, Maynard & Co.,
15 Beacon st. Boston, Mass.,
Dear Sir:

Will you let me buy back from you the "three-and-a-bit" of my books which I publish?

They cannot be worth much to you, measured by the law of diminishing returns in royalties, but I have the author's fondness for them, and want to keep them with those I have brought out as "the Charlton Co.,"——which is simply Mr. Gilman and myself.

Some day I hope to have a "uniform edition," when the Charlton Co. can afford it.

If you are willing to do this what would be the price, plates, bound copies, and all?[37]

Yours sincerely,

627 W. 136th st.<br>[New York, N.Y.]<br>March 19th. 1919.

Dear Mr. Vance,[38]

Yes, I got your letter of Feb. 24th [asking for an article on "The Future of the Marriage Relation"], and have been doing what you suggested.

You only said "Now think it over, and possibly you can do something for us that will be unusually good."

You will not be offended, I hope, if I say that I have done several pieces of work on suggestions of yours, only to have them returned, and at present, I am too busy with regularly engaged syndicated editorials to put in time on uncertainties. It is quite a new experience for me to get a salary, and if it does as well as the syndicaters think it will I shall find my work really pay—which it never did before.

Besides this I have been laughed at by some of my writing friends, women really less known, because they say I work too cheaply. They get two and three hundred dollars for an article, have done so for years.

One editorial friend cheerfully put it—"You can't sell yourself, that's all."

You see I do not know much about the business end, never did. Do you pay other writers of my standing as you do me? If so there is no reason I should get more. But if you do pay them more, why not me?

Professor Montague[39] of Columbia says he divides feminists into two schools, those who uphold monogamous marriage and those who teach free relations, and that I am the leader of the first school. So I think I could do something you would like on that line, if you want it.

Yours sincerely,

[New York, N.Y.]
March 23rd, 1919.

[To Anne Henrietta Martin][40]

... You will be pleased to hear that I am at last embarked on a line of work that really promises to PAY!

I'm doing some newspaper syndicate work, just started, but with excellent prospects. This helps with both lectures and magazine articles, one hand washing the other as it were.

I amm [*sic*] beginning to arrange for the fall trip well in advance this time, and have offered Colorado three weeks in November. Denver, Boulder, and Colorado Springs are hopeful of having "Gilman Weeks." Montana comes in before that, and now I'm hoping to get to California, and, of course, to stop over in Nevada.

Cordially yours,
Charlotte Perkins Gilman.

627 W. 136th st.
[New York, N.Y.]
Friday May 9th. 1919.

Dear Mr. Vance? [*sic*]

I have written a new opening [to the article on marriage], and carried on the re-arrangement about half through, a little more perhaps.[41]

The last part seemed to be about what I wished to say, so I left it. This makes the paper about a page too long,—but you can easily cut out one if you wish.

I know I do not do this sort of article as well as my own work. Such merit as I have is in the power of original thought, or seeing connections and relations, and a sometimes happy trick of expression which comes as natural as breathing when the thought flows freely.

But when I have to load up with a lot of arbitrarily gathered fresh material, and then as arbitrarily stick it together, the result is not good. That's why I never try to do that kind.

I do have important ideas sometimes, lots of 'em.

And I do have a sort of style of my own. But that's all.

There are hundreds of professional writers who can collect facts and piece them together. I enjoy and appreciate their work, when it is good. But they very seldom blossom into ideas.

Perhaps one reason is that ideas are not wanted.

The distinctive value of my views on marriage lies mainly in the position that it is a natural relation, based on biological law. To show that monogamy is natural and right, to point out what are the essential errors of our marriage laws and customs and how to change them, to put the "New Morality" in its right place as merely the old immorality on a pedestal, to show up the fallacy in "Birth Control,"[42] to shed light on the whole matter, this seems to me as well worth doing as telling what this writer has said or that legislature done. . . .

I have very honestly and laboriously tried to furnish what you wished for in this paper, but you didn't need to tell me it is not very good. . . .

Excuse this long and doubtless unnecessary screed—its not a common offense from me.

> Still cordially yours,
> Charlotte P. Gilman.

> 629 W. 136th st.
> New York City.
> Sept. 15th. 1920.

Dear Mrs. Roantree,[43]

You asked for some publicity material, and with great distaste I have endeavored to manufacture some. . . .

It occurs to me that something might be done by asking a number of Syracuse women "What Mrs. Gilman Means to You?" That would make good newspaper stuff, and if you only asked friendly ones it ought to help the lectures.

Then some one might make little funny or sharp extracts from my books or the Forerunner, call 'em "Gilmanisms," perhaps some paper would run a few. I'm not much good at this publicity stunt, if I were I should be richer! . . .

I am willing to do anything I can to help, except give interviews—that I will not do, ever, no matter how favorably intended. You see I am particularly anxious for you people to make a real success of this, so that I can convince other clubs that I am not an Expense Account only. . . .

How about a sermon, on the 3rd, to get more folks roused up? I love to preach better than anything, have done it often.

> Most cordially,

627 W. 136th st.
New York City.
Dec. 1st. 1920.

Marshall, Jones & Co.
Summer st.
Boston. Mass.,
Dear Sirs,

I hear from Mr. Chester Lane,[44] that there is a possibility of your being interested in my books. This possibility I do not overestimate I assure you.

At present I own all my books, having bought in from Small Maynard C., those they had. . . .

My ultimate purpose—do not be alarmed, it is remote—is to have a uniform edition, a set of "works." . . .

A competent critic and writer, Miss Amy Wellington, long on Current Literature, has prepared a brief biography of me, from the point of view of literary study and estimate.

Such a biography, accompanied by the new volume of verse, and with the earlier volume reprinted, uniformly with the new, might find a market. I have frequent and urgent demands for the poems, but it has been out of print for about a year. . . .

For new books I have two in mind. One is a sort of "Social Primer," an un-technical kind of social philosophy, suited to a quite popular study, hopeful and practical. . . .

The other is a book of serious verse, in varied forms, bringing out as has never yet been attempted the historic drama we call "the woman question": This has nothing to do with the suffrage movement, nor yet with all that oscillating confusion we miscall "feminism." If I do it, and do it well, it will be something new in literature, and useful in putting safe foundations under our changing views. . . .

Yours sincerely,

627 W. 136, New York
Dec. 23rd. 1920

To James H. Barry,[45]
And his Good Wife Also:

Year after year your message of good will
Has found me silent and neglectful still

But now with sudden gratitude I jump
And send arrears of "thank yous" in a lump!

Your friendship for my father and for me—,
Your labor for humanity at large—
Unnumbered kindnesses that angels see—
Surely your lives have well fulfilled their charge!

I specially remember your strong hand
Of helpfulness when I was poor, alone,
Condemned and criticized, my work unknown,
You helped me give it to the world, and so
Assisted the one worship that I know—
Fulfillment of true service; this I bless
More than all other many kindnesses.[46]

Charlotte Perkins Gilman.

627 W. 136th st.<br>New York City.<br>May 16th. 1921.

Dear Mr. Holt,[47]

... "Prejudice, Antipathy and Judgement" I've written on before, but not printed as far as I can discover. This is a brand new article any how, and you can change the name to be quite safe. . . .

How about a little one on "The Terrible Super-State," showing how similar it is to our much dreaded and long opposed Federal Government; how normal in political evolution. This could show also that the doubt of managing the conflicting interests of dissimilar peoples is settled by our well-established habit of doing that very thing among our own "dissimilar peoples."

There is no subject which appeals to me at present as much as this obvious and pressing matter of world union.

Yours cheerfully,

19th [illegible]—'23[48]<br>380 Washington Street<br>Norwichtown, Conn.

My dear Alice [Stone Blackwell]—[49]

... Behold my new address! . . . To me the change is delightful. I increasingly hated New York and its swarms of jostling aliens.

It is bad enough here, but I don't see them—living in the old part of the town. I'm Connecticut born, and it is all very homelike and pleasant.

I'm writing a book on "His Religion and Hers"—and have two articles under that title coming out in the Century, March & April I believe. . . .

I love to think of you—your great parents—the whole splendid family. They contribute one of the high spots in my experience, a race of giants, full of the social spirit.

I hope you keep well and are able to look far beyond these discouraging days.

Always your loving friend,<br>Charlotte P. Gilman

380 Washington Street<br>Norwich Town, Conn.<br>Dec. 28. '23

[To William Haslam Mills]

My dear friend—

It is good to hear from you—brings up my pleasant days in London and your many kindnesses. . . .

Yes, I'm coming to England again—some day; but it costs, more than ever, and I'm not yet able to travel for the fun of it. I'm a "glossopod" you remember—I travel on my tongue!

Yes, there is great need of what I try to teach—now that all the tempestuous struggle for "the vote" has lapsed with pointless indifference to the use of it. The women have no program—no purpose to vote for. And we need them more than ever. . . .

With loving remembrance and good wishes for the new year——

C. P. Gilman

380 Washington st.<br>Norwich Town. Conn.<br>July 6th. 1925.

[To E. A. Ross]

O Eminent Sociologist,

    Effective and Agreeable Writer

        and Excellent Friend,

        Greetings! [. . .] I don't know how long it is since I've written you, but just now I found on my desk among the "not immediates" yours of about two years ago, with kind words about my last book and most gratifying news of family triumphs. . . .

I have some new lectures I'd like you to hear; The Falsity Of Freud; Americans and Non-Americans; and Standards and Programs. Shall you be "at home" about the last week of March? . . .

. . . I have started in a feeble way on my Autobiography, but it does not interest me as much as it ought to. My real interest is in ideas, as you know. Here is one I think you will care for and can perhaps do something about. You know my suggestions about "Standardising Towns["]—? . . .

Well—that has got to be done for Nations.

You know how we all love, honor and brag about our own land? And it never occurs to us that nations vary in value to the world, some useful, some of small account, some deleterious. My proposition is to prepare some sort of list of "Points" in which different peoples visibly excel, as for instance, Art; Science; Music; Warfare; Invention; Discovery; Benevolence; Refinement; Honesty; Progressivness; Political development;—points to be agreed upon by some competent authorities, and then a group of the principal nations classified under that list.[50]

My suggestion to editors was to get an able man of each land to write the braggingist article he could on his own people's attainments, say twelve of 'em, publish them monthly, and then have the facts checked off by an international group of historians—(fine fighting there!) and the whole bunch measured and rated.

I tried it in a loose tentative fashion. I don't know enough to undertake it seriously—something like the enclosed.[51] [Of] course any list would be violently disagreed with, but instead of mere bragging and lying there would be in the popular mind something to judge by. You'll be amused by my estimate of Ireland's achievements, but as a nation, what have they contributed to the world besides a few writers? . . .

Did the Turks ever do anything good? I think of them as a purely predatory people, and an injury to the world.[52] . . .

I think your "naturalists" comment on Ward's Gynocentric theory[53] extremely shallow. He gave instances enough from birds and quadrupeds . . . to rest the whole thing on. Except for the special decorations and fighting machinery of the male, and his seasonal pugnacity, the female is the equal in all race activities, and adds her increasing power as a race-builder. Of course it's her "psyche" if you wish to call it that. See what a nice thing I've got on Freud—. Sex is not the "Life Force." Life existed for ages, and reproduction went on, billion-fold, before sex was developed. It is not essential to life, nor to reproduction, but to the improvement of species. So there!

With cordial regards to Mrs. Ross, your old friend,

C. P. Gilman

380 Washington Street
Norwichtown, Conn.
7-28-'25

Dear English Walling—[54]

We are so pleased to hear from you again, and to know that you are in Connecticut. How far is Westport? Couldn't you motor over and see us? We'd love to have you. . . .

I shall be glad to contribute to the book you contemplate, if I can write anything favorable along the lines you propose. The nearest thing fit which I see at present is a little discourse on the feeble way in which people have allowed Bolshevism to completely overshadow and discredit genuine Socialism!!

I'm not "discouraged"—no believer in Social Evolution can be, but I do think that the movement toward socialization, first perverted by Marx and then defiled by Bolshevism, has been set back for years. Maybe fifty years!

Also, being made into a class-struggle etc., the behavior of the noble workingman has been such as to quite dull the sympathy which used to make some people socialists!

Perhaps a little quiet analysis of what ails us—in regard to Socialism, and indication of the real principles and orderly advance, beneficial to all classes—would be useful: "What Hinders Socialism," say.

I've looked you up on map and timetable. You'd better come by train I guess—& stay over night—how about it?

Cordially—

C. P. Gilman

380 Washington St.
Norwich Town. Conn.
12-4-'25

[To E. A. Ross]
Now see here!

Can't you come down here for over Sunday after the A.S.S. (!) meetings in N.Y.?[55] If you will I'll come to the City of Dreadful-all-the-time and bring you triumphantly home with me. . . .

<u>Do</u> come and see us. I tremendously want to talk with you. Also, as a Proud Mother, show you my Katharine's pictures and casts; and, as a grandmother her two lovely children.

I've read the India article—think you overestimate the power to "unite" of those various wide-split and often furiously antagonistic millions.[56]

The only language they have in common is <u>English</u>!

O—come and <u>talk</u>!

Your old friend.

C. P. Gilman

380 Washington Street<br>Norwichtown, Conn.<br>Sept. 11th 1928

Dear Dr. Ross;

Are you there? Or traversing the globe in a new direction? . . .

I've written a book on Ethics. Popular Ethics.[57] . . .

In all the flood of popular science so eagerly lapped up—so widely bought at $4.00 a volume—there is as yet no popular ethics. I have produced it. It is with Brandt & Brandt—as good agents as any in New York. But I'm desperately anxious about it. It seems to me that if they could have a really valuable opinion to show the publishers it might make a difference in their attitude. . . .

I've called it <u>Pernicious Adam</u>, the general thesis being that man is the only animal <u>both</u> individual and social, and conscious of both; and that his problem in conduct is the balancing of self-interest and social-interest; what we call "evil" in our "dual nature" being the persistence of an artificially nourished self-interest in a highly socialized state of culture—i.e., "the old Adam."

I think you'd like it, and see its tremendous application.

Would you be willing to read it? Or some of it? And give an opinion (—if it's a good one!)[58]

Warm regards to all of you from your old friend,<br>C. P. Gilman.

380 Washington Street<br>Norwichtown, Conn.<br>Sept. 11th. 1928—

Dear Cousin Lyman;

After getting your kind note I wrote to Mr. Brandt; and at last have heard from "Bernice Baumgarten"[59] of the book department that he has turned over the mss. to them. I've been writing an earnest little letter to Miss B. suggesting that in all our flood of popular science there's nothing on Ethics; no popularizing of that immensely necessary subject; and that if this book "went" at all it would find an eager market. Here's all this mass of young people, repudiating old standards and finding no new ones.

Now do you mind if I brag to you a little? You know all my work and, I hope, take an interest in it outside of the cousinly feeling. I've never bragged much about any of my books, though Women and Economics was wildly influential. The poems I never claimed to be "poetry" save in a few instances; but they were useful to, and used in many a pulpit. The autobiography is not a good piece of work—I did not enjoy doing it. The last one, about Religion, was just one view, sound enough but not general. Human Work, my greatest so far, was not so handled as to reach the general reader. Concerning Children has been touchingly useful—mothers have told me with tears in their eyes how it has helped them, and it is still quoted in the child culture course at Teacher's College. The Home was amusing enough but mainly critical. And so on. You see I have enough, counting those in the <u>Forerunner</u> worth saving, to make a shelf of twentyfive. It's a respectable output. But I've been so be-labelled with the various "causes" I conscientiously worked for, that few have recognized the real value of the contribution to social understanding.

With such summary in view I trust you will not think me a megalomaniac when I call this book [<u>Social Ethics</u>] great.

If it is what I think it is, it is one of those books that marks a fresh stage of thinking; it establishes a new basis of measurement in human conduct, it gives a reason [for] the floundering young minds that do not see <u>why</u> a given act is right or wrong.

It is written in an easy colloquial style, well within the range of easy reading if there is any interest at all in the subject matter.

I've just written to Miss Baumgartner [*sic*]—not as boastfully as this, but urging that it had the possibility of a large sale in our present state of mind—and suggesting that if it did not impress her it might help to have it read by some one interested in Ethics. What do you think of that idea? And do you know any one likely to take a large view of the book from the side of its social importance. . . . Would you be willing to look at the Introduction, chapters list, and two or three chapters?

It's a shame to bother you with it but I'm a bit desperate in my anxiety for a suitable presentation. I'm so incapable of "selling myself," always was. And I know this is big. . . .

Love to all of you, young and not so young—from your affectionate
Cousin Charlotte.

380 Washington St.
Norwich Town. Conn.
Feb. 14. 1930.

Dear Mr. [Parker] Whitney,[60]

You have perhaps forgotten these facts; The Outlook published an article of mine, called Fashion, Beauty and Brains on the 7th of August, 1929. It had not been paid on acceptance and after waiting some weeks further, into September, I wrote requesting payment.

On September 20th I was sent a check for $75.00, which is half of what you paid for a former article—and that was half of what I have been in the habit of receiving, from other publications.

I wrote protesting against this reduction and you replied, Sept. 30th. 1929. "The cut was not intentional and you may expect an additional check for $75.00 in a few days."

Since then I have made two visits to the city, have taken the trouble to call at your office and have failed to find you or the check promised.

It is now one hundred and thirty-seven days since Sept. 30th. May I urge that this long overdue payment be made soon?

Yours sincerely,

380 Washington st.
Norwich Town. Conn.
June 21, 1932.

Dear Dr. Ross—

This is sad news indeed.[61] That brilliant beautiful woman—so brave and strong, so more than competent in so many ways—I can't think of her gone! But there is no quicker way—clean and swift—and her children there. I don't like to think of your not being there—its hard however it happens.

And your heart uncertain too—what ails us all today, that more go by heart disease than any other! You two certainly have lived normal lives. And such <u>good</u> ones. When your time comes you ought to fairly purr—to think of the splendid service you have done the world. . . .

There's a verse of mine—

> "Get your work done, to remember!
> Nothing can take it away!
> So shall the sun of December
> Shine brighter than early May!" Yes sir! . . .

. . . I would come to see you if I could—and hope you'll come here if & when you can.

Your cordially admiring old friend—
Charlotte Perkins Gilman.

380 Washington Street
Norwich Town, Conn.
Aug. 18th. '32

Dear Cousin Lyman;

I'm asking a favor, a real one.

Can you arrange to come and visit us, long enough to have considerable talk and to look over some books, letters, pictures, etc.[62]

I want you to be my literary executor——if you will.

You see I'm convinced that "Human Work," followed by my "Ethics," which I am re-writing, will make an impression—some time! I may not be here.

There is my wretched autobiography, furnishing at least data, for later use; poems enough for a second volume, heaps of stuff. It might be really a sizable business proposition—I want your advice. . . .

Your affectionate Cousin—
Charlotte P. Gilman

Dec. 16th. '32

Dear Cousin Lyman,

"The Yellow Wallpaper" was included in "Masterpieces of American Fiction," by Howells, Boni, Liv[e]right & Co., and in "American Mystery Stories." . . .

I can bestow upon you one of the original copies—from The New England Magazine, also. And I never got a cent for it! An agent placed it & took the pay, only $40.00. . . .

Cousin Charlotte

380 Washington St. Norwich Town. Conn.
August 16th. 1933.

Dear Dr. Ross,

I've been invited to speak for the World Fellowship of Faiths in Chicago, Sat. Sept. 9th., and by hook and by crook I'm coming. There are special trips from New York on astonishingly low terms, with three days lodging in Chicago, at Hotel Morrison. . . .

Now then I want awfully to see you. We've been friends for forty years, yessir! And, as I'm now seventy-three and not on the road as I used to be, maybe I'll never get out your way again.

Being pinched [financially] flat as a pancake, like everybody else, I'm coming on a shoestring, and a very short shoestring at that. Does not allow for any extras. So I'm wondering if there is any liberal church or Ethical Society or Summer School on "The Body and Soul of Society" in Madison which would engage me . . . even if it was for expenses only.[63] . . .

I hope you are well as I am, and that you want to see me as much as I want to see you.

Your affectionate old friend,
Charlotte Perkins Gilman.


April 25th. 1934.

Dear Lyman,

Thanks for sending on the Farrar note.[64] Too bad he didn't take it. "Extraordinary" may mean <u>anything</u>—I've seen extraordinary books—of no real value.

If you would be good enough to try this W. W. Norton with the ms. it would save two transfers. . . . If you see him will you say how much your Bobbs Merrill man liked it—said it ought to be required reading for college courses. . . .

Always gratefully—
Cousin Charlotte.

Figure 6. Charlotte Perkins Gilman, ca. 1919. Courtesy of the Schlesinger Library, Radcliffe Institute, Harvard University.

# 6

# Famous Correspondents

## "not a man in America whose praise . . . I would rather win!"

Charlotte Perkins Gilman was, as one biographer confirms, "a part of the international currents and movements that shaped the new ideas of her time," this despite the fact that "she lived on the margin of intellectual life" and was "an accepted member of the intellectual establishment" only "through some personal contact with those" firmly residing among its ranks (A. J. Lane 230). Gilman's contact with some of the leading writers and intellectuals of her day, as well as with other famous and influential people, was often facilitated through letters. Particularly interesting is her correspondence with men who served in some capacity as mentors to her: William Dean Howells, Lester Frank Ward, and Charles Fletcher Lummis. While each of these relationships was unique, it is notable, and perhaps not surprising, that all of them were fraught with underlying tensions fueled in some way by Gilman's unconventional ideas about womanhood.

As "a personal embodiment of the institution of letters" (Brodhead 81–82), William Dean Howells (1837–1920) was one of Gilman's most distinguished correspondents. Editor of the *Atlantic Monthly, Harper's,* and *Cosmopolitan;* esteemed novelist; and authority on American literary realism, he was someone whose patronage would be valuable and whose approval would mean a great deal to an aspiring writer. Gilman first came to Howells's attention as the author of the 1890 poem "Similar Cases." An ardent Nationalist like Gilman, Howells appreciated the poem's social critique. He wrote to her on June 9, 1890, that he had read the piece "many times with unfailing joy" (qtd. in Gilman to Martha Luther, June 17, 1890; see chapter 2). In her reply, Gilman assured Howells that "there is not a man in America whose praise in literature I would rather win!" (June 16, 1890). She would later confirm that Howells's commendation made her feel "like a real 'author' at last" (*Living* 122). Howells continued to express admiration for Gilman's work for the rest of his career; a typical compliment came in 1894: "you speak with a tongue like a two-edged sword. I rejoice in your gift fearfully and wonder how much more you will do with it" (July 11, 1894, qtd. in Hill, *Gilman* 254). The two finally met in March 1897, when Howells came to hear her address the Single Tax Club in New York City, and they and their families would socialize often over the ensuing years.[1] In her memoir, Gilman called her friendship with Howells "a special pleasure" (*Living* 222).

Undoubtedly, Gilman enjoyed his friendship and patronage, and she appreciated the way "he reached out a strong hand" to new authors (Gilman to Houghton, October 20, 1898, qtd. in Scharnhorst, *Gilman* 43). Yet Howells's support of Gilman was given at arm's length: while he did occasionally solicit her work directly, generally he "used his influence to get her work brought out by other publishers than those with which he was directly associated" (Karpinski 203). When she sent him the manuscript for "The Yellow Wall-Paper" in 1890, for example, he passed it along to Horace Scudder of the *Atlantic Monthly,* who rejected it. While Howells himself engaged in a lifelong struggle with nervous exhaustion (which drove him, in fact, to leave his post at the *Atlantic Monthly*), and while his own daughter, Winifred, had died in the care of S. Weir Mitchell only the year before, in 1889, Howells also held an old-fashioned admiration for traditional femininity despite his support of woman suffrage. Ultimately, it seems that Howells admired Gilman's work but was unable fully to stand behind it. "I am afraid that the acceptance of Mrs. Stetson's satire is mostly confined to fanatics, philanthropists and other Dangerous Persons," he wrote. "But that need not keep us from owning its brilliancy" (qtd. in Scharnhorst, *Gilman* 43). Gilman's opinion of Howells's work was mixed. She admitted to Martha Luther that "Howells never was a favorite of mine," his work being "of small artistic value" and driven by ineffective "moralism" (July 27, 1890; see chapter 2). However, she would later praise his utopian romance, *A Traveler from Altruria* (1894), both privately in a letter to her cousin Marian and publicly in the *Impress.* Despite his occasional standoffishness and her own ambivalence about the quality of his fiction, Gilman appreciated his patronage and approval and seemed genuinely to look upon him "with grateful admiration and warm good will" (Gilman to Howells, October 17, 1919).

Similarly complex was Gilman's relationship with Lester Frank Ward (1841–1913), a paleobiologist and a pioneer in the field of American sociology. The author of several volumes treating various aspects of sociology, Ward was an opponent of the social Darwinism so popular during the late nineteenth century and a favorite of women's rights advocates because of his "gynaecocentric theory," which held that women were the primary sex of the species and that they originally controlled both sexual selection and reproduction. "Woman *is* the race," Ward wrote in 1888, "and the race can be raised up only as she is raised up" ("Our Better Halves" 275). This essay was one of two sources Gilman would later cite as the basis for her arguments in *Women and Economics.* Ward initiated an acquaintance with Gilman in 1894 when he wrote to ask for additional copies of *In This Our World.* Soon afterward he offered to organize a reception in her honor at the upcoming Women's Suffrage Convention in Washington, D.C., in 1896, where they first met in person. He was a particular fan of "Similar Cases" and would famously add a fourth stanza of his own while using the poem to attack social Darwinist Benjamin Kidd. Gilman wrote to him that she was never more pleased "in relation to my work": "I felt like the stone in David's sling" with "a grudge against the giant!—and chuckling as it sped" (January 1, 1896).

Gilman described Ward in the *Impress* in 1894 as "a great man, a clear, strong, daring thinker" (qtd. in Scharnhorst, *Gilman* 47) and called his gynaeconcentric theory "the greatest single contribution to the world's thought since Evolution" (*Living* 187). He was similarly admiring of her. "Ward saw Gilman," however, "as a poet, whose creativity provided grist to his mill. . . . [H]e did not see her as a peer contributor to sociological theory" (Allen 70), and this would lead to increasing tensions between them. Gilman was a vocal champion of Ward, yet he was slow to recognize her use of his theories in her own work. In addition, despite their many points of agreement, Ward was not particularly enthusiastic about Gilman's attempts to debate matters of theory. And fundamentally, Ward saw "economic dependence for women [as] a consequence—not a cause—of androcentric culture," while Gilman attributed women's subjection centrally to their economic inequality with men (Allen 75). Thus, while their friendship began on a high note, and while Gilman would eulogize Ward warmly after his death in 1920, beneath the surface their relationship was less than amicable.

Like Ward, Charles Fletcher Lummis (1859–1928) was a mentor who ultimately failed to appreciate Gilman as his equal. Lummis was the founder and editor of *Land of Sunshine* (later *Out West*), a magazine that promoted the literature and culture of southern California and the Southwest. Lummis presided over a community of writers, historians, anthropologists, and other western intellectuals; under his mentorship Gilman rubbed elbows with the likes of Edwin Markham, Joaquin Miller, Ina Coolbrith, Mary Austin, and David Starr Jordan. Grace Channing Stetson, also part of this community, would establish her own professional relationship with Lummis. In 1894 Gilman reviewed *Land of Sunshine* in the *Impress,* and in August 1895 she made her first contribution to Lummis's magazine. The following month, having left California for Hull House, she penned her first extant letter to Lummis. Gilman and Lummis would go on to have a collegial, even affectionate correspondence for several years, with Lummis dubbing her "the brightest woman I ever knew, who never yet found a theory that I could accept as logical" (Lummis journal entry, August 14, 1904). His reviews of Gilman's work were enthusiastic, despite his opinion that her style was like "white-hot metal in a sand mold, and no filing" ("In Western Letters" 348). Though he often disagreed with her ideas, he admired her for her uncompromising intellect: "The vital thing about her is that she has the wherewithal to think, and uses it; and makes other people go through more or less of the motions, according to their equipment"; she was thus "rather disquietous to napping intelligences" ("In Western Letters" 350).

Lummis was one of the few public figures to defend Gilman when the California press vilified her for so-called unnatural motherhood and the perceived love triangle among Gilman, Walter, and Grace. (Walter would write in 1900 to thank Lummis for this defense, for Katharine's sake.) Indeed, beyond socializing with Gilman, the Lummises also spent time with Walter, Grace, and Katharine after Gilman had left the state. "I am glad to have you all hob-a-nobbing there at the ends of the earth and wish I was in it too," Gilman wrote Lummis on October 14, 1895. Throughout the 1890s Gilman periodically visited Lummis at his home in Los Angeles. On one occasion, March 24, 1890, he took three cyanotype photographs of her (labeled facetiously "Women," "Economics," and "Both"); she signed some books for him and inscribed a poem in his guest book, ending with the line, "Long may I come!" (Lummis, House Book 347). This amicable relationship began to sour, however, as the years wore on, and as Gilman became less invested in her literary association with California, her career blossoming on the world stage. When she wrote him on November 22, 1910, to express her support after his divorce from his second wife, his defensive response, while couched between a friendly salutation and the complimentary closing, "Always Your Friend," was a biting rebuff: "your pious advice is a bark up the wrong stump," he snapped (November 27, 1910). It is unclear whether they corresponded after this incident. What is known is that Lummis became increasingly embittered after his divorce, more openly hostile toward women in general, and less tolerant of those women (particularly his protégées) whose success exceeded his own.

Beyond these mentor figures, Gilman's famous correspondents included fellow writers, editors, activists, and even an actress (not surprising, given Gilman's longtime love of the theater). This chapter thus includes letters to a range of well-known individuals such as Whitman biographer Horace Traubel, actress Annie Russell, socialist and author Upton Sinclair, and women's rights activists Carrie Chapman Catt and Margaret Sanger. Though Gilman very likely corresponded with other famous friends, such as Susan B. Anthony, Elizabeth Cady Stanton, and

Jane Addams, none of her letters to these individuals are known to have survived.

Box 401 Pasadena Cal—
Mon. June 16th. 1890.

To Mr. Wm. D. Howells—[2]
Dear Sir,

I thank you most sincerely for your kind note received this morning. Among all the pleasant things I had hoped for in my work this particular gratification was never imagined. And the best part of it is that there is not a man in America whose praise in literature I would rather win!

With genuine gratitude for a very genuine pleasure—

Yours sincerely,
Charlotte Perkins Stetson.

1673 Grove St. Oakland
Tues. Jan. 11, 1892

[To Prof. Edwin Markham][3]
Dear Sir,

Can you oblige us by reading or speaking for the New Nation Club[4] next Friday—the 22nd?

We had a most agreeable evening last week, but missed you. . . .

Would you like to speak—to prepare a paper,—or to merely read something this time, and let me put you down for a later date as speaker?

I wish you would do that—look over the calendar, and make arrangements between now and June 1st, to help the cause by lending it your brain and voice when you best can. We would like much to have you for this week if possible. . . .

Hoping for an early and favorable reply,

Sincerely yours,
Charlotte Perkins Stetson
(Chair. Pro. Com. N. N. [Program Committee New Nation] Club.)

Hull House Chicago Ill.
Sept. 4th. 1895—

[To Charles F. Lummis][5]
Writer of most enjoyable letters,

Here is a book for thee. If you get another, via San. Francisco, put it where 'twill do the most good—this is for you, bearing my hand if not seal. . . .

Have you been to see Mr. Stetson's pictures yet? You'd better.

Please send my sunshine to this address.

When Kier Hardie[6] comes to L.A. go to hear him—he's a man....

I'll send you further produce when there is any.

Serenely—

Charlotte Perkins Stetson

Hull House Chicago<br>Oct. 14th. 1895—

[To Charles F. Lummis]

O Amazing Editor!

... Yes, I will send you some stuff when genius burns that way.

My present career, while nutritious in the extreme, is not wholly palatable and in no way conducive to literature. Still, we will see.

What you say of my people gives me keen pleasure—it makes the life there seem more real when I hear of it from another beholder.

Yes, the damsel Katherine [*sic*] <u>is</u> a nice youngster, though I say it that shouldn't....

It all gives me a hilarious sense of friendly inter-parentage—rather vague, but pleasant. Also as I am very proud of my miscellaneous people and think them most superior, and as I likewise esteem you folks, I am glad to have you all hob-a-nobbing there at the ends of the earth and wish I was in it too. Someday—

Sincerely—

Charlotte Perkins Stetson

The Elm Street Settlement<br>80 Elm Street<br>Chicago, Jan. 1st 1896

Lester F. Ward,[7]

Dear Sir,

I am exceeding proud that you should want my book, and will forthwith send not one but two copies—(they are but fifty cents!) to the address you give....[8]

Nothing has ever pleased me more in relation to my work, than the use which I heard you made of "Similar Cases" in a recent lecture.... I felt like the stone in David's sling—supposing said stone to had [*sic*] a grudge against the giant!—and chuckling as it sped.

I shall be in Washington at the approaching W. [Women's] Suffrage Convention—23rd to 29th—my first visit to the city.

With deep respect for a name well known to me—(I know Prof. Ross of Stanford)

Yours sincerely—

Charlotte Perkins Stetson

on local train—

Mon. Jan. 16th, 1896

Chicago—

Mr. Lester F. Ward,

Dear Mr. Ward,

Your letter gives me great pleasure. I shall be very glad to meet you, and your friends also, in such time as is my own.

My "duties" are to represent three Californian Societies at the Convention; but beyond an address Monday Evening—(the 27th) and some talking to the Judiciary Committee of the House, I do not know what lies before me.

Sunday would be a free day in any case I should think. . . .

With thanks for the pamphlets which I prize much—

Yours sincerely

Charlotte Perkins Stetson

Hotel Arno

Washington D. C.

Fri. Jan. 24th 1896.

Prof. Lester F. Ward—

Dear Mr. Ward.

I was delighted to get your lecture and the <u>Forum</u> article. The latter I read this morning at the convention, with intense satisfaction—somewhat neglecting the treasurer's report. Therefore the former remains—save that I did look at the poem part, and went to bed quite puffed up with pride and joy.

I am to preach Sunday a.m. at the People's Church—Mr. Kent is their regular incumbent I believe; and Sunday afternoon at the Convention—Church of our Father—in lieu of Anna Garlin Spencer[9] who has telegraphed of illness and cannot come.

So I ought to be fairly well talked out by the time I get to your house, and that will give you some little chance!

I shall return here after the service—it begins at 3—and await you. With much pleasant anticipation,

Yours sincerely—

Charlotte Perkins Stetson.

The Elm Street Settlement,
80 Elm Street,
Chicago, Feb. 10th 1896.

Dear Mr. Ward,

I received your check for twelve dollars of which I re-enclose two, as I sent only the twenty you ordered.

It is a great pleasure to me that you think well of the little book.

My English edition—T. Fisher Unwin—comes out this spring. I await it with much interest. . . .

Mrs. Campbell[10] joins me in warm regards to yourself and Mrs. Ward.

Sincerely—

Charlotte Perkins Stetson

Drummond's Hotel
Glasgow, Scotland.
Sept. 14th, 1896.

[To Charles F. Lummis]

Respected Editor and

  August Craftsman—

If I can get to Southern California this winter do you know of any manner of thing whereby I could acquire—say $5.00 a week? Literary thing, I mean. . . .

I've been six years getting over a seven year's illness, and it don't work as fast as I'd like to see it.

Disease—Failure of the Head!

My sprightly muse does not hop about as I like to see her—she does but flop convulsively now and then—without spirit enough to do up her hair.

I am advised to get me to a nunnery or some such, if I would save the pieces. Now were I in Los Angeles I could—methinks—do some of my usual preaching, for a consideration; and also write a little—praising God[?] and California from a hammock the rest of the time. . . .

I'm having fine times over here—save that I've not been well. My Works seem well and favorably known to such folk as I would most care to have know them. And my lecturing goes just as well here as at home. But alas! It does not pay as well—nay, not at all. Still, my fame waxeth, and I begin to feel quite a considerable Person.

I was invited to dinner at Mr. Hyndman's, to meet Liebknecht, Justin McCarthy & George Meredith.[11] And couldn't go!!!

However, life is long. (and George Meredith is longer—I may see him again!) The least I get out of lecturing is travel, entertainment, and experience. That's something surely. . . .

Best regards to the family
Sincerely
Charlotte Perkins Stetson

20 West 32nd st.
New York City.
Dec. 10th. 1896.

Dear Mr. Ward—

I want to thank you for those last two pamphlets you sent me—one about Ethics and one about somebody's Principles of Sociology. I enjoyed them—the latter particularly.

I've been three months in England and Scotland, and had a very satisfying visit. Stayed a few days with Alfred Russell Wallace[12] and enjoyed it immensely. He arranged some lectures for me, and took the chair. I felt so small—to stand up and lecture before that great man!

He spoke of you, most warmly. I am here in New York for the winter probably, and shall perhaps get down your way before spring. I'm much interested in this Congress on Motherhood they are arranging there—it is one of my favorite subjects in lecturing. . . .

Sincerely and cordially—
Charlotte Perkins Stetson.

c/o Mrs. Wm. Dow.
473 Orchard St. Chicago
May. 20th. 1897.

[To Charles F. Lummis]
My Cherished Editor—

Lo! here is a Poem![13] I think it will please you. It pleases me so I chuckle in my bed at night to think of it.

And it belongs to Land of Sunshine—Bless it! and to no other. . . .

Sincerely—
Charlotte Perkins Stetson

18 West 32nd Street
New York,
Feb. 24th 1898.

Dear Mr. Lummis:

Here is a short tale for you, and some verses also—I am seeking to kill one bird with two stones!

Have you seen me blooming out lately? New England, Atlantic, Scribner, Chap-Book—quite a <u>début</u>.

And two books have I in press, a nice new edition of the poems, same name "In This Our World," and a direful prose work on "Marriage and Economics" or "Women & Economics."

You see I have found a publisher—Small, Maynard & Co. 6 Beacon St. Boston. They've just been doing Whitman—a splendid complete edition. Nice folks.

I've scrabbled along this winter living from pen to mouth as usual, and am still scrabbling.

You may hear from me occasionally during the summer—in verse and prose. . . .

Sincerely—
Charlotte Perkins Stetson

18 West 32nd Street,
New York, March 8th 1898.

Dear Mr. Howells,

Do you know these stories by my friend and co-mother Grace Ellery Channing-Stetson?[14]

I think that you will care for them—perhaps for the two I have marked in the brief "contents."

A Roman reviewer calls them better than Verga's[15] (—have I his name right!) and they have met with the warmest commendation in Italy. That ought to speak well for their truth, ought it not?

Sincerely—
Charlotte Perkins Stetson.

18 West 32nd Street
New York,
April 1st. 1898.

Dear Mr. Lummis:

Here's "<u>Tomorrow</u>" again—you needn't apologize, I'm all the better pleased to have it come out in the fine June number![16]

But my feelings <u>are</u> hurt at not being asked to participate in your Western Writers League![17] Don't I still sign "Pasadena" in hotel registers! Am I not introduced on platforms as Mrs. Stetson of California! Don't I write everything I can think of for that blessed country and delight to put things in your magazine because it is California's— even if it doesn't "pay" much! People abused me for sending "Their Grass" to you—said I could have done better. I told 'em I couldn't— that it was Californian and belonged there and that was all that mattered. And here I'm not even mentioned in your galaxy of famous authors!

O hear my cries! Behold my tears! Well—I'll forgive you, <u>if</u> you will take occasion to read ponder and inwardly digest the first article[18] in the April Harpers; and <u>give that man what he deserves</u>. No one in the country can do him justice but you.

And how in the name of all reason can Harpers—Harpers New Monthly Magazine, have published such foul vile weak illiterate silly ghoulish stuff as that!!!!

This is a condition of pardon for forgetting that I am Californian as much as Grace Channing—to say nothing of the ten minutes time I've sacrificed [*sic*] to copying this poem again!

Sincerely—and with suspended hostilities—
Charlotte Perkins Stetson.

18 West 32nd Street,
New York,
April 15th, 1898.

Dear Mr. Lummis,

. . . I have been hovering for years over a series of little stories all set in Pasadena—not of the scenery, nor the history, nor the local character, but of the new life which that great country can so well let grow at last—and, if you liked 'em, they surely belong in the leading magazine of that country. You see if I ever do anything worth while it has to be my own kind—not from choice but from necessity.

I suppose some day you'll be bigger—have more room—want larger things. When I get one of these done I'll send it you for a sample. And if those don't do, perhaps other things will.

The "Western phase" which most appeals to me is its opening for human progress—and all my work is at bottom "dynamic sociology."

I'm getting slowly on in it too; and if my work can help in the least to show the beautiful opportunities of our dear land—that's better than any kind of "pay." As to photo—I haven't one available. But if you'll subtract half a dollar from my next remittance and send it to Thor's (T h o r s) 14 Grant Ave. San Francisco, you can get that best one I've ever had—the one that is in my book.

Notman[19] in Boston took the one in the April <u>Bookbuyer</u>—do you prefer that. (They took 'em for nothing too—asked the privilege!) . . .

Cordially yours—
Charlotte Perkins Stetson

<u>179 W. 76th St., New York</u>
Chicago Ills.
Nov. 28th. 1900.

Dear Prof. Ward

. . . An Italian translation of <u>Women and Economics</u> is being made, by the Contessa Pironti, of Naples, and I am repeatedly urged to send a "bibliography of my authorities."

My principal authority is You—but I have read a number of works on sociological lines, for years and years past—without definitely remembering them. You know my head has been weak for fifteen years or so. Could you, who know the field, and who have read my book, give me a little list of reliable authorities whose facts would bear out my position? . . .

I will not claim to have read them—but do not wish to appear to have invented my facts as well as propounded an especial theory. If I am asking too much—don't do it!

With cordial remembrance of past kindness—

Yours sincerely—
Charlotte Perkins Gilman.
(ex-Stetson!)

179 W. 76th st. New York.
1-15-1901.

Dear Prof. Ward;

Thank you for your kind letter. I am quite relieved to find that I need not struggle to supply an impossible bibliography to that book. . . .

Did you really think I did not know your books? I own the Dynamic

Sociology and mean to have the "Psychic Factors" some time. And you should hear me refer other people to them!!

How do I like it this time? Very well indeed, thank you.[20] Circumstances alter cases. Strongminded girls should be allowed to "sow their wild oats"—have their work free and full and have it early—they'll be willing enough to marry later. . . .

Very cordially—

Charlotte Perkins Gilman

Twilight Park.

Haines Falls. N.Y.

June 26th, 1902

[To Charles F. Lummis]

Writing? Of course I am. At 2 cts a word thank you. Just short stuff for "Success" at present, and there's another book coming; that one I was doing at Las Casitas and didn't get on with. A book on "Work." How you will despise it! I haven't done much since "Concerning Children" (someone told me you had fun with that, but I didn't happen to see it—haven't seen a copy of Land of Sunshine—Out-West for ever and ever). . . . When ever I write anything I think you'll like I'll send it, probably. . . .

Katharine has had a terrible time this spring—pneumonia, pleurisy, and scarlet fever, one down t'others come on—three months in bed nearly.

But she's gaining now, up here in the cool Catskills: I wish it were our Sierras!

Cordially always—

Charlotte Perkins Gilman

SummerBrook

Hurricane P.O.

Essex Co. N.Y.

Aug. 21st, '02

[To Charles F. Lummis]

And why not write for "Success"? Marden[21] is doing well with it I think, perhaps you did not know it had changed. . . .

Katharine is vastly benefitted by three months mountain air, and so am I. She sails soon for Italy—to stay with her father and dear Grace for a while. The change will do her great good we all feel. . . .

Yours cordially—

Charlotte Perkins Gilman

Woodstock, N.Y.

June 30th 1903.

Dear Mr. Ward;

. . . [I] hasten to tell you that I am no[w] well enough to read your books, with no more pleasure than before, for I always enjoyed them; but with an ease I have not known for twenty years!

My health is vastly improved. I can read—even study a little. This summer I am learning German; in view of the Woman's Congress at Berlin next June. . . .

We bought Pure Sociology at once.[22] I already have the Dynamic Sociology[23]—and I pitched into that woman chapter first because you asked me to tell you what I thought of it—and Mrs. Helen Campbell was eagerly waiting for the book and I hadn't time for the whole of it then.

Now I am trying to arrange with some big magazine to write an article on that tremendous theory of yours—it ought to be popularized at once. Will you tell me if anyone else is doing it anywhere? And what, in your judgment would be the best place for such an article?

I was a little grieved in reading your statement that no one had taken up your theory—for I had stoutly defended it in my book Women and Economics. But perhaps you didn't consider that book of sufficient importance to mention.

Or perhaps you haven't read it. I instructed the publisher to send you advance sheets of it—so sure I was that you would be interested, but evidently I overrated your interest. . . .

Yours cordially—

Charlotte Perkins Gilman.

179 West 76th Street, New York.

Jan. 20th. 1904

Dear Professor Ward,

. . . I want to tell you what I think of your Gynaecocentric Theory. You asked me to let you know. I think it is the most important contribu-

tion to the "woman question" ever made—(not excepting my own beloved theory)—and therein of measureless importance to the world.

Moreover I mean to make it the recognized basis of a new advance
in the movement of women.

On the W. S. A. [Women's Suffrage Associaton] Convention held
in Washington this winter, Feb. 11th to 17—I am to make it the subject
of my address; and also in the International Congress of Women held
in Berlin in June. . . .

It is a continuing surprise to me to find so little recognition of this
great theory of yours in the reviews of your book or any other place. . . .

I want to make the people feel what a great work you have done in
this one thing—to say nothing of all the rest of your work!

Very Cordially—

Charlotte Perkins Gilman

179 West 76th Street, New York

7-19-'04.

Dear Mrs. Spring—[24]

I was so pleased to get your letter! . . .

Yes, all is well with me. I have a happy home at last, a dear dear husband, and my daughter is a tall lovely girl of nineteen, studying art.
Next June I speak on Woman's day in Oregon; and <u>may</u> get down to
Los Angeles. If so I hope I shall see you there, and Jeannie[25] too—give
him [*sic*] my cordial regard please.

I'm sending you a lecture circular, so you can see what I'm doing.

Quite a string of books now—and plenty more where they came from!

I saw dear Grace Channing Stetson in Rome; she is fairly well, and
working always. . . .

It's a good world anyhow!

Love to you,

Charlotte Perkins Gilman.

179 West 76th Street, New York.

8-4-'04.

Dear Prof. Ward—

I have thought of what seems to me a fine argument in support
of your Gynaecocentric Theory, namely: That since the establishment
of the two sexes, each with specially adapted organs; both have gone

on differentiating in species, the female equally with the male; but she has also differentiated in steps of tremendous importance in her special functions—developing order marsupalia and order mammalia—introducing new organs and functions of enormous value to progress—whereas the male has merely inherited the rudiments of these new organs—and has developed nothing in the way of commensurate improvement on his part.

Am I right in this?

It shows her not only the original organism, not only equal in modification to species, but leader in modification to sex.

Can you refer me to any material—not difficult to study—wherein I may get at some of the simpler and more prominent facts as to early organisms? I expect to have a good deal of fighting to do as I continue to advocate your theory, and would like some special ammunition.

Always admiringly your friend,<br>Charlotte Perkins Gilman.

[n.d., ca. 1906]

[To H. G. Wells, Spade House, Sandgate, Kent, England]

Happy New Year! I haven't read the American book[26] yet, but will—and converse thereon. I'm "agin" you on <u>Paid Motherhood</u>—see <u>The Independent</u>, soon.

C. P. Gilman

179 West 76th Street, New York.<br>3-15-'06

Dear Professor Ward—

I am grateful to you for the most complimentary reference in your <u>Independent</u> article;[27] which I prize the more now that you have sent it to me. . . .

By the way I was grieved to see in <u>Pure Sociology</u> that you have not read my <u>Women & Economics</u> or if you have, did not notice my explicit reference (page 171) to your Forum article of 1888; because you say that to your knowledge no one has ever advocated your theory; and I've done my humble best at it, in lecture book and article these many years.

All my biological friends scoff at you, and say you have not the facts to rest the theory on—that they know no instance of a creature with the tiny transient male—the first stage of detached existence. Mr. Holt[28] has three replies which he calls "withering." I don't think they'll "wither" much; and the matter needs wide and thorough discussion.

I hear you have been called to the chair of Sociology at Brown. Power to your elbow!

Cordially and admiringly—
Charlotte Perkins Gilman.

313 W. 82.—New York.
2-1-'07

Dear Professor Ward;

I am sending you a copy of <u>Human Work</u> with some marked passages. I truly think it will interest you to see how largely I have followed the same lines of thought you have covered so much more fully; and that one or two points may have fresh suggestions perhaps.

My head is getting stronger at last—for more than twenty years I have been unable to study, or indeed to read anything requiring continued attention—and one of the big pleasures long deferred is reading your books. So far—except for the Phyllogenetic forces in Pure Sociology; and some of the shorter papers you were so kind as to send me— I have not really read you at all. Mr. Gilman and I are beginning at the wrong end now, with Applied Sociology. He has read all the others.

I hope you enjoy as you ought the Himalayan heights you have won—the glorious view—the light—the clear stimulating air; and, best of all, the sure knowledge that this big joy is for us all—and will be reached by all. . . .

It was a keen pleasure and a lasting good to come to the meetings— thank you sincerely for the opportunity. Dr. Ross came home to dinner with us—Prof. Giddings[29] was summoned by telephone and called— we had a delightful evening.

He appreciates you—Edward Ross!

So do I.

Charlotte Perkins Gilman

313 West 82nd Street, New York
12-9-'07

Dear Mr. Traubel—[30]

I wish you would write me quite frankly about mother[31]—Mrs. Campbell—as if I really were her daughter. I feel that it must be extremely hard for you to have her ill in your house so long, and yet my hands are tied at present. As soon as she is able to come I can keep her here for a while, and will gladly; but what I want to do—and can't—is to send on money for her. I write, rather foolishly, just to say that I feel the obligation, but am unable to meet it.

And I want to know more definitely about her. A card—of Dec. 4th—says she has bronchial grip now. It must be very hard for her—brave though she is.

I am ashamed to be so helpless—but we are "in the trough of the sea" just now, like plenty of others.

Do send me a word.

Would you like this for The Conservator?—(The "Little White Animals").[32]

Cordially—

Charlotte Perkins Gilman

5-21-'08

My Dear Mrs. Yorke—[33]

At about 6 o'clock this evening, my estimable second maid, a person of indefinite understanding and a voice lacking in richness, gave me a long circumstantial account of much telephoning in my absence.

The final consummation—as transmitted to me by this inadequate maid—was that Mr. Gilman and I were invited to lunch—on Sunday next—by—"Annie Russell."

On the strength of this pleasing rumor Mr. Gilman and I shall rush gaily forth to Short Hills next Sunday morning, bringing with us two appetites, many thanks, and one play!

If—as is a plain possibility—we are in any way misled, a postal card arriving Saturday will stave off this incursion.

In case we hear nothing further—you must abide the event!

If the case is as stated, per telephone and per maid—I'm extremely obliged to you for giving me this opportunity.

Yours most appreciatively—

Charlotte Perkins Gilman.

313 West 82d Street, New York

9-5-'08

Dear Professor Ward;

I cannot remember if I thanked you for your paper on The Sociology of Political Parties—if I didn't, I do now.

There are two things I've been meaning to mention to you—to ask about.

1. May it not be shown that the overthrow of the matriarchate resulted in many cases in the complete extinction of those races most violently androcentric, as well as in the visible decadence of so many others; and that in the centers or center of the earliest civilization the women still held a position of comparative freedom?

2. As a hypothesis accounting for the overthrow of the matriarchate—: Assume a matriarchal settlement under exceptionally good conditions—good climate, abundant food—peace & plenty. Under good conditions, females are produced.

   Assume an excess of females. (Under the difficult conditions of previous human life there had been an excess of males with combat for selection by females as in other animals.)

   Having now good conditions and surplus females, the male becomes increasingly valuable.

   The dominant females, already the industrial power and used to tribal communism, now establish <u>a voluntary polygyny</u> agreeing to maintain one male to each small group of females.

   If this were done, the male being now supported by the group of females and held in high esteem, is in a position to develop, naturally, the excessive indulgence, cruelty, pride, etc. which would so lead to the more injurious effects of unchecked masculine rule. This hypothesis seems to me simple and genetic— requires no telic process—no determined action.

   Good condition—excess females. Excess females—male at premium. Male at premium—females establish polygyny. Polygyny—over development of maleness. Predominant maleness— androcracy. Androcracy—the world as we have it.

How's that?

It has always been a puzzle to me, to see how the female, the unquestioned dominator of all previous life, could have been suddenly—or gradually—overthrown.

But from a peaceful promiscuity with matriarchal dominance to a voluntary polygyny, the females agreeing to share rather than to compete—seems to me a very possible step.

And polygyny produces the characteristics which lead to further masculine dominance.

Hoping you are well—

Charlotte Perkins Gilman.

3-31-'09

Dear Mrs. Yorke—

. . . Would you like to look at another play of mine?[34] This one is called "Interrupted." It is more of a "star" play than the other—so may appeal to the managerial mind the more readily.

I saw you in The Stronger Sex. The people who think you can only do "fair and feeble" parts should note that lady with the pistol!

Whether I write it or not I do want to see you in something you thoroughly enjoy, sometime.

This is—so to speak—the first draught of my play; I thought, if it found favor, I could modify it to suit demands. . . .

Yours with warm admiration

Charlotte Perkins Gilman

224 Riverside Drive

New York

6-24-'10

Dear Mr. Bynner—[35]

Thanks for your kind note, and for the Subscriber [to the Forerunner]—now come to hand.

But what I am writing for is to express my keen delight in your bit of verse ["Hills of Home"] in the July Century.

That's a poem. It reaches way in and catches you on the inside.

I quite caught my breath when I read it, and read it again to see if that clutch was really there.

"Before I met this flesh and bone

And followed and was lost."

The way life stretches out on either side of those two lines is marvellous.

That is a great little poem—it will live.

Please come and see me again some time.

Cordially—

Charlotte P. Gilman.

8-31-'10

My Dear Mr. Sinclair:[36]

I carried your ms. yesterday to Hamptons Magazine, and left it with "our Mr. Young"—who signed for it.[37]

I read it all; the last installment rather hurriedly, the rest carefully.

I have as you know a real belief in your genius; and an admiration for some of your work; but since you ask my opinion of this I must say frankly that I object not only to what seems to me an unnecessary explicitness of detail; but, most extremely, to the publication of such intimate matters regarding your wife.

Yours sincerely—
Charlotte Perkins Gilman

On train—nearing Denver
11-22-'10

[To Charles F. Lummis]
I'm sorry, Brother—

Very sorry—, for lots of things. Among them that I had not time enough to see old friends in the Loveliest Land.

You have strong years yet before you, wise ones, I hope. Can't you go into the desert for a season—come out Clean—and build a piece of Life that your children will be lovingly proud of?[38]

Your friend—
Charlotte Perkins Gilman

224 Riverside Drive
New York City
May 3rd. '11

Dear Mr. Bynner:

I shall be very glad to have you come next Sunday after noon, for a walk if it is pleasant and a talk in any case; also a home-made servant-less supper afterward. . . .

I am still reciting those two or three perfect verses of yours—to the invariable appreciation of my friends—"Name me no names for my disease—"[39]

Have you read my Man Made World? (Androcentric Culture?) And how does it strike you. I shall value your opinion.

Cordially—
C. P. Gilman.

7-19-'11

Dear Mr. Bynner,

. . . Your long poem[40] is a long poem; which Poe would consider harsh criticism I suppose.

I like the spirit of it.

I like the sort of Atlas-lift with which you strive to seize and carry the Great New Theme. . . .

It seems to me that you are pushing steadily on with the Real Life of our times; and your work is not the "poems distilled from other poems"—which "shall pass away."[41] . . .

I hope to see you again.

Charlotte Perkins Gilman.

12-28-'14

My dear Mary Austin,[42]

Your card is found on our return from "going home for Xmas"— Houghton's home.

I will come with pleasure to lunch on Wed. Jan. 5th, at 1 P.M.

We have had no "evenings" this season. Houghton has been doing night work—or you'd have heard from us before now.

Cordially—

Charlotte Perkins Gilman

12-30-'14

My dear Miss Paul,[43]

I'm sorry, but I can't afford it—either time or R.R. fare [to attend a meeting of the National Advisory Council].

But if any affluent sympathiser would engage me for a "Parlor Talk" Fri. or Sat. or any other engagement offered ($50.00) why I'd come and stir up sentiment beforehand.

As this is too short notice to expect any such golden opportunity I'll have to regretfully decline.

(I'm not stingy—but I am mighty hard up this year.)

Cordially,

C. P. Gilman

627 W. 136.

Oct. 17. 1919

Dear Mr. Howells,

I am pleased and honored that you should wish to use <u>The Yellow Wallpaper</u> in the book as you ask.[44] Did you know that that one piece of "literature" of mine was pure propaganda? I was once under Dr. Weir Mitchell's treatment, at 27. He sent me home to "Live as domestic a life as possible; have your child with you all the time; lie down an hour after each meal; have but two hours intellectual life a day; (!) and never touch pencil, brush, or pen as long as you live."

I tried it over one summer, and went as near lunacy as one can, and come back.

So I wrote this,—and sent him a copy.

He made no response, but years after some one told me that he had told a friend "I have altered my treatement [*sic*] of neurasthenia since reading The Yellow Wallpaper." Triumph![45] Please—did you ever receive either one of the bound volumes of the first year of my precious Fore-runner? That first year was precious any how; fourteen numbers, and covers bound in. I did want you to notice my baby, and tried twice—letter and book.

As you may know I wrote that little magazine—all of it—for seven years. Stopped Dec. '16. Some of it was pretty good. And it was a large piece of work anyhow;—21,000 w[or]ds a month. Also I had to work a lot more, on the side, to pay for the privilege of publishing a magazine! But I am well pleased. Some day I'll publish a lot of it, in book form. . . .

Yours with grateful admiration and warm good will—

Charlotte Perkins Gilman.

380 Washington Street
Norwichtown, Conn.
Nov. 22, 1930

My dear Mrs. [Carrie Chapman] Catt,[46]

I have just returned from a round of little visits and then the State Convention of the League. My late arrival at your luncheon was due to there being four "Sherry's" in New York—and my gross lack of sense in not telephoning beforehand to find out which was the right one.[47] I stayed over in N.Y. especially to attend—wanted to see something of you, and of other old friends too—all of which I missed; and then had to sneak away even while you were speaking, to take my train.

By this time you must be fairly swamped with gratitude for your lavish gifts. How like you to distribute so widely what was given to you for your long and splendid work. I have always most honestly admired the clarity and strength of your mind, your calm wisdom and patience, and breadth of vision. One of the highest compliments of my own life was when you put me at the head of your list of "the twelve greatest women" of our country. Of course I did not appear in the list that was officially prepared, because in the twelve professions they selected no place was given to a social philosopher. But your good opinion I valued.

I think the League of Women Voters the most worthwhile thing to belong to now; and was much impressed at this convention with the person[n]el and spirit shown. You may be immensely proud of your children!

As for me I am in excellent health and spirits. My husband and his brother inherited the old homestead here, and barely enough money to run it. I love the beautiful old town, the pleasant people. My last book—His Religion and Hers—came out in 1923, Century Co. Every now and then I have an article or bit of verse somewhere, but not often. The modern taste does not enjoy my work, you see, the "readers" are just out of college. Just at present I am warmly interested in getting before the League a little "Know Norwich"—"Know Hartford"—and so on book, with a table of comparison on the "points" chosen, see enclosed tentative outline.

You see it seizes on two "handles" to promote action, local pride and the competitive instinct.

You remember the fine work done in Kentucky when it was shown how low she stood in literacy and in care of tuberculosis. These little books would have tables in the back, of each town using them, all marked as to their standing, so that any town could see at once where it stood in comparison. The best town and the worst would be shown—a spur to activity. I've been speaking to various Leaguers about it, and to the Convention, and found much interest.

It was a pleasure to see you—I wish it could have been longer.

Thanking you once more for your gift, your old friend

Charlotte P. Gilman

380 Washington Street
Norwich Town, Conn.
May 26, 1932.

My dear Mrs. Sanger;[48]

Thank you for your kind letter, and for the enlargement of my modest expense account duly received.

It was a pleasure to be there, and we both know that all this pressure steadily counts.[49] Each succeeding "failure" is like another wave of a rising tide.

I was very sorry to hear that you were ill—but not surprised.[50] The amount of force you put into this work—quiet, steady, ceaseless lifting—is an enormous expense. The excellence of the management—so smooth and apparently easy, impressed me as an old campaigner. Success is sure, but not immediate.

—I <u>like</u> you. With cordial admiration,

C. P. Gilman.

380 Washington St.[51]
Norwich. Town. Conn.
November 1st. 1933.

Dear Mrs Catt,

. . . I'm sending you two peace flag songs I made years ago, and some other stuff I thought you would like to look at. . . .

It is, as I think I said before, a keen distress to me that I have no chance to speak for these things. As you know I have real power to stir and convince. I'm to speak at the Birth-control Convention (—<u>that's</u> a thing we've got to have if there is ever lasting peace!) on Jan. 17th, and in the evening Forum At John Haynes Holmes' church Feb. 4th. Perhaps we might meet. . . .

With affection and admiration,

[C. P. Gilman]

Figure 7. Charlotte Perkins Gilman, ca. 1911. Courtesy of the Schlesinger Library, Radcliffe Institute, Harvard University.

# 7
# The Twilight Years
### "my writing . . . simply doesn't come"

On the occasion of her sixtieth birthday, Gilman wrote of her plans for a "New Life" that would entail "Emergence, Achievement, Triumph." Though her career was on the wane, she characteristically struck an optimistic note and reaffirmed her desire to do her "full duty" (July 3, 1920, *Diaries* 851). She would continue to be driven by this sense of duty, and by her optimism, for the remainder of her life. In 1922 she and Houghton moved from New York City, where they had lived since 1900, to Norwich Town, Connecticut. With both of their careers in decline, their financial situation became precarious. To help defray expenses, they raised their own food in a large garden, which Gilman tended avidly. Despite worries over money and mounting tensions with Houghton's brother and sister-in-law, with whom they shared a home, Gilman was for the most part content with her personal life. Professionally, however, she became increasingly disappointed.

By 1920, the Progressive Era movements with which Gilman had been involved had lost their steam; with the passage of the Nineteenth Amendment, the women's movement was similarly fading. While her own interest in particular causes had cooled (she was less interested in working on behalf of groups, such as women and laborers, whom she saw as progressively able to "work for themselves"), she remained as committed as ever to "stimulat[ing] the social consciousness and clarify[ing] popular thought on social relationships" (Gilman to L. L. Bernard, September 26, 1927). Her theories and her interests, however, were largely out of step with the times. Added to this was the simple fact that Gilman was no longer young, and she did not always speak to the younger generations' concerns. As she complained to Alice Stone Blackwell, "These very young readers editors & critics have no use for minds over thirty!" (October 24, 1930). In particular, she was frustrated with young women, whom she roundly dismissed as "painted, powdered, high-heeled, cigaret smoking idiots" (Gilman to Katharine, December 19, 1931). Simply put, she was "out of harmony with the aspirations of many women of the 1920s" and 1930s (A. J. Lane 345).

Though it became more and more difficult for her to find an audience, Gilman did continue to work during this period. She embarked upon the occasional lecture tour, addressed the League of Women Voters gratis, and even had a "Gilman Week" of lectures in Hartford in 1933. She also received recognition and accolades from such respected public figures as Carrie Chapman Catt and Zona Gale. In 1923 she published *His Religion and Hers: A Study of the Faith of Our Fathers and the Work of Our Mothers,* a major piece of nonfiction that earned scant recognition. Then came a string of disappointments. In 1925 Gilman began her autobiography, which she tried and failed to place in the late 1920s. She would pick up the manuscript again in the early 1930s, and again in the months before her death, but she did not live to see its publication in 1935. She completed *Unpunished,* her first and only detective novel, in 1929; though written in a popular genre she hoped would sell, it did not find a publisher during her lifetime. Most disappointing for her was the failure of *Social Ethics* to see print, for she claimed that on that book, along with *Human Work,* she would "rest [her] claim to social service" (*Living* 332). The "flat failure" of these "last three attempts" left her disheartened: "There's nothing to prevent my writing," she revealed to Alice Park, "but it simply doesn't come" (February 28, 1932). Her lectures similarly saw a decline. In 1928 she confessed to Park, "Lectures have fallen off a lot. Guess I'm a has-been" (June 29). Four years later she confirmed that "No one seems to want my lectures now. . . . Gratifying, isn't it" (Gilman to Park, February 28, 1932).

While Gilman faced the very real problem of earning a livelihood, more profoundly she believed that she had something important to offer and that her work was needed more than ever. Though she bemoaned her lack of a "pulpit" (Gilman to Blackwell, April 1, 1932), she never lost her resilience or her drive to fulfill what she saw as her duty. Even as late as 1931, she would make this note to herself:

> To do:  Same job. To see and to say.
> Same tools: Voice and pen. (*Diaries* 854)

Her determination was reflected in another entry the following year: "There may be some years of good work yet. Get at it. Write something, as often as possible, as well as I can" (*Diaries* 855). To her old friend Alice Park, she followed the complaint that there was no use in writing "if I can't be published" with the announcement that she had been invited to contribute to a book and that she was "really pleased that in the tide of falsehood and grossness which floods the press there is still any call for my special views" (July 18, 1930). This positive attitude was echoed on the personal level: having been diagnosed with inoperable breast cancer in January 1932, she would write to Park the following year, "How's your health, my dear? Mine is excellent" (September 20, 1933).

In these twilight years, Gilman's disappointment with having fallen out of favor was balanced by her own and others' recognition of her accomplishments. Throughout the 1920s and the early 1930s she received hundreds of requests from publishers and editors of anthologies, prayer books, and high school texts requesting permission to reprint some of her poems and essays. She almost always granted permission. She crowed to her cousin Lyman Beecher Stowe that she had been at the top of Zona Gale's list of "Immortals" for having been "a social force and a shaper of policies for betterment for years" (February 18, 1933). She would be remembered shortly after her death by longtime friend Harriet Howe as "the greatest personality that I had ever seen," someone who "had given me the greatest of all gifts,—the courage of my convictions" (Howe 211). Looking back on her long career, Gilman wrote to Alice Stone Blackwell that she was satisfied with her own contributions: "The immortality I believe in is for the race, for our continuing ascending humanity. To that progress you and I and the others have contributed, in it we live" (April 15, 1934).

> 627 W. 136th st.
> New York City.
> Oct. 3rd. 1921.

My dear Dr. Dunn[ing],[1]

I think you will be amused at the blows to my 61-year-old vanity involved in my "Report."

In the earlier one I was marked "feet and posture perfect for age," which pleased me much because I have striven all my life to stand erect and high-chested, and to keep my feet free and healthy. Also this time you said such nice things about my feet that I came home and bragged cheerfully, quoting you as stating that they were "the best out of 18 thousand cases" you had examined.

And now, alas! comes the second report, for the first rating, saying "Posture slightly drooping," and as to those superior feet merely this cold and cruel word "Corns"! . . .

> 627 W. 136th st.
> New York City.
> Dec. 4th. 1921.

My dear Miss Hill,[2]

Here in my conscience-crushing heap I find your letter of last July, asking for some word of how work came to be done. I saved the letter for a fitting time to answer—and there never is any.

As to the circumstances under which "my things were written["]— there was no particular requirement. The poem called "Heroism" for instance, was written on the train between Chicago and Milwaukee, where I was going to address an Ethical Society on "The Heroes We Need Now."

Many of them sprang from some prose essay, the main thought suddenly presenting itself in verse. Some were in letters to friends who seemed to need such a word. As to "how they were worked out"—they were not, they simply arrived, bringing their garments with them, written just as they stand, with hardly a word of alteration.

I am not a poet, you see, I'm only a preacher, whether on the platform or in print, and the fact that sometimes the thought appears in verse is but a natural expression. As to "how the ideas have come," I do not know. Probably as a result of a definite concentration on human service, from the age of sixteen. Very early I made the "Two Prayers" which later came into the verses enclosed.

Now you know all I do about it.

Dec. 29th—or 30th. 1926.
Norwich Town, Conn.

My dear little Grandson;[3]

I have your beautiful letter with Christmas decorations; and the one with songs on it—about the Slumber Boat. . . . I had no idea you could write so well. . . .

Here we had a big snow storm, deep and drifted and then a long warm rain, so one needed rubber boots to walk in. One boy I met in the rain said he stepped in up to his knee! He had a poncho, but no umbrella. Papa will tell you what a poncho is. Will you please give my love to Mama and tell her I will write to her later.

Your loving grandmama.

To a Neglected Grandson.
A Sadly Belated Birthday Letter.[4]
[n.d.]

There was once a grandmother so sinful and queer
She could not remember the day of the year
When beloved relations had chanced to be born!
Such conduct is worthy of pity and scorn.

From her youth absentmindedness oft was her curse,
And now in her age it grows visibly worse.

So Excellent Grandson, of whom I am fond,
I make here a suggestion, for birthdays beyond.
As you see one approaching, a fortnight before,
Just drop me a post-card, a word, nothing more,
The briefest inscription, as "How is your health?"

Or "I hope you are happy and rolling in wealth".
I'll say "Why does my Grandson emit this brief holler"?
And then I'll remember and send you a dollar.

380 Washington st.
Norwich Town. Conn.
Sept. 26th. 1927.

Mr. L. L. Bernard,
Faculty Exchange,
Univ. of Chicago.
Dear Sir,
 In answer to your letter of Sept. 10th.[5] here are some notes. . . .

I.  Charlotte Anna Perkins, born July 3rd, 1860, in Hartford, Conn. Have lived in Hartford, Conn., Providence, R.I., Apponaug, R. I., in the country near Rehoboth, Mass., back and forth among three places. In 1888 I moved to California, spending three years in Pasadena, three in Oakland and one in San Francisco. In 1995 [*sic*][6] I went to Chicago; traveled about, lecturing, in various states and in England, until 1900 when I settled in New York until 1922, then removing to this town. Work in youth[:] painting[,] teaching painting, drawing, common branches, and gymnastics; this with private pupils and classes.

II.  Am now most interested in the specific qualities of different races, and the effect of promiscuous interbreeding among them, as it applies to our immediate national problems; and also, with the weakening of religious beliefs and the collapse of "morals," in the need of a scientifically based ethics as a foundation for social efforts. As to changes in interest and activities, I am far less interested in working for women since they became able to work for themselves; similarly with the "labor movement," my interest is less as the power of the worker increases. As to legitimate socialism, that movement is so hopelessly retarded for the present by the follies and excesses of Communism and the ghastly example of Russia, that it is hardly worth while to discuss it. Have not taught in institutions save in occasional lectures.

III. My "teachers in sociology" were many writers on the natural sciences, on history, and various lines of social conditions, errors, and needs—no college instruction. The governing impulse was a natural interest in human life and progress, a clear perception of glaring evils, and a generalizing mind. Beginning at about sixteen I read and studied with a view to better understanding of the nature of society, and its possible improvement. Of special "influence" the only conspicuous one was Lester F. Ward. His gynecocentric theory, as first outlined in The Forum, and Geddes and Thompson on "The Evolution of Sex" were the only references I could think of when trying to add a bibliography to <u>Women and Economics</u>, my first book.[7] For the most part such work as I have done is only my own thinking.

IV. Researches[:] I have made none. Of lectures I have given some thousand or more, in repeated visits in all but four of our states, and on five European lecture trips. All these were along sociological lines, with much on the position of women, as I held her aborted social development to be one of the main checks to our normal progress.

Of essays and articles there have been a great number, widely distributed. I cannot possibly list them as suggested; practically all of them on social questions.

Books as follows:

1. <u>Women and Economics</u>. . . . This is the most widely known and influential. . . .
2. <u>In This Our World</u>. Verse. . . .
3. <u>Concerning Children</u>. Some useful educational suggestions.
4. <u>The Yellow Wallpaper</u>. A story, psychopathological study.
5. <u>The Home</u>. A decidedly novel criticism of the home as an economic institution, with serious charges.
6. <u>Human Work</u>. The most important of my books. . . .
7. <u>The Manmade World</u>. . . . Shows result of male dominance in social progress.
8. <u>Moving the Mountain</u>. A shortrange possible Utopia outline.
9. <u>The Forerunner</u>. . . .

9. [*sic*] <u>Our Brains and What Ails Them</u>. A study of the action of social institutions on the development of the human mind. . . .

10. <u>Social Ethics</u>. Showing ethics to be essentially a social science, and our deficiency in understanding it due to the persistence of primitive individualism.

11. <u>The Dress of Women</u>. Showing how large a part of the obstruction of human progress is due to the blind sequacity of women in following "the fashion."

12. <u>Growth and Combat</u>. Treats of the basic difference between the competitive combative tendencies of the male, and constructive tendencies of the female in their effect on human progress. . . .

13. <u>His Religion and Hers</u>. A similar analysis, showing how our death-based religions may be traced to the hunting and fighting activities of men in which death was the climax; and showing the possible effect of a religious view coming through the minds of women with whom birth, with its ensuing love and service was the main climax of life.

14. Am now engaged in a study of Ethics with the hope of clarifying and popularizing that most needed of sciences.

V. Member of American Sociological Association. . . .

VI. I can think of no other information other than is covered by the above. In a lifetimes work I have sought to stimulate the social consciousness and clarify popular thought on social relationships.

C. P. Gilman

380 Washington Street
Norwichtown, Conn.
Oct 24th 1927.

Mr. Baker Brownell[8]
Dear Sir;

I shall be very glad to write the article you suggest, for the series on Contemporary Thought, and will see that you get it before Xmas.

Yours with much interest in the undertaking.

C. P. Gilman.

By the way—did you ever read my "Human Work"? That's my most important contribution to the change in social thought.

February 3rd. 1928.
380 Washington St.
Norwich Town. Conn.

For the Contributor's Column,
Dear Atlantic,

Having thus belatedly just read an article in your issue of last December, called "The Paradox of Humanism," by Mr. Joseph Wood Crutch[9] I am moved to protest at the combined ignorance of both author and proof reader, in allowing such a laughable error to appear in your pages as calling the ant "he."

Mr. Krutch seems to have learned somewhat of the characteristics of that amiable insect, but refers to the creature through two long paragraphs with some twenty repititions [*sic*] of he, him, his, and himself. In some slight casual reference, this might be excused on the ground that "he" is the most frequent usage, but this is an extensive specific description. We are told that "he" makes no demands for himself which will interfere with the prosperity of the colony which he inhabits; whereas, the briefly wedded and then lost male ant never is any part of the colony. We are told "His industry and foresight have always been admired," whereas he shows neither[,] save as one chosen out of many may evince foresight. Still more amazing is it to learn that "he has never achieved a control over the processes of reproduction which enables him to see to it that just the right number of each type of citizen shall be born"; and again, that "he" has consented "to remain sexless, while certain specialists are endowed with powers of reproduction."

In plain fact "he" never does anything save that one out of wasted thousands fertilizes the "queen ant." The "sexless" ones are female, and can lay eggs when isolated and reduced to extreme measures. There was more knowledge than this in the ancient Hebrew who said "Go to the ant thou sluggard, consider her ways and be wise." . . .

If you do not wish to print this protest in the interests of cooperative motherhood, please return it to me, and oblige.

Yours truly

380 Washington Street
Norwich Town, Conn.
June 29th 1928

[To Alice Park][10]
Yesm'!

. . . Have written a really big book, "Pernicious Adam. A study in Ethics."

Have also just written a short thing—"God for a Day"—funny. Am in pretty good health, very good considering, and absolutely <u>sunk</u> in the garden. All May the planning and planting, all June the weed-weed-Weeding. I've changed my mind about the word "fighting" as applied to weed. If the desire to kill and desperate efforts thereto, against the ceaseless pressure of an en-enemy [*sic*], a million-headed enemy which rises up like Anteus[11] is not a fight, what is it?

Also the slaying of bugs and worms of all sorts. Anyhow we do it, and indulge our baser passions.

Autobiography has not got out yet. Ethics only in agents hands since May 1st. She's been trying to serialize it—unsuccessfully.

But I've got to write something saleable soon—for my other family. Houghton the angel—has been carrying on while I've spent two winters on books.

Had a left-arm neuritis last winter but cured it absolutely with Iodex-methyl salycilate.[12] Good stuff. <u>No</u> ideas in my head except garden. It's been a dark rainy season and the weeds are awful.

Don't know when I'll be West again—lectures have fallen off a lot. Guess I'm a has-been. One publisher said, apropos of the autobiography "Mrs. Gilman is not as well known as she was ten years ago"!!!

Still yours affectionately
C. P. Gilman.

380 Washington Street
Norwich Town, Conn.
Sept. 5th. 1928.

Dear Alice [Park],

I've just had such a pleasant visit in Miss Eddy's boardinghouse.[13] She asked Grace Stetson and "a friend," and was pleased to have me so listed.

There were <u>twelve</u> old lady boarders before we arrived to swell their numbers. "Old Lady No. 13"—and 14. . . . But I was the village cut up. They admired to see me jump over a chair, and run up stairs two steps at a time! . . .

I might say that Miss Eddy seemed well—for her. (What <u>does</u> ail her, by the way?) . . . And do you know what dreadful blow broke Sarah Eddy in her young power, and turned her strong vivid pictures into cotton wool?

I was amazed at the clear vigor of her early work. The change is pitiful. . . .

Your old friend
Charlotte P. Gilman . . .

380 Washington St.
Norwich Town. Conn.
April 3rd. 1929.

My dear Mr. Williams,[14]

There are two lives of Ambrose Bierce announced in last Sunday's New York Times. Why another? Why any? . . .

Mr. Bierce and I never met personally, and [I] should have refused to meet him had the opportunity offered. He was the Public Executioner and Tormentor, daily exhibiting his skill in grilling helpless victims for the entertainment of the public, for wages.

He was an early master in the art of blackening long-established reputations of the great dead, or such living persons as were unable to hit back effectively, and at his best in scur[r]ilous abuse of hard-working women writers. As a member of the Pacific Coast Women's Press Association during its first years I had excellent opportunity to judge.

Why any man worth the name should find pleasure, or be willing to make profit, in coarsely contemptuous vilification of these women striving to earn a living, is hard to explain. As an exhibition of ingenious malice his "roasts" were spread before the public, as once the torture and execution of criminals; but his victims were not criminals. I recall at this distance his repeated reference to a young Jewish writer named Lezinksky as "the lezinsky"; and also a choice descriptive phrase in which he referred to "the cotton-stuffed bosoms" of the women writers. Nice man.

Save as an extreme expression of the infamous misuse of journalism he gives no excuse for biography, certainly not in the cheaply-piled thick horror of his stories.

Yours sincerely,<br>Charlotte Perkins Gilman

Aug. 21st. 1929

Dear Harold [Channing]—[15]

Seems to me you have a trifling juvenile birthday coming off soon! Here I am gaily bragging that "next year I shall be seventy"!—and athletic even yet.

Those athletic early years, with an undignified, nimble activity ever since have certainly kept me limber. As I remember you were more distinguished for strength than agility. You were occupying your leisure by digging a well when I first came to Pasadena. Do you ever think of that fine masquerade we had? I've quite forgotten what I wore, but still boast of the parti-colored zany suit I made you. Mighty good times we had in those days, didn't we. I'm sorry enough not to get out your way as I did, but if people do not want my lectures, how can I travel! . . .

Here's hoping you are well and happy and will stay so!

With good will—<br>Charlotte P. Gilman.

380 Washington Street<br>Norwich Town, Conn.<br>Sept. 5th. 1929.

Dear Alice Park—

Another book off my hands! Just a story, this time. Ethics not taken anywhere yet—

And now I'm timidly assailing the letter pile. Among 'em is yours of March 9th, with enclosures: Child Labor verses on front page—and various others.

One Carey McWilliams of L.A. recently wrote to me asking for reminiscences of Ambrose Bierce!!! I gave him some![16] He's trying to write a "life" of the creature, and there are two out already. . . .

I'm pretty well, and so is the good man. We did have such a nice time with you in '27!

With love—<br>C. P. Gilman.

Dec. 31st. '29

Dear Harold [Channing],

. . . I'd like to have had you at hand last night. I was doing a X-word puzzle, and got stuck. . . . Grace gets lovely ones in the Herald-Tribune, and sometimes gives me a bunch. I carry them on my travels, light and entertaining.

But I don't travel much these days. Only one real lecture last year—as I remember.

I hope you are keeping well, and it makes me feel comfortable to think of you in a real house—<u>with</u> a bathroom—instead of the little shack!

Cordially—

C. P. Gilman.

380 Washington st.
Norwich Town. Conn.
June 23rd. 1930.

My dear Mr. Schmallhausen [*sic*]:[17]

"Sex and Civilization" must have been a real success for you to contemplate another symposium so soon. But if it was successful why has there been no second royalty? The first one was very satisfactory, but as in the historic yacht-race there was no second.

My "Women and Economics" was published in 1898. Olive Schreiner's "Woman and Labor" after the Boer War.[18] She was one of the greatest women of the age, far greater than I in literary power, but unless you refer to the suggestions in "The Story of an African Farm," and the far-reaching vision of her "Dreams" my work on the economic dependence of women and its results antecedes hers.

Don't you think "The Truth About Women" is a pretty large order? Seems to me if you called it, "Some Truth About Women" it would command more respect—or perhaps "More Truth" etc. As a matter of biological and sociological fact the subject has hardly been touched yet. We are so obsessed with the conspicuous interpersonal relations that we fail to study a race crippled and retarded by misplacing its sexes.

As to parasitism, it is as old as other forms of life, almost a favorite trick in nature. If you'll let me call it "Parasitism and Civilized Vice" I'll do it, and cover your point just as well. You mean twentyfive typewritten pages I suppose, about 7500 words that would be. I should like a contract with details.

Yours cheerfully,

July 18th, 1930.<br>380 Washington St.<br>Norwich Town, Conn.

[To Alice Park]
Patient Friend,

Yours of May 12th, with many interesting enclosures, duly received, read, appreciated and buried!

I'm just digging 'em out now—a terrible heap. . . .

As to my autobiography—I have three books now with no takers; that, The Ethics, and a sort of detective novel.

The last is not very good, but better than some I read.

The Ethics is a valuable book, next to Human Work. . . .

So if you could come a-visiting we'd feed you well! I'm thin and brown as an Indian, but keep well right along. Seventy—and can still jump over a chair!

Am not writing at present. What's the use—if I can't be published! But I have an order ahead, a contribution to a book of many authors— "More Truth about Women." I am really pleased that in the tide of falsehood and grossness which floods the press there is still <u>any</u> call for my special views.

Love and good wishes from your old friend—C. P. Gilman.

380 Washington st.<br>Norwich Town. Conn.<br>Sept. 24th. 1930.

My dear Mr. Schmalhausen,

. . . I think you show real breadth of mind in including such views as mine in your proposed book, the bulk of which I doubt not will be markedly different. Perhaps you will draw the line at my most disrespectful remarks about the "modern" views; but then other of your chosen authors, including your self, have been quite merciless toward what you consider fallacious.

I have given much attention to your request for a definite statement as to "normality," and have tried to meet it. If I were discussing the normality of as widely used a function as digestion I should not base it on a study of one dyspeptic species. It seems to me that you sex-enthusiasts airily disregard the evidence from the entire living world outside of us, also the evidence of the results of centuries of conscience-free indulgence among Oriental peoples who have never been interfered with by "Puritanism." Further that no effort has been made to get down to cases and show [by] convincing figures a clear relation between the degree of sex-indulgence enjoyed and the social value or personal health and happiness of the individual.

That women are as over-sexed as men I advanced in 1898, but in the 999,999 cases out of my hypothetical million, this "male psychology" and "female psychology" are quite clear. Our confused condition is pathological, and will pass with better understanding, and time for better breeding.

It has been rather difficult to write again what I've been discussing for some fifty years with out much repitition [*sic*], some was unavoidable.

Yours—reasonably,

C. P. Gilman

380 Washington St.

Norwich Town, Conn.

Oct. 24th, 1930

Dear Alice [Stone Blackwell]—

What a noble and beautiful book you have made, about a noble and beautiful life.[19] It is a pleasure to read, for anyone, an invaluable record for the ignorant and shallow young people of today to study; and to us who are old enough to remember many of the great people you so well describe it is a deep gratification. I only saw and heard your mother once, but never forgot her—beauty, power and peace—a gift of God, she was. I was very fond of your father. How kind he was to me, how hospitable and helpful. And I particularly remember his brave cheerfulness—coming down every morning to declare it a "holiday"—going out as gaily as a boy, to his work in the Woman's Journal. What a gorgeous heritage! You are rich indeed in two such parents, and your own efforts have carried on the noble work, the endless work, to "make the world better." Those were the loveliest last words I ever knew of.[20]

I had your Easter card—and your kind words about my unwelcome address in Ford Hall.[21] I'd love to have a real good talk with you about mixing races.—Saw that little thing you had in the N.Y. Times about the little girl wishing the aliens were all deported, "bag & baggage."[22] It did not seem to me a fair argument to answer her by taking out the great inventions and other contributions of different races. "Humanity" is a spiritual and material growth, to which all breeds of human animals contribute. The accumulated wealth of art and science, discovery and invention, increases down the ages and should be enjoyed by all the peoples of the earth. But to thank China for her movable type, her silk and porcelain, does not intermixture with her people [*sic*].

The special gifts of the different races are from three main causes: their stock, their environm[en]t, their culture. When transplanted to another environment, immersed in another culture, and mixed with another stock, their "gifts" are lost!

That all races should help one another, and spread wide the advantages of each among the others, is right. Mixing them does not promote the advantages. Did you read Gino Speranza's "Race or Nation?"[23] A most valuable book. As an Italian-American he was singularly able to see the problems from both sides at once.

I'm not writing much now. Have failed to place my last three books,—a very poor Autobiography, a book on Ethics, and a story. These very young readers editors & critics have no use for minds over thirty!

I remember the first time I saw you—a bright-eyed handsome girl, at your desk in the office. And you printed one of my earliest poems— "In Duty Bound." My very first, "One Girl of Many"[24] was printed in "The Alpha"—do you remember that little Washington paper? It was a defence of the "fallen woman." And now they are falling all over the place and enjoying it!! Here's love and gratitude to you!

Charlotte P. Gilman

July 28th 1931

My dear Harold [Channing],

An envelope addressed to you has been lying about on my desk for months. It gives rise to a haunting conviction that perhaps I never wrote to thank you for that exquisitely packed collection of X-word puzzles![25] It's quite likely, I'm that kind of a sinner, old & hopeless! So I'll send these much belated thanks, with my customary apologies.

We are having a soaking summer, whereas last year was a baking one.

I keep thinking of "Bishop Hatto.—" "The summer and autumn had been so wet That in winter the corn was growing yet."[26] . . . Still my garden flourishes, and we flourish on eating it. About 28 edibles this year. . . .

Grace is coming for a visit as soon as I can induce her thereto. I'm much worried about her—but what can I do! . . .

Have you read "Humanity Uprooted"?[27] It's great, a wise wide-reaching book, and excellent reading.

Hoping you are well and busy—which means happy—

Your old friend—

Charlotte P. Gilman.

July 28th 1931

380 Washington Street

Norwichtown, Conn.

And still you call me "Mrs. Gilman"—and still I call you Alice
Dear Alice [Stone Blackwell],

I have here a pleasant Easter card from you, and kind words as well, suggestions that I might write for the newspapers if I can find no publishers for anything else.

I could, of course, if I had anything to say that they would take. You are quite right about the usefulness of it—if it be only to make "a millionaire manufacturer sick," but I almost never have "available" ideas. At present there is no "urge," no wish to write. If there was I could lay up mss. for posthumous publication.

I am well, happy, disgustingly contented. All summer I work in the garden, a throw-back common to the aged I believe! But I have begun to give lectures, free, to the League of Women Voters, anywhere in Connecticut—and that I enjoy hugely.

Love to you, old friend!

C.P. Gilman

380 Washington Street

Norwich Town, Conn.

1931 Dec. 28th

Dear Harriet,[28]

It is very sweet of you to remember me, and I am always pleased to hear from you. . . . What a range of work you college women are undertaking! It is more than necessary for us to understand some rational psychology, and I don't doubt it has to begin this way; but the effect

of this volume of study on "the maternal mind," each woman an ama-
teur, with unbridled power over the one-two-three children she has to
practice on, is pretty dangerous I think. Do you remember any of my
stuff about child culture? . . . You see I think that the mother-&-child
relation should be simple; primitive if you like, with as much understanding and sympathy as is possible in individual cases; but that the
subtleties of education should be carried on outside the home by those
fitted for it by nature & training, and in a broader more dispassionate
atmosphere. But all this eager learning will help toward that larger process; just as the more women study "Home Economics" the more able
they are to see its essential limitation.

Yes ma'am, I'd love to talk things over with you. There is to be a
Birth-Control issue of The Nation in January. About the 20th I
believe—in which I have a contribution—"<u>Birth Control, Religion,
and The Unfit</u>." Rather amusing. . . .

I'm "doing fine" . . . weigh 123—which is corpulence for me. . . .

Love to you all from<br>C. P. Gilman.

380 Washington St.<br>Norwich Town, Conn.<br>February 28th. 1932.

My dear Alice [Park],

(Guess we've loved each other long enough to be Alice and
Charlotte!) Thanks for your nice letter and enclosures. . . .

Speaking of gund [*sic*] for children, my friend Susa Young Gates,
lost a daughter that way, accidentally shot by a brother![29] He was too
small to be blamed, but Oh dear!

The proposition of the Milwaukee lady to pay alimony to her husband if he would stay away from home is very pleasing. . . .

I am well, better than for many years, and disgracefully contented,
but not writing,—no urge at all. The flat failure of my last three
attempts—and even the last one printed is now dead, I've bought the
plates back and some copies—seems to have checked the supply. There's
nothing to prevent my writing, but it simply doesn't come. Oh well, I've
done something to promote social progress, mustn't be greedy.

No one seems to want my lectures now. I'm speaking for the League
of Woman [*sic*] Voters for expenses only—and at that there are almost
no calls. Gratifying, isn't it. Also I've offered to speak for the League of

Nations Assn. for expenses; gave a fifteen minute radio talk for them, and one other address.

We are squeezed pretty flat by "the depression," like most people, the worst of it is that I[,] meaning Houghton![,] can no longer do anything for my people in Pasadena. . . .

Your old friend,

C. P. Gilman

380 Washington St.

Norwich Town.Conn.

March 1st. 1932.

Dear Mr. Huebsch,[30]

I'm more pleased than disappointed with your letter, for my hopes [of publishing "Social Ethics"] were not strong as to publication, and you do recognize power and truth in the book. Probably nothing but an expensive "boom" beforehand would set that work going, spectacular talk about its answering many of our pressing problems, commendations such as those of The Westminster Gazette on "Women and Economics" (—see circular enclosed,) claims as to "the first woman philosopher," and the like—all of which costs money.

Sincere thanks for the noted points for change. I've just been reading the thing over . . . with a view to revision; but have come to the conclusion that except for such minor alterations as you suggest, and a few others, with a bit of condensation here and there, I can not better it. It is a social philosophy, well reasoned and clearly connected, and save for illustrations it <u>has no date</u>—at least as long as we remain in our present stage of economic development. . . .

[I]f I can do no more while alive I mean to place them in some public libraries and universities, for I do think the book will find its place in time. (See Einstein!)

With cordial thanks for your kind interest,

Charlotte Perkins Gilman

380 Washington Street

Norwichtown, Conn.

April 1st., 1932

Thank you again, dear Alice [Stone Blackwell],

. . . Thank you for <u>Unity</u>,[31] with the article on not growing old. If you saw my activities in the garden—vegetable garden mind you!, not merely flowers; or the easy way in which I can cover five or six miles—we are a mile & a half from "the center" and I can do it twice in a day & not mind it—you wouldn't think I needed much encouragement! That is what makes it so hard not to be <u>used</u>—not to have "a pulpit." . . .

Look here! Couldn't you come and make me a visit? I'd just love to have you, and you'd find it very comfortable and quiet. What good times I used to have with you and your splendid father! "This is a holiday!"—every morning. I'm so glad I'm English too—as far back as a long genealogy.

Yours lovingly—

C. P. Gilman

Feb. 1st. 1933

On Board Steamer New Hampshire

Dear Cousin Charles,[32]

We are returning from a delightful visit with Lyman & Hilda, in their gorgeous home on the river. Such a fine time as we have had! Theatres, moving pictures, and Amazing Buildings—a mile high, more or less. Did I tell you Lyman is going to be my literary Executor? I'm immensely pleased that he is willing and feel sure he will do wonders with the stuff. He's getting on famously with his Beecher book,[33] he read us several chapters and it is mighty good. He certainly has the gift of biography. . . .

Mon. evening they gave a party for me, in which I was allowed to perform. Perched on a rug-covered steamer trunk I stood up and discoursed for an hour or so, and read various verses. That's my idea of a nice party—where I can do most of the talking! About 60 guests, I think. I wish you could have been the 61st!

They speak of you with affection—and so do we dear Cousin Charles. Keep well, and maybe we shall see each other again.

Your loving Cousin

Charlotte.

380 Washington st.

Norwich Town. Conn.

1933. Feb. 18th.

Dear Cousin Lyman,[34]

Mrs. Stetson has just sent me a clipping from—I think—the World-Telegram, headed "Zona Gale Lists Her Nine Immortals," among present women.

"I should head the selection with the name of Charlotte Perkins Gilman" said Miss Gale. "Here is a woman who has been a social force and a shaper of policies for betterment for years. It is incredible that she should not be named." She spoke of Hoover's showing that "the purpose of food is to feed people, not to be exploited for financial gain." "Well" continued Miss Gale, "twenty five years ago this was the spoken theory of Mrs. Gilman. Moreover she anticipated Woodrow Wilson's League of Nations in her formulation of articles for world federation. This was an initial step by an American for the integration of the world." ...

Z.G. made a good list: Jane Addams, Julia Lathrop, Grace Abbott, Mary Macdowell, Frances Perkins, Carrie Chapman Catt, Anna Shaw, and Dr. Mary E. Wooley. ...

Love to both of you, dear cousins, from your affectionate

C. P. Gilman

380 Washington st.
Norwich Town. Conn.
February 23rd. 1933.

Dear Cousin Lyman,

Dear Cousin Lyman—(had to get up for something and began all over again,)—<u>did</u> you tell Mr. Shively that mss. was un-begun and unfinished, that I had not even corrected it myself—and so on? It was only intended for you to read and advise about. Alas! I fear me you didn't read it at all.

However, as Mr. S. seems favorably impressed I won't worry. But, if you havn't, do please tell him that it was a scrambled reduction of a previous book and open to all kinds of improvements. Also, if there is talk of publishing it, I want them to read Human Work too, it <u>should</u> come before the Ethics, preferably.

Be assured however that I shall be only too thankful to get anything out, and I feel that you have accomplished miracles to so far interest a favorable publisher. Maybe it is just as well that I did not "place" him when he spoke to me after my talk, I was so cheerfully convinced that nothing of mine had any show nowadays, that all the "readers" were young things just out of college who had no use for any pre-war stuff. (Unless bottled.) ...

With love to Hilda, your affectionate cousin,

Charlotte P. Gilman

380 Washington St.
Norwich Town, Conn.
Sept. 20th. 1933.

Dear Alice [Park],

Your kind suggestion about western lectures couldn't be followed this time. But there is talk of getting me back there this fall or winter, and if that comes to anything I'll let you—& Katharine—know. . . .

The Chicago possibilities were along lines of League of Women Voters & League of Nations work; but you know I'm open to anything. . . .

How's your health, my dear? Mine is excellent.[35]

I took the boat from New London to New York; round trip $4.00; had to go Labor Day night, and when we telephoned for a stateroom there were none! So I sat up all night, part of the time in a comfortable chair, took my train from N.Y. about 10 a.m. Ar. in Chi. 8.30 or so a.m: took my suitcase to Hull House where I was to stay one night, then took street car to the Fair & spent the day there—mostly on foot. That giant thermometer stood over 900. Came back, had a bath, a good dinner, and was lively in the evening. Pretty tough old lady. . . .

We are up against it <u>hard</u>. Don't know how to buy our winter coal. You see Francis pays nothing on the common expenses now. H. has to carry it all. His legal income is painfully little, all dividends are next to nothing, and as for me I've had no work for several years,—writing or speaking. But we live largely on the garden, bless it!

Thanks so much for providing an efficacious friend for poor Hattie Howe.[36] She came near being a genius—a pitiful life.

Yours with grateful affection
C. P. Gilman.

380 Washington st.
Norwich Town. Conn.
Nov. 2nd. 1933.

Dear Lyman—

Look here, I've had an idea! I think I told you my "Yellow Wall Paper" came out in the Oct. <u>Golden Book</u>.

Why wouldn't that make a <u>gorgeous monologue</u>! Stage setting of the room <u>and the Paper</u>, the four windows—the moonlight on the paper—changing lights, and <u>movement</u>—and the woman staring![37]

I could do it myself, in a drawing room and make everybody's flesh creep, but I think it would make a real Emperor Jones'y[38] thing on the stage. . . .

Perhaps Kate Hepburn would consider it—though she's pretty young. Oh if Nazimova would! She's not dead is she?[39]

Maybe your August mama-in-law would know somebody—has she read it? . . .

Love to both of you
Cousin Charlotte

The Wauregan Hotel
Norwich Conn.
Jan. 22nd. 1934.

My Very dear Cousin [Ellen "Nellie" Day Hale]—[40]

Next to Houghton you are far and away the dearest.

I wish I hadn't wasted so much time talking nonsense—and abusing other relatives. There was so much to say of my lovely memories of you when I was 15–16–17. You were so kind! My mother wasn't. She "did her duty" with ceaseless devotion, but strove to make me self reliant by "inhibiting" all tenderness. A Pity. I needed it. And you were so heavenly kind to all the brothers! . . .

It was a deep pleasure to see you. I had really been afraid you had slipped away from us without our knowing. We only heard about Phil—and Edward much later—by accident.[41]

So—I'm grateful for a glimpse of you, and hope for another, for there was some talk of my coming again. . . .

Love to you, dear Cousin, <u>love sixty years long!</u>—

Charlotte Perkins Gilman.

Houghton loves you too.

The Wauregan Hotel.[42]
Norwich. Conn.
Sun. Feb. 11th. 1934

Rev. John Carruthers,
Dear Dr.

My daughter has written as to dates and charges for my lectures. If 200.00 <u>net</u> is guaranteed I will risk coming, hoping to make more while there, there is some possibility of opportunities up the coast. . . .

My regular charge is $100.00. but in these times I would take $75.00 or even $50.00 when necessary. Educational and progressive work was always half price. If circumstances justified it a number of small engagements might be made at low prices.

Last Sunday I spoke on "Our Transient Sexolatry" at Dr. J. H. Holmes Community Forum in New York. It was warmly received. Other recent titles are "Youth, Age, & Foolishness," "Fashion, Brains and Beauty," and, referring to a just finished book on Social Ethics, "The Social Body and Soul." Also another important one, "Religion Cleared Up."

Yours cheerfully,

April 15th, 1934.

Dear Alice [Stone Blackwell],

I have two kind cards to thank you for—Christmas and New Years! It is always nice to know you're there. What a pleasant provision of nature it is that as we grow older our old friends diminish in numbers, new ones do not hold as closely, the young workers do not need us, and it becomes easier and easier to step out!

Have you any belief in personal immortality? I have not, not any interest in it. It seems to me a petty idea. But I have a profound confidence in God, the kind of God I see; and am absolutely contented to accept the order of nature.

The immortality I believe in is for the race, for our continuing ascending humanity. To that progress you and I and the others have contributed, in it we live. Do you remember Whitman—?—"no words can say how utterly at peace I am about God and about death."[43]

So here's love to you, my dear; congratulations for good work done—and glorious hopes for humanity!

Charlotte Perkins Gilman

Figure 8. Charlotte with George Houghton Gilman, ca. 1920. Courtesy of the Schlesinger Library, Radcliffe Institute, Harvard University.

# 8
# The Final Chapter
## "a restful sense of finality"

In January 1932, at the age of seventy-one, Charlotte Perkins Gilman was diagnosed with breast cancer. The extant letters corroborate her contention that she took the news in stride. "I had not the least objection to dying," she remarked in her autobiography (*Living* 333). When she asked her doctor how long she had left to continue writing her book *Social Ethics,* he estimated "a year and a half." Her only concern, she insisted, "was for Houghton. . . . He suffered a thousand times more than I did" (333). On May 4, 1934, Houghton, to whom Gilman had been married for thirty-four years, died suddenly from a cerebral hemorrhage. He was sixty-six.

As the letters in this chapter demonstrate, Gilman's attitudes toward death and dying were both pragmatic and progressive. She believed in death with dignity and was a proponent of assisted suicide. Houghton's death, she remarked, was "a blessed way to go" (Gilman to Alice Park, May 26, 1934). "Whatever I felt of loss and pain was outweighed by gratitude for an instant, painless death for him, and that he did not have to see me wither and die" (*Living* 334). Because Gilman rejected the concepts of immortality and afterlife, she did not console herself with the belief that she and Houghton would someday be reconciled. Rather, while there is little doubt that she grieved the loss of her husband as friend, lover, and companion, her intellectual response to his death was rational and detached. There was no point, she believed, in either spilling tears or wallowing in self-pity. Instead, she began to prepare for her own death.

Four months after Houghton's death, Gilman relocated to Pasadena to spend her remaining time near her daughter and grandchildren. Before she left the East, Gilman also needed to visit friends whom she would never again see. She informed Katharine that she couldn't possibly fly west before August: "I want to make some goodbye visits among friends here" (June 4, 1934). Gilman arrived in California in September 1934, but it was not until the following March that she broke to Katharine the news about her illness and her intended suicide. "K. rather dreads my 'self-help,'" Gilman wrote to Lyman Stowe, "but I think it a real duty. For a decent person of some standing to protest against our inhumane absurdities ought to rouse serious discussion and promote change of thought" (March 29, 1935). With the time she had left, Gilman determined to live as normal a life as her disease would allow. She lectured before various groups, which provided both a small income and the opportunity to stay intellectually alive. She also began informing old friends, via letters, of her "proposed exit," as she termed her suicide (Gilman to Lyman Stowe, March 29, 1935). In a letter to her cousin Katharine Seymour Day, Gilman announced her "prospective departure for parts unknown! Cancer," she wrote matter-of-factly. "One woman in eight has it—why not I? . . . I'm emaciated, I'm weak, but quite calm and cheerful. Eat with pleasure, sleep well—nothing to complain of!" (May 22, 1935).

Though she was soon plagued by shingles, "a horrid disease—a loathsome disease—a painful irritating disease," she wrote to Stowe in June, the cancer itself had caused little discomfort (June 14, 1935). To her longtime friend Edward A. Ross, Gilman wrote that although she had "had the best behaved cancer you ever saw . . . 'complications' have set in . . . so I'm going to go peaceably to sleep with my beloved chloroform" (August 15, 1935). She was gratified by the support she received, not only from Ross but from friends in general. "I find the people I've mentioned it to are not shocked," she wrote to Lyman Stowe. "The world does move. Its only that we are timid about openly facing it" (April 12, 1935).

The response from friends to her planned suicide was, without exception, supportive. Gilman's lifelong friend Martha Luther Lane offered compassion and understanding: "Of course I think you have a right to plan a decent exit," she wrote. "Some day we shall find a decent way of getting out of the world without establishing a precedent in which there might be changes" (April 30, 1935). Another longtime friend, Martha Bruère, wrote, "My dear Charlotte, you cannot die—too much of you has become part of this lovely world—too many of us have made your work ours" (June 9, 1935). Women's rights activist Carrie Chapman Catt wrote to acknowledge Gilman's contributions "for the woman's cause in this world" and offered assurance "that you will leave behind you an influence too valuable to measure" (May 28, 1935). Gilman's longtime friend and physician, Dr. Edward Shelby, sympathized with her suffering and wrote of her planned suicide that "I do not think it wrong and I do not blame you for making such a decision or for carrying it out." He also regretted that "the law would not permit me to lend a hand" when his patients requested assistance in ending their suffering and reminded her that "only a brave heart can carry out such a plan" (March 26, 1935).

Perhaps buoyed by the support that poured in during her final months, Gilman found the strength to write a pro-euthanasia article titled "The Right to Die," with the request that it be published posthumously. It appeared in the November 1935 issue of *Forum* magazine, and with the exception of the brief comments in her published memoirs, it marked her last public statement on suicide, a topic she had addressed many times over the years. It was also her most eloquent essay on the subject. With her suicide imminent, Gilman shifted from theoretician to practitioner: "The record of a previously noble life is precisely what makes it sheer insult to allow death in pitiful degradation. We may not wish to 'die with our boots on,' but we may well prefer to die with our brains on," she remarked ("Right" 299). Moreover, "a civilized society" has the ability to devise "suitable legal methods" that might be enforced "when the sufferer begs for release or when the mind is gone and the body going" (300). She concluded by arguing that "Death is not an evil when it comes in the course of nature, and when it is administered legitimately it is far less than the evil of unnecessary anguish" (300).

By her seventy-fifth birthday, on July 3, Gilman weighed just one hundred pounds. She celebrated the occasion with "friends, gifts, [and] a cake." Katharine presented to her mother "a bottle of whiskey" and "apricot cordial!" much to Gilman's delight. "I often have a little whiskey & water when too tired to eat, and the other I consider the nicest confection man ever made," she remarked to Stowe (July 10, 1935). Even in her final days, Gilman showed the ability to appreciate humor. At the end of her last documented letter, written to Edward A. Ross two days before her suicide, Gilman included a joke. "'Why is a bustle like a historical novel?' 'It is an artificial construct based on a stern reality,'" she wrote with obvious amusement (August 15, 1935).

On the evening of August 17, 1935, Charlotte Perkins Gilman calmly inhaled a lethal dose of chloroform and died peacefully in her Pasadena bungalow. Her suicide note, which she incorporated into her autobiography, explained her actions: "When all usefulness is over, when one is assured of unavoidable and imminent death, it is the simplest of human rights to choose a quick and easy death in place of a slow and horrible one. . . . Believing this open choice to be of social service in promoting wiser views on this question, I have preferred chloroform to cancer" (*Living* 333–34). Her old friend Hattie Howe observed the following about Gilman's death: "Indomitable, valiant, she was never vanquished, she even conquered death. Death did not seize her, an unwilling victim. She went resolutely to meet it, with serene self-determination, as she met all things, gallantly, like a soldier on the field of battle" (Howe 216).

> 380 Washington St.
> Norwich Town. Conn.
> May 26, 1934

Dear Alice [Park],

Yes, dear, [Houghton's death is] a great loss, a great pain. But <u>every</u> married pair faces it—we all have to. . . .

It was a blessed way to go. May we all fare as well! And I'd rather bear the loneliness than to have left him to face it. Thirty four years of happiness—only a few to go alone.

I shall come to California to end my days—as soon as I can pull out of the property mess here. Dear Houghton left very little—he had done so much for my people—and others.—So it's essential that I get some work out there, and I think I can. . . .

Shall hope to see something of you. If I get up to Santa Barbara, to

say goodbye to my aged cousin Charles E. Stowe, now failing fast, I'll
stop over and see you if you're there.

Yours with grateful affection for long kindness,
Charlotte P. Gilman—

380 Washington St.
Norwich Town. Conn.
May 26th, 1934.

Dear Anna [Waller][1]

Thank you for your loving letter. How pleased he [Houghton] would
have been to know you thought of him so appreciatively.

It eases my pain to think of his beautifully swift going; no long
anxiety, pain, distress for me—just gone. Except for friends to grieve a
while there is no one to be sorry for but me, and that's a small matter.

It is a clean pain. A great loss. What of it? Every married pair must
face it—every one! And few can look back on so much unbroken happiness. Pity if I can't bear what everyone bears. The world is full of wid-
ows. And I haven't long empty years to bear it in, like dear Grace. She
had far greater pain. . . .

I hate to add to Katharine's load; but it cannot be helped. We have
plenty of companions in distress, these hard years.

If I can find more work to do, in California, I'll hang on as long as I
can. If not I do not propose to stay any longer than I choose! . . .

Your old friend
Charlotte Perkins Gilman.

380 Washington st.
Norwich Town, Conn.
[c. June 1934]

[To Walter Stetson Chamberlin]
You darling Boy![2]

How dear of you to write to me, with such tenderness and appreciation. I'm pleased and grateful. There have been ever so many letters;
some very sweet and wise, but I value yours most of all.

You see he [Houghton] was very fond of you. Of course we expected
that I would go first; and in such case he meant to go to Pasadena,
where there would still be somebody to love him.

And then, as you know, we planned to go together, and have a little
home there.

Now there is nothing to come but half a Grandmother! It really seems as if half of me was gone. But as long as I am able to do any work, writing or lecturing or anything, of course I must hang on.

I don't know how I shall live out there. It seems absurd to have a house just for one old lady. Probably a room. I'd like what I think every grown up person has a right to—two rooms and a bath. Boarding is easy, but sometimes complicated, on account of the boarders!

But anyhow it will be somewhere near you dear people. . . .

It is a real disappointment to me that you and Dorothy could never visit us here, see this lovely old town and our ancient house. However, thats only one thing!

With love and thanks for your dear letter,
Grandmama

127 N. Madison St.
Pasadena. Cal.
Dec. 14th. 1934.

Dear Zona [Gale],

My husband is dead.

I sat at home, reading, waiting for him to return from an evening of bridge at his quiet elderly club. A telephone call, "an accident," "a fall in the street," "unconscious," a car came for me. I "stood at attention" as I always do in sudden danger, went down town calmly to a little office opening on the street,—he lay on the floor at my feet, dead. May 4th. 1934[.]

Three dreadful months of sorting, packing, destroying, giving away. A restful month of visits with dear friends. Then I came here to live, and die. Because, for which I am grateful, and strictly in confidence if you please, the doctors give me but a year or two.

There was enough left of what used to be a comfortable little competence to keep me in contentment for the time remaining. I'm very pleasantly situated in a rooming house in this most desirable location; library near, shops and restaurants, and my daughter and brother within easy walking distance. I'm living on $30.00 a month comfortably.

Now here is what I'm writing about. My last book, A Study in Ethics, is in process of declination by publisher after publisher. On this book, with Human Work, I am willing to rest my claim to service. And it is particularly important now, with the old bases of conduct wavering and new ones so weak.

But these book venders want my Memoirs. Memoirs! Me! Most of my life has been a vague unhappy blank, with one clear purpose and intermittent accomplishment—work. A few years ago I did undertake to write my life, and very poor stuff it is. The opening chapters are good, while [I] was alive, very strongly alive. Then came that mis-marriage and the blank years; why Zona, I counted up, subtracting my working time from the rest of the time, and that early error in mating cost me pieced together twentyfive years of not merely helpless idleness but black misery.

After marrying Houghton there was peace and happiness. Slowly I recovered. It has been several years now since the recurrence of that blackness [...]

I have been reading "Birth."[3] The divine tenderness of insight with which you followed the formless Goodness of that lovely soul to its release stirred in me a sudden hope.

Will you write my life?[4]

I'll send you the one I wrote, for facts and dates. I'll tell you anything you want to know.

I think you have seen better than any one else what I have tried to do, and measured better than any one else what I have done. If you could do this I feel that it would stir an interest in my other books, now all out of print. I have enough later poems to make another book like In This Our World—for which I've had unfillable orders for years....

And, for the sake of the work, the scrappy, imperfect, desperately earnest work I have done, I hope you'll do this for me.

Your loving friend,

127 N. Madison st.
Pasadena, Cal.
Jan. 6th. 1935

[To Lyman Beecher Stowe and Hilda Stowe]
You <u>Dear</u> People!

I <u>will</u> put a capital D. to it! It is such a warm spot in my heart—the memory of all your loving kindness....

I continue [to] be considered a model of health and vigor—by the other old ladies who inhabit this house. There are nine of them now! And my top floor residence continues to give me warm satisfaction. (No, 8 of them, I am the 9th!)...

I am sitting as I write by my double glass doors, one open, looking out on tall pointsettias, a great bush of marguerites, oranges, roses, and such.... I do love it here.

Mostly I cook for myself now. . . . I'm as contented as a pig. Three times a week I go to dinner with Katharine. The children seem to like me. Yes, I'm as comfortable as need be, and as happy as I've any right to expect. . . .

Your loving and grateful Cousin Charlotte

127 N. Madison Ave.<br>Pasadena, Cal.<br>Jan. 11th, '35.

My dear Alice [Stone Blackwell]:

You will be grieved to hear that I have lost my husband. He died, suddenly—cerebral haemorrhage—on May 4th.

34 years of happiness, we had together—that is enough to be thankful for. And that he had no anxiety—no pain—and no loneliness to bear.

There remains a tiny income for me, enough to see me through I think, and I have come out here to be with my daughter, and the two grandchildren; also an aged brother and a young nephew.

I love California, and this beautiful little city is more like home to me than any place on earth.

So you may feel quite easy in your mind about me—which is, nowadays, more than one can say of most friends. As to grief, a clean final grief, that can be borne, as you well know.

I hope you keep well my dear; and know that as long as you live you are doing good as far as you can reach.

It has been an honor and a pleasure to know you, and to remember your lovely mother, you[r] noble and sublimely cheerful father.

Your loving old friend<br>Charlotte Perkins Gilman

127 N. Madison Ave.<br>Pasadena, Cal.<br>Mch. 29. 1935

Dear Lyman,

. . . Good News! Zona Gale has cordially consented to do—I don't quite know what—with my biography! Don't brag about it yet for she may fall out—people do. But if she writes the kind of thing she would write—nothing could be better for our plans. Then if Amy Wellington can get the poem's [*sic*] together—with a foreword—(have you read what she said of me in her "<u>Women Have Told</u>"?) I wouldn't ask a better start there. . . .

I have told Katharine [about my cancer]. She is quiet and brave—but it is a blow. We have a plan for me to come to the house next but one which her friend Miss Waller is buying—really for her; so that she can see the last of me as it were—Doctor now says six months. And I say probably less!

K. rather dreads my "self-help," but I think it a real duty. For a decent person of some standing to protest against our inhumane absurdities ought to rouse serious discussion and promote change of thought.

I hope to see you again and in any case to write you again; but I want to say now how deeply, how warmly grateful I am for all your cousinly kindness. . . .

Thank you dear boy, from my heart. I feel happy about your work. You have a distinct place in the world, with your special gift, and chosen field of work, and are gaining in power—and in charm. . . .

Your affectionate Cousin Charlotte

127 N. Madison Ave.<br>Pasadena, Cal.<br>Mch. 29th. 1935

My dear Cousin Lyman—

You've been <u>such</u> a comfort to me! As I've said before, and what heavenly kind things you said about me at that "Reunion"! I'm ashamed to have made so scant and poor a response but nothing came to me to say except on grounds of descent in the male line only. When I looked at that array of outsiders—adopteds, marrieds, and such; as well as diluted descendants—it seemed to me the Beecher stock was running rather thin!

Our greatgrandfather was certainly a "prepotent sire," but then he had a "prepotent dam" to help him; two perhaps—the second was good stock, too. Anyhow, they <u>did their work</u>—and that keeps.

I'm going to pieces pretty fast now. Getting very weak and horribly tired of coughing. You see the critter is scrabbling around in my lungs—most inconvenient. I'm hoping to get over to the house by Katharine in about a fortnight. She is simply angelic! If you have another Beecher meeting next year do have her bring Frank and the children—they would love it.

I meant to have prepared for Miss Wellington a nicely typed set of poems—! Not strong enough.

Do you think, (instead of "flowers"!) you and Hilda could help in having them typed?

I think the book "Gilman's Poems" Book I. In This Our World, Book II. "Here Also" will at least cover expenses. . . . It really is unusual work. Miss W. [Wellington] will write a foreword I suppose.

Here is my—Valedictory. I don't know just what should be done with it—but I want it published.

I'd like some discussion—sermons—articles—etc. . . . . Use your judgement dear—but I want it put before the people fairly. Of course the papers here will be nasty about it—they always are. . . .

Charlotte Perkins Gilman.

April 5th. '35

Dear Amy [Wellington]—

I don't know what to say about the nonsense verse.[5] These "duets" I think very funny; and "The Dream of old," albeit nonsense is good poetry. "The Melancholy Rabbit" is a gem—if I did do it.

Maybe later they'll get out some "miscellany"—maybe I'll never achieve this "revival" at all! Anyway, send the stuff back to Lyman—what you don't use. The main thing of course is the real book—"Gilman's Poems."

C. P. G.

Pasadena Ca<br>Fri. April 12. 1935

Dear Cousin Lyman,

I'm giving Katharine's address, because it may not be at all convenient to "answer the door" at my house! I expect to be alone in it a good deal—but there's a telephone by my bed, connecting with K.'s, as well as "general"—move over there tomorrow. There will be a restful sense of finality when I settle down in that bed!

I find people I've mentioned it to are not shocked by my proposed exit. The world does move. It's only that they are timid about openly facing it. . . .

Zona Gale came—a mere half hour! She took my copy of the Auto-biography—some picture[s] & letters.[6] And I'm going to send her a full set of The Forerunner—to look over. I don't know just what she means to do. She stopped again for a few moments in the afternoon, bringing Mr. Breeze [*sic*] . . . and Hamlin Garland.[7] . . .

Well my dear boy, I am still cheerful and comfortable. Not an ache or a pain or a worry!

Love to both of you from<br>Cousin Charlotte.

223 S. Catalina Ave.<br>Pasadena Cal<br>April 22nd. 1935

Dear Alice [Park]—

Two nice letters from you and no answer! And now I have a piece of bad news for you, my dear.

I set out to tell you while you were here, asking if you'd like to know if you were never to see me again—and you said "yes and no"—so I let it go by.

But will now state that my being here in the middle of June is dependent on how my "cough" gets on—that is on how comfortable or vice versa I am. Said cough is due to cancer; which I discovered in the breast early in 1932.

I have more than doubled the life limit they gave me then; but now it is rambling around in the lung space—which interferes with breathing! As you probably know I do not intend to die of any slow and disagreeable disease, not I; but to go peacefully asleep when I get ready.

So far I have had <u>no</u> pain from the thing; not even discomfort. Last fall the area began to swell; but Xray treatment stopped that completely. So I haven't been disfigured, even.

Also I have had no mental distress from it—took it like a lamb—or a clam. The doctor was <u>so</u> surprised!

You see it gets one woman in eight—one man in ten—and—consistent humanitarian that I am—why not me!

Here I have a whole nice little house to live in next door but one to Katharine, who is taking care of me with heavenly kindness. A big green yard—flowers—trees—a long chair under a blossoming orange tree, bees & birds and sunshine—the family close by—I am thoroughly enjoying my new position of Distinguished Invalid! But if it begins to hurt—or to choke—off I go! As it is I mustn't talk much, or laugh—make me cough. . . .

Yours cheerfully,
Charlotte P. Gilman.

223 S. Catalina Ave,
Pasadena Cal.
April 23. 1935

Dear Cousin Lyman,

. . . Now about Grace. At present she is a load on my mind.[8] You see I have loved her for nearly 60 years. She is old, heavily disabled, poor, and <u>alone</u>. Here she would have a favorable climate—her early home; Katharine, whom she dearly loves; and the grandchildren. Moreover there is a third old lady here, Katharine's "Aunt Augusta," Miss Senter, who lived close to Grace and has been a most intimate friend since—1876 or 7. We three have been Katharine's "three mothers". . . .

Now Miss Senter has a seriously affected heart—We are all three on our last legs; and presently Katharine will be left triply orphaned as it were. I'm probably off first; there will be a lot of unpleasantness about "the order of my going"; and if she has Grace here it will be an enormous comfort to her. The three of us who love her will enjoy a re-union, though brief; and it will be an immense relief to me to feel that my already overstrained daughter is not alone with her burden. . . .

I understand there is really more chance for pictures than there has been for some years.[9] If Grace, somewhat refreshed, could write something to revive knowledge of and interest in Mr. Stetson's work—published in the fall and followed by an exhibition and sale, that would be salvation for our harassed family. . . .

I shan't try to talk to her—not at all, just write, when necessary.

I can't talk and she can't hear! . . .

Spend my time in a cushiony long-chair under a blossoming orange tree, enjoying the mockingbirds and flowers. . . .

C. P. Gilman.

223 S. Catalina Ave.
Pasadena Cal.
May 22nd. 1935

Well, my Kind Cousin [Katharine Seymour Day],

I'm writing "p.p.c."[10] letters to various friends announcing my prospective departure for parts unknown! Cancer. Began in the breast, early in 1932. Now rambling about to suit itself. They gave me a year and a half—and I've made it three and a half and not dead yet!

It was because of this that I was so earnest to have one more chance to say what I had to say. Thanks to your friendly efficiency I had it, and am grateful. I've just been writing to Mrs. Green to thank her, I did enjoy her house, a lovely place to speak in.

You know I find cancer not at all dreadful, so far. No pain, and, such is my temperament, no fear or repugnance. One woman in eight has it—why not I? It began in the breast; was apparently quite discouraged there by assiduous Xrays, and is now distributing itself in other places— still with no pain. I'm emaciated, I'm weak, but quite calm and cheerful. Eat with pleasure, sleep well—nothing to complain of! Am living in a little house next door but one to Katharine, in my beloved Pasadena. She brings me my breakfast in bed; I go there to dinner & supper.

Amusingly enough I mustn't talk much, nor laugh!—makes me cough more.

Even here I had a "class" for six weeks; a swan-song as it were. I write letters mornings, when feeling up to it, and spend my afternoons under a tall orange tree—full of bees. The white petals drift down softly. A large back garden; plenty of roses and other flowers—the whole quiet street is a garden for that matter.

Mocking birds sing day and night—but do not keep me awake.

So I'm really having a very pleasant time, every comfort, and the happiness of loving daughter and grandchildren.

I'd like to see you my dear. You've been very good to me, and besides I like you!

Cousin

Charlotte

223 S. Catalina Ave.

Pasadena, Cal.

May 27th. 1935

My dear Cousin Lyman,

What miracles have you and Hilda wrought—for I'm sure she's had a hand in it—that you should move the immovable at last! I am deeply touched and grateful by your goodness.

The third of this little group of old friends [Augusta Senter] is on her last legs also—a heart that is liable to stop any time. She is deaf too. We are a sorry bunch of old ladies! But I flatter myself that if this extraneous enemy had not attacked me I should have continued to be a very agile old party for some years yet!

Katharine is so glad to see Grace again. She has been more of a mother to her than I have, in many ways; has influenced her character more, I think. . . .

We here [*sic*] that Grace plans to arrive on the 11th of June. That was her wedding day; and, by sheer oversight, mine too, to Houghton. . . .

With love and gratitude

C. P. Gilman—

June 14th 1935.

223 S. Catalina

Pasadena, Cal.

Dear Lyman and Hilda,

. . . Katharine has told you I guess of my latest affliction—Shingles! It is a horrid disease—a loathsome disease—a painful irritating disease, and weakening beyond words. Why Lyman—I haven't been dressed since it hit me. I've been so weak I could hardly turn in bed. It attacked the left arm shoulder & neck; and constant application of witch hazel proved most relieving. As a matter of fact it was a fairly comfortable light attack—if I'd been well, I shouldn't have minded it much. Rapidly healing now, thank goodness. . . .

Then comes this amazing Appleton proposition [to publish the autobiography]. How could Zona be so deluded! And how delude them! It's hypnotism! Can it be that all previous decliners were mistaken?—Anyhow I'm thankful. Now if they'll take the poems to[o] they'll be fine for the Xmas sale; the two together ought to make a splash—as I hoped. . . .

But <u>why</u> should they call it a "splendid autobiography!" It isn't. . . .

You're quite right about Miss W. [Wellington] getting a third of the royalties—but I doubt if she will accept! Or Zona either. I tell you Lyman its worth while, dying, just to learn what friends one has. . . .

With grateful love—

Cousin Charlotte.—

223 So. Catalina Av.

Pasadena, Calif.

June 21, 35

Dear Mrs. Coats,[11]

I am sorry to disappoint you, and my old friend Mrs. Park, but I absolutely refuse to be listed as a "California woman." I have done so before, and shall do so as long as I live, (—which will not be long!) I shall have to leave one of these old melodramatic "curses" for everyone who does it after I am dead. There are two sufficient reasons. Firstly, I am <u>not</u> a California woman. I was born in Hartford, Conn., and have lately been living in that state for twelve years. I lived in Rhode Island for fifteen years. I lived in New York, N.Y. for 22 years. None of those states try to claim a casual resident as their own.

I spent seven years in California—less than any of these.

I will not be falsely represented. It is a pitifully small business, for a state to grab at tourists, visitors, temporary visitors, as its own—shall we call Robert Louis Stevenson "a Samoan man?" "A Samoan author?"

My second reason is this. I did seven years of work—some of my best work—in California, creditable enough for any community. I was black guarded by the California press, fairly kicked out of the state—a discreditable failure!

Then I became favorably known, in America and in Europe. They have repeatedly tried to claim me as "a California writer." Never with my consent....

There now. Aimee Spurr[12] tells me you are a very nice person! I know you mean kindly by me and thank you. But I'm sitting up in bed—trying to answer letters, and raging over this old grievance.

Wishing you success and with friendly personal greetings,

C. P. Gilman

223 S. Catalina Ave.
Pasadena Cal.
June 25th. 1935

My dear Lyman,

. . . I'm a lot better—of the shingles. It was left arm, shoulder & neck. Glad it was not the right! Practically cleared up as to the external horror, but the arm still pretty helpless yet, prickles & stings if I use it, and is <u>cold</u>! Have to keep it wrapped up extra.

Grace is here, sharing my little house. I cannot say how grateful I am to you and Hilda for doing it—and I know it was owing to you. She has two rooms; I have two rooms, kitchen and bath in common....

It is doing her good already. She has a brother here—ineffectual person—but she is fond of him; and to him it is a great happiness to see her.—

Katharine is as pleased as I thought she would be. And Mrs. Senter, friend of 60 years, who was at death's door with heart disease, is better, and very happy to see her. We all think the rest and change will prolong life for Grace.

So you see it is a very large happiness to five people.

I don't try to talk to her. Write things that are necessary, but mostly hold hands and smile and play anagrams! . . .

I continue to be happy, comfortable, and immensely grateful. . . .

> With love
>
> Cousin Charlotte

July 10 (?) 1935.

Dear Lyman,

More thanks for improving the contract. Katharine . . . is immensely impressed with her "advance royalty." I'm <u>thankful</u> for it! For when I drop out this will tide 'em over another month or so. Of course I [will] pay for typing the poems! And any other necessary bills. . . .

Yes I had a lovely birthday—friends, gifts, a cake—and a fine sense of wealth, in your present. <u>What</u> do you think K. bought me out of it! A bottle of whiskey . . . [and] apricot cordial! I often have a little whiskey & water when too tired to eat, and the other I consider the nicest confection man ever made—not a drink.

And a bathroom scale I asked for. I was fondly hoping to find out how little I weighed—I'm nothing but bones and wrinkles—and to my disgust, I weighed 100! . . . I still enjoy eating, sleep pretty well, have little to complain of but fathomless ex[h]austion—at times. And a wriggling physical irritability—when I <u>can't</u> get comfortable. . . .

Love & thanks to you & Hilda—

> C. P. Gilman

> 223 S. Catalina Ave.
> Pasadena, Cal.
> July 11th 1935.

[To E. A. Ross]
My dear old friend,

Here is a post card on which please send me your address! Because I want to send you my Autobiography, coming out this Fall—Appleton

Century Co.—with accumulated thanks for all your valuable—and enjoyable—books given to me. . . .

Me, I'm living next door but one to my daughter, in this lovely land. She is my wholly desirable nurse. For I've been dallying with a cancer for three years and a half. No pain at all, so far; nothing to complain of till lately; but now I'm just bones and drapery! and can't sit up long. Comfortable & happy all the same.

With long and pleasant memories of your many kindnesses—

Your cheerful old friend

Charlotte P. Gilman.

[P.S.] Mr. Gilman died suddenly May 4th, 1934. I'm so <u>glad</u> he does not have to see [me] through this!

223 S. Catalina Ave.[13]

Pasadena. Cal.

Aug. 5th. 1935

My dear Zona [Gale],

Will you take a gift with a string to it? I want you to keep my precious set of <u>Forerunners</u>—but I want you to leave 'em in your will to my family! You see there are so few of the bound sets! Three or four at the outside. Just leave 'em to Lyman Stowe—he will know addresses and which grandchild wants them—if they do at all.

I feel as if you were one of the few people in the world who would really enjoy having them. I think there were some papers, too—things to look over in connection with the book—please return those. . . .

As for me I am approaching the stepping off place very closely—a matter of a few weeks more or less. I see no reason whatever in prolonging an increasingly uncomfortable existence. As soon as I'm too weak to totter to the bathroom—off I go. I know what it means to be "tired to death." And O my dear! <u>What</u> a comfort it will be to go to sleep! Isn't it good to be so perfectly confident about God!

What's that lovely bit of Whitman (my mind is almost as feeble as my body) "I have no words to express how absolutely at peace I am, about God and about Death."[14] Me too!

I've always loved you, etherial [*sic*] Zona. You are not like the rest of us. . . .

Love and gratitude from your old friend,

Charlotte Perkins Gilman.

223 S. Catalina Ave.
Pasadena. Ca.
August 5th. '35

My very dear Cousin Lyman,

. . . I'm so weak now that my head wo[b]bles on my neck! Have to have a little pillow for it when I'm propped up in a chair. And its laughable to see me totter out to my cot under the orange tree—I only sit for an hour or so to rest my joints. No pain at all. And yet the unutterable weariness—such physical humiliation—I <u>won't</u> be bedridden! What's the use! All that holds me is my little "allowance"—Katharine will miss that sorely. But I am not going to stay even for that. Did I tell you my last very definite suggestion for the title [of the autobiography]. I think it fine.

The "Living"
of
Charlotte Perkins Gilman.
By Herself.

You see I refer to my "Living" all the way through the book.

Well my dear boy—take comfort in thinking how <u>good</u> to me you have been, and do remember Katharine.

With grateful love.
Cousin Charlotte

[August 12, 1935]

Dear Alice [Park],[15]

. . . I'm about done with writing—and most everything else. A matter of days now, I think. Still no pain, but much distress, utter weakness, and an ebb tide feeling there is no dodging.

Love to you my dear and years of thanks. It was good to see you again, and your splendid daughter—and the boy.

Charlotte Perkins Gilman

Aug. 15th 1935.
223 S. Catalina Ave.
Pasadena, Cal.

[To E. A. Ross]
My Very dear Old Friend,

I was <u>so</u> pleased to get your letter. Cheerfulness? Why not? I've had the best-behaved cancer you ever heard of—no pain at all. But in June I had shingles, which is a devilish disease, and now "Complications" have set in, nephritis and dropsy, and a fairly laughable weakness; so I'm going to go peacably to sleep with my beloved chloroform. I'm getting "fed up" with sheer weakness. . . .

I'm glad you are so rich in the Ross Clan—you being The Ross!

I alwa[y]s did admire & like the Scotch—and despise the Irish!

Did you ever think when the New Wave opened and Little England, Little Scotland, Little Portugal, little Holland and Sweden and Norway and Denmark put to see [*sic*] in their cockleshells and helped themselves [to] the new land, little Ireland never produced one boat!!! Preferred to sit still and holler about being oppressed!

Well—goodbye—

Charlotte Perkins Gilman

[P.S.] (Say do you know this lovely one? A Latin professor had a nervous niece in charge for some out door celebration. Her name was Henrietta, Etta, Ette. Thunder storm came up. Ette much alarmed, he must get a vehicle & send her home. All he could find was a bus, already full, but he squeezed her in, remarking as it left—"Et in terra pax homnibus"!)[16]

---

This from the President of Yale:
"Why is a bustle like a historical novel?" "It is an artificial construct based on a stern reality."

# Notes

## Abbreviations

| | |
|---|---|
| AESL | Arthur and Elizabeth Schlesinger Library, Radcliffe Institute, Harvard University, Cambridge, Massachusetts |
| BANC | Bancroft Library, University of California, Berkeley |
| BARN | Barnard College Library, New York |
| BRL | Braun Research Library, Autry National Center/Southwest Museum, Los Angeles |
| COL | Rare Books and Manuscript Library, Columbia University, New York |
| HBSC | Harriet Beecher Stowe Center Library, Hartford, Connecticut |
| HL | Houghton Library, Harvard University, Cambridge, Massachusetts |
| HOR | Horrmann Library, Wagner College, Staten Island, New York |
| HUNT | Huntington Library, San Marino, California |
| JHL | John Hay Library, Brown University, Providence, Rhode Island |
| KL | Kroch Library, Cornell University, Ithaca, New York |
| LL | Lilly Library, Indiana University, Bloomington |
| LOC | Library of Congress, Washington, DC |
| NUL | Northwestern University Library, Evanston, Illinois |
| NYPL | New York Public Library |
| PM | Pasadena Museum of History, Pasadena, California |
| RIHS | Rhode Island Historical Society, Providence |
| SL | Sheidan Libraries, Johns Hopkins University, Baltimore |
| SSC | Sophia Smith Collection, Smith College, Northampton, Massachusetts |
| SUL | Stanford University Library, Palo Alto, California |
| UCLA | Department of Special Collections, Charles E. Young Research Library, University of California, Los Angeles |
| UIL | University of Illinois Library, Urbana-Champaign |
| URL | University of Rochester Library, Rochester, New York |
| VCL | Vassar College Libraries, Poughkeepsie, New York |
| WHM | Women's History Museum and Educational Center, San Diego, California |
| WHS | Wisconsin Historical Society, Madison |

WSC     Private Collection of Walter Stetson Chamberlin, Los Alamos,
        New Mexico

## Introduction

1. Of particular note in this regard are Barton and Hall, Decker, Gaul, and Hewitt.

2. Among those scholars who have noted that epistolary conventions are often used to negotiate differential power relationships between the writer and recipient is Susan K. Harris; see *The Cultural Work of the Late Nineteenth-Century Hostess* 56.

3. See Decker for a particularly useful analysis of this phenomenon.

4. About the fact that Gilman saved her correspondence, M. A. Hill writes, "It was almost as though she realized her published writing would be one type of legacy. Another would be the record of her life [preserved in her letters]—compelling, disquieting, and very real" (*Journey* 22).

5. For further discussion of the material dimensions of epistolary exchange, see Decker 37–56, Gaul 26–29, and Sharon M. Harris's discussion of the "interruptive discourse" used by women whose writing was done amid domestic labors (24).

6. Gilman dated her letter "8-9-'15"; because she frequently transposed the numbers for month and day, it is unclear whether she composed this letter on August 9 or September 8.

7. Scholars frequently note this aspect of published letter collections. Modern readers of such a volume, Decker points out, "have no part in what is now a chronologically distant exchange" (7). While the letters printed herein have lost what initially defined them, i.e., "their existence as direct communications from one unique sensibility to another" (Spacks 70), we have striven to include letters that illustrate the personal, cultural, and historical contexts through which Gilman navigated.

## Chapter 1

1. Family Correspondence, Gilman Papers, AESL. Mary Beecher Foote Perkins (1805–1900) was Gilman's paternal grandmother.

2. Catherine was Gilman's aunt Catherine Perkins Gilman (1836–79).

3. Frederic Perkins (1828–99) was separated from Gilman's mother, Mary Westcott Perkins. A notation on the letter in Gilman's hand reads, "1871–2?" All letters to Frederic Perkins are taken from the Family Correspondence, Gilman Papers, AESL.

4. *The Princess and the Goblin* (1881) was written by Scottish novelist and poet George Macdonald (1824–1905).

5. A notation on the letter in Gilman's hand reads: "[18]'74 or 5 I guess."

6. The quotation is from *The Lady of the Lake* by Scottish novelist and poet Sir Walter Scott (1771–1832).

7. The quotation is from Genesis 49:4: "Unstable as water, thou shalt not excel; because thou wentest up to thy father's bed; then defiledst thou it: he went up to my couch."

8. Gilman's cousin and future second husband, Houghton Gilman, was twelve

years old in 1879; Gilman was nineteen. All letters to Houghton Gilman, whom she sometimes referred to as "Ho," are taken from the Family Correspondence, Gilman Papers, AESL.

9. Gilman is referring to news about the sudden death of Houghton's mother.

10. Houghton had written that his absent father was returning home after learning of his wife's death.

11. Gilman is quoting lines from "The Merry Bard" by English author William Makepeace Thackeray (1811–63).

12. Family Correspondence, Gilman Papers, AESL. Caroline Robbins (1822–98) was Gilman's aunt. The Pitchers were Gilman's downstairs neighbors.

13. For further information on "Perkins & Company Designers" see Knight, "An Amusing Source of Income." The enterprise yielded a profit of $373.

14. Letters to Martha Luther Lane in this and other chapters were taken from two sources. While the majority are from the Charlotte Perkins Gilman Letters, RIHS, the April 17, 1935, letter, quoted in the introduction to chapter 8, is from the General Correspondence, Gilman Papers, AESL. Unless otherwise noted, all salutations that begin "Dear Martha" refer to Martha Luther Lane. Gilman and Lane enjoyed a lifelong friendship. "With Martha I knew perfect happiness," Gilman wrote in her memoir. "Four years of satisfying happiness with Martha, then she married and moved away." Gilman was devastated by Martha's decision to marry, calling it "the keenest, the hardest, the most lasting pain I had yet known" (*Living* 80).

15. Avis: The title character in American author Elizabeth Stuart Phelps's (1844–1911) *The Story of Avis* (1877), which explores the conflict between the pursuit of art and conventional marriage.

16. Halicarnassus: Gilman's nickname for Charles A. Lane, to whom Martha would become engaged in the autumn of 1881. The city of Halicarnassus, today known as Bodrum, is located in southwest Turkey, overlooking the Aegean Sea.

17. Providence resident Sam Simmons and his brother Jim were students at Brown University.

18. In Arabian mythology, a fisherman placed an Afrite, a powerful demon, in a corked bottle.

19. Parnassus: The sacred, mythological mount in Greece where Apollo and the Muses lived.

20. These lines are from "To Lucasta, on Going to the Wars," by English poet Richard Lovelace (1618–58).

21. These lines are from the essay "Self-Reliance" (1841), by American transcendentalist writer Ralph Waldo Emerson (1803–82).

22. In the fall of 1881, Gilman was successful in persuading Dr. John P. Brooks, author of *Exercise-Cure. The Butler Health Lift; and What It is and What It Will Do* (1884), to open the Providence Ladies' Sanitary Gymnasium.

23. This quotation and those that follow are from Emerson's essay "Friendship" (1841). The sentence quoted by Gilman in the following paragraph actually reads, "Why should I cumber myself with regrets that the receiver is not capacious?" The quotations in the next several paragraphs following this one are also from "Friendship."

24. bête noir: a bane

25. Gilman is apparently being facetious; there is no "Chace" breed of cats.

26. The Grimalkin of Shakespeare's *Macbeth* was one of the witch's familiar spirits, and the cat, the reputed companion of these unsavory characters, often received this name.

27. The correct title of the weekly paper is *Illustrated London News.*

28. Gilman has circled the paragraph beginning "Private!" and ending with "home!"

29. Gilman is paraphrasing the poem "Divided" by English poet Jean Ingelow (1820–97). The lines actually read:

And yet I know past all doubting, truly,—
A knowledge greater than grief can dim,—
I know, as he loved, he will love me duly,—
Yea, better, e'en better than I love him.

30. "Aunt Catherine" is most likely Gilman's great-aunt Catharine E. Beecher (1800–1878), who devoted her professional life to advancing educational opportunities for women and to advocating kindergarten for children.

31. "That man" was Jim Simmons. Her fear that Martha was falling in love with Simmons likely fueled Gilman's desire to distance Martha from him. Martha, however, was being courted by Charles A. Lane, to whom she would become engaged in October.

32. Martha married Charles A. Lane of Hingham, Massachusetts, on October 5, 1882.

33. Mrs. Grundy was a character in British playwright Thomas Morton's *Speed the Plough.* The allusion is used to describe a person who is overly priggish.

34. Caroline Hazard (1856–1945) was a philanthropist, educator, and author. Educated by private tutors at Mary A. Shaw's School in Providence, and later, in Europe, Hazard assumed the presidency of Wellesley College in 1899.

35. Addenda to the Gilman Papers, AESL. At the top of the letter, in Gilman's hand, is the following notation: "After Martha Luther's engagement. This to one Sam Simmons a friend of several year's standing. I had so few——."

36. Family Correspondence, Gilman Papers, AESL. Gilman met her first husband, Charles Walter Stetson (1858–1911), on January 11, 1882. The letters dated February 21 and February 22, 1882, are also taken from the Family Correspondence, Gilman Papers, AESL.

37. Gilman's "lost friend" was Martha Luther Lane.

38. One of the few known female poets of ancient Greece, Sappho was born sometime between 630 and 612 B.C.E. and spent much of her life studying the arts on the isle of Lesbos.

39. Gilman crossed out from "pure and high" through "should most enjoy" and resumed the letter the following day.

40. General Correspondence, Gilman Papers, AESL. Hedge, a resident of Cambridge, Massachusetts, was a longtime friend of Gilman's.

41. Gilman sustained injuries to her genitalia after falling onto a chair when she climbed atop a piano to set a clock in the Providence Ladies Gymnasium. In her diary entry for March 18, 1882, she reports that the fall resulted in "a violent bruise" and a "profusely bleeding cut just in the 'middle.'" Despite the scare, Gilman noted that she would be "blest with an entire holiday till Thurs.!" and that she enjoyed receiving "Delicate attention!" (*Diaries* 113).

42. Family Correspondence, Gilman Papers, AESL. Thomas Adie Perkins (b. 1859) was Gilman's only surviving sibling. This letter was inscribed in Gilman's hand and inserted in the back of her diary for 1883. Julia was Thomas's wife.

43. Here and in the next sentence, Gilman is paraphrasing a line from Emerson's 1841 essay, "Self-Reliance."

44. Gilman began working as a governess to Eddie Jackson, a young Providence boy, on July 16. Originally overjoyed at the prospect of steady employment, she soon confided to her diary that Eddie was "a despicable boy" (222). She remarked in her autobiography over forty years later, "[I] learned more about the servant question in that time [I was a governess] than most of us ever find out" (*Living* 69).

45. Martha's son, Charles Chester Lane, was born on August 6, 1883.

46. Private Collection, Walter Stetson Chamberlin. Gilman had spent considerable time with Brown during her stay in Ogunquit, Maine, the previous summer and noted in her diary that during one of their walks he allowed her to "try [out] his [loaded] revolver" (207). She also took time to comfort and counsel Brown after he confided that he had often contemplated suicide.

47. Gilman's daughter, Katharine Beecher Stetson Chamberlin, inserted and circled the comment "A happy courtship!"

## Chapter 2

1. Emily Perkins Hale (1829–1912) was the wife of Unitarian minister and author Edward Everett Hale. The paternal grandmother to whom Gilman alludes in the third sentence of the letter was Mary Foote Beecher Perkins (1805–1900), daughter of the renowned Presbyterian minister Lyman Beecher (1775–1863). Gilman's maternal grandmother, Clarissa Fitch Perkins, who was born circa 1790, had died in 1873. This letter and others to Aunt Emily are taken from the Hale Family Papers, SSC.

2. Zona Gale Papers, WHS. Silas Weir Mitchell (1829–1914) was the American physician who in 1887 treated Gilman for neurasthenia, an emotional and psychic disorder characterized by debilitating fatigue, loss of energy and motivation, feelings of inadequacy, and psychosomatic symptoms. Renowned for his treatment of nervous disorders, Mitchell was the author of medical publications such as *Wear and Tear* (1871) and *Fat and Blood* (1877) as well as several novels and volumes of poetry.

3. In his preface to the 1867 edition of *The Guardian Angel,* American author and physician Oliver Wendell Holmes (1809–94) argued that inherited attributes determine character from generation to generation.

4. Unitarian minister Henry Westcott, Gilman's maternal grandfather, was a descendant of Stukely Westcott (1592–1677), a planter and colonizer who, along with

Roger Williams, was among the thirteen original proprietors of the Providence Plantations and the Colony of Rhode Island.

5. Gilman's maternal grandmother, Clarissa Fitch Perkins, married Henry Westcott in 1826.

6. Gilman's mother, Mary Westcott Perkins, was born in 1828 and died in 1893.

7. Gilman's paternal grandfather, Thomas Clap Perkins (1798–1870), was a lawyer in Hartford, Connecticut.

8. Gilman's paternal grandmother, Mary Foote Beecher Perkins, was born in 1805 and died in 1900.

9. Gilman's father, Frederic Beecher Perkins, was born in 1828 and died in 1899.

10. Dr. Buckland's Scotch Essence of Oats was purported to treat, among other things, insomnia, paralysis, opium habits, drunkenness, neuralgia, sick headaches, sciatica, and nervous dyspepsia.

11. The following note was later appended in Gilman's hand at the bottom of the letter: "He kept me a month. Found nothing the matter apparently. Sent me home with this prescription: 'Live as domestic a life as possible. Have your child with you all the time. Lie down an hour after each meal. Have but two hours intellectual life a day. Never touch pen, brush, or pencil again as long as you live.'

---

I did it, that summer, and came to the edge of insanity. To save others I wrote *The Yellow Wallpaper*. Sent Dr. Mitchell a copy. No answer. But years later I heard that he said he had changed his treatment of neurasthenia after reading T. Y. W.!!" No evidence has been discovered, however, that would corroborate Gilman's claim.

12. Charles Walter Stetson Papers, BANC. Rebecca Steere Stetson was Gilman's mother-in-law.

13. Martha's daughter, Margaret, was born on October 18, 1886.

14. William Gillette (1853–1937), an actor, playwright, and director, made his first stage appearance in 1875, when he was a student at Yale. Gilman first made his acquaintance in 1886, when she cowrote a play with Walter Stetson that she hoped Gillette would produce. He declined.

15. Gilman is quoting from *Life and Sayings of Mrs. Partington and Others of the Family* (1854) by American humorist Benjamin Penhallow Shillaber (1814–90).

16. In an 1861 letter to a friend, English writer Edward FitzGerald (1809–83) wrote of Elizabeth Barrett Browning's death: "Mrs. Browning's Death is rather a relief to me, I must say: no more Aurora Leighs, thank God! . . . She and her Sex had better mind the Kitchen and their Children." Robert Browning (1812–89) read the letter many years later and wrote a scathing poetic response, titled "To Edward FitzGerald" (1889), even though Fitzgerald was already deceased. See Levine.

17. These lines are from a poem about loss that Gilman wrote to Martha on December 13, 1881, after learning of her engagement to Charles Lane. See Knight, "'But O My Heart.'"

18. See Knight, "New Evidence."

19. Gilman's "charming cousin," Marian Parker Whitney (1861–1946), earned her Ph.D. from Yale in 1901 and joined the faculty at Vassar College in 1905 as a professor

of German. This letter and others to "Cousin Marian" Whitney are taken from the Marian Parker Whitney Papers, VCL.

20. American author Delia Lyman Porter (1858–1933) wrote such works as *The Blues Cure and Other Stories* (1892), "Mr. Freeman at Home" (1893), *An Anti-Worry Recipe and Other Stories* (1905), and *A Year of Ideals for Every-Day Living* (1909).

21. In December 1890 the American Art Galleries in New York City opened an exhibition that featured the work of Stetson and two other artists. See Eldredge.

22. brown study: a reverie

23. Gilman enjoyed a thirty-year friendship with American author and editor William Dean Howells (1837–1920).

24. Joanne Karpinski identifies the "apostle" as Edward Bellamy. Howells's "favorable review" helped to propel Bellamy's novel to prominence.

25. Originally serialized in *Harper's Weekly* between March and November 1889, Howells's *A Hazard of New Fortunes* was published in one volume in 1890.

26. The social purity movement, which emerged in the late 1870s, had a moral and social agenda that sought to regulate prostitution, discourage divorce and illegitimacy, control venereal disease, and promote sex education. Some members of the movement also advocated eugenics, including racial extermination and mandatory sterilization of various racial groups.

27. There is evidence to corroborate Gilman's account of Walter's reaction to "The Yellow Wall-Paper." An offprint copy of the story's 1892 appearance in the *New England Magazine,* obtained through private sale, contains the following inscription in Stetson's hand: "This story seems to me a masterpiece! I've read it a half dozen times, first and last, and each time it fairly makes me shudder. Ch. W. S." See Knight, "'Only a Husband's Opinion.'"

28. Augusta Senter had been a friend of Grace's since the late 1870s. Gilman became acquainted with Senter in 1890, and they remained friends until Gilman's death in 1935.

29. The line is from "The Cat and the Mouse in Partnership," by Jacob Ludwig Grimm and Wilhelm Carl Grimm, in *Grimm's Fairy Tales* (1812).

30. Whitney attended private schools in the United States and Europe. She authored and edited several German and French grammars and textbooks. Gilman's "furrin tongues" is a play on "foreign tongues."

31. We thank Cynthia J. Davis for sharing this letter with us. A transcript of this letter was filed with the Providence Supreme Court on October 27, 1892, and was entered as "Exhibit 1" in the divorce proceedings between Gilman and Walter Stetson.

32. We thank Cynthia J. Davis for sharing this letter with us. A transcript of this letter was filed with the Providence Supreme Court on October 27, 1892, and was entered as "Exhibit 2" in the divorce proceedings between Gilman and Walter Stetson.

33. Howells briefly assumed editorship of *Cosmopolitan* in 1891. His utopian romance, *A Traveler from Altruria,* was published in 1894.

34. Benjamin R. Phelon Family Papers, RIHS. "Cousin Mary" was Mary D. (Robbins) Phelon (1862–1907).

35. Just weeks earlier, Gilman had sent Katharine east to live with Walter.

36. In her diary entry of June 18, 1894, Gilman wrote the following upon learning that Walter and Grace had married: "I feel so glad I put on my terracotta robe and a 'coiffure.' Reporter from The Call seeks to interview me on the above theme, in vain" (*Diaries* 588). See also *Living* 167–68 for Gilman's reaction to the reporter.

37. The *Impress* was a short-lived literary weekly featuring articles, poems, editorials, reviews, and short stories. Gilman was elected president of the Pacific Coast Women's Press Association in September 1893.

38. Helen Stuart Campbell (1839–1918), author, reformer, and home economist, was a close friend of Gilman's, sharing her concern about the poverty of women and children. Active in the early home economics movement, Campbell helped to organize the National Household Economics Association, and many of her writings emphasized the devastating effects of low wages on women. Her works include *The Problem of the Poor: A Record of Quiet Work in Unquiet Places* (1882); *Prisoners of Poverty: Women Wage-Workers, Their Trades and Their Lives* (1889); and *Darkness and Daylight, or Lights and Shadows of New York Life* (1893).

39. Philanthropist and educator Sarah Brown Ingersoll Cooper (1835–96) pioneered in the nineteenth-century kindergarten movement. She was the sister of the political activist and orator Robert G. Ingersoll, who led a spirited defense of agnosticism. It was Cooper who came to Gilman's aid in 1895, when she left California for Chicago. On the eve of her sixty-first birthday, Cooper was the victim of a murder/suicide at the hands of her daughter, Harriet, who suffered from acute depression. This letter and others to "Mrs. Cooper" are taken from the Sarah Brown Ingersoll Cooper Papers, KL.

40. Modeled after Hull House, the Chicago Commons was founded in 1894 by American theological sociologist Graham Taylor (1851–1938) and offered a kindergarten, classes, and a civic forum for the discussion of current events.

41. Scottish-born James Kier Hardie (1856–1915), a socialist and labor leader, became one of the first representatives of the Labour Party in the British House of Parliament.

42. Harriet Howe was a women's rights activist from San Francisco and member of the Los Angeles Nationalist Club's program committee. She boarded with Gilman in 1891–92, and the two were close friends. Her posthumous tribute to Gilman, "Charlotte Perkins Gilman: As I Knew Her," appeared in *Equal Rights: Independent Feminist Weekly* in 1936.

43. John Vance Cheney (1848–1922) was an American poet. Eugene Field (1850–95), also an American writer, was best known for his humorous essays and his poetry for children.

44. Lucinda Hinsdale Stone (1814–1900) was an activist on behalf of equal educational rights for women. She taught courses for women at the University of Michigan in Kalamazoo, and in 1873 she organized the first comprehensive women's club in Michigan.

45. The Italian slum area of Chicago where Hull House was located was dubbed Little Sicily or Little Hell.

46. In her memoir, Gilman characterized Lester F. Ward (1841–1913), a prominent

sociologist and the country's leading Reform Darwinist, as "quite the greatest man" she had ever known (*Living* 187). See Allen.

47. Ward's *The Psychic Factors of Civilization* was published in 1893.

48. Susan B. Anthony (1820–1906) crusaded tirelessly for women's rights. Anna Howard Shaw (1847–1919), the first female Methodist minister in the United States, was also a physician, a suffragist, and a popular lecturer.

49. Anthony was affectionately referred to as "Aunt Susan" by her supporters.

50. During the convention, a spirited debate took place over what became known as the "Woman's Bible Resolution," resulting from Elizabeth Cady Stanton's characterization of passages from Scripture—those referring to women—as "The Woman's Bible." Some members of the National American Woman Suffrage Association felt that the reference to "The Woman's Bible" was offensive and compromised their work on behalf of suffrage. A resolution was brought to the floor that asked delegates to affirm "That this Association is non-sectarian, being composed of persons of all shades of religious opinion, and that it has no official connection with the so-called 'Woman's Bible' or any theological publication." Despite an impassioned appeal by Anthony, who spoke against the resolution, saying it would amount to "a vote of censure upon a woman [Stanton] who is without a peer in intellectual and statesmanlike ability; one who has stood for half a century the acknowledged leader of progressive thought and demand in regard to all matters pertaining to the absolute freedom of women," it passed by a vote of 53–41. For the full text see Stanton.

51. Hale Family Papers, SSC. Edward Everett Hale (1822–1909) practiced liberal theology as a Unitarian minister. He was also a social reformer and a prolific writer, best remembered today for his short novel, *The Man Without a Country* (1863).

52. Addenda to the Gilman Papers, AESL. The letter below dated April 23, 1897, is also taken from the Addenda.

53. In May 1894, Frederic Perkins married his first love, Frankie Beecher Johnson, to whom he had been briefly engaged during his youth. As Gilman notes in her autobiography, Johnson had been married to Perkins's uncle James Beecher. With the marriage between Johnson and Perkins, Gilman wrote, "my father became my great-uncle, my great-aunt became my mother, and I became my own first-cousin-once-removed" (*Living* 191).

54. Carrie Chapman Catt (1859–1947) was a suffragist, peace advocate, and founder of the League of Women Voters.

55. Sydney Richmond Burleigh (1853–1931) was an American artist—particularly of watercolors—and an active member of the Providence Art Club.

56. Summer Brook Farm in the Adirondack Mountains of upstate New York was a commune that, Gilman wrote, attracted "interesting people of a progressive tendency" (*Living* 230). Green Acre, in Eliot, Maine, earned its name from American poet John Greenleaf Whittier, who found inspiration in its beautiful setting overlooking the Piscataqua River. With the backing of Sarah Jane Farmer, a partner in the hotel, Green Acre became a center for the study of religions and today focuses on the establishment of world peace, gender equality, racial unity, and spiritual transformation.

57. Nellie Hale was Gilman's cousin Ellen Day Hale (1855–1940), a successful artist and author. This letter and others to members of the Hale family are taken from the Hale Family Papers, SSC.

58. Day Papers, HBSC. This letter to Alice Hooker Day (1847–1928) is an example of epistolary rhyme, a device that Gilman used often during her youth and occasionally as an adult.

59. Day Papers, HBSC. Cousin Katharine was Katharine Seymour Day (1870–1964).

60. Here Gilman paraphrases "Chant-Pagan" (1903), a poem by British author Rudyard Kipling (1865–1936), which begins:

Me that 'ave been what I've been—
Me that 'ave gone where I've gone—
Me that 'ave seen what I've seen—
'Ow can I ever take on
With awful old England again

61. Gilman's uncle Edward Everett Hale died on June 10, 1909, of unspecified causes.

62. Charles Walter Stetson died in Rome at the age of fifty-three.

# Chapter 3

1. Letters in this chapter were taken from two sources. While the majority are from the Grace Ellery Channing Papers, AESL, those dated February 17, 1922, January 5, 1924, October 13, 1925, and February 15, 1928, are from the Grace Ellery Channing Stetson Collection, BRL.

2. In Victorian times there was a common superstition that May was an unlucky month in which to be married. One poem about marriage contains the ominous line, "Marry in the month of May, and you will surely rue the day." The superstition dates as far back as pagan times, when the festival of Beltane was celebrated with orgies.

3. Organized in 1874, the Woman's Christian Temperance Union advocated total abstinence from alcohol. The Young Woman's Christian Temperance Union was an offshoot of its parent organization.

4. English philosopher and economist John Stuart Mill (1806–73) was an advocate of women's suffrage. Among his many books are *On Liberty* (1859) and *The Subjection of Women* (1869).

5. Gilman's poem "One Girl of Many" was published in the February 1, 1884, issue of *Alpha*.

6. The Alpha Doctrine holds that the Bible is God's revelation and is the primary means by which God communicates with humanity.

7. Today the Stone Lea is a bed-and-breakfast. It was originally opened to guests in 1880.

8. Gilman was preparing to move to Pasadena, near Grace's family.

9. William Gillette's 1888 novel, *A Legal Wreck*, was first produced as a play. It was

advertised as an "Intensely Interesting, Highly Amusing, Laughable, and Pathetic Novel."

10. Grace's older sister, Mary Channing Saunders Wood, was the same age as Gilman.

11. Dorothy was Mary Channing Wood's daughter.

12. Emily Parkhurst founded the Pacific Coast Women's Press Association in 1890. Gilman presented a lecture titled "She Who Is to Come."

13. "A Conservative" originally appeared in *Life* in 1892.

14. Gilman reports in her autobiography that she was visited by a reporter from the *San Francisco Examiner* when it became public that Charles had filed for divorce. Despite Gilman's insistence that the divorce was not newsworthy, the *Examiner* published a full-page story. See Gilman, *Living* 142–43.

15. Scrofula is a tuberculous infection of the skin of the neck.

16. Mary Perkins was terminally ill with cancer.

17. Delle was Adeline E. Knapp, a reporter for the *San Francisco Call*, with whom Gilman had a tempestuous two-year relationship. Mrs. Howe was Harriet Howe (see chapter 2, note 42). The identity of Miss Sherman is unclear.

18. Paul Tyner worked on the short-lived *Impress* magazine with Gilman and Helen Campbell in 1893–94 and was, for a time, a romantic interest of Gilman's. Mary A. Hill reports that in a letter to her future husband, Houghton, Gilman remarked about Tyner: "Once I thought I should marry this worthy man. Then I found his weakness of character" (*Charlotte Perkins Gilman* 41).

19. South African author and feminist Olive Schreiner (1855–1920) was one of Gilman's favorite writers.

20. Jane Addams (1860–1935) was a social reformer who, with Ellen Gates Starr (1859–1940), founded Hull House in Chicago. The Hull House settlement, which eventually grew to thirteen buildings and a playground, attracted a number of prominent reformers, including Gilman, Florence Kelley, Julia Lathrop, Dr. Alice Hamilton, and sisters Grace and Edith Abbott, who assisted with the settlement activities.

21. See note 20 above. Starr worked to reform child labor laws and to promote better wages and working conditions for immigrant factory workers.

22. Benjamin Kidd (1858–1916) was an English social philosopher whose most controversial work, *Social Evolution* (1894), launched a strong attack against socialism. The *New York Nation* was founded in 1865 by Edwin L. Godkin, whose biting criticisms of various social issues caused the magazine to be dubbed "the weekly day of judgment."

23. English author Charles Kingsley (1819–97) wrote *The Water-Babies: A Fairy Tale for a Land Baby* (1863) for his son Grenville. Although *Water-Babies* was a children's tale, it broached serious issues such as child labor and poverty. Scottish poet and novelist George MacDonald (1824–1905) published *Phantastes: A Faerie Romance for Men and Women* in 1858. It is the story of a young man's quest across fairy land and won praise for its richly dreamlike quality and beauty of prose.

24. See chapter 2, note 50. Stanton (1815–1902) originally published *The Woman's Bible* in 1895. The impetus behind the two-volume edition, which featured essays and

commentaries on the Bible, was to promote a critical discussion of biblical texts that were used to degrade and demoralize women.

25. Whitman (1819–92) actually wrote in "Song of the Open Road" (1856), "I am larger, better than I thought, / I did not know I held so much goodness."

26. Gilman is referring to the fourth (1867) edition of Whitman's *Leaves of Grass.*

27. Grace had written with the news that her mother, Mary Jane Tarr Channing (1818–97), had died.

28. Gilman enjoyed socializing with Elizabeth Cady Stanton and her daughter, Harriot Stanton Blatch.

29. Grover Cleveland was the twenty-second and twenty-fourth president of the United States. He married Frances Folsom in 1886 when she was twenty-one.

30. Most forcefully advocated in Henry George's *Progress and Poverty* (1879), the single tax was intended to counter economic inequality and redistribute wealth through taxing rent collected from land along with profit earned through land speculation (both considered unearned income), while leaving wages and interest untaxed. Gilman had "real respect for the Single Tax as a useful fiscal reform, though overrated in its hoped-for results" (*Living* 219). However, addressing single-tax advocacy groups led her to label them too "narrowly intense"; she complained that they rendered her "a stamping ground whereon to exploit their own doctrine" (*Living* 219, 220). See also Gilman's diary entries for February 14 and 15, 1896, and March 20, 1897 (*Diaries* 609, 666).

31. Grace's story "The House on the Hill-Top: A Tale of Modern Etruria" appeared in *Scribner's Magazine* in August 1893.

32. Grace's husband, Charles Walter Stetson, to whom Gilman had been married from 1884 to 1894, died in Rome on July 20, 1911, of complications stemming from intestinal surgery. He was fifty-three. Stetson's body was cremated and his ashes scattered in the Mediterranean Sea.

33. Gilman is referring to the "Great Salem Fire" on June 25, 1914, which burned 253 acres and nearly 1,400 homes and businesses, leaving 20,000 people homeless and 10,000 workers unemployed.

34. American children's book author and illustrator Lucy Fitch Perkins (1865–1937) was best known for her popular "Twins" series. American author Zona Gale (1874–1938) was a novelist, journalist, and short-story writer. Her gloomy realistic novels of life in the Midwest, which won critical acclaim in their time, include *Birth* (1918), *Miss Lulu Bett* (1920), and *Papa La Fleur* (1933). Gale's dramatization of *Miss Lulu Bett* opened on Broadway in 1920 and won the Pulitzer Prize for drama in 1921. Margaret Wilson was likely the American writer (1882–1973) whose poetry and short fiction had appeared in periodicals in the early twentieth century. She was awarded the Pulitzer Prize for *The Able McLaughlins* (1923).

35. Katharine married the artist Frank Tolles Chamberlin in 1918.

36. *His Religion and Hers: A Study of the Faith of Our Fathers and the Work of Our Mothers* was published by the Century Company in 1923.

37. Charlotte later had a major falling out with Francis Gilman and his wife, Emily, with whom she and Houghton shared a house in Norwich Town, Connecticut.

38. Alexander Black (1859–1940) was an author, journalist, and longtime friend of Gilman's.

39. International PEN was founded in 1921. Its membership is composed of poets, playwrights, essayists, editors, and novelists; hence the acronym PEN.

40. Rebecca West (1892–1983) was the pseudonym of London-born author, socialist, and feminist activist Cecily Isabel Fairfield. West's articles appeared in the *New Yorker, New Republic, Sunday Telegraph,* and *New York Herald Tribune.* She also wrote several novels and nonfiction works. The Mormon friend was likely Susa Young Gates (see note 42 below).

41. Lilian Whiting (1859–1942) was an American critic, journalist, editor, and the author of numerous books. Praiseworthy letters from Howells, Hale, and Bellamy remain in the Gilman Papers, AESL. Edward Bellamy (1850–98) was best known for his utopian novel, *Looking Backward* (1888).

42. Susa Young Gates (1856–1933), daughter of American Mormon leader Brigham Young, was a writer, publisher, educator, missionary, and a trustee of Brigham Young University. Active in local and national women's organizations, she was the mother of ten sons and three daughters.

43. Katharine's daughter Dorothy was born on October 10, 1918.

44. Eva LeGallienne (1899–1992) was a noted actress, a director, and a founder of the American repertory theater. She became a major star on Broadway at the age of twenty-one.

45. In 1927 Universal Pictures released a silent film of Harriet Beecher Stowe's *Uncle Tom's Cabin,* starring actor James B. Lowe (1879–1963). It was one of the most expensive silent films ever made.

46. Iodex is an anti-infective iodine salve; methyl salicylate is a compound used in pain-relieving ointments.

47. Gilman had an acrimonious relationship with William Randolph Hearst, stemming from articles in the Hearst-owned *San Francisco Examiner* in the early 1890s focusing on Gilman's separation and divorce from Charles Walter Stetson. Gilman was so incensed by the invasion of privacy and the perpetuation of "yellow" journalism that she vowed never to write for a Hearst publication. See Knight, "Gilman, Hearst, and Ethical Journalism."

48. This article is likely "Fashion, Beauty and Brains," published in *Outlook* in August 1929.

49. Gilman enjoyed the fact that Herford had sung her praises; she repeated his remark in a letter to Katharine dated July 25, 1928. Herford (1863–1935) was a noted English writer and illustrator who also worked in New York City as an editor for *Life* magazine in the 1920s. In his July 9, 1929, letter to Gilman, Herford wrote: "I think of you whenever I think of what is most worth contemplating in womankind. And 'In This our World['] is never out of reach of my hand—I was refreshing my memory of Mr. Rockyfeller's [*sic*] Prayer the other day apropos of The New Life which by the way has a real dime embedded in the cover so firmly that I doubt if even the practiced digits of John D. himself could extract it." Gilman originally published the poem "Rockefeller's Prayer" in 1891 in the *Wasp.* It is a scathing indictment of John D. Rockefeller (1839–1937), who purportedly once stated that his wealth so exceeded

his means of spending it that he had to seek divine guidance about how to dispose of it.

50. The nation was transfixed by news of the kidnapping on March 1, 1932, of the twenty-month-old son of aviator Charles Lindbergh and Anne Morrow Lindbergh. Charles Augustus Lindbergh III was found murdered ten weeks later.

51. In this letter, Gilman invoked for herself the Greek name Sophronia, which means "wisdom" and "knowledge."

52. *Death Lights a Candle* (1932) was one of several mysteries written by American author Phoebe Atwood Taylor.

53. Gilman's *Human Work* was published by McClure, Philips, & Co. in 1904 and was reprinted in 2005 by AltaMira Press.

54. For Catharine Beecher see chapter 1, note 30.

55. A close friend of Houghton's, Rev. Alexander Hewes Abbott (1880–1955) would eventually preside at Houghton's funeral service and defend Gilman's then-unorthodox decision to have her husband cremated.

56. George was the name Emily and Francis most often used when referring to Houghton.

57. American actress Katharine Hepburn (1907–2003) starred in *A Bill of Divorcement* opposite John Barrymore in 1932. Gilman was acquainted with Katharine Hepburn's mother, Katharine Houghton Hepburn (1878–1951), a prominent suffragist and birth control advocate who worked with Margaret Sanger to promote the American Birth Control League, the forerunner of today's Planned Parenthood Federation of America. In 1934, Mrs. Hepburn took Gilman to see her daughter perform in a play, most likely *The Lake* (see Gilman's letter to Katharine dated January 27, 1934, in chapter 4).

58. Katharine Hepburn appeared in the film *Little Women*, based on the 1868 novel by American author Louisa May Alcott, in 1933.

59. Houghton died the following evening from a cerebral hemorrhage. He was sixty-six. Gilman's allusion to "Bronx" is a pun on "bronchs," an abbreviation for "bronchial."

60. Gilman had been diagnosed with breast cancer in January 1932.

61. This letter was written on Houghton's stationery, which read "George H. Gilman, Counsellor at Law."

62. Gilman is referring to the transcontinental flight she took to California from the East Coast.

63. In this letter, Gilman playfully invoked for Grace the name Amelia, which in Latin means "industrious" or "beloved." See also note 51 above.

64. Colorado Boulevard is the main street through Pasadena.

65. Grace's sister, Mary Saunders Wood, had died on September 17, 1934, at the age of seventy-three. Clarence was Mary's second husband.

66. Gilman is referring to Augusta Senter, a friend for more than forty years.

67. Harriet Beecher Stowe (1811–96) was Gilman's great-aunt; Stowe's sister Mary was the mother of Gilman's father, Frederic.

68. Gilman is alluding to Ecclesiastes 12:5, which suggests that the weakness of the aged is so debilitating that even the weight of a grasshopper is too much to bear.

69. Gilman had delivered a series of talks to a Sunday school class of women during December; by request, she extended it into the new year.

70. Gilman's second volume of poems, *The Later Poetry of Charlotte Perkins Gilman,* was published posthumously in 1996.

71. Gilman had not yet told her daughter that she had breast cancer and planned to commit suicide.

72. Gilman sometimes referred to her son-in-law by his middle name, Tolles. Anna was Katharine's close friend Anna Trumbull Waller, who owned the property at 239 South Catalina Avenue where Gilman lived in Pasadena at the time of her death. The house has since been relocated and designated a Historic Landmark.

73. Gale (see note 34 above) ultimately declined to write Gilman's biography. However, she did contribute the foreword to Gilman's memoir, *The Living of Charlotte Perkins Gilman,* published posthumously in 1935.

74. Lyman Beecher Stowe (1880–1963) was a grandson of Harriet Beecher Stowe. An accomplished author in his own right, he served as Gilman's literary executor from 1932 until her death in August 1935.

75. Katharine's "third" mother was Pasadena resident and longtime Gilman friend Augusta Senter.

76. Amy Wellington (1873–1948) was an American feminist author and onetime editor of *Current Opinion.*

77. Grace suffered significant hearing loss in her later years.

## Chapter 4

1. Family Correspondence, Gilman Papers, AESL. Katharine was nine when this letter was written. While the majority of letters in this chapter are from the main collection of Gilman Papers, the following letters are taken from an Addenda to the Gilman Papers, which was acquired by the Schlesinger Library separately from the main inventory: August 5, 1913, April 6, 1919[?], and December 16, 1926. The letter dated September 23, 1911, is from Walter Stetson Chamberlin's private collection.

2. London-born John Burns (1858–1943) was an engineer who became outraged by the treatment of Africans when he went to work for the United Africa Company. Convinced that socialism would remove the disparities between races and classes, he founded the Social Democratic Federation, which he later left. A leader of the London Dock Strike, he lobbied on behalf of the dockworkers and raised large sums of money from various trade unions to help the strikers.

3. Charles Fletcher Lummis (1859–1928) was an American author, editor, photographer and activist. For eleven years he was editor of the regional magazine *Land of Sunshine* (renamed by Lummis as *Out West*). Gilman's "Wind and Leaves" appeared in the March 1897 issue of *Land of Sunshine.*

4. Gilman's article "The International Congress of Women" appeared in the September 1899 issue of *Ainslee's.*

5. There is no extant correspondence between Gilman and Katharine from 1900 to 1910. Katharine spent those years in various cities, including New York, where she lived with Gilman and her second husband, George Houghton Gilman; Rome, Italy,

where her father, Charles Walter Stetson, was living; and Philadelphia, where she studied at the Pennsylvania Academy of Fine Arts.

6. Charles Walter Stetson had died in Italy on July 21, 1911.

7. American sociologist Edward Alsworth Ross (1866–1951) earned his Ph.D. from Johns Hopkins University in 1891 and was the nephew of sociologist Lester F. Ward. He taught economics at Stanford University from 1893 to 1900 but was fired for opposing the use of Chinese immigrants in the building of the railroads. From 1906 to 1937 he was a professor of sociology at the University of Wisconsin. His best-known works are *Social Control* (1901) and *Principles of Sociology* (1920). In his autobiography, *Seventy Years of It: An Autobiography of Edward Alsworth Ross* (1936), he refers to Gilman as "the most brilliant woman" he had ever known (57).

8. Gilman's characterization of Katharine's pregnancy as "a heavenly thing" is ironic, given her well-documented struggle with depression during and after her own pregnancy.

9. Gilman is quoting Irish author and satirist Jonathan Swift (1667–1745), who wrote, "The best doctors in the world are Dr. Diet, Dr. Quiet and Dr. Merryman."

10. *Red Hot Dollars,* starring Charles Ray, was released in 1919. *The Copperhead,* starring Lionel Barrymore, debuted in 1920.

11. Gilman's cousin Robert Brown left an estate of half a million dollars when he died. Extant correspondence suggests that he left Charlotte and Katharine a small amount. See also Gilman's letter to Katharine dated August 18, 1921.

12. Katharine was pregnant with her second child, Walter Stetson Chamberlin, who was born on April 2, 1920.

13. Emily Dunning Barringer (1876–1961), who supported medical education for women, women's suffrage, and reforms for the treatment of incarcerated females, earned her M.D. from Cornell University Medical School in 1901. Her autobiography, *Bowery to Bellevue: The Story of New York's First Woman Ambulance Surgeon,* was the basis for the 1952 film *The Girl in White.*

14. Sir Philip Gibbs (1877–1962) was an English journalist and author.

15. Gilman's article "Making Towns Fit to Live In" appeared in the July 1921 *Century.*

16. Hamilton Holt (1872–1951) was an American educator, author, and editor.

17. American poet Leonora Speyer (1872–1956) was awarded the Pulitzer Prize in 1927 for her collection of verse *Fiddler's Farewell.*

18. Pickford was twenty-eight when *Through the Back Door* was released in 1921.

19. Robert Bruère was director of New York's Bureau of Industrial Research and associate editor of the *Survey.* His wife, Martha Bensley Bruère, was the author of such works as *Mildred Carver* (1919) and *Increasing Home Efficiency* (1913).

20. Maxfield Aley was the managing editor of the *Century.*

21. American author Inez Haynes Gillmore Irwin (1873–1970) was a prolific fiction writer and a winner of the O. Henry Award in 1924. Much of her fiction addressed women's issues, including divorce, single motherhood, and the workforce. Chester Lane was Martha Luther Lane's son.

22. Harold Channing (1869–1946) was the younger brother of Grace Ellery Channing Stetson.

23. Gilman is apparently referring to an engraving by the German artist Albrecht Dürer (1471–1528).

24. Gilman's hopes had been raised by discussions with the editor of *Century* magazine about the possible republication of the *Forerunner*, which folded in 1916, and a reprint edition of *Human Work*.

25. British *Pathe* was founded in London in 1902.

26. Wellington (see also chapter 3, note 76) survived this illness, and others that would plague her through the years, but she never wrote the biography to which Gilman refers. Zona Gale was later courted by Gilman to write her biography, but she, too, declined (see chapter 3, note 34). In the final months of Gilman's life, Wellington tried to help Gilman publish a second volume of poems, but that edition was not published until 1996. Gale contributed the foreword to Gilman's memoir, *The Living of Charlotte Perkins Gilman*, published posthumously in 1935.

27. Houghton's aunt Louise had resided in Norwich Town with her brother, William, who was Houghton's father. William Gilman had died in March.

28. Gilman's article "Cross-Examining Santa Claus" appeared in the December 1922 *Century*.

29. A Morris chair, designed by William Morris and introduced in the 1860s, is one early type of reclining chair.

30. The book was *His Religion and Hers: A Study of the Faith of Our Fathers and the Work of Our Mothers*, published by the Century Company in 1923.

31. Eskay's was a popular food supplement in the early 1900s. Nujol is an oral laxative.

32. Maggie was the third wife of Gilman's brother, Thomas. Gilman, whose own finances were precarious, frequently sent money to her brother, who was living with his family in Idaho at the time of this letter.

33. Katharine's husband was building an art studio behind their house.

34. Gilman published articles on "His Religion and Hers" in the March and April issues of *Century*.

35. Gilman arrived in New York from her trip west on Wednesday, March 28, 1923.

36. Veronal is a long-acting barbiturate used medicinally as a sedative.

37. Johan Kristoffer Hansen Bojer (1872–1959) was a popular Norwegian novelist and dramatist who often wrote about the lives of the poor farmers and fishermen of Trondelag.

38. The J. B. Pond Lyceum Bureau was located at Fourth Avenue and Seventeenth Street in New York City.

39. Delia's identity is unclear; it is Gilman's views on sexually transmitted diseases that make this passage noteworthy.

40. Gilman's article "Toward Monogamy" appeared in the June 1924 *Nation*. As a major voice of the literary community, the International PEN seeks to promote intellectual cooperation and understanding among writers; to create a world community of writers that would emphasize the central role of literature in the development of world culture; and to defend the freedom of expression wherever it may be threatened (see also chapter 3, note 39).

41. Gilman is playfully referring to her "bowels."

42. i.e., "poisoned"

43. Roger Williams (see chapter 2, note 4), an English Puritan clergyman and founder of the American colony of Rhode Island, returned to England in 1643 and secured a colonial charter incorporating the settlements of Providence, Newport, Plymouth, and Warwick, which were known as the Providence Plantations in Narragansett Bay.

44. Thomas's third wife, Maggie, had purchased a loom with which to make rugs.

45. Ellis Parker Butler (1869–1937) was an American writer and humorist.

46. Ginn and Company was a Boston-based educational publisher. Gilman apparently means "Okinawa" when she writes "Yokonawa."

47. American politician Robert LaFollette (1855–1925), who served as both governor of and senator from Wisconsin, ran as a Progressive candidate in the 1924 presidential election.

48. Gilman's brother survived prostate surgery.

49. The silent film *The Last Laugh* (1924) tells the story of a self-confident hotel porter who is unfairly demoted to a lavatory attendant.

50. "Charlotte Perkins' Leap" refers to a deep chasm across which Gilman used to leap when, in her early twenties, she visited Ogunquit during summer vacations.

51. Gilman's article "Wash-Tubs and Women's Duty" appeared in the June 1925 *Century.*

52. Gilman's article "The Noble Male" appeared in the July 1925 *Forum.*

53. Cecil B. DeMille's *The Ten Commandments* was originally released in 1923. DeMille released a remake of the film in 1956.

54. Jame Cruze's 1925 silent film epic, *The Pony Express,* is the story of a passionate rivalry between two men. L. Frank Baum's *The Wizard of Oz,* one of the most successful American stage extravaganzas of the early twentieth century, was first produced at New York's Majestic Theatre.

55. Wellington's *Women Have Told: Studies in the Feminist Tradition,* which included a chapter on Gilman, was eventually published by Little, Brown in 1930.

56. The poem "Twigs" was published in *Life* magazine in February 1924.

57. As an experiment in utopian living inspired by the Arts and Crafts movement, the Byrdcliffe Arts Colony was founded in 1902 on fifteen hundred acres of south-facing mountainside above Woodstock, New York, in the Catskill Mountains. The Arts and Crafts movement stressed reform of social, environmental, and economic conditions to combat the slums and degradation fostered in the nation's industrial regions, and Byrdcliffe offered a utopian enclave for artists and writers.

58. Gilman is most likely referring to her manuscript of "Social Ethics." See note 61 below.

59. Emma Lucy Gates Bowen (1880–1951) was a gifted pianist and opera singer who performed for a while with the Chicago Opera Company.

60. Gilman's article "Woman's Achievements since the Franchise" appeared in the October 1927 *Current History.*

61. Gilman left a revision of the ethics book, retitled "A Study in Ethics," in manu-

script at the time of her death. The book was originally serialized in 1914 in the *Forerunner* under the title *Social Ethics*.

62. Aunt Carrie was Charles Walter Stetson's sister Caroline Stetson Baxter Lindsey. She died in December 1927.

63. Charlotte's great-aunt Harriet Beecher Stowe (1811–96) published *Uncle Tom's Cabin* in 1851. Thereafter it was adapted for the stage, and theater performances reached a peak in the 1890s. Stowe received no profits from the dramatization of her work.

64. Jane was Charles Walter Stetson's sister. Another sister, Carrie, had passed away a month earlier, in December 1927.

65. Katharine turned forty-three on March 23; Gilman's grandson turned eight on April 2. It is unclear who had the third birthday that Gilman missed.

66. Kallah was the name of a teachers' convention that was held in Babylonian academies.

67. Thomas Dudley (1576–1653), a British colonial governor of Massachusetts Bay Colony, was born in Northampton, England. A convert to Puritanism, he became an outspoken advocate of its strictest tenets.

68. Republican Herbert Hoover (1874–1964), thirty-first president of the United States, easily defeated Democrat Al Smith in the 1928 election.

69. Gilman is likely referring to American author Thomas Beer (1889–1940).

70. Gilman was writing the detective novel *Unpunished*. Her efforts to publish the book were unsuccessful, and it remained unpublished until 1997.

71. Novelist, playwright, and journalist Edgar Wallace (1875–1932), one of Britain's most prolific authors, produced popular detective and suspense stories. In his time he was considered "the king" of the modern thriller, selling five million books a year.

72. The National Society of Magna Charta Dames and Barons was instituted in 1909 as a nonprofit lineage society. Lifetime membership is by invitation only and is based upon lineal blood descent from one or more of the twenty-five Sureties for the Magna Charta or from a Baron, Prelate, Knight, or other influential person present on the meadow of Runnemede, England, in June 1215 on behalf of the Charter.

73. Patricia Wentworth (1878–1961) was the pseudonym of mystery writer Dora Amy Dillon Turnbull, who wrote more than seventy mystery novels. *The Dower House Mystery* was published in 1925.

74. We have been unable to identify Mr. Tapley.

75. The Gamut Club was originally a men's club composed of musicians and artists.

76. The Hatfield Gallery, located in the Ambassador Hotel in Los Angeles until its demolition in 2006, was founded by American artist Dazell Harvey Hatfield (1893–1963).

77. Charlotte sent Katharine a check for $500 on January 12, 1930.

78. The quotation is from Lewis Carroll's "The Hunting of the Snark" (1876).

79. "To Isadora Duncan" was the name of a poem Gilman wrote in tribute to the American dancer (1878–1927). Gilman attended a performance by Duncan in 1915 and published a highly favorable review of it in the April 1915 *Forerunner*.

80. Sherry's Restaurant opened its doors in 1898 and quickly became one of New York City's most famous eateries.

81. Katharine appended the following note to the back of the envelope in which this letter was sent: "Mama must be wrong about my father—He was b. 1858—March. 25—I was b. Mar. 23 1885 so two days after my birth I think he would have been 26 so was 25 when I was b. My mother b. 3 July 1860 was 24 when I was b. and would have been 25 July 3 1885." Katharine's math is also faulty, however. Her father would have been twenty-six when she was born; he turned twenty-seven two days later.

82. Caroline M. Seymour Severance (1820–1914), known to her intimates as Madam Severance, was active in abolitionist causes in the years before the Civil War. After the war she joined Elizabeth Cady Stanton and Susan B. Anthony in support of the growing women's suffrage movement. She founded the Los Angeles Chapter of the Friday Morning Club in 1875 and served as its first president.

83. Isabella Beecher Hooker (1822–1907), the daughter of Lyman Beecher, married John Hooker in 1841. In 1868 she helped organize the New England Women's Suffrage Association, and in 1871 she organized a convention in Washington, DC, to lobby for a constitutional amendment that would give women the vote. She also joined forces with Victoria Woodhull denouncing Henry Ward Beecher, her half brother, for allegedly engaging in an adulterous affair with a married woman, Elizabeth Tilton.

84. Gilman actually attended a dinner in honor of H. G. Wells (1866–1946), not H. B. Wells. H. G. Wells was an English novelist, journalist, sociologist, and historian who was most famous for his works of science fiction. His best-known books include *The Time Machine* (1895), *The Invisible Man* (1897), and *The War of The Worlds* (1898).

85. Gilman describes her meeting with Dreiser in *Living* 304.

86. South African author Olive Schreiner (1855–1920) published *Women and Labor* in 1911. Her short-story collection *Dreams* was published in 1891.

87. In a letter to Katharine Seymour Day dated June 1, 1932, responding to her request that Gilman play the part of Harriet Beecher Stowe in an upcoming pageant to raise money for the Mark Twain Memorial, Gilman writes that she was "hotly interested" in playing Stowe and that she had "a muslin dress of about that period" that she could wear, along with a "full petticoat." She also suggested that Day secure "some little grey curls to pin behind [her] ears." Day Papers, HBSC.

88. In her undated thank-you note to Gilman, pageant director Inez Temple wrote: "I cannot get over the feeling that I have presented a pageant in which Mrs. Stowe has taken a part. She has really been here in our midst and it seems almost as though we are withholding from you your due, so completely have you yielded [your] place to her. . . . I could hardly believe it, after I had suggested that you take the part, that you had consented to do it. Now, it is a milestone in my pageant efforts to have made the opportunity for Hartford to see you in the role. If there had been nothing else in the pageant, it would have been a memorable event." General Correspondence, Gilman Papers, AESL.

89. Gilman included a sketch of a knotted tassel to illustrate her theory of "breeding out."

90. Alice Locke Park (1861–1961) was one of the leaders of the women's suffrage

campaign in California and a correspondent for the *Woman's Journal*. She served as Gilman's California agent, without fee or commission.

91. John Haynes Holmes (1879–1964) was a prominent Unitarian minister, pacifist, and social activist, and head of New York's Community Church, which boasted a multicultural congregation. By 1930 the church had attracted more than eighteen hundred members representing thirty-four nationalities.

92. Gertrude Atherton (1857–1948) was an American novelist and short-story writer and a friend of Gilman's.

93. Gilman met American poet Edwin Markham (1852–1940) in the early 1890s, before he gained national recognition with "The Man with the Hoe" in 1899. Markham's poem was inspired by the painting *L'homme à la houe* by French artist Jean-François Millet (1814–75).

94. The play Gilman saw with Mrs. Hepburn was most likely *The Lake*, in which Katharine Hepburn was starring. It was a critical and commercial failure.

95. Gilman was contemplating a trip to California and was attempting to line up lectures.

96. The poem "Casabianca," by English author Felicia Hemans (1793–1835), tells the story of a young boy, son of an admiral, who, because he is unable to gain the permission of his unconscious father, perishes in an explosion on a ship by his refusal to abandon his post during a battle.

97. Katharine Hepburn married Ludlow Ogden Smith, whom she met at Bryn Mawr College, in 1928. They divorced in 1934. Hepburn starred in the film *Spitfire* the same year.

98. Gilman's cousin Nellie Hale painted the portrait of Gilman in 1877. It is now part of the collection at the Smithsonian National Portrait Gallery in Washington, DC (see also chapter 2, note 57).

99. In a June 15, 1934, letter to Katharine, Gilman had asked about the possibility of taking a room in a boardinghouse run by a Miss Mills.

## Chapter 5

1. Barrow Family Papers, HL. Samuel June Barrows (1845–1909), a graduate of Harvard Divinity School, was a pastor in Dorchester, Massachusetts, from 1876 to 1881; an editor for sixteen years of the *Christian Register;* a Unitarian; and a Republican congressman from 1896 to 1898.

2. Percy Bysshe Shelley (1792–1822) was a major figure among the British romantic poets. Fragments were a common product of the romantic imagination. Ironically, Shelley's last fragment, written before his drowning death, was titled "The Triumph of Life."

3. Brander Matthews Papers, COL. See Oliver and Scharnhorst. James Brander Matthews (1852–1929) was an American author of novels, short stories, plays, poems, biographies, and essays as well as a professor of dramatic literature at Columbia College (now Columbia University). He was a prominent figure in the theatrical and literary circles of New York City, Paris, and London.

4. Oliver and Scharnhorst note that in his "Prattle" column of October 16, 1892,

Bierce "had ridiculed the poet Ina Coolbrith, claiming that she had been fed full of local adulation and had, as a result, formed much too high an opinion of her literary abilities. Published three days before Gilman wrote Matthews, this essay was no doubt the 'most recent specimen' of Bierce's 'delicate touch' that she enclosed with her letter" (44 n. 7). Matthews responded that "any one as far removed from the seat of war" as he was "can express any opinion or make any suggestion likely to be of service to those better acquainted with the circumstances" (41).

5. Jeanne C. Smith Carr Papers, HUNT. Carr was one of several "mothers" whom Gilman informally adopted after the death from cancer of her biological mother, Mary Westcott Perkins, in March 1893. Carr, a botanist, was married to Ezra Slocum Carr, a physician and professor of natural sciences and chemistry. The Carrs settled in Pasadena and named their home, which was renowned for its beautiful gardens, "Carmelita." Jeanne Carr is credited with having greatly influenced the career of Scottish-born naturalist and conservationist John Muir (1838–1914). The two enjoyed a long friendship and a lively epistolary relationship, which became the subject of Muir's volume *Letters to a Friend: Written to Mrs. Ezra S. Carr, 1866–1879*, published by Houghton Mifflin in 1915.

6. Gilman's "specimen" is the first printing of her volume of poems *In This Our World* (1893).

7. William Lloyd Garrison (1838–1909), son of the abolitionist William Lloyd Garrison (1805–79), was a prominent advocate of women's suffrage and the single tax. Gilman mentions meeting him in *Living* 240. All letters to Garrison are taken from the Garrison Family Papers, SSC.

8. On the single tax see chapter 3, note 30.

9. William Dean Howells Papers, HL. Mrs. Howells was Elinor G. Mead Howells (1837–1910), the wife of American author William Dean Howells.

10. The book was published as *Women and Economics* in 1898.

11. On Ross see chapter 4, note 7. All letters to Ross are taken from the Edward Alsworth Ross Papers, WHS.

12. The *New York Nation* declared *Women and Economics* "the most significant utterance on the subject [of sexual oppression] since Mill's 'The Subjection of Women'" (qtd. in Scharnhorst, *Gilman*). For additional reviews see Scharnhorst, *Gilman* 54–56.

13. American economist Thorstein B. Veblen (1857–1929) is best known for *The Theory of the Leisure Class* (1899). He coined the term "conspicuous consumption" to refer to purchases designed to flaunt one's income or accomplishments.

14. Ross was fired from Stanford University in 1900 (see also chapter 4, note 7).

15. Gilman had read Veblen's *The Theory of the Leisure Class* earlier in the year.

16. British-born writer Vernon Lee (1856–1935), the pseudonym of Violet Paget, split her time between England and Italy. An ardent advocate of women's rights and social reform, Lee contributed the introduction to the Italian edition of *Women and Economics*. The Gilman Papers, AESL, also contain two reviews by Lee in Italian of *La donna e l'economia sociale* (*Women and Economics*).

17. Gilman's account of the request for a bibliography in *Women and Economics* differs in her autobiography. Rather than identifying Vernon Lee as the source of the

request, she writes that "Dr. E. A. Ross . . . asked why I had not put in a bibliography. I told him I had meant to, but when it came to making a list of books I had read bearing on the subject, there were only two! One was Geddes's and Thompson's [*sic*] *Evolution of Sex,* the other only an article, Lester F. Ward's, in that 1888 *Forum*" (*Living* 259). W. Scott published Sir Patrick Geddes and Sir J. Arthur Thomson's *The Evolution of Sex* in London in 1889. Geddes (1854–1932), a Scottish biologist and sociologist, and Thomson (1861–1933), a Scottish zoologist and naturalist, proposed a gender theory based the characteristics of sperm and egg; i.e., the female egg was associated with passivity and submissiveness, while the mobile male sperm suggested progressive and creative tendencies.

18. Emma B. Sweet Papers, Department of Rare Books and Special Collections, URL. Emma Biddlecom Sweet (1862–1951) was a lifelong suffragist and advocate for other progressive causes. A distant cousin of Susan B. Anthony, she worked as Anthony's secretary from the mid-1890s until 1906.

19. The speaking engagement would most likely have been for Rochester's Political Equality Club, for which Sweet held various offices during this period. Gilman and Sweet agreed on a lecture date of November 1. In her October 24, 1903, letter to Sweet confirming the date of the engagement, Gilman mentioned the success of *Women and Economics:* "Women & Economics has just reached me in Russian. That book is now being eagerly read in six great nations—(no, one is a little one— Holland!)"

20. Severance Collection, HUNT. On Severance see chapter 4, note 82.

21. Fenyes Papers, PM. Watercolorist Eva Fenyes (1849–1930) was a patron of early California art and held popular art salon gatherings for artists, writers, and members of the cultural elite at the Fenyes mansion in Pasadena.

22. In 1888 Gilman rented a small cottage at Orange Grove Avenue and Arroyo Drive in Pasadena for ten dollars a month. By the early twentieth century the vicinity of Orange Grove Avenue was known as "Millionaires' Row" because of the opulent homes erected there, including the Fenyes mansion, which was built in 1905.

23. Dr. Elgin R. L. Gould (1860–1915) was a reformer who sought to build safer tenement housing for the poor. All letters to Gould are taken from the Elgin Ralston Lovell Gould Papers, SL.

24. "Kitchen Dirt and Civic Health" was published in the *Independent* in December 1904.

25. General Correspondence, Gilman Papers, AESL.

26. Mabel Hay Barrows Mussey (1873–1931) was a dramatic director and dancer and the daughter of Unitarian minister and congressman Samuel June Barrows (1845– 1909) and Isabel Chapin Barrows (1845–1913), an ophthalmologist and reformer. The Gilmans had vacationed with the Musseys in previous years. All letters to Mussey are taken from the Barrow Family Papers, HL.

27. Gilman's "New Baby" was her self-published magazine, the *Forerunner,* which was published between 1909 and 1916.

28. General Correspondence, Gilman Papers, AESL. British citizen Margaret Damer Dawson (1875–1920) was founder of the Women's Police Service and the editor of the *Woman Worker* in London.

29. General Correspondence, Gilman Papers, AESL. Miss Williams was Anna L. B. Williams of 246 North Mentor Avenue in Pasadena.

30. Gilman had met English journalist William Haslam Mills (1874–1930), chief reporter for the *Manchester Guardian*, and his wife, Evelyn Travers Mills, during one of her trips to England. Evelyn Mills died in 1914. All letters to Mills are taken from the Women's Rights Collection, SSC.

31. England entered World War I in September 1914.

32. In the February 1915 *Forerunner*, Gilman argued that because "Commercial growth has given us some of the blackest, ugliest, sickest and wickedest cities, for which Americans should wear the sackcloth and ashes of shame" (53), score cards should be developed to rate each town on such criteria as health, beauty, public spirit, educational facilities, etc.

33. Maida Herman Solomon Papers, AESL. Solomon (1891–1988) was a 1912 graduate of Smith College and a pioneer in the field of psychiatric social work.

34. General Correspondence, Gilman Papers, AESL. Eleanor Daggett Karsten (1872–1946) was one of the leaders of the International Committee of Women for Permanent Peace, founded in 1915.

35. The Woman's Peace Party was founded in Washington, DC, in January 1915 by Jane Addams and Carrie Chapman Catt. In April 1915, representatives from the Woman's Peace Party participated in the International Congress of Women held at The Hague in The Netherlands, during which the ICWPP was founded.

36. General Correspondence, Gilman Papers, AESL. Rose Pastor Stokes (1879–1933) was born in Russia. Her family immigrated to England in 1885 and later to Cleveland, Ohio. Stokes joined the Socialist Party and moved to New York, where she became active in politics and a vocal opponent of U.S. involvement in World War I. In 1917 Stokes was arrested and charged under the Espionage Act for criticizing the U.S. government. Gilman circulated a petition on behalf of Stokes, urging that her case be reconsidered. Her case was appealed, and eventually the government dropped its case against her.

37. General Correspondence, Gilman Papers, AESL. The treasurer of Small, Maynard responded to Gilman's letter on January 25, 1919, asking her to make an offer for the stock and plates on the four books the company had published (*The Yellow Wall-Paper, In This Our World, Women and Economics,* and *Concerning Children*). On February 28, 1919, Gilman wrote to ask if they would accept $500 for the stock, plates, and copyrights: "You see you have had the books about twenty years now, and I hope have made enough to pay for the investment. I do not wish to be mean about this; if it is not enough please say so." Small, Maynard countered with an offer of $600, to which Gilman agreed.

38. General Correspondence, Gilman Papers, AESL. Arthur T. Vance, editor at the *Pictorial Review*, requested revisions to Gilman's article "What Is Going to Happen to Marriage." See also Gilman's letter in this chapter to Vance dated May 9, 1919.

39. William Pepperell Montague (1873–1953) was a professor of philosophy at Columbia University.

40. Anne Henrietta Martin Papers, BANC. Martin (1875–1951) was an American educator, author, and suffragist who was active in the National Woman Suffrage Association, the National Woman's Party, and the Women's International League for Peace and Freedom. She was chair of the Department of History at the University of Nevada for several years.

41. See note 38 above.

42. Gilman approved of birth control not only because it offered women reproductive and economic freedom but also because it could be used to support a eugenic agenda. However, she also argued that the purpose of sex was procreation, not pleasure. Her reference here to "the fallacy in 'Birth Control'" may reflect either her worry that freer access to birth control led to licentious behavior or her anxiety that native-born white women's use of birth control to limit family size masked a threat from the high birthrate among immigrants and others whom she would have seen as "unfit" to reproduce.

43. General Correspondence, Gilman Papers, AESL. Mrs. Lula T. Roantree was an affluent resident of Syracuse, New York.

44. General Correspondence, Gilman Papers, AESL. Chester Lane, the son of Gilman's lifelong friend Martha Luther Lane, was born on August 6, 1883.

45. James H. Barry Papers, BANC. Born in New York City, Barry (1856–1927) was raised in San Francisco. He founded the weekly journal *The Star* in 1884 as a vehicle to fight against government corruption, and he was a particular advocate of labor reform. Appointed by President Woodrow Wilson as Naval Officer of Customs at San Francisco, he served from 1913 until 1921. He was a friend of Gilman's father, Frederic Beecher Perkins.

46. In 1894, after enduring years of taunts, barbs, and insults from author Ambrose Bierce about both her work and her personal life, Gilman published "A Reproach to San Francisco," an essay taking him to task, in *The Star* (unfortunately, no copy of this essay is extant and no further bibliographic information is available). Thus, during a period in which she was vilified in the press for her divorce, her "unnatural motherhood," and her relationship with Adeline Knapp, Barry gave her a venue to strike back. In his letter of January 7, 1921, thanking Gilman for this poem, Barry wrote that the verse "recalls the past—brings back the days when 'The Star' first began to twinkle; when your father and I—he was so good yet so misunderstood—were associated together in fighting for the right as we saw the right; when you, then little more than a girl, but a brave girl, were doing the same thing in a somewhat different way." James H. Barry Papers, BANC.

47. General Correspondence, Gilman Papers, AESL. Hamilton Holt (1872–1951) graduated from Yale University in 1894 and was a journalist and editor of *Independent* magazine and *Harper's Weekly*.

48. The month is illegible; however, Charlotte and Houghton Gilman moved into the Norwich Town house, which they shared with Francis and Emily Gilman, in September 1922.

49. American journalist and human rights activist Alice Stone Blackwell (1857–1950) was the daughter of Henry Brown Blackwell and Lucy Stone. A graduate of

Boston University, she served as an editor of *Woman's Journal* from 1881 to 1917. All letters to Blackwell are taken from the National American Woman Suffrage Association Records, LOC.

50. In his October 3, 1925, reply, Ross informed Gilman that her idea had already been proposed by American geographer and eugenicist Ellsworth Huntington in his 1915 book, *Civilization and Climate.*

51. Ross later returned Gilman's enclosure in a letter to Gilman dated October 3, 1925, because, according to Ross, "you may want to use it again." The outline, however, has not been located in either the Gilman Papers at the Schlesinger Library or the Ross Papers at the Wisconsin Historical Society. Ross Papers, WHS.

52. Gilman's nativist leanings have been well documented. See, e.g., Lanser, and Knight's "Charlotte Perkins Gilman and the Shadow of Racism." In his October 3, 1925, reply to Gilman's letter, Ross aligned himself with Gilman's position on the Irish and the Turks: "I agree with you about Ireland. The Irish are often brilliant but they will accomplish little until they break away from priestly domination. You are altogether right about the Turks. I have yet to hear of a Turk interested in ideas of evincing scholarly proclivities. They are a bonehead stock and that is why they have never been able to supply decent government to their subject peoples." Ross Papers, WHS.

53. Ross wrote hundreds of articles and nearly thirty books. The precise source of his "comment" on Ward's gynocentric theory is unclear.

54. Anna Strunsky Collection, HUNT. American socialist William English Walling (1877–1936) was born into a wealthy family of former slaveholders in Kentucky. Educated at the University of Chicago and Harvard Law School, he joined the Hull House settlement before moving to New York. In 1905 he married Anna Strunsky, a Russian Jew, who had been imprisoned as a revolutionary. Walling helped to found the National Women's Trade Union League in 1903. In August 1908, Walling and his wife witnessed the riots in Springfield, Illinois, where a white mob attacked local African Americans. The following year he helped to found the National Association for the Advancement of Colored People.

55. Ross served as president of the American Sociological Society in 1914 and 1915.

56. Ross's article "The United States of India" appeared in the December 1925 *Century.* In a November 26, 1927, letter to Ross, Gilman asked whether the book *Mother India,* by American journalist Katherine Mayo, was reliable. Ross's December 1, 1927, response was unequivocal: "It is a book that presents the truth. . . . I rejoice that the damnable system of female subordination—the worst which now exists anywhere—has been shown up." Ross Papers, WHS.

57. Gilman was unsuccessful in securing a publisher for *Social Ethics.* The volume, edited by Michael R. Hill and Mary Jo Deegan, was published posthumously in 2004.

58. On September 15, 1928, Ross agreed to read the manuscript. He also informed Gilman that he would be away for eight months beginning in November, when he and his wife would be "going around the world with the Floating University." On

October 15 he wrote Gilman that his impending trip had left him with "a thousand things to see to" and that he had only read about 25 percent of the book. While he enjoyed her writing style, which he characterized as "terse, fluent, and pollucid [*sic*]," he opined that she was sometimes "too lavish in ideas" and that the "ideas of secondary importance . . . compete with and detract from your dominant idea." He also counseled Gilman to rely more on secondary sources to advance her theory and suggested that the book would not attract an academic audience since it failed to "follow the accepted line of ethical speculation" by such figures as Plato, Shaftesbury, Hume, Kant, and Spencer. Ross Papers, WHS.

59. Bernice Baumgarten (1902–78) was employed as a literary agent by the New York firm of Brandt and Brandt. All letters to Lyman Beecher Stowe are taken from the Family Correspondence, Gilman Papers, AESL.

60. J. Parker Whitney was editor of *Outlook*. General Correspondence, Gilman Papers, AESL.

61. In a letter dated June 15, 1932, Ross informed Gilman that his wife of forty years, Rosamond Simons Ross, had passed away: "You will be pained to learn that Mrs. Ross died unexpectedly while I was in the South Seas. She passed away April 6th of heart failure owing to a clot. Her boys and their wives were with her and she experienced no pain." Ross also informed Gilman that he had been forced to cut short his trip to the South Seas because of his own health crisis: "I am only just now back from four months absence in . . . Tahiti, enforced by my heart going bad and hence inability to go on." Ross Papers, WHS.

62. Lyman Beecher Stowe and his wife, Hilda, visited Gilman in early December 1932 to discuss her proposal that Lyman assume the position of literary executor. When Gilman was diagnosed with breast cancer in January 1932, the matter of publication became more urgent.

63. In a letter dated August 29, 1933, Ross informed Gilman that he had "been unable to find any remunerative speaking engagement" on her behalf. Ross Papers, WHS.

64. Lyman Beecher Stowe, who was serving as Gilman's literary executor, wrote Gilman on April 21, 1934, to report that John C. Farrar of Farrar and Rinehart had rejected Gilman's manuscript on ethics. Farrar suggested that Stowe submit the manuscript to Norton, but Norton, too, declined to publish the manuscript. Family Correspondence, Gilman Papers, AESL.

# Chapter 6

1. For Gilman's views on the single tax see chapter 3, note 30.

2. See chapter 2, note 23. All letters to Howells are taken from the William Dean Howells Papers, HL.

3. Edwin Markham Archives, HOR. Gilman would later grow disenchanted with Markham.

4. After the publication of Edward Bellamy's utopian romance, *Looking Backward, 2000–1887* (1888), New Nation clubs were formed throughout the United States

and resulted in the founding of the *Nationalist* monthly, which was in publication from 1888 to 1891. Bellamy later founded the *New Nation,* a journal that was in print from 1891 to 1894.

5. Letters to Lummis in this chapter were taken from two sources at BRL. Those dated September 4, 1895, October 14, 1895, May 20, 1897, February 24, 1898, and April 1, 1898, are from the Marion Parks Collection. Those dated September 14, 1896, April 15, 1898, June 26, 1902, August 21, 1902, and November 22, 1910, are from the Charles Fletcher Lummis Manuscript Collection.

6. For Hardie see chapter 2, note 41.

7. Lester F. Ward (1841–1913) is best remembered today for his pioneering work in sociology and his support of women's rights. A Civil War veteran, Ward was employed by the United States Treasury from 1865 to 1881. In 1882 he went to work for the U.S. Geological Survey, and in 1905 he accepted a faculty appointment at Brown University, where he remained until his death. His published works include *Dynamic Sociology* (1883), *Outlines of Sociology* (1898), *Pure Sociology* (1903), and *Applied Sociology* (1906). All letters to Ward are taken from the Lester Frank Ward Collection, JHL.

8. For an illuminating discussion of the Gilman-Ward friendship and Ward's influence on Gilman, see Allen.

9. Anna Garlin Spencer (1851–1931) was an American educator, feminist, Unitarian minister, and a leader in the women's movement. Her books include *Woman's Share in Social Culture* (1913) and *The Family and Its Members* (1922).

10. For information on Helen Stuart Campbell see chapter 2, note 38.

11. Karl Liebknecht (1871–1919) was a German socialist and a co-founder of the Spartacist League and the Communist Party of Germany. He was abducted and executed by members of the right-wing militia, the Freikorps, in 1919. Justin McCarthy (1830–1912) was an Irish-born author, journalist, and politician. George Meredith (1828–1909) was an English novelist and poet who is credited with launching the literary career of Thomas Hardy.

12. English author and social scientist Alfred Russel Wallace (1823–1913) originated independently the theory of natural selection.

13. Gilman is referring to the poem titled "Their Grass!" which appeared in the July 1897 *Land of Sunshine.*

14. On the back of the letter, Howells inscribed the following: "Mrs. Stetson's 'co-mother' is married to Mrs. Stetson's divorced husband. Mrs. Stetson attended the wedding and gave her young daughter to her 'co-mother' as a wedding present. Mrs. S's father's mother was Lyman Beecher's daughter I think. Mrs. S. is a cousin of Mr. Edward Everett Hale's." William Dean Howells Papers, HL. There is no truth to Howells's contention that Gilman attended the wedding or gave her daughter to the couple as a "wedding present"; Gilman was living on the West Coast at the time of the wedding in 1894, and Stetson and Channing married in the East.

15. Italian novelist Giovanni Verga (1840–1922) depicted the Sicilian middle class with sympathy and documented the poverty and struggles of Italian peasants. Gilman is probably referring Howells to Grace's story "The House on the Hill-Top," which appeared in *Stories of Italy,* published by Scribner in 1893.

16. Gilman's poem "Our Tomorrow" appeared not in June but in the May 1898 issue of *Land of Sunshine*.

17. In 1897, in an attempt to recruit contributors to his fledgling magazine *Land of Sunshine*, Lummis organized a syndicate of western writers with strong allegiance to the region who agreed to send him their work on western themes in exchange for stock in the venture in lieu of cash payments. After this gentle prodding, he invited Gilman to join this group of supporters, none of whom expected actually to receive any funds as a result.

18. Gilman is referring to "Photographing a Wounded African Buffalo," by Arthur C. Humbert. The piece was accompanied by graphic descriptions of the hunt and by several grisly photographs of the dying buffalo.

19. Scottish-born photographer William Notman (1826–91) had studios in Boston, Montreal, and Toronto. His eldest son took over the business after his father's death.

20. Gilman is responding to Ward's question about how she likes marriage the second time around.

21. Orison Swett Marden (1850–1924) founded *Success Magazine* in 1897. The magazine encountered financial difficulties and was suspended in 1912. In 1918, however, Marden launched a new *Success*, which was still growing in circulation at the time of his death.

22. Ward's *Pure Sociology*, a treatise on the origin and spontaneous development of society, was published by Macmillan in 1903.

23. Ward's *Dynamic Sociology*, which argued that social progress depended on a planned society overseen by a benevolent government that would provide universal education and an end to poverty, was originally published by Appleton in 1883.

24. Rebecca Spring Papers, SUL. Rebecca Buffum Spring (1811–1911) was the daughter of Arnold Buffum, the first president of the New England Anti-Slavery Society. Spring and her husband, Marcus, were Quaker activists who founded the Eagleswood School in New Jersey in 1853. A utopian community for intellectuals, artists, and abolitionists, the school was visited by such figures as Louisa May Alcott, Henry David Thoreau, Ralph Waldo Emerson, and Horace Greeley. Longtime friends of Lydia Maria Child, Margaret Fuller, and Elizabeth Palmer Peabody, the Springs became increasingly involved in liberal political and social causes, including lobbying unsuccessfully for the acquittal of abolitionist John Brown, who was executed in 1860. In her autobiography, Gilman describes visiting the ninety-nine-year-old Spring in California: Spring was "shriveled and shrunken . . . her eyes mere buttonholes." When Gilman asked Spring what she did with her time, Spring responded, "'I read nov-els [*sic*]. When I was young they would not let me read them, and now I read them all the time'" (*Living* 111).

25. Jeanie Peet was Rebecca Spring's daughter, who lived in southern California. After her husband's death in the late 1890s, Spring moved to California from the Northeast.

26. H. G. Wells Correspondence, UIL. Wells published *The Future of America* in 1906. See chapter 4, note 84, for more on Wells.

27. Ward cited Gilman in "The Past and Future of the Sexes," which appeared in the March 1906 *Independent*.

28. For information on Holt see chapter 5, note 47.

29. American sociologist and educator Franklin Henry Giddings (1855–1931) had expressed criticism of Ward's theories.

30. Papers of Horace and Anne Montgomerie Traubel, LOC. Horace Traubel (1858–1919) was Walt Whitman's biographer and author of the nine-volume *Walt Whitman in Camden*. He also founded the *Conservator*, a journal dedicated to the preservation of Whitman's legacy, which was in print from 1890 to 1919.

31. "Mother" was Gilman's longtime friend, writer and reformer Helen Stuart Campbell (see chapter 2, note 38). In a letter to Traubel dated November 17, 1907, Gilman again expressed her concern about Mrs. Campbell: "It makes my heart ache that I can't take her right here and keep her—but our home is full—(and our purse empty!) at present. Hard sledding for a good many people just now."

32. Gilman's poem "The Little White Animals" appeared in the *Conservator* in 1907 and in the *Forerunner* in 1910. The date of her letter, however, invites confusion, since she alludes to a card dated December 4, yet her poem appeared in the October issue of Traubel's journal. Our best guess is that the *Conservator* was behind schedule and that the date of her letter is correct.

33. Mrs. Yorke was Annie Russell (1864–1936), a British-born American actress who won acclaim for her 1881 performance in *Esmerelda* in New York City. She married English actor Oswald Yorke in 1904. All letters to Russell are taken from the Annie Russell Papers, NYPL.

34. In a letter dated September 27, 1909, Gilman thanked Russell for the "safe return of 'Interrupted'" and remarked that because the *Forerunner* was demanding so much of her time, "plays have temporarily ceased to exist!"

35. Witter Bynner (1881–1968) was an influential early-twentieth-century American poet. A Harvard graduate, Bynner counted among his literary acquaintances Mark Twain, Henry James, D. H. Lawrence, and Edna St. Vincent Millay. All letters to Bynner are taken from the Witter Bynner Papers, HL.

36. Sinclair Collection, LL. Upton Sinclair (1878–1968) was an American socialist and the author of more than eighty books, the most famous of which is *The Jungle* (1906). He was a muckraker and ardent reformer who ran unsuccessfully as the Democratic candidate for governor of California in 1934.

37. It is unclear to which manuscript Gilman is referring. "Our Mr. Young" likely refers to William Young, editor of *Hampton's Magazine*. Sinclair's marriage to the wife mentioned by Gilman ended in 1911.

38. Gilman's letter evoked a strong retort from Lummis, who was offended by her "pious advice," offered in sympathy upon hearing of his divorce. Bristling at her solicitude, Lummis responded in a letter dated November 27, 1910, which read, in part:

> I have lived in the desert for a long time; and have watered it with my life blood, and have brought up a crop of flowers. No weeds grow there, because neither the atmosphere nor I are propitious. I do not need to go over to the des-

ert "for a season" to get clean; for I keep clean anywhere, and have populated the desert which others made desolate.

As a speaker and writer you seem so successful that I would not, if I were in your place, crowd out any auditors. Any fool can listen. Most do. The wise make themselves listened to, at so much per.

I shall be very glad to do something which my children will "be lovingly proud of." I suppose that when their grandchildren go around and see the California Missions and remember who made it possible for them to see them, they won't feel sorry that I didn't belong to the Friday Morning Club. I presume that when my children travel through the Indian Reservations of the Southwest, they will not blush to find in every one where my tracks have changed the direction of our government policies. I presume that the Southwest Museum and the Lummis Museum will not cause any of my posterity to feel obliged to change their names. . . .

I realize that your letter was not meant to be impudent, but was only friendly, so I send back my "Hello" in the same spirit—but with this vague suggestion that your pious advice is a bark up the wrong stump; and that one reason why women don't vote and won't vote is because they believe everything they hear.

39. Gilman is quoting the opening line of Bynner's poem "Hills of Home."

40. It is unclear to which poem of Bynner's Gilman is referring.

41. Gilman is quoting Whitman's preface to the 1855 edition of *Leaves of Grass*.

42. Mary Hunter Austin Collection, HL. Gilman first met American writer Mary Austin (1868–1934) in Pasadena in the early 1890s; the two became reacquainted in New York in the early 1900s. Although both women decried the tendency of male authors to depict women characters in a negative light, Austin was also critical of Gilman's fiction—particularly her use of didacticism—complaining that everything Gilman "wrote was in the same key" (326).

43. Alice Stokes Paul (1885–1977) was one of the leaders of the American suffragist movement that resulted in the passage of the nineteenth amendment. National American Women Suffrage Association Records, LOC.

44. Howells had requested permission to reprint "The Yellow Wall-Paper" in *Great Modern American Stories* (1920).

45. See chapter 2, note 11.

46. General Correspondence, Gilman Papers, AESL. On November 6, 1930, Catt wrote to inform Gilman that she had been awarded $5,000 by the *Pictorial Review* for its "Achievement Award," from which she was giving ten fellow suffrage and peace reformers, including Gilman, $100 apiece. She wrote, "It is a great thing for an old lady like me to have $5,000 to share with other reformers. My dear Mrs. Gilman, here is your $100 and may it bring you something of comfort and enjoyment." Catt Papers, LOC. In a letter to Katharine dated November 21, 1930, Gilman wrote that receiving the gift left her "feeling quite cocky" and that "It was very gratifying to me to be in a big group of progressive women again." Family Correspondence, Gilman Papers, AESL.

47. See chapter 4, note 80.

48. Margaret Sanger Papers, LOC. Sanger (1879–1966) championed birth control as a way for women to exercise control over their lives and health. She served as chair of the National Committee on Federal Legislation for Birth Control alongside Katharine Houghton Hepburn (the mother of actress Katharine Hepburn), who chaired the organization's Legislative Committee.

49. At Sanger's invitation, Gilman had traveled to Washington, DC, earlier in the month to address a committee of the House of Representatives on the topic of birth control.

50. Sanger suffered from tuberculosis.

51. General Correspondence, Catt Papers, LOC.

# Chapter 7

1. General Correspondence, Gilman Papers, AESL. According to Gilman's letter to Katharine on October 15, 1921, Dr. Emily Dunning-Barringer at the Life Extension Institute performed the examination.

2. General Correspondence, Gilman Papers, AESL. Caroline M. Hill held a PhD in Psychology from the University of Chicago. Hill was compiling an anthology of poems and had asked Gilman and other "living American poets" to "tell something of the circumstances under which they have done their best work, how the ideas have come to them and been worked out."

3. Family Correspondence, Gilman Papers, AESL. Gilman's grandson, Walter Stetson Chamberlin (1920–), who retired in 2007 from the Los Alamos National Laboratory in New Mexico, has taken a role in shaping his grandmother's legacy.

4. Gilman was notoriously forgetful about family birthdays.

5. General Correspondence, Gilman Papers, AESL. Gilman was responding to letters dated September 9 and 10, 1927, from L. L. Bernard at the University of Chicago, requesting data about herself and "the institutions" at which she had taught, for inclusion in a volume titled "History of Sociology in the Universities and Colleges of the United States." Bernard had provided a "Suggested Outline for Data" that he wished respondents to follow.

6. The correct date is 1895.

7. While *Women and Economics* was Gilman's first theoretical treatise, it was preceded by two books: *Art Gems for the Home and Fireside* (1888) and a volume of poetry, *In This Our World,* first published in 1893.

8. Baker Brownell Papers, NUL. American author and educator Baker Brownell (1887–1965) solicited from Gilman an article on "Feminism and Social Progress," which appeared in his volume *Problems of Civilization* (1929).

9. General Correspondence, Gilman Papers, AESL. Joseph Wood Krutch (1893–1970) was an American naturalist, writer, and critic. Gilman misspelled "Krutch" in her first reference to the author's name but spelled it correctly elsewhere in her letter.

10. On Park see chapter 4, note 90. All letters to Park are from the Alice Park Archive, WHM.

11. Antaeus, the son of Gaia and Poseidon, was a giant whose strength made him

appear to be invincible. He challenged strangers to wrestle with him and conquered each of them through defeat or death. Antaeus remained unbeatable until Hercules discovered that Antaeus's strength came from contact with the earth, his mother. Hercules finally prevailed by lifting Antaeus off the ground until his strength was exhausted.

12. See chapter 3, note 46.

13. Sarah J. Eddy was an American artist, writer, and photographer. Her book *Friends and Helpers* (1899) advocated humane education. Eddy also painted a famous portrait of eighty-year-old Susan B. Anthony in 1902.

14. UCLA. It was actually American journalist Carey McWilliams (1905–80) that Gilman wrote to, whom she mentions in her September 5, 1929, letter to Alice Park. McWilliams was also an editor and lawyer who was active in progressive causes. His book *Ambrose Bierce: A Biography* was published in 1929.

15. Addenda to the Gilman Papers, AESL. For information on Channing see chapter 4, note 22.

16. Bierce had viciously attacked a number of women writers in California, including Gilman, in the early 1890s. See Oliver and Scharnhorst.

17. General Correspondence, Gilman Papers, AESL. Psychologist Samuel Daniel Schmalhausen published a number of books examining contemporary behavior, including *Why We Misbehave* (1928); *Sex in Civilization* (1929), coedited with Victor Francis Calverton and introduced by Havelock Ellis; *The New Generation: The Intimate Problems of Modern Parents and Children* (1930), coauthored with Calverton and Bertrand Russell; and *Woman's Coming of Age* (1931), coedited with Calverton. Gilman's essay "Sex and Race Progress" was published in *Sex in Civilization*, and her "Parasitism and Civilized Vice" appeared in *Woman's Coming of Age*.

18. There were two Boer wars in South Africa, one in 1880–81 and the other in 1899–1902. Both were between the British and the settlers of Dutch origin (called Boers, Afrikaners, or Voortrekkers) in South Africa and resulted in the end of the two independent republics they had founded.

19. On Alice Stone Blackwell see chapter 5, note 49. Blackwell's "noble and beautiful book" was her 1930 biography of her mother, Lucy Stone (1818–93), published by Little, Brown and Plimpton Press.

20. Lucy Stone's last words to her daughter were "make the world better." Lucy Stone died in Dorchester, Massachusetts, on October 18, 1893.

21. In a December 30, 1929, letter, Gilman invites Blackwell to attend this January 17, 1930, lecture, in which, she says, "I am to be the chopping block in a discussion on 'Racial Prejudice'! Doubtless most of the audience will be Alien."

22. The *New York Times* published Blackwell's letter to the editor, titled "America for Americans?" on September 28, 1930. Blackwell summarizes "an amusing little play" she had seen in which a girl wishes all foreigners deported, forgetting that she is wearing a wishing ring. "An energetic baggage agent" then magically enters her home, shipping the telephone back to Scotland, "the country of Alexander Graham Bell; the radio to Italy, the birthplace of Marconi," etc. Finally the girl herself is ordered to leave by "American Indians in feather headdresses," so she reverses her wish and vows no longer to think "Unfriendly Thoughts" (E2).

23. *Race or Nation; A Conflict of Divided Loyalties* was published by Gino Charles Speranza (1872–1927) with Bobbs-Merrill in 1925.

24. Gilman's memory is faulty. Her first poem was "To D.G.," which appeared in the May 1880 *New England Journal of Education.*

25. Gilman had, in fact, written to Harold Channing on March 1, 1931, to thank him for sending her a "prodigious bunch of puzzles."

26. Gilman is quoting from "God's Judgment on a Wicked Bishop," by English poet Robert Southey (1774–1843).

27. *Humanity Uprooted,* by Maurice Hindus, was published in 1929 by Jonathan Cape and Harrison Smith.

28. General Correspondence, Gilman Papers, AESL. Harriet is Harriet Park Kobold, daughter of women's rights activist Alice Park.

29. For information on Susa Young Gates see chapter 3, note 42.

30. Papers of B. W. Huebsch, 1893–1964, LOC. Benjamin W. Huebsch (1876–1964) was editor of the *Freeman,* a liberal weekly, and later editor and publisher at Viking Press.

31. The journal *Unity* was associated with the World Congress of Religion, founded in Chicago at the 1893 World's Fair.

32. Family Correspondence, Gilman Papers, AESL. Charles Edward Stowe (1850–1934), who also went by "Charley," was the son of Harriet Beecher Stowe. He was ordained as a Congregationalist minister in 1878, and from the mid-1850s until the late 1890s he was minister of the Congregational Church in Simsbury, Connecticut, not far from his parents' Hartford home.

33. Lyman Beecher Stowe's *Saints, Sinners and Beechers* was published by Bobbs-Merrill in 1934.

34. All letters to Lyman Beecher Stowe are taken from the Family Correspondence, Gilman Papers, AESL.

35. Gilman had been diagnosed with breast cancer in January 1932.

36. For information on Howe see chapter 2, note 42.

37. In a letter dated November 3, 1933, Lyman responded that he "should think the 'Yellow Wallpaper' might make an excellent monologue" but admitted that he knew "very little about such matters." He also made it clear that he did not have time to try to secure an actress to perform the role: "I am in the last mad rush on my Beecher book *Saints, Sinners, and Beechers* which is due the 15th of November for publication in February." Family Correspondence, Gilman Papers, AESL.

38. Gilman is referring to Eugene O'Neill's *The Emperor Jones,* first staged in 1920 and influenced by German expressionism.

39. Alla Nazimova (1879–1945), a Russian-born actress of American theater and film, moved to New York in 1905.

40. For Hale see chapter 2, note 57.

41. Nellie Hale's brothers—and Gilman's cousins—Philip and Edward Jr. died in 1931 and 1932, respectively.

42. General Correspondence, Gilman Papers, AESL.

43. Gilman is paraphrasing section 48 of "Song of Myself" from Whitman's

*Leaves of Grass:* "No array of terms can say how much I am at peace about God and about death."

# Chapter 8

1. Waller Papers, BARN. Anna Trumbull Waller was a close friend of Katharine's. See Gilman's letter to Grace dated March 20, 1935.

2. This letter is taken from the private collection of Gilman's grandson, Walter Stetson Chamberlin.

3. Gale's realistic novel, *Birth,* set in the Midwest, was published in 1918.

4. In response to Gilman's request, Gale wrote: "I <u>want</u> to do it—I am honored and proud beyond words. . . . We are off to Honolulu now—a thousand things have happened. . . . I <u>know</u> what that loss of Houghton means to you. I love you, I quote you every time I speak. O but could I do it as it should be done? . . . I want to see you—to talk of this—you dear, and precious friend—you great woman—" (March 8, 1935). Gale eventually agreed instead to write the introduction to Gilman's autobiography. General Correspondence, Gilman Papers, AESL.

5. Gilman had recruited Amy Wellington to prepare an edition of Gilman's verse for posthumous publication. The volume was finally published in 1996.

6. Among the material entrusted to Gale was a copy of the letter Gilman wrote to Dr. S. Weir Mitchell on April 19, 1887, in which she described her history of neurasthenia. See Knight's "'All the Facts of the Case.'"

7. Mr. "Breeze" was actually William L. Breese, husband of American writer Zona Gale (1874–1938). American realist writer Hamlin Garland (1860–1940) is best remembered today for his stories about the hardships endured by midwestern farmers.

8. In a letter dated April 16, 1935, Lyman Beecher Stowe informed Gilman that Grace Ellery Channing Stetson was "making every effort to finance a trip out to see you." He expressed concern that Grace's visit "would be a great strain" on Gilman, in part because Grace had recently grown "deafer than ever," and asked Gilman to "tell me definitely whether you are anxious to have Mrs. Stetson come out to see you." General Correspondence, Gilman Papers, AESL.

9. Gilman is referring to paintings by Charles Walter Stetson.

10. "p.p.c." is the acronym for the French *pour prendre congé,* "to take leave" or "I am leaving." We are indebted to Cindy J. Hall for providing both the translation and interpretation of this abbreviation. Hall notes that in his *Dictionary of Phrase and Fable* (1898), English editor E. Cobham Brewer (1810–97) remarks that "p.p.c."—or "paid parting call" in English—was "sometimes written on the address cards of persons . . . when they pay their farewell visits." Hall further notes that "Pour Prendre Congé" is the title of a poem by American writer Dorothy Parker (1893–1967) that appeared in the July 1927 *New Yorker.*

11. Alice Park Archive, WHM. Daisy Bannerman Coats, a longtime resident of California, was involved in a number of arts and civic organizations, including the Los Angeles Chapter of the Friday Morning Club, the National Woman's Party, and the Historical Society of Southern California.

12. Aimee Spurr (1884–1967), who resided in California, was one of Gilman's friends.

13. General Correspondence, Gilman Papers, AESL.

14. In section 48 of "Song of Myself" from *Leaves of Grass,* Whitman wrote, "No array of terms can say how much I am at peace about God and about death."

15. Park typed the final letter she received from Gilman with the following notation at the top: "Mrs. Gilman's last letter to me mailed August 12. She died Aug. 17, 1935." Alice Park Archive, WHM.

16. The Latin puns on a phrase from the Mass, "et in terra pax hominibus," which translates as "and on earth, peace to mankind."

# Bibliography

Allen, Judith A. "'The Overthrow' of Gynaecocentric Culture: Charlotte Perkins Gilman and Lester Frank Ward." *Charlotte Perkins Gilman and Her Contemporaries.* Ed. Cynthia J. Davis and Denise D. Knight. Tuscaloosa: U of Alabama P, 2004. 59–86.

Altman, Janet Gurkin. *Epistolarity: Approaches to a Form.* Columbus: Ohio State UP, 1982.

Austin, Mary. *Earth Horizon.* Boston: Houghton Mifflin, 1932.

Barry, James H. Letter to Charlotte Perkins Gilman. 7 Jan. 1921. James H. Barry Papers, Bancroft Library, University of California, Berkeley.

Barton, David, and Nigel Hall, eds. *Letter Writing as a Social Practice.* Amsterdam: John Benjaminis, 1999.

Bernard, L. L. Letters to Charlotte Perkins Gilman. 9 Sept., 10 Sept. 1927. General Correspondence, Gilman Papers, Arthur and Elizabeth Schlesinger Library, Radcliffe Institute, Harvard University, Cambridge, Massachusetts.

Brewer, E. Cobham. *Dictionary of Phrase and Fable.* Philadelphia: Henry Altemus, 1898.

Brodhead, Richard. *The School of Hawthorne.* New York: Oxford UP, 1986.

Brooks, John P. *The Butler Health Lift and What It Will Do.* n.p., 1880.

Bruère, Martha Bensley. Letter to Charlotte Perkins Gilman. 9 June 1935. General Correspondence, Gilman Papers, Arthur and Elizabeth Schlesinger Library, Radcliffe Institute, Harvard University, Cambridge, Massachusetts.

———. *Mildred Carver.* New York: Macmillan, 1919.

Campbell, Helen S. *Darkness and Daylight, or, Lights and Shadows of New York Life.* Hartford: A. D. Worthington, 1893.

———. *Prisoners of Poverty: Women Wage-Workers, Their Trades and Their Lives.* Boston: Roberts Bros., 1889.

———. *The Problem of the Poor: A Record of Quiet Work in Unquiet Places.* New York: Fords, Howard & Hulbert, 1882.

Catt, Carrie Chapman. Letter to Charlotte Perkins Gilman. 6 Nov. 1930. Papers of Carrie Chapman Catt, Library of Congress, Washington, DC.

———. Letter to Charlotte Perkins Gilman. 28 May 1935. General Correspondence, Gilman Papers, Arthur and Elizabeth Schlesinger Library, Radcliffe Institute, Harvard University, Cambridge, Massachusetts.

Chamberlin, Katharine Beecher Stetson. Letter to Lyman Beecher Stowe. 20 Aug. 1935. Beecher-Stowe Collection, Arthur and Elizabeth Schlesinger Library, Radcliffe Institute, Harvard University, Cambridge, Massachusetts.

Channing, Grace. "The House on the Hill-Top: A Tale of Modern Etruria." *Scribner's* Aug. 1893: 135–50.

———. "The House on the Hill-Top: A Tale of Modern Etruria." *Stories of Italy.* New York: Scribner's, 1893. 151–208.

Crecelius, Kathryn. "Authorship and Authority: George Sand's Letters to Her Mother." *Writing the Female Voice: Essays on Epistolary Literature.* Ed. Elizabeth C. Goldsmith. Boston: Northeastern UP, 1989. 257–72.

Davis, Cynthia J. *Charlotte Perkins Gilman: A Living.* Stanford, CA: Stanford UP, 2009.

Decker, William Merrill. *Epistolary Practices: Letter Writing in America before Telecommunications.* Chapel Hill: U of North Carolina P, 1998.

Dickinson, Emily. Poem 636. *The Complete Poems of Emily Dickinson.* Ed. Thomas H. Johnson. Boston: Little, Brown, 1960. 314–15.

Dunning Barringer, Emily. *Bowery to Bellevue: The Story of New York's First Woman Ambulance Surgeon.* New York: Norton, 1950.

Earle, Rebecca, ed. *Epistolary Selves: Letters and Letter-Writers, 1600–1945.* Aldershot, UK: Ashgate, 1999.

Eldredge, Charles C. *Charles Walter Stetson: Color and Fantasy.* Lawrence: U of Kansas, 1982.

Emerson, Ralph Waldo. *Essays.* Boston: Houghton, Mifflin, 1841.

Gale, Zona. *Birth.* New York: Macmillan, 1918.

Gaul, Theresa Strouth, ed. *To Marry an Indian: The Marriage of Harriet Gold and Elias Boudinot in Letters, 1823–1839.* Chapel Hill: U of North Carolina P, 2005.

Gilman, Charlotte Perkins. *Art Gems for the Home and Fireside.* Providence: J. A. and R. A. Reid, 1888.

———. "A Conservative." *Life* 4 Feb. 1892: 68.

———. "Cross-Examining Santa Claus." *Century* Dec. 1922: 169–74.

———. "The Dancing of Isadora Duncan." *Forerunner* Apr. 1915: 101.

———. *The Diaries of Charlotte Perkins Gilman.* Ed. Denise D. Knight. Charlottesville: UP of Virginia, 1994.

———. "Fashion, Beauty and Brains." *Outlook* Aug. 1929: 578–79.

———. "Feminism and Social Progress." *Problems of Civilization.* Ed. Baker Brownell. New York: D. Van Nostrand, 1929. 115–42.

———. *Forerunner* 1–7 (1909–16). Rpt. New York: Greenwood, 1968.

———. "His Religion and Hers." *Century* Mar. 1923: 676–83; Apr. 1923: 855–61.

———. *His Religion and Hers: A Study of the Faith of Our Fathers and the Work of Our Mothers.* New York: Century, 1923. Rpt. Westport, CT: Hyperion, 1976.

———. *Human Work.* New York: McClure, Phillips, 1904.

———. *The Impress.* Gilman Papers. Arthur and Elizabeth Schlesinger Library, Radcliffe Institute, Harvard University.

———. "The International Congress of Women." *Ainslee's* Sept. 1899: 145–51.

———. *In This Our World.* 1893. 3rd. ed. Boston: Small, Maynard, 1898.

——. "Kitchen Dirt and Civic Health." *Independent* 8 Dec. 1904: 1296–99.

——. *The Later Poetry of Charlotte Perkins Gilman.* Ed. Denise D. Knight. Newark: U of Delaware P, 1996.

——. Letter to Alice Stone Blackwell. 30 Dec. 1929. National American Woman Suffrage Association Records, Library of Congress, Washington, DC.

——. Letter to Harold Channing. 1 Mar. 1931. Addenda, Gilman Papers, Arthur and Elizabeth Schlesinger Library, Radcliffe Institute, Harvard University.

——. Letter to Katharine Seymour Day. 1 June 1932. Day Papers, Harriet Beecher Stowe Center Library, Hartford, Connecticut.

——. Letters to Martha Luther Lane. 16 Mar. 1889, 20 Jan. 1890. Charlotte Perkins Gilman Letters, Rhode Island Historical Society, Providence.

——. Letters to Martha Luther Lane. 30 Apr., 9 June 1935. General Correspondence, Gilman Papers, Arthur and Elizabeth Schlesinger Library, Radcliffe Institute, Harvard University.

——. Letter to Annie Russell. 27 Sept. 1909. Annie Russell Papers, New York Public Library.

——. Letters to Lyman Beecher Stowe. 23 Apr., 27 May 1935. Family Correspondence, Gilman Papers, Arthur and Elizabeth Schlesinger Library, Radcliffe Institute, Harvard University, Cambridge, Massachusetts.

——. Letter to Emma Biddlecom Sweet. 24 Oct. 1903. Emma B. Sweet Papers, Department of Rare Books and Special Collections, University of Rochester Library, Rochester, New York.

——. Letter to Horace Traubel. 17 Nov. 1907. Papers of Horace and Anne Montgomerie Traubel, Library of Congress, Washington, DC.

——. "The Little White Animals." *The Conservator* Oct. 1907: 116.

——. *The Living of Charlotte Perkins Gilman: An Autobiography.* New York: Appleton-Century, 1935. Rpt. Madison: U of Wisconsin P, 1990.

——. "Making Towns Fit to Live In." *Century* July 1921: 361–66.

——. "The Nobler Male." *Forum* July 1925: 19–21.

——. "One Girl of Many." *Alpha* 1 Feb. 1884: 1.

——. "Our Tomorrow." *Land of Sunshine* May 1898: 251.

——. "Parasitism and Civilized Vice." *Woman's Coming of Age.* Ed. Samuel D. Schmalhausen and V. F. Calverton. New York: Liveright, 1931. 110–26.

——. "A Reproach to San Francisco." *Star* [n.d., 1894]: n.p.

——. "The Right to Die." *Forum* Nov. 1935: 297–300.

——. "Rockefeller's Prayer." *Wasp* 21 Nov. 1891: 2.

——. "Sex and Race Progress." *Sex in Civilization.* Ed. V. F. Calverton and Samuel D. Schmalhausen. New York: Macaulay, 1929. 109–23.

——. *Social Ethics: Sociology and the Future of Society.* Ed. Michael R. Hill and Mary Jo Deegan. Westport, CT: Praeger, 2004.

——. "Their Grass!" *Land of Sunshine* July 1897: 64.

——. "To D.G." *New England Journal of Education* May 1880: 331.

——. "To Isadora Duncan." *The Later Poetry of Charlotte Perkins Gilman.* Ed. Denise D. Knight. Newark: U of Delaware P, 1996. 141.

——. "Toward Monogamy." *Nation* 11 June 1924: 671–73.

———. "Twigs." *Life* 21 Feb. 1924: 4.

———. *Unpunished.* Ed. Catherine Golden and Denise D. Knight. New York: Feminist P, 1997.

———. "Wash-Tubs and Woman's Duty." *Century* June 1925: 152–59.

———. "Wind and Leaves." *Land of Sunshine* Mar. 1897: 152.

———. *Women and Economics: A Study of the Economic Relation between Men and Women as a Factor in Social Evolution.* Boston: Small, Maynard, 1898.

———. "The Yellow Wall-Paper." *New England Magazine* Jan. 1892: 647–56. Rpt. New York: Feminist P, 1973.

Hale, Edward Everett. *The Man without a Country.* Boston: Ticknor and Fields, 1863.

Harris, Sharon M. Introduction. *American Women Writers to 1800.* Ed. Harris. New York: Oxford UP, 1996. 3–30.

Harris, Susan K. *The Cultural Work of the Late Nineteenth-Century Hostess: Annie Adams Fields and Mary Gladstone Drew.* New York: Palgrave, 2002.

Hemans, Felicia Dorothea. "Casabianca." *The Poetical Works of Felicia Dorothea Hemans.* London: Oxford UP, 1914. 396.

Herford, Oliver. Letter to Charlotte Perkins Gilman. 9 July 1929. General Correspondence, Gilman Papers, Arthur and Elizabeth Schlesinger Library, Radcliffe Institute, Harvard University, Cambridge, Massachusetts.

Hewitt, Elizabeth. *Correspondence and American Literature, 1770–1865.* Cambridge: Cambridge UP, 2004.

Hill, Caroline M. Letter to Charlotte Perkins Gilman. 16 July 1921. General Correspondence, Gilman Papers, Arthur and Elizabeth Schlesinger Library, Radcliffe Institute, Harvard University, Cambridge, Massachusetts.

Hill, Mary A. *Charlotte Perkins Gilman: The Making of a Radical Feminist, 1860–1896.* Philadelphia: Temple UP, 1980.

———, ed. *A Journey from Within: The Love Letters of Charlotte Perkins Gilman, 1897–1900.* Lewisburg, PA: Bucknell UP, 1995.

Holmes, Oliver Wendell. *The Guardian Angel.* 1867. 16 Nov. 2004. <http://www.worldebooklibrary.com/eBooks/Gutenberg/etext01/ange11.htm>

Howe, Harriet. "Charlotte Perkins Gilman: As I Knew Her." *Equal Rights: Independent Feminist Weekly* 5 Sept. 1936: 211–16.

Howells, William Dean, ed. *The Great Modern American Stories.* New York: Boni and Liveright, 1920.

———. *A Hazard of New Fortunes.* New York: Harper, 1890.

———. *A Traveler from Altruria.* New York: Harper, 1894.

Humbert, Arthur C. "Photographing a Wounded African Buffalo." *Harper's* Apr. 1898: 655–63.

Ingelow, Jean. *The Poetical Works of Jean Ingelow.* New York: John W. Lovell, 1863.

James, P. D. Foreword. *800 Years of Women's Letters.* By Olga Kenyon. New York: Penguin, 1992. vii–viii.

Karpinski, Joanne B. "When the Marriage of True Minds Admits Impediments: Charlotte Perkins Gilman and William Dean Howells." *Critical Essays on Charlotte Perkins Gilman.* Ed. Karpinski. New York: G. K. Hall, 1992. 202–21.

Kipling, Rudyard. "Chant-Pagan." *The Five Nations.* New York: Doubleday, 1909. 159–62.

Knight, Denise D. "'All the Facts of the Case': Gilman's 'Lost' Letter to Dr. S. Weir Mitchell." *American Literary Realism* 37.3 (2005): 259–77.

———. "An Amusing Source of Income: Charlotte Perkins Gilman and the Soapine Connection." *Advertising Trade Card Quarterly* 8.2 (2001): 8–12.

———. "'But O My Heart': The Private Poetry of Charlotte Perkins Gilman." *Charlotte Perkins Gilman: Optimist Reformer.* Ed. Jill Rudd and Val Gough. Iowa City: U of Iowa P, 1999. 267–84.

———. "Charlotte Perkins Gilman and the Shadow of Racism." *American Literary Realism* 32.2 (2000): 159–69.

———. "Charlotte Perkins Gilman, William Randolph Hearst, and the Practice of Ethical Journalism." *Charlotte Perkins Gilman and Her Contemporaries: Literary and Intellectual Contexts.* Ed. Cynthia J. Davis and Denise D. Knight. Tuscaloosa: U of Alabama P, 2004. 46–58.

———. "New Evidence about the Origins of Gilman's 'The Giant Wistaria.'" *American Literary Realism* 40.2 (2008): 173–79.

———. "'Only a Husband's Opinion': Walter Stetson's View of Gilman's 'The Yellow Wall-Paper'—An Inscription." *American Literary Realism* 36.1 (2003): 86–87.

Lane, Ann J. *To Herland and Beyond: The Life and Work of Charlotte Perkins Gilman.* New York: Pantheon, 1990.

Lane, Martha Luther. Letter to Charlotte Perkins Gilman. 30 Apr. 1935. General Correspondence, Gilman Papers, Arthur and Elizabeth Schlesinger Library, Radcliffe Institute, Harvard University.

Lanser, Susan S. "Feminist Criticism, 'The Yellow Wallpaper,' and the Politics of Color in America." *Feminist Studies* 15 (1989): 415–41.

Levine, George. "Rich, Lazy, and (At Least Once) Inspired." Rev. of *With Friends Possessed: A Life of Edward FitzGerald,* by Robert Bernard Martin. *New York Times Book Review* 21 Apr. 1985: 11.

Lummis, Charles Fletcher. House Book. Lummis Manuscript Collection. Braun Research Library, Autry National Center/Southwest Museum, Los Angeles.

———. "In Western Letters." *Land of Sunshine* May 1900: 346–52.

———. Journal. Typescript. Lummis Manuscript Collection. Braun Research Library, Autry National Center/Southwest Museum, Los Angeles.

———. Letter to Charlotte Perkins Gilman. 27 Nov. 1910. Charles Fletcher Lummis Manuscript Collection, Braun Research Library, Autry National Center/Southwest Museum, Los Angeles.

Markham, Edwin. *The Man with the Hoe.* San Francisco: A. M. Robertson, 1899.

Matthews, Brander. Letter to Charlotte Perkins Gilman. 28 Oct. 1892. Brander Matthews Papers, Rare Books and Manuscript Library, Columbia University, New York.

Mitchell, S. Weir. *Fat and Blood: And How to Make Them.* Philadelphia: Lippincott, 1877.

———. *Wear and Tear or, Hints for the Overworked.* 5th ed. Philadelphia: Lippincott. 9 Nov. 2004. <http://www.gutenberg.org/dirs/1/3/1/9/13197/13197-h/13197-h.htm>

Oliver, Lawrence J., and Gary Scharnhorst. "Charlotte Perkins Gilman v. Ambrose Bierce: The Literary Politics of Gender." *Charlotte Perkins Gilman and Her Contemporaries: Literary and Intellectual Contexts.* Ed. Cynthia J. Davis and Denise D. Knight. Tuscaloosa: U of Alabama P, 2004. 32–45.

Perkins, Frederic. Letter to Charlotte Perkins Gilman. N.d. Folder 26. Family Correspondence, Gilman Papers, Arthur and Elizabeth Schlesinger Library, Radcliffe Institute, Harvard University, Cambridge, Massachusetts.

Porter, Delia Lyman. *An Anti-Worry Recipe and Other Stories.* Boston: American Tract Society, 1905.

———. *The Blues Cure and Other Stories.* New York: A. D. F. Randolph, 1892.

———. "Mr. Freeman at Home." *Scribner's* Nov. 1893: 612–22.

———. *A Year of Ideals for Every-Day Living.* Boston: Pilgrim, 1909.

Ross, Edward Alsworth. Letters to Charlotte Perkins Gilman. 3 Oct. 1925, 1 Dec. 1927, 15 Sept. and 15 Oct. 1928, 15 June 1932, 29 Aug. 1933. E. A. Ross Papers, Wisconsin Historical Society, Madison.

———. *Principles of Sociology.* New York: Century, 1921.

———. *Seventy Years of It: An Autobiography of Edward Alsworth Ross.* New York: Appleton-Century, 1936.

———. *Social Control: A Survey of the Foundations of Order.* New York: Macmillan, 1901.

———. "The United States of India." *Century* Dec. 1925: 136–49.

Scharnhorst, Gary. *Charlotte Perkins Gilman: A Bibliography.* Metuchen, NJ: Scarecrow, 1985.

———. *Charlotte Perkins Gilman.* Boston: Twayne, 1985.

Schreiner, Olive. *Dreams.* London: T. Fisher Unwin, 1891.

———. *Women and Labor.* New York: Frederick A. Stokes, 1911.

Shelby, Edward. Letter to Charlotte Perkins Gilman. 26 Mar. 1935. General Correspondence, Gilman Papers, Arthur and Elizabeth Schlesinger Library, Radcliffe Institute, Harvard University, Cambridge, Massachusetts.

Shillaber, Benjamin Penhallow. *Life and Sayings of Mrs. Partington, and Others of the Family.* New York: J. C. Derby, 1854.

Spacks, Patricia Meyer. *Gossip.* New York: Knopf, 1985.

Speyer, Leonora. *Fiddler's Farewell.* New York: Knopf, 1926.

Stanton, Elizabeth Cady. *Woman's Bible.* 1898. <http://www.gutenberg.org/dirs/etext06/wbibl10.txt>

Stetson, Charles Walter. *Endure: The Diaries of Charles Walter Stetson.* Ed. Mary A. Hill. Philadelphia: Temple UP, 1985.

———. Letter to Charles Fletcher Lummis. 28 May 1900. Charles Fletcher Lummis Manuscript Collection, Braun Research Library, Autry National Center/Southwest Museum, Los Angeles.

Stowe, Harriet Beecher. *Uncle Tom's Cabin.* Boston: John P. Jewett, 1852.

Stowe, Lyman Beecher. Letters to Charlotte Perkins Gilman. 3 Nov. 1933, 21 Apr. 1934. Family Correspondence, Gilman Papers, Arthur and Elizabeth Schlesinger Library, Radcliffe Institute, Harvard University, Cambridge, Massachusetts.

Swift, Jonathan. *Hints toward an Essay on Conversation*. 1713. Reprinted in *Jonathan Swift: Selections*. Ed. Harden Craig. New York: Charles Scribner, 1924.

Temple, Inez. Letter to Charlotte Perkins Gilman. n.d. General Correspondence, Gilman Papers, Arthur and Elizabeth Schlesinger Library, Radcliffe Institute, Harvard University, Cambridge, Massachusetts.

Vance, Arthur T. Letter to Charlotte Perkins Gilman. 20 May 1909. General Correspondence, Gilman Papers, Arthur and Elizabeth Schlesinger Library, Radcliffe Institute, Harvard University, Cambridge, Massachusetts.

Ward, Lester F. "Our Better Halves." *Forum* Nov. 1888: 266–75.

———. *The Psychic Factors of Civilization*. Boston: Ginn, 1893.

Wellington, Amy. *Women Have Told: Studies in the Feminist Tradition*. Boston: Little, Brown, 1930.

Wells, H. G. *The Invisible Man*. New York: Stover, 1897.

———. *The Time Machine*. London: William Heinemann, 1895.

———. *The War of the Worlds*. London: William Heinemann, 1898.

Wentworth, Patricia. *The Dower House Mystery*. New York: Small, Maynard, 1925.

Whitman, Walt. "Song of Myself." *Leaves of Grass and Other Writings*. Ed. Michael Moon. New York: Norton, 2002. 26–78.

———. "Song of the Open Road." *Leaves of Grass and Other Writings*. Ed. Michael Moon. New York: Norton, 2002. 126–35.

# Permissions Acknowledgments

Grateful acknowledgment is made to the following for permission to publish materials from their holdings:

The Bancroft Library: Letters from the James H. Barry Papers, the Anne Henrietta Martin Papers, and the Charles Walter Stetson Papers published courtesy of The Bancroft Library, University of California, Berkeley.

The Barnard College Library: Letter from the Waller Papers published courtesy of the Barnard College Library, Overbury Collection.

The Braun Research Library: Letters from the Charles Fletcher Lummis Manuscript Collection, the Grace Ellery Channing Collection, and the Marion Parks Collection published courtesy of The Autry National Center/Southwest Museum, Los Angeles.

Christopher and Melinda Ratliffe: Painting of Charlotte Perkins Stetson and Katherine by Charles Walter Stetson published courtesy of the private collection of Christopher and Melinda Ratliffe.

The Harriet Beecher Stowe Center: Letters from the Katharine Seymour Day Papers published courtesy of The Harriet Beecher Stowe Center, Hartford, Connecticut.

The Horrmann Library: Letter from the Edwin Markham Archives published courtesy of the Horrmann Library, Wagner College.

The Houghton Library: Letters from the S. J. Barrows Family Papers, the Witter Bynner Papers, and the Howells Family Papers published by permission of the Houghton Library, Harvard University.

The Huntington Library: Letters from the Mary Hunter Austin Collection, the Jeanne C. S. Carr Collection, the Caroline Severance Papers, and the Anna Strunsky Walling Collection published by permission of The Huntington Library, San Marino, California.

The John Hay Library: Letters from the Lester F. Ward Papers published courtesy of the Brown University Library.

The Kroch Library: Letters from the Sarah Brown Ingersoll Cooper Papers published courtesy of the Division of Rare and Manuscript Collections, Cornell University Library.

The Lilly Library: Letter from the Sinclair Collection published courtesy of the Lilly Library, Indiana University, Bloomington, Indiana.

The National Portrait Gallery, Smithsonian Institution: Painting of Charlotte Perkins Stetson Gilman by Ellen Day Hale published courtesy of the Smithsonian Institution.

The New York Public Library: Letters from the Annie Russell Papers 1874–1941, Manuscripts and Archives Division, published courtesy of the New York Public Library, Astor, Lenox and Tilden Foundations.

Northwestern University: Letter from the Baker Brownell Papers published courtesy of the Northwestern University Archives.

The Pasadena Museum of History: Letter from the Fenyes-Curtain-Paolheimo Papers published courtesy of The Pasadena Museum of History.

The Rare Book and Manuscript Library: Letter from the Brander Matthews Papers published courtesy of the Rare Book and Manuscript Library, Columbia University.

The Rare Book and Special Collections Library: Autographed postcard from the H. G. Wells Correspondence published courtesy of the University of Illinois at Urbana-Champaign.

The Rhode Island Historical Society Library: Letters from the Benjamin R. Phelon Family Papers and the Charlotte Perkins Gilman Letters published courtesy of the Rhode Island Historical Society.

The Schlesinger Library, Radcliffe Institute: Letters from the Charlotte Perkins Gilman Papers and the Addenda to the Gilman Papers, and the Grace Ellery Channing Papers, published courtesy of the Schlesinger Library, Radcliffe Institute for Advanced Study, Harvard University, Cambridge, MA. Photographs from the Charlotte Perkins Gilman Papers also published courtesy of the Schlesinger Library.

Sheidan Libraries: Letters from the Elgin Ralston Lovell Gould Papers published courtesy of Special Collections, Sheidan Libraries, The Johns Hopkins University.

The Sophia Smith Collection: Letters from the Hale Family Papers, the Garrison Family Papers, and the Women's Rights Collection published courtesy of the Sophia Smith Collection, Smith College, Northampton, Massachusetts.

Stanford University Libraries: Letter from the Rebecca Spring Collection published courtesy of the Department of Special Collections and University Archives, Stanford University Libraries.

The University of Rochester Library: Letter from the Emma B. Sweet Papers published courtesy of The Department of Rare Books and Special Collections, University of Rochester Library.

Vassar College: Letters from the Marion P. Whitney Papers, published courtesy of Special Collections, Vassar College Libraries.

Walter Stetson Chamberlin: Letters from the private collection of Walter Stetson Chamberlin.

The Wisconsin Historical Society Archives: Letters from the E. A. Ross Papers and the Zona Gale Papers and the frontispiece photograph from the Zona Gale

Papers published courtesy of the Wisconsin Historical Society, Madison, Wisconsin.

The Women's History Museum: Letters from the Alice Park Archive published by permission of The Women's History Museum and Educational Center.

We are also grateful to the following for the use of materials in their holdings:

The Library of Congress: Letters from the National American Woman Suffrage Association Collection, the Papers of Carrie Chapman Catt, the Papers of Charlotte Perkins Gilman, the Papers of B. W. Huebsch, the Margaret Sanger Papers, and the Papers of Horace and Anne Montgomerie Traubel published with thanks to the Library of Congress.

Charles E. Young Research Library, UCLA: Letter from the Carey McWilliams Collection of Material About Ambrose Bierce, published with thanks to the Department of Special Collections, Charles E. Young Research Library, UCLA.

# Index